Windows Programming Power with
# Custom Controls

# Windows Programming Power with
# Custom Controls

**Paul Cilwa and
Jeff Duntemann**

THE CORIOLIS GROUP

| Publisher | Keith Weiskamp |
|---|---|
| Editorial Director | Jeff Duntemann |
| Cover/Interior Design | Bradley Grannis |
| Editor | Shannon Bounds |
| Production Coordination | Lisa Eads |

**Library of Congress Cataloging-in-Publication Data**

Printed in the United States of America

10 9 8 7 6 5 4 3 2 1

# Table of Contents

# Chapter 10    The Text File Editor Control    305

# Chapter 11   The IniData Control   389

# Preface

There was a time (and it wasn't so long ago) when every new computer that a computer company designed was designed utterly, completely from scratch. The digital logic was created from individual logic gates or (only a few years earlier) from individual transistors and resistors. Power supplies were created with custom-designed power transformers, custom-designed voltage regulators, and even custom-designed on/off switches and circuit breakers. Each computer had a mass-storage device that no other computer had.

And you wonder why computers used to cost so much: It took a team of engineers *years* to create each individual model. Such talent doesn't come cheap—and so your average computer could cost more than the building that housed it.

Remarkably enough, each time a new computer design was needed, the engineers picked up their pencils and started designing power transformers again. This cycle wasn't broken until the early 1980s, when the market for computers got large enough that price competition forced prices down into four figures. Out of that merciless competition arose a suite of standard components for a standard computer family called the "PC." The CPU standardized early on. Power supply output voltages were very much the same, and in time even the power-supply cabinets converged on a standard set of dimensions, right down to the screw holes. Huge task-specific chips emerged, with one chip for video, one chip for bus control, one chip for keyboard control, and so on, until the motherboard shrank to a smallish piece of circuit board material with scarcely a dozen monster chips on it, instead of hundreds of little ones. Motherboards became largely inter-changeable, with only the CPU speed and memory capacity differing as the technology progressed.

In this environment, *anyone* could create a custom computer. Pick a power supply, pick a motherboard, pick a case, pick a keyboard, pick a disk drive—and they all fit together, even though no two components had been made by a single manufacturer. Designing a computer became less a matter of invention than simple assembly.

It may well be that the engineers who used to spend their professional lives designing one power transformer after another were really into power transformers on a total lifestyle basis and genuinely enjoyed it—but we'll bet that it hasn't been long since you stared at the Shell sort or data entry routine on your screen and wanted to scream, *I've done this before! I don't want to do it again!*

You're in good company—and we'd like to offer you a way off the treadmill.

## Software Components

Ideally, when you needed a data entry line, you'd just reach into your "software parts box" and pull one out. Reusable code like this has been a sort of Holy Grail for many years; much sought after, but just as elusive as ever. The reasons that interchangeable software parts have been so long in coming are complex, but mostly they cook down to the fact that standard software parts need a "standard chassis" to plug into. Software is more than just pushes and pops, calls and returns. An application is also a set of assumptions about how things work and what things mean, and those assumptions have an *enormous* influence on the shape of the software that embodies them.

For interchangeable software components to work, they need an all-inclusive, highly standard set of assumptions to act as a foundation from which to work. Until very recently, no such standard set of assumptions existed. In the past two or three years, however, Microsoft's Windows 3.1 operating environment has become so universal in the PC world that its suite of conventions and assumptions has been accepted as the sort of "standard application chassis" into which standard software components can be plugged. These software components are known as *custom controls,* but as we'll show later in the book, they aren't just buttons and edit lines but can be much broader in scope.

Windows has become very much the mainstream. The components have been a little longer in coming. The time for them, however, is *now.*

○   ○   ○

*You can create a component* once*, and use it over and over in any Windows 3.1 application without running into an ugly web of nasty conflicts.*

○   ○   ○

Not every part of an application makes a suitable software component. Each application has unique aspects that must be implemented from scratch in order to solve a given problem. However, with some discipline and a little foresight, you can adopt an application design style that makes the best use of existing software components—your own or those devised by others—to cut your development time considerably.

Basically, it's a design and coding philosophy that lets you spend your time doing the *fun* stuff; and then when you need to do the dull stuff, simply pull the dull stuff out of a drawer.

This book will help you adopt a software components mindset for your C/C++ Windows programming. You'll be amazed at the time you will save.

## Who This Book Is For

This book was created primarily for Windows programmers working in C or C++. It's about a new slant on Windows programming, and it assumes that you know a little bit about Windows programming to begin with.

The custom controls presented in this book, however, aren't limited to any specific C/C++ compiler, or even the C/C++ language. In particular, you can load and use the VBX forms of the controls described here from Visual Basic. In the near future, you'll also be able to use the VBX controls from several new Windows development environments from a number of vendors.

VBX controls are increasingly becoming the "standard parts" of the Windows platform for *all* development tools—not just Microsoft's visual languages.

If you're a Visual Basic user, you don't necessarily have to be able to read or modify the C code embodying the controls. They're fully finished and ready to use, although we emphasize that studying the code in detail can make you a *much* better Windows programmer, whether you ever write a line of your own C/C++ code or not.

## What You'll Need

Windows custom controls are easy to create. If you're an experienced Windows programmer, you already know how to create an application window—and a custom control is, after all, just a window that implements the well-defined custom controls API.

To compile any of the source code in this book, you'll need a C compiler and linker capable of producing Windows DLLs. Any of Microsoft's C compilers from version 6.0 to the latest (Visual C++) will do. You can also use one of the compilers from Borland (Borland C++ or Turbo C++), Symantec, or other vendors. You will need the Windows SDK or equivalent, which comes bundled with most C/C++ compilers for the PC that support Windows development at all.

In addition, if you wish to compile the visual (VBX) forms of the controls presented here, you'll need certain files available only in the professional version of Visual Basic 3.0. VB 3.0 contains the Control Development Kit (CDK) which contains essential portions of the visual layer that makes VBX controls what they are.

○   ○   ○

*All of the source code to the controls presented in this book is presented on the diskette bound into the back cover of the book. There is no additional diskette to send away for.*

○   ○   ○

## How to Use This Book

We've designed this book to work on several levels. You can treat it as a software tools package, by loading the controls from the bound-in diskette and simply using them according to the instructions in Appendix A.

You can use this book as an introduction to the design and creation of custom controls, whether or not the example custom controls interest you at all. The process is laid out in great detail, and we feel that the approach of building a control in layers, such that a non-visual custom control lies at the heart of the somewhat more complex visual controls, is original and has not been described in print before.

Even if you know a little bit (or maybe a lot) about the creation of custom controls, you can use the example controls presented here as starting points for producing more specific or more ambitious controls to support one of your current projects.

The very *best* way to use this book, of course, is to curl up in your cushy chair with a box of Triscuits within easy reach and read it from one end to the other. Take notes; use your highlighter pen liberally. *Think.* In the process, you'll learn a lot about how controls work and how to write them, but perhaps more than anything else you'll learn a strategy for building on what you've already built, and wasting as little effort as possible in creating your software components.

◦　◦　◦

*Productivity is the watchword, and we've tried to present you with a way of working that will make you much more productive as a Windows programmer, regardless of the environment you're using.*

◦　◦　◦

## How to Use the Code

The custom controls presented in this book can be used by standard Windows apps created through SDK-style development, or those created using the "visual" environments such as Visual C++ or Visual Basic. With only a couple of exceptions, each of the controls has been implemented two ways: as a "standard" (SDK-style) control, and as a visual (VBX) control. The exceptions will be noted in the text.

The executable forms of the controls (both SDK-style and visual) can be used as is. You can use the source code forms to derive new and different controls from the ones presented.

Finally, just reading the code can be a wonderful brush-up on the internal operation of custom controls, whether or not you read the explanatory copy in detail.

# What's Inside

Here's a very brief summary of each of the book's eleven chapters:

Chapter 1: *A New Way to Think About Windows Programming* explores the question of why Windows programming is so hard, and introduces the notion of software components as a solution to simplifying the complexity of Windows development.

Chapter 2: *Custom Controls as Software Components* presents an overview of both Windows and its custom controls, and explains why custom controls make nearly ideal software components.

Chapter 3: *Inside a Custom Control* develops a workable "Skeleton" custom control that does nothing itself, but provides a platform to build on in later chapters.

Chapter 4: *Using Custom Controls* explains the different ways that custom controls may be used, and helps you develop an effective strategy for building them into your own applications.

Chapter 5: *Creating a Panel Control* develops a simple but interesting 3-D control that displays information with a raised or sunken appearance.

Chapter 6: *The Virtual Listbox Control* presents a listbox that can display 32K *items*—not simply 32K of total data size, as with the listbox that comes with Windows.

Chapter 7: *The Pagelist Control* develops a control that lets a user select one or more page icons from a horizontal list of such icons—similar to page selection in Aldus PageMaker.

Chapter 8: *The Browser Control* shows how to design and build a read-only list browser that can be bound to the Visual Basic Data control for examining records in a database.

Chapter 9: *The Text File Viewer Control* presents a basic text display box that can manage up to 32,767 lines, and provides a foundation for the full text editing control developed in the next chapter.

Chapter 10: *The Text File Editor Control* builds on the text viewer in Chapter 9 to create a complete text editor capable of handling up to 32,767 lines of text, with full Clipboard support and all common text editing features.

Chapter 11: *The IniData Control* presents a special-purpose edit control that manages Windows INI files, including a special feature to encrypt selected items in an .INI file to keep unauthorized users from altering them.

# 1

# A New Way to Think About Windows Programming

t was H.L. Mencken who said, "The public should not witness the making of laws, nor sausages." Laws? Sausages? Hah. How about software? Now there's a scary thought: The world's power users lined up at a railing, looking down upon a huge pit where row upon row of nerdy individuals sit hunched over their keyboards, bashing out "product." Would you buy software after that?

Or would you stop on the way home and pick up a slide rule?

1

**P**eople who know engineering but don't know software can regularly be read in trade journals, bemoaning the lack of quality in the industry's products. *How can our electronics be so good and our software so bad?* "Good question," is the usual answer. It's really not just a "good question," but a very simple and very important one. Not everyone will agree on a single answer, but there are some pretty obvious component answers that the people who write software for a living will generally agree upon.

# Running Hard and Losing Ground

One of the most important answers is this: *We never have time to learn the process well before it changes*, often radically. Just when we were mastering CP/M on the 8-bit 8080, the 16-bit IBM PC appeared, bringing new registers and that accursed hammerlock of segments and offsets. Just when we were mastering IBM PC programming on the 8088, the 286 brought protected mode, extended memory, the A21 line, and gross befuddlement. Very few people had figured out the 286 before the 386 appeared and changed everything, with 32-bit registers, greatly improved memory management, Virtual-86 mode, an unthinkably vast memory space, "flat model," and numerous brand-new instructions. Concurrently we were struggling first with DOS, then multitaskers like TopView and DesqView, then progressively more powerful and more prolix versions of Windows. The shortcomings of Windows led IBM to introduce OS/2 2.x, and OS/2 2.x led Microsoft to accelerate its development of Windows NT.

No matter how hard you run, you just can't seem to keep from falling behind.

◦   ◦   ◦

*The majority of Windows programmers are desperately trying to learn Windows at the same time that they are desperately trying to produce "live"—that is, money-making—code. If much Windows code seems as though it were written by amateurs, that's because...it is.*

◦   ◦   ◦

## Learning as You Go

Programming is a far more highly skilled profession than it used to be, due to all this piling up of technology upon technology. Where do those skills come from? The schools haven't been a great deal of help for many reasons, chief of which being that our educators haven't had any more time than our programmers to get ahead of the race. Even the seminar folks, although half a step ahead of the universities, are still a step-and-a-half behind the latest releases.

Mostly, programmers teach themselves.

You who are reading this book are probably in that "class." You know the drill: There is a spec, often a good one, and you know it well. Often, you wrote it. The problem isn't with the spec, but with the fact that there are seven hundred to a thousand API calls and a multitude of interlocking factoids that define the platform you're developing for. You know about a third of that from your last project. So you start with what you learned on your last project, and you begin building the application from the inside out, working from that precious familiar ground. As soon as you move away from familiar territory, you begin spending about half your time furiously researching a dozen different books (written by people barely half a step ahead of where you are) and the other half wondering why your application is throwing GP faults at you.

Layer by painful layer, your application happens. Each of those layers is in fact a layer of intellectual scar tissue. The quality of the work varies widely, in rough proportion to how long you had worked before you got to any given section. By the time you get it "done," you know a lot more than you did when you began. But by no means do you know it *all*, and before you begin the *next* project, the platform vendor produces another major release...with another 250 API calls and a totally revamped memory manager.

The people who keep shouting, "Design! Ya gotta have a design!" obviously haven't had to write any live code in years. You can't design when you don't understand the underlying technology. Sure, you can design "blind," but you end up abandoning the design a week into the work, and even if you create a new design, you end up abandoning that one within a month as well.

⚬   ⚬   ⚬

*By your fourth or fifth project, the lights are beginning to come on...*
*...then* bang! *You're promoted to management.*
*The new guy they hire begins back at Square One.*
*The circle is unbroken.*

⚬   ⚬   ⚬

## The Atomic Trap

There are some non-obvious consequences to learning Windows programming this way. The application's quality is uneven. Early code will be clumsy while later code could be quite good. This makes possible a very subtle class of bugs that comes from the differences between multiple gestalt understandings of the problem and its solution. Each conceptual "Aha!" that happens to the programmer will alter his or her grasp of the process, and change the direction and nature of that process subtly but irreversibly. Sadly, layers of scar tissue don't always function gracefully with one another—and you can't totally eliminate such bugs without rewriting much or most of that early, awkward code.

How many shops will give people time to rewrite that early code? Damned few. Scar tissue it was written, and scar tissue it will remain.

Much worse, however, are the programming habits that this process tends to unconsciously reinforce in the programmer. As described above, programmers build applications layer by layer, atom by atom, because they don't yet have the experience to look ahead and see the solution from a height. Those lucky few who persist long enough to obtain that gestalt understanding of the Windows API may well continue building their code like this, simply because it was the way they learned and really the only way they know how.

Furthermore, this atomic methodology builds in programmers the expectation (often but by no means *always* true) that each time they go through the coding process, they can do things a little bit better by doing them a little bit differently. So progress happens, atom by atom—at least until the next technological earthquake throws the programmer back to the Stone Age to begin again.

This brings us to the single most significant casualty of the Atomic Trap: Software reuse.

○   ○   ○

*Continuous striving to produce better code doesn't always produce better code—but it usually produces code that is different from and incompatible with earlier efforts.*

○   ○   ○

## The Curse of the Riflesmith

Rifles were once considered high technology, and in that earlier era they were created almost literally as works of art. A riflesmith would spend a great deal of time on the barrel, trying for the utmost precision, straightness, and finish. To the barrel he would fit the stock, and to the stock the other parts, one by one, shaping each one to precisely fit all the parts that came before. Each rifle *was* a work of art, and the longer the riflesmith worked, the better his rifles tended to be.

Each rifle, however, was different from every other, not in function, but in form. Each piece was hand-shaped to fit every other piece, and a hammer from one rifle would not quite fit into any other rifle. If that hammer ever broke, the rifle itself was useless unless you could get a riflesmith to somehow hand-fit a new hammer into the rifle. And because the original gestalt process of creating the rifle could not be recreated, *even by the original riflesmith*, a replacement hammer was rarely if ever as good as the one originally created with the rest of the rifle.

Does any of this sound the least bit familiar?

One of the fundamental turning points in the evolution of technology happened when rifles ceased to be works of art and instead became exercises in mass production. A rifle was created as a set of standardized parts, each with fixed dimensions that had to be created within specified tolerances. These parts were made individually such that each part was identical to every other part of its kind, and then all the parts were assembled into absolutely identical rifles.

One of these standardized rifles was not necessarily better than a hand-made "work of art" rifle. Most were strictly average and many, in fact, were marginal. Most worked well enough to be accepted by their users, however, and they were *tremendously* cheaper than one-off rifles.

This story has been told many times in the software development literature. The value of standardized parts in manufacturing is inarguable— it underlies the entire technological and economic foundation of our civilization. We can plainly see the echoes of the riflesmith in the way Windows programmers (and programmers for other complex platforms like OS/2 and OSF/Motif) currently produce their applications. Why, then, aren't we learning the same lessons? Why isn't software produced from standardized parts?

Why can't we reuse what we wrote last week?

No one will agree completely on a single answer to this question. In our view, the Curse of the Riflesmith lives on for these reasons:

• What we wrote last week is simply not as good as what we wrote this week. For the reasons presented above, programmers rarely if ever top out on any learning curve.

• Because software is so often created "atom by atom," programmers do not develop the sense of seeing software as separable into standardized parts.

• Because software doesn't "move," it doesn't break itself down obviously into individual parts "by inspection." Two programmers will rarely agree on what should be included in or left out of a given function.

- Because software does not break down into parts by inspection, it must be broken into parts by convention, and in our fractious industry such a convention has not yet emerged.
- Because there is such diversity in software tools such as languages, linkers, and debuggers, the framework within which standardized software parts are created must be defined *by the platform*, and not by individual languages or coding methodologies. In other words, as valuable as they are, *objects are not enough*.

# The Importance of Interconnections

Some people argue with considerable validity that software is not machinery, like a rifle or a punch press, but is instead a statement of logic. If there is a better metaphor for software in the "hard" world of manufacturing, it's probably somewhere in the realm of electronics, where digital circuits are also statements of logic, and where standardized parts have existed for almost eighty years.

Readers who have worked in or read much about electronics will be familiar with the "7400" series of integrated circuits. Well over a hundred different packages contain different assortments of logic gates, flip-flops, counters, and special functions common in digital work, like seven-segment display decoder/drivers. The inputs and outputs of each IC are well-defined and standardized. The digital designer essentially chooses them from a catalog with the assumption that they work and that their internal operation can be ignored in the context of designing the system under development.

They are genuinely "logic components." In the 7400 IC are four NAND gates. In the 7404 IC are four NOT inverters, and so on. The correspondence to program logic seems agonizingly close.

We are not the first writers to perceive this. Brad Cox, in his excellent book *Object-Oriented Programming: An Evolutionary Approach*, draws a direct comparison between objects and integrated circuit logic. His company even went so far as to trademark the term "Software IC" for its line of object-oriented libraries that provide "drop-in" logic for its object-oriented C compiler.

Cox's book is worth reading, both for his very strong arguments in favor of software reuse, and also to set you wondering why so few people are using Objective-C and its Software ICs. The problem is one of perspective:

⊙   ⊙   ⊙

*Interchangeable components are interchangeable not because of what they are, but because of what they plug into.*

⊙   ⊙   ⊙

## The Platform as Arbiter

This seems obvious to us, but it may not be obvious to everyone. What do Cox's Software IC's plug into? Mostly, they plug into Objective-C programs. If you're not using Objective-C, you can still use Software ICs, but the process is not as straightforward, and much of the ease of reuse is lost. This is not a criticism of Objective-C, which is a brilliant piece of work and deserves far more attention from the industry than it has received. Sadly, the vast majority of C programmers have never even heard of it, so its benefits are not available to them.

The metaphor isn't exact, but I think the situation is similar to making hardware ICs specific to a particular insertion tool. That is, if you can't hook the IC into the insertion tool, you can't use the IC—which is absurd.

TTL ICs like the 7400 series are interchangeable because of the standard conventions by which they are connected—in other words, "what they plug into." TTL ICs require a standard power supply of 5V. There is a well-defined spec for how the input and output pins respond to incoming signals and outgoing logic levels. The connections make them interchangeable. They are independent of any particular method of connection. Their "platform," if you want to call it that, is the body of physical laws governing electronics.

If there were only one language compiler of any consequence in the industry, we could make do with selling objects in that language and calling them "software components." They would not really be *software* components, however—they would be *language* components, because they would embody and be limited by all the assumptions and limitations contained in the language to which they must be linked.

To be considered true software components, code modules that we write must transcend the peccadilloes of *all* languages. For that to happen, the platform itself must be the arbiter of control and interface among the software components that we write and the applications that use them.

In today's parlance, a *platform* consists of an operating system overlaid by a user-interface layer. There are dozens of platforms that operate on desktop machines, but only three truly major ones: DOS/Windows, OS/2 PM, and Mac. (Unix taken as a whole might also be a major platform, but it is splintered into numerous incompatible platforms that do not as individuals command any significant PC market share.) For the purposes of this book, we'll be speaking of the DOS/Windows platform, which has the largest market share of any platform now available on desktop machines.

o     o     o

*To be a "standardized part," a software componenet must plug into the platform, and be available to any application or application development environment that respects the rules of that platform.*

o     o     o

# Component Programming for Windows

It may be true that Microsoft didn't have software components in mind when they defined the interface to Windows 3.x code modules known as *controls*. The name gives it away; controls do not have to be "controls" in the sense of user-interface elements like buttons and edit lines. Nonetheless, software components are what they are, and software components are what the industry is increasingly using them for.

Windows itself comes with a number of standard controls, which are all user-interface elements: Buttons, edit lines, panels, check boxes, and so on. What is important about Windows controls, however, is not the standard controls but the standardized interface that those controls present to Windows. This interface allows third-party developers to create controls that drop into and merge seamlessly with the Windows environment.

Controls were used sparingly, and generally as controls, until Microsoft first released Visual Basic in 1991. Visual Basic's control implementation was not fundamentally different from the one Windows defined, but the Visual Basic development environment encouraged programmers to think of controls as general-purpose software components. Visual Basic's Timer control was not really a control at all, but was an invisible machine that generated events after presettable intervals. With Visual Basic as an example, the third party market got started, and today there are hundreds of custom controls on the market, some of which are not controls in even the remotest sense of the word.

Why did Visual Basic make the difference? Probably because *Visual Basic fundamentally breaks the riflesmith paradigm of software creation.* Software is created by dragging components from a toolbar and dropping them onto a window. Code takes a back seat to the arrangement of components on a window. It's more like electronic assembly than crafting rifles: first the components are mounted on a chassis using drag-and-drop; then the components are wired together using Basic code as the connecting wiring.

◦   ◦   ◦

*Visual Basic's innovation has little or nothing to do with Basic, but
everything to do with treating software as standard components from
which an application is created.*

◦   ◦   ◦

Visual Basic controls are different enough from "standard" controls to
present some problems. We'll explain the dual nature of Windows controls
in the next chapter, and also explain how to circumvent those problems.

## Not Just Visual Basic

This book is not about Visual Basic, and the use of custom controls as
software components is not limited to Visual Basic or even Visual C++.
Windows custom controls may be used by any compiler that understands
the Windows controls API. Any C, C++, and Pascal compilers that generate
Windows applications at all have the ability to use Windows custom controls. Custom controls are generally stored in Windows DLLs, which are
language independent.

In short, Windows controls plug into Windows, not into any specific
language. This being the case, one or at most two varieties of a single
control (visual and standard) can serve the entire Windows software development industry.

*Now* we have software components, and can begin to think about
Windows software development in software component terms.

## The Software Components Design Mindset

No two programmers design their software in exactly the same way. Our
point in this book is not to present a design methodology, but simply to
show some simple changes in mindset that open the design process to the
use of software components. Most design methodologies are "component-
friendly"; that is, structured and object-oriented design both deal with well-
defined and highly decoupled modules.

As we pointed out earlier in this chapter, many Windows applications
are not designed so much as secreted, layer by layer, much as an oyster
secretes a pearl. Using software components in Windows programming is, if
anything, a return to more desirable methods of design and coding. These
are the skills you should develop:

- *Learn to see your application as an assemblage of independent blocks of functionality, not as "lines of code."* Ironically, many people who used to do this while developing for DOS lose the skill in negotiating the morass of the Windows API. Define your application in terms of functional blocks whose coupling is as close to zero as possible.

- *Learn to aggressively generalize wherever possible.* Generality is the soul of reuse. When defining a functional block, watch out for application-specific aspects. When you find them, see if they can be pulled out and placed somewhere else. If generalization seems difficult, it may be that your functional blocks are simply too large and complex. Split them and simplify the individual blocks. This may increase the overall number of functional blocks, but it will also increase the number of functional blocks that you can reuse in your next project.

- *Implement truly general functional blocks as custom controls.* Developing this skill is much of what this book is about. The process of creating a custom control from a functional block pretty much "seals off" the functional block as a zero-coupled component. A custom control may still be application-specific in what it does, but it will at least not be structurally tied to one larger block of code.

- *Whenever possible, migrate application-specific aspects to the connections between generalized functional blocks.* This is subtle. Parameterize blocks to generalize them, and then embody application specificity in the parameters that you pass to your generalized blocks. Try to create as few application-specific functional blocks as possible, since these are difficult to reuse in later projects.

- *Absolutely lose the "not invented here" mindset.* Ego can hurt you. Building your own components is a necessary skill, but no less important is the skill of integrating the components of others into your applications. If you can't shake the notion that other people's code simply *can't* be as good as your own, you deserve whatever you get.

- *Be aware of what's available in the third-party market.* Oddly, this may be the most difficult part of component-oriented design. To the best of our knowledge there is not yet any industry-wide catalog of third-party custom controls. You'll have to keep your eyes open, scan the ads in industry publications, and speak to other people who are working with custom controls.

- *Create your own catalog of custom controls.* If you program for Windows full-time, you will in the course of a year or two produce a fair number of custom controls. Document them thoroughly, and keep a notebook of the quirks and unusual aspects of the controls that you create. You'll be surprised how easy it is to forget about a modest piece of code that you create and perfect in an afternoon and then plug into an application. If you forget about 'em, you can't re-use 'em. If you discover third-party or public-domain controls that prove useful, include them in your catalog along with notes on how they are integrated with what you were doing.

These are the basic skills of component-oriented software development. You can apply them while using any design methodology you might choose. Rather than being a new way of working, they're simply a way of returning to an older notion of good coding practice, now made possible by the Windows custom controls API.

# A Survey of Today's Software Component Scene

The third-party market in custom control software components didn't really happen until Microsoft released Visual Basic in quantities running into the hundreds of thousands. All at once, the demand for control components grew to the point where it could support numerous small concerns.

It's instructive to take a look at what has already been put on the market. The survey here will show you the breadth of imagination represented by the software components already for sale. This list is by no means complete or even especially representative. There are now hundreds of standard and VBX components for sale on the open market. We've simply chosen a few that we have worked with and admire. Look in the smaller ads of nearly any programmers' magazine and you'll find dozens more.

## FarPoint's Spread/VBX

Figure 1.1 shows a very powerful custom control from FarPoint Technologies. They have implemented a complete spreadsheet in VBX form, with the ability to display cell data as ordinary alphanumeric text, times or dates, buttons, or bitmapped images. The figure shows the Spread/VBX control installed on a Visual Basic form, and being used for fairly traditional display of a mortgage amortization table.

The Spread/VBX control allows elaborate formatting of cells, cell locking, loading, saving, and printing of the sheet, printing of a portion of the sheet, the attaching of formulas to cells, and a great deal more.

**Figure 1.1  The FarPoint Technologies' Spread/VBX custom control.**

| Payment | Due Date of Payment | Principal in This Payment | Interest in This Payment | Balance After This Payment | Extra Principal This Payment | Principal Paid So Far |
|---|---|---|---|---|---|---|
| 1 | | 101.43 | 889.00 | 139898.57 | 0.00 | 101.43 |
| 2 | | 102.07 | 888.36 | 139796.50 | 0.00 | 203.50 |
| 3 | | 102.72 | 887.71 | 139693.78 | 0.00 | 306.22 |
| 4 | | 103.37 | 887.06 | 139590.41 | 0.00 | 409.59 |
| 5 | | 104.03 | 886.40 | 139486.38 | 0.00 | 513.62 |
| 6 | | 104.69 | 885.74 | 139381.69 | 0.00 | 618.31 |
| 7 | | 105.36 | 885.07 | 139276.33 | 0.00 | 723.67 |
| 8 | | 106.03 | 884.40 | 139170.30 | 0.00 | 829.70 |
| 9 | | 106.70 | 883.73 | 139063.60 | 0.00 | 936.40 |
| 10 | | 107.38 | 883.05 | 138956.22 | 0.00 | 1043.78 |
| 11 | | 108.06 | 882.37 | 138848.16 | 0.00 | 1151.84 |
| 12 | | 108.74 | 881.69 | 138739.42 | 0.00 | 1260.58 |
| 13 | | 109.43 | 881.00 | 138629.99 | 0.00 | 1370.01 |
| 14 | | 110.13 | 880.30 | 138519.86 | 0.00 | 1480.14 |
| 15 | | 110.83 | 879.60 | 138409.03 | 0.00 | 1590.97 |
| 16 | | 111.53 | 878.90 | 138297.50 | 0.00 | 1702.50 |
| 17 | | 112.24 | 878.19 | 138185.26 | 0.00 | 1814.74 |
| 18 | | 112.95 | 877.48 | 138072.31 | 0.00 | 1927.69 |
| 19 | | 113.67 | 876.76 | 137958.64 | 0.00 | 2041.36 |

FarPoint's product contains several additional custom controls, but none are as ambitious as Spread/VBX itself. The other controls in the package include a formatted date control, formatted time control, formatted picture control, a formatted read-only text viewer, and numeric entry fields for both integer and floating-point values.

**Spread/VBX**
FarPoint Technologies, Inc.
585A Southlake Boulevard
Southport Office Park
Richmond, VA 23236
(804) 378-0432

## MicroHelp's HighEdit

What FarPoint did for spreadsheets, MicroHelp has done for word processors. The HighEdit custom control is a middling word processor embodied as both a standard (DLL-based) and visual (VBX-based) component. The word processor is similar to Microsoft's Word for Windows, including many similar options on the menus and in the toolbar. Figure 1.2 shows a HighEdit window with some text in the window.

**HighEdit**
MicroHelp, Inc.
4359 Shallowford Industrial Parkway
Marietta, GA 30066
(404) 516-0898

## Sheridan Software's Data Widgets

Visual Basic 3.0 introduced the concept of a *bound data control*; that is, a control that could be connected to a database file existing independently of the control on disk. Microsoft implemented some simple bound data controls itself, but the third party market quickly began introducing new and more powerful bound controls for database work.

**Figure 1.2  MicroHelp's HighEdit word processor component.**

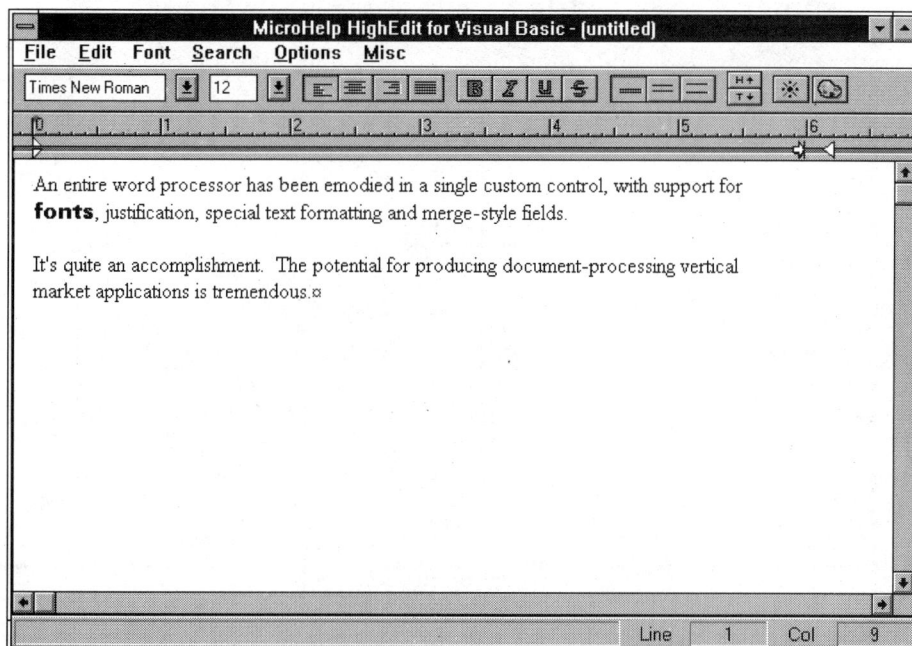

One such package is Data Widgets from Sheridan Software. The product is a collection of several bound data controls, all of them cooperating with Microsoft's own Data control, which is a part of Visual Basic 3.0. The major control in the package is a data grid that can be linked to Microsoft's Data control. This provides you with a data display similar to that used in Microsoft's Access database. (See Figure 1.3.)

One Widget is an improved data control that provides speed navigating with the VCR buttons, as well as a bookmark button to save a place in a table during a browse operation. Another intriguing bound data control is a data-aware drop-down listbox, which displays fields from a table in list box format and allows a user to select one item from the listbox by double-clicking on the item. The drop-down listbox Widget is shown with the larger Data Grid Widget in Figure 1.3.

The Data Widgets product contains a similar control that is an editable combo box, and an option button that can be bound to a field in a database to set or display the value in the bound field.

The controls in the Data Widgets product may be used *unbound*; that is, without any stated connection to a database table or query, but in that case they lose a considerable amount of their power.

**Figure 1.3  Sheridan Software's data-aware listbox Widget.**

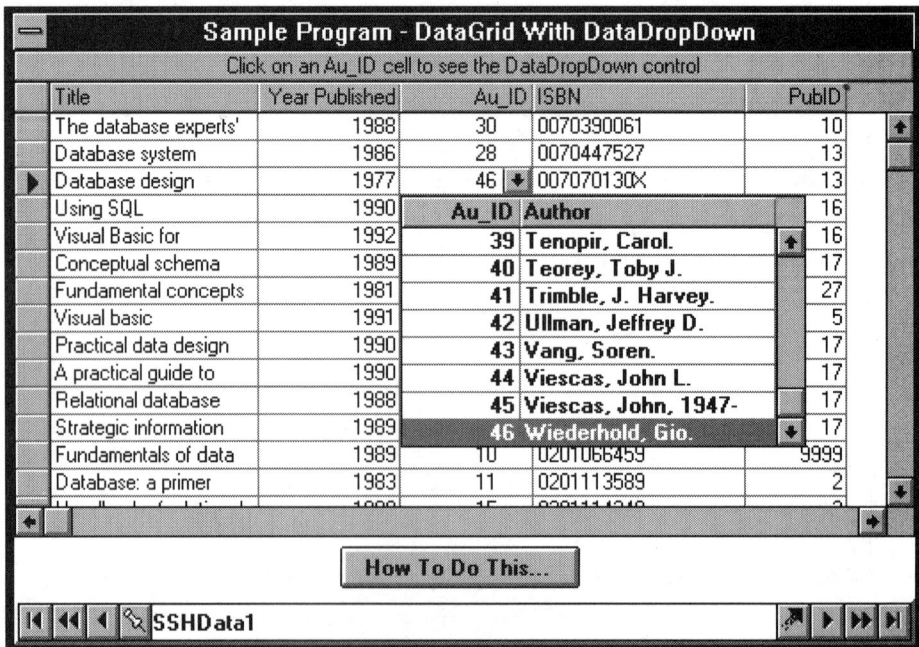

| Title | Year Published | Au_ID | ISBN | PubID |
|-------|---------------|-------|------|-------|
| The database experts' | 1988 | 30 | 0070390061 | 10 |
| Database system | 1986 | 28 | 0070447527 | 13 |
| Database design | 1977 | 46 ↓ | 007070130X | 13 |
| Using SQL | 1990 | | | 16 |
| Visual Basic for | 1992 | | | 16 |
| Conceptual schema | 1989 | | | 17 |
| Fundamental concepts | 1981 | | | 27 |
| Visual basic | 1991 | | | 5 |
| Practical data design | 1990 | | | 17 |
| A practical guide to | 1990 | | | 17 |
| Relational database | 1988 | | | 17 |
| Strategic information | 1989 | | | 17 |
| Fundamentals of data | 1989 | 10 | 0201066459 | 9999 |
| Database: a primer | 1983 | 11 | 0201113589 | 2 |

Sample Program - DataGrid With DataDropDown

Click on an Au_ID cell to see the DataDropDown control

| Au_ID | Author |
|-------|--------|
| 39 | Tenopir, Carol. |
| 40 | Teorey, Toby J. |
| 41 | Trimble, J. Harvey. |
| 42 | Ullman, Jeffrey D. |
| 43 | Vang, Soren. |
| 44 | Viescas, John L. |
| 45 | Viescas, John, 1947- |
| 46 | Wiederhold, Gio. |

How To Do This...

SSHData1

**Data Widgets**
Sheridan Software
65 Maxess Road
Melville, NY 11747
(516) 753-0985

# Some Ideas for Custom Control Software Components

A lot of programmers have told us that they really didn't obtain a truly useful understanding of any technology until they went off and completed a project embodying that technology. Furthermore, that project had to be *useful* in its results, and not simply a lab exercise like the ones done in college.

So in this section we're going to suggest a number of components that (to the best of our knowledge) do not yet exist in custom control form. They could be implemented in either standard or visual form, or both.

- **A Parser component**. This control could be implemented either without any visual expression (like the VB timer) or with both visual and non-visual modes of operation. In essence, this control would accept a string, and would parse the string into the string's component substrings. The substrings would then be stored in an internal array, much as the elements of a listbox are stored in an internal array. In fact, it makes sense to extend a listbox by adding parser machinery to it. That way, the programmer would have the option of letting the application user select one or more substrings from the listbox display, if choosing one of the substrings were part of the application's spec. A "mute" parser (that is, one without any display capability) would be smaller and no less useful.

- **A Mini-Midi Composer**. It could be fun and useful to have a control that presents the user with a staff and allows the user to edit a short musical sequence for output to a MIDI (Musical Instrument Digital Interface) port.

- **A Label Printer component**. Now that self-adhesive labels have been made relatively standard in terms of sizes and sheets (through Avery's domination of the label market), you could easily build a component that displays text or bitmaps on standard individual labels or sheets of labels. People who have made label printer software choose software based on Avery's catalog numbers. A cross-reference table relating Avery's part numbers to identical labels from other manufacturers would be a useful extra.

- **A Bar Coding component**. Build on your label printer component, and create a component that accepts alphanumeric data through a method, and outputs that data as bar coding patterns to a specified label type.

- **A Bar Code Reader**. While you're immersed in bar code lore, identify a popular bar code reader wand and create a component that watches its port for data and accepts bar code information and makes it available to the host program.

- **A "Shipper's ZIP" component**. Start with a simple edit box that prompts for a ZIP or Canadian Postal Code. Then validate the code against a table of legal codes, and optionally against a state/province code passed into the component through a method. (That is, let the component test to see if ZIP code 85255 is in Iowa.) Apart from devising a compact encoding scheme for the table of legal codes, that's almost trivial. To make the component truly compelling (and commercially marketable) devise a compressed, installable table for the component to read, containing current, dated shipping schedules from all the major couriers; for example, the USPS, Federal Express, DHL, Airborne, and so on. Pass a list of parameters into the component through a method (things like weight, contents type, maximum delay to delivery, and so on) and let the component select the least expensive shipper and return a shipping cost for that shipper. The real challenge here lies in creating a fairly easy way to encode the shipping rate tables into a binary module of reasonable size, and also a way to let the user easily install an updated table as needed. To make it real Buck Rogers stuff, build a mini-terminal into the component that allows the component to dial into your support BBS weekly or monthly, and check to see if a new table is available; if so, download it and install it automatically!

- **An Invoice component**. Nearly all businesses have to invoice clients or customers, and one or a series of ready-to-run invoice components would be a great head start in creating a vertical-market business manager application. Now that Microsoft has released the Access database engine and standardized the API for "data-aware" controls, you could create a data-aware invoice component that automatically stored orders and order items in database tables.

Doubtless, you'll unearth countless other ideas for reusable components as you build your skills in creating custom controls. It's high time to begin discussing what controls are, how they work, and most important, how you can build some of your own.

# 2

# Custom Controls as Software Components

The key to understanding a complicated system, no matter how tangled a conglomeration of whatevers it might be, lies in knowing how far back to stand while you look it over. Windows has a nasty reputation for complexity, but a lot of that probably stems from people standing too close while they study it. Put your nose down in the device contexts first off, and you'll be lost. Better to take ten steps back and then turn around and start to close in on it, little by little, taking good notes as you go.

n this chapter we'll stand back and explore the basics of custom controls. As you read on, you'll discover that custom controls provide an ideal way to create software components for creating Windows apps. We'll also show you the key differences between custom controls designed for standard environments and controls designed for visual environments.

## The Essence of Windows—The Big Ear

Microsoft Windows can be thought of as an operating environment in the active voice, just as good old DOS is an operating environment in the passive voice. DOS is a troll lying half-asleep under a bridge, waiting for orders. When you make an INT21H DOS call, you're yelling down to the troll and ordering him to get to work on something. Unless you yell down under the bridge, DOS the Troll just sort of sits there with one ear cocked, waiting.

Windows, on the other hand, takes a far more active role in things. Windows listens to the keyboard, listens to the mouse, shuffles memory around, and when something happens, it taps your program on the shoulder and says something like, "User just hit a key, Boss. Whatcha gonna do about it?"

These little advisements from Windows are called, most appropriately, *messages*. A Windows application is, at the core of it all, a continuous program loop, constantly checking to see if a message has arrived from The Next Level Up. Typically, in your Windows program you'll have a message-poll function call followed by a (usually large) *switch* or *case* statement. Down the length of this *switch* statement are options that correspond to every Windows message that your application must be able to respond to. For each message, there is a response of some sort, typically a function call.

There are, of course, a near infinity of details lying just beyond the resolution of this very simple explanation. But that's really all a Windows program is.

○   ○   ○

*A Windows program is an "ear" to listen for a Windows message, and a big* switch *statement to sort out the program's response.*

○   ○   ○

## Custom Controls Basics

The message/switch mechanism lies at the heart of every Windows program. In fact, a message loop like the one just described lies inside every window that an application can display. A Windows application has a single main window, and any reasonable number of child windows. As above, so below: The child windows have their message loops as well. This similarity between application windows and custom controls means you have less to learn about writing custom controls than you might think.

○   ○   ○

*If you can write an application window procedure, you have the pro-gramming knowledge to write a custom control.*

○   ○   ○

A child window does not have to be a full-blown window with a menu bar and a title and all the other folderol possessed by the main window. A child window can be as simple as a rectangular area of the screen with no adornment at all. It can even be *invisible*—no Windows law says that every window must be seen at all times, or any time at all.

Dialog boxes are child windows, as are the buttons and list boxes that populate them. Screen components like buttons, list boxes, and edit lines are what the user uses to control the program, and so such components have come to be called *controls*. Windows provides a number of "canned" controls: static (an empty frame), button, edit line, scroll bar, listbox, and combo box. This is a good list, but a somewhat thin one. Any control not supplied in the can with Windows is called a *custom control*. There is a thriving third-party market in Windows custom controls, and it's thriving for a very good reason.

○   ○   ○

*Every software component you buy is a component that you don't have to write for yourself.*

○   ○   ○

Buy what you can, and write what you must. Then you'll be covered for every eventuality. The important thing to remember is the Big Secret of Custom Controls:

○   ○   ○

*A custom control, at its heart, is just a window.*

○   ○   ○

Keep this in mind, and the mystique of custom controls is less likely to spook you.

## The Great Divorce

This being said, you can begin to explore the differences between custom controls and ordinary windows that belong to any Windows application. The differences are fewer than you might imagine. A control is very much like your main application window. Both are based on the message loop mechanism that we described earlier; both must respond gracefully to critical Windows creation messages such as *WM_CREATE* and *WM_DESTROY*, as well as the dozens of messages that arrive in between.

○    ○    ○

*Most of the differences between controls and ordinary windows is not structural but rather a matter of coupling.*

○    ○    ○

*Coupling* is a software engineering term that indicates the measure of conceptual connectedness between two pieces of code. Think of coupling as the sort of secret insider-understanding that happens among members of some sort of in-group. Some years ago, hip teenagers in Southern California had a term for something they considered worthy of admiration: *tubular.* Say "tubular" to them ("totally tubular" in the superlative), and they'd think of Eddie Money or some other rock star; you might still be thinking about lengths of PVC pipe. This new meaning of "tubular" was not in any dictionary, and it became a stumbling block for understanding between members of the L.A. younger set and the rest of humanity. The teenagers all knew what it meant, however, and in this respect they were conceptually coupled to one another in ways that the rest of us were not.

Undocumented and nonstandard assumptions shared between two pieces of code increase the coupling between them. One such matter of coupling happens through global variables. If your application defines a number of global variables, and its child windows make use of those global variables, your child windows are fairly tightly coupled to the main window. Take the child windows out of their "home" application and drop them into a different one, and they will continue reaching for global variables that are no longer there. Needless to say, they won't work correctly or (more likely) at all.

Custom controls, on the other hand, may make *no* such global assumptions about an application, except those assumptions enshrined in the Windows architecture and API. A control must be completely independent of any particular application.

○   ○   ○

*Think of controls as windows that have been divorced from any particular application, and which may be used within any application without changes of any kind.*

○   ○   ○

Obviously, such windows must be of fairly general application. A three-way button control hard-labeled "White, Wheat, or Rye" may not be globally coupled to any particular application, but it won't be of much use outside of delicatessen management systems. Better to make a generic three-way button and let the application provide the labels.

## One Copy, Many Instances

There's another major and far more subtle requirement that all custom controls must meet: They must be *re-entrant*. We'll deal with the details of accomplishing this later on. For now, you simply need to know what it means and why.

A control typically exists in a separate DLL file. This single DLL file is not linked to any specific application, and may be called from any Windows application that knows about and wishes to use the control. If you have three or four Windows applications running at once, they may all be using a single DLL file containing your fancy button control. Any single application, because it has only one thread of execution, will only be executing any given control once at any single time. However, as soon as you allow multiple applications to share a single control, the chance arises that two or more applications will execute the single code block of a control at the same time.

Sharing the code isn't a problem. However, a control's data must be stored in a separate *instance* of the control; one instance for each separate place a control is present in each application. You must write your controls so that they do not store information in static data.

○   ○   ○

*Each and every instance of a control must have its own copy of any data internal to the control.*

○   ○   ○

Of course, if you write your controls to be statically linked into a single application, this restriction does not apply. However, if your controls are to be stored in DLLs and shared by more than one application, they *must* be completely re-entrant.

## Two-Way Communication

To avoid "sneak paths" and unwanted coupling that destroys the generality of a custom control, all programmatic communication to the control must be through messages exactly like the ones Windows sends an application's main window. In fact, controls receive the same messages that an application does.

You are free to define new messages, just as Microsoft did with the *LB_* messages (for listboxes) and the *EM_* messages (for edit boxes). Likewise, the control's only communication with its parent is via messages. Mostly these are notification messages (which are subsets of the *WM_COMMAND* message), but a control can send specially defined messages to its parent as well. This two-way message traffic follows the general path outlined in Figure 2.1.

## Summary: The Black Box

A custom control, at its heart then, is just a window, very much like your main application window. It is based on a message loop, and must respond to messages sent down to it from its parent entity. A custom control must have near-zero coupling to any particular application, since its primary purpose for being is to act as a software component that may be dropped into any application that requires the services that the custom control provides. Because a custom control exists in a DLL, and that single DLL-based copy may be used by numerous applications executing at once

**Figure 2.1  The two-way message system for communicating with a standard control.**

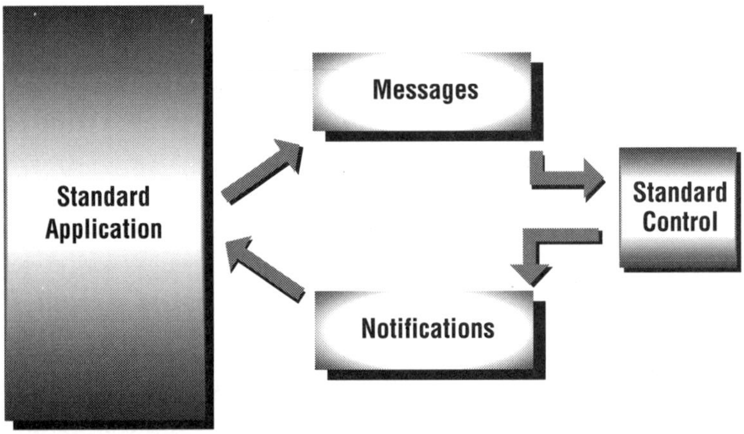

through Windows cooperative multitasking, custom controls must be entirely re-entrant.

In creating a custom control, what you are designing is basically a black box. You have to define, with utter lack of ambiguity, the following aspects:

• What the box's input data will be.

• How the box's appearance will react to this data.

• What response should be given to external events (user input, system events).

• What data may be extracted from the box.

This is less difficult than it appears.

# A Confusion of Interfaces

The word "interface" comes up a lot in Windows work, and never more than in work involving custom controls. We'd better lay out the various kinds of interface right now so that they won't pile up on you later on and cause mass confusion.

◦　◦　◦

*Generally, there are four kinds of interfaces in Windows custom controls work: User interfaces, application interfaces (APIs), integration interfaces, and development environment interfaces.*

◦　◦　◦

*User interfaces* are those aspects of a control that interact with the application user. The "button-ness" of a button control (that is, the fact that it can be pressed with a mouse click) is its user interface.

*Application Program Interfaces* (APIs) are sets of function calls and semantic assumptions that shape the way a piece of code is used by "outsiders"; that is, people who use the code but cannot modify it. The familiar set of INT 21H DOS calls are most of DOS's API. The Windows API is vastly more complex, consisting of hundreds of function calls and a host of assumptions about the way memory and pointers are used.

*Integration interfaces* are the ways that a control is integrated with an application that uses it. In most non-visual Windows work this means resource scripts. In a visual environment, the integration interface is an "active interface"; the programmer drags the control from a toolbar to the target form.

*Development environment interfaces* are the ways that a control is manipulated from inside any of the various development environments that understand custom controls. With some special set-up work, Windows custom controls can be loaded and edited from a dialog editor like Borland's Resource Workshop.

○   ○   ○

*If written to support Microsoft's VBX API conventions, a control can be loaded into an interactive development environment like Visual Basic, and be added to an application using the "drag-and-drop" machinery supported by Windows.*

○   ○   ○

## Integrating Controls

Ordinarily, you integrate custom controls into an application through resource scripts. It's a whale of a lot easier to tack custom controls onto a dialog, however, if you can edit the dialog visually through a dialog editor like the one in Microsoft's SDK or Borland's Resource Workshop. The snag is that a "bare" custom control isn't recognized as a control by the dialog editor. The dialog editor just sees it as another DLL, and has no way to tell how large the control is, what color it is, (things like that). You have to build some extra machinery into a custom control that allows the dialog editor to "ask" the custom control certain things about its aspects. The dialog editor uses the control's answers to manipulate instances of the control on-screen and attach them to dialog boxes being edited.

Microsoft's SDK dialog editor requires that each custom control resides, all alone, in its own DLL. Borland's Resource Workshop allows multiple controls in a single DLL, but you must keep in mind that a multi-control DLL cannot be edited with Microsoft's dialog editor.

You'll have to deal with all of these different sorts of interfaces in designing and perfecting your custom controls.

# Standard Controls Versus Visual Controls

With the advent of visual programming environments (primarily Visual Basic and Visual C++), suddenly the original method of realizing Windows applications has become *standard, conventional,* or even (to some folks' point of view) *old-fashioned*. Yet the non-visual environments (such as Borland's) are still going strong—you yourself may be a proponent. Either way, you need to understand how the original, or standard controls, differ in their implementation from the newer, visual controls—and how a single control implementation can work in *both* environments!

Controls intended for Microsoft's visual environments have additional requirements over those for standard controls. For example, while the code for standard controls can reside in a static link library, visual controls *must* reside in a DLL. Normally, DLLs containing visual controls have file extensions of .VBX, although this isn't an absolute requirement.

In addition to the messages understood by standard controls, visual controls also implement *properties, methods*, and *events* in a fashion highly suggestive of traditional OOP objects. These aspects impose a new structure on the "control-ness" of the visual control, and provide a framework through which those aspects may be manipulated from the visual environments. Properties, for example, are simply "state variables"; that is, data containing definitions of aspects of individual control instances. Properties define how large a control is, where it falls on the screen, what its caption and colors are, and so on. Standard controls have such aspects as well, but a visual control organizes these aspects into a table that the visual environment can easily access for examination and update by the visual programmer.

Methods, in keeping with the OOP tradition, are actions that a control may take on command from elsewhere in the program. For example, the *Refresh* method supported by most visual controls makes the control redraw itself on the screen. The *SetFocus* method, when called, gives the focus to the control.

Events are a little like methods in reverse; they are function calls initiated by the VB environment when some circumstance triggers the event. The call is made to code that the programmer "attaches" to the event through code editors within the visual environment. When a button control is clicked, for example, the click action triggers the *Click* event. If the visual programmer has attached some code to the *Click* event through the visual environment, that code will be executed.

## Controls within Controls

On the surface, it appears that visual controls are nothing at all like standard controls. In truth, everything that a standard control must do, a visual control must do also.

○   ○   ○

*Visual controls are supersets of standard controls and may be designed
so that a standard control is actually contained inside the visual control, performing those tasks that both types of controls have in common.*

○   ○   ○

This is the approach we have taken in this book. It allows a control to work
both as a standard and as a visual control with relatively little work.

In a visual control, the functional hand-off between the two types of
controls is accomplished by a special layer of code that lies between the
visual environment and the standard control contained within it. This layer
is composed of descriptions of the properties, methods, and events supported by the visual control, and of message-switching procedures that
perform appropriate translations before passing messages on. For example,
the assignment of a new value to a property should result in an appropriate
message being sent to the underlying standard control. It works in the
opposite direction as well: A notification from the standard control should
translate to an event trigger within the visual layer above it. We've sketched
out how this layer operates in Figure 2.2.

## Playing Visual Environment Catch-Up

There is something you should know regarding the difference between
Microsoft's Visual Basic and Visual C++ visual development environments. At the time of this writing, Visual Basic 3.0 is current, yet Visual
C++ 1.0 only supports VB 1.0 visual controls. Since all the most interesting abilities of visual controls were added *after* VB 1.0, that means that
those controls cannot be used by the current 1.0 release of Visual C++.
The VBX forms of the controls in this book require those advanced
features, so until an updated version of Visual C++ is released, the VBX
forms of these controls will only be useful in Visual Basic.

The first three releases of Visual Basic followed on one another's heels
*very* quickly, and in writing this book we made the assumption that
Microsoft will not let Visual C++ 1.0 reign for very long. Perhaps by the
time you read this, a new Visual C++ will have replaced the initial release,
and Visual Basic 3.0-style visual controls will be fully supported. Even if
Visual C++ 1.0 hasn't been updated, we don't think you will need to wait
for very long. Don't forget, *of course,* that this only applies to visual (VBX)
controls; the standard controls will *of course* work within any C/C++
compiler supporting DLLs and the Windows SDK conventions.

**Figure 2.2  How visual and standard controls are designed.**

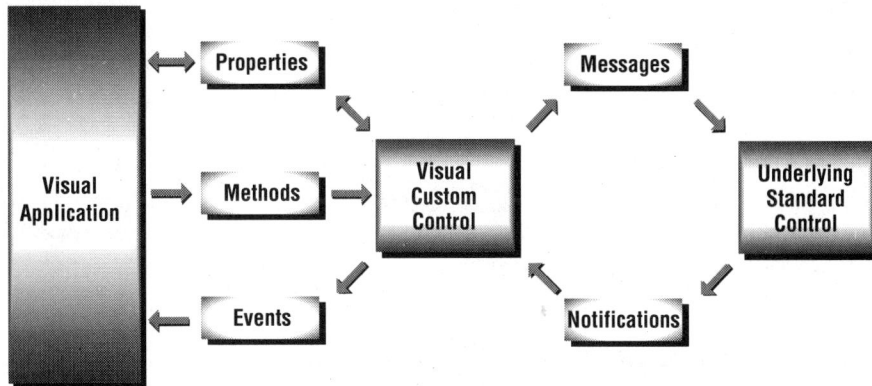

## Just Visual?

It is possible to create a control that can *only* be used from the visual environments. In such a case, the visual interface layer described above is actually the only "layer"; when messages arrive from the development environment, they are acted on directly instead of being passed on to a deeper layer. The advantage is the elimination of the overhead of a layer of code. The disadvantage is that the control can then never be used from a conventional environment.

Keep in mind that companies other than Microsoft may come out with competing Windows-hosted visual programming environments. They may or may not use VBX-style controls, but they will likely be compatible with all the conventional controls out there...including yours, if you don't nix the possibility up front by designing for the visual environments only.

One case where VBX-only controls make sense is when the control exists to encapsulate some function that would be difficult to achieve in the visual environment, but is relatively simple in C or Pascal. For example, a Visual Basic program can access the Windows API, but it is clumsy and un-Basic-like to do so. There are also pitfalls in translating between Visual Basic strings and native Windows strings, because each environment stores strings differently. A custom control that encapsulates, say, access to .INI files would save a Visual Basic programmer from having to use the *GetPrivateProfileString()* API function and hassling with string conversions to retrieve initialization data.

Note that the controls in these examples address shortcomings specific to Visual Basic in the here and now. Such controls would not be useful in Visual C++ or in a visual implementation of some other language—and a future release of Visual Basic might address the conflict somehow and make the controls completely unnecessary.

○　　○　　○

*We feel that you're better off hedging your bets, swallowing the (minor) overhead of that intermediating layer, and creating your controls to serve both the conventional and the visual markets.*

○　　○　　○

That's the approach we'll be taking as we present controls throughout the rest of this book.

# 3

# Inside a
# Custom Control

In this chapter we'll develop a useful custom control template. You'll be able to use this flexible template to create powerful, working controls in later chapters. As you progress through this book, you'll learn how to use messages with custom controls, how to store properties, and how to package a control so that it can be used by Windows applications whose resources are managed by Borland's Resource Toolkit, Microsoft's Dialog Editor, Visual C++ App Studio, or even Visual Basic.

**W**e'll refer to the control template we create as the Skeleton control. This control will require a number of source files. As we develop the control, we'll take you inside each important source file used. Then, in later chapters, we'll show you how to derive powerful controls from the Skeleton.

# Creating a Skeleton Control

Whether you are creating a simple or a complex control, it's best to do so within a consistent framework. This design approach will help you to use the control easily and locate its important components in case you wish to make changes. Here are the three components we'll include in each control we develop:

• A standard window-support function

• Initialization and termination functions

• A function for each major message that must be processed

All of these components could be kept in a single module. However, this approach would conflict with the modular programming techniques that have been shown to be superior.

○   ○   ○

*Even simple controls are likely to contain many lines of code just to handle Windows system messages. Therefore, we'll want to design our controls using a number of files to make them as efficient and as flexible as possible.*

○   ○   ○

With this philosophy in mind, we'll create separate control modules and store them using the filenames listed in Table 3.1.

## Getting the Big Picture

Before you begin any programming project, you'll want to make sure you understand its "big picture." Take a moment to examine the functions listed in Table 3.1. Also, view Figure 3.1 to get an idea of how the different files work together to create our Skeleton control. As we work through this chapter, we'll show you how each of these modules is designed and coded.

**Table 3.1   Modules Used in the Skeleton Control**

| Module | Description |
| --- | --- |
| INTERNAL.H | Private header file (includes SKELETON.H). This file defines all of the internal constants, structures, and function prototypes needed for the Skeleton control. |
| SKELETON.H | Public header file for the Skeleton control. In later chapters this file will be renamed to develop other custom controls. |
| MAIN.C | Provides the message dispatcher and *LibMain()* function for implementing a control as a DLL. |
| PAINT.C | Provides the functions for displaying a control. |
| DIALOG.C | Supplies the support dialog boxes for Dialog Editor, Borland Resource Workshop, and so on. |
| VISUAL.C | Supplies the visual environment layer for using a control with Visual Basic or Visual C++. |
| HELP.C | Provides access to the Windows Help Engine for the visual environments. |
| SKELETON.DEF | The module definition file. |
| SKELETON.RC | The resource script file for creating the control. |

**Figure 3.1   The file components of the Skeleton control.**

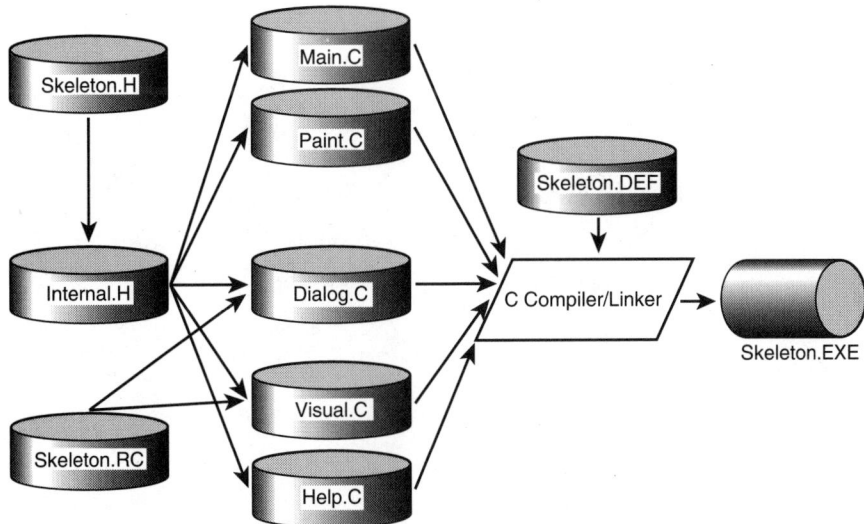

# Creating the Header Files

As you can see from Table 3.1, our Skeleton only requires two custom header files—INTERNAL.H and SKELETON.H. Each module will include INTERNAL.H, which contains internal constants and prototypes. Because this header file is only included by the modules that define the Skeleton control—MAIN.C, PAINT.C, and so on—it is considered a *private* **#include** *file*.

INTERNAL.H will also **#include** the public header file for the control (SKELETON.H in this chapter), as well as any other header files that are needed by the modules. Because Microsoft's Visual C++, C/C++ 7.0, and Borland/Turbo C++ all feature pre-compiled headers, there's no benefit in maintaining a separate header list with specific **#include** statements for each module.

## INTERNAL.H

INTERNAL.H is used by each of the modules in the Skeleton custom control. Unlike SKELETON.H (or its custom equivalent), INTERNAL.H will not be distributed with the custom control DLL or VBX. Here is the complete file:

```
#include <windows.h>
#include "Skeleton.H"
#ifndef NONVISUAL
#include <vbapi.h>
#endif
#include <custcntl.h>
#include <string.h>
#include <direct.h>
#include <stdlib.h>

#ifdef MAIN
HINSTANCE LibInstance = 0;
char far * ClassName = "Skeleton";
#else
extern HINSTANCE LibInstance;
extern char far * ClassName;
#endif

typedef struct
   {
   struct
      {
      UINT : 16;
      } CustomStyles;
   struct
      {
```

```
        UINT TabStop: 1;
        UINT Group: 1;
        UINT Thickframe: 1;
        UINT SysMenu: 1;
        UINT HScroll: 1;
        UINT VScroll: 1;
        UINT DlgFrame: 1;
        UINT Border: 1;
        UINT Maximize: 1;
        UINT ChipChildren: 1;
        UINT ClipSiblings: 1;
        UINT Disabled: 1;
        UINT Visible: 1;
        UINT Minimize: 1;
        UINT Child: 1;
        UINT Popup: 1;
        } StdStyles;
    } STYLEBITS, FAR * LPSTYLEBITS;

typedef struct
    {
    HFONT   Font;
    } MYDATA, far * LPMYDATA;

void far pascal PaintMe (HWND Window, HDC dc, LPMYDATA MyData);

#define IDC_STATIC 0
#define IDC_CAPTION 101
#define IDC_ID 102
#define IDC_BORDER 103
#define IDC_DISABLED 104
#define IDC_GROUP 105
#define IDC_TABSTOP 106
#define IDC_HSCROLL 107
#define IDC_VSCROLL 108


HSZ far pascal GetAboutPropertyString (HCTL Control);
HWND far pascal PopupAbout (HWND Window);
void far pascal RegisterVbPopups (void);
void far pascal UnregisterVbPopups (void);
LPSTR far pascal HelpFileName (void);
BOOL far pascal vbm_Help
    (
    HWND Window,
    BYTE HelpType,
    BYTE i,
    PPROPINFO Properties[],
    PEVENTINFO Events[]
    );
```

Let's start at the top. Notice that we've included SKELETON.H immediately after the WINDOWS.H file. This will ensure that SKELETON.H won't require other external include files. (SKELETON.H can be **#include**d with other programs, so it must stand alone as a "public" **#include** file.)

After the **#include** statements, we are testing to see if MAIN is defined (**#ifdef** MAIN). This test is done to determine if we need to allocate the variables *LibInstance* and *ClassName* or provide an external linkage to them. (MAIN will be defined in MAIN.C but not in the other modules.) *LibInstance* will be set in MAIN.C to hold the DLL instance handle; many Windows API functions require this value. *ClassName* will be referred to any time the name of the control class is needed. In this example, the string assigned to *ClassName* is "Skeleton."

◦   ◦   ◦

*Each time you derive a new control from the Skeleton control, you'll need to change the string assigned to* ClassName.

◦   ◦   ◦

The *STYLEBITS* structure describes the various bits in the *dwStyle* doubleword used when a control is created. This structure is available through the *GWL_STYLE* index of *GetWindowLong()*, as we'll see shortly. It's much easier to check these bits as Boolean values than to manually perform the bitwise masking that is otherwise necessary. If you add a custom style to your control, you'll want to add both the bit description to *STYLEBITS.CustomStyles* and the more traditional **#define** of a hexadecimal value equivalent to the setting of that specific bit. We'll be doing this in future chapters as we develop actual custom controls.

The *MYDATA* structure is used to store the information each instance of this control needs to do its job. Most controls will make extensive use of this structure, but the Skeleton control only needs to store a font handle here. Remember, in one application, all instances of a given control share the same data segment. Thus, you cannot use global variables to keep instance-specific data. By attaching a unique *MYDATA* structure to each instance, we'll be able to get around this constraint.

The function prototypes which follow the *STYLEBITS* declaration allow functions that reside in other modules to be called from MAIN.C. Note that only **far** functions are prototyped here. In each of the modules you'll find "local" functions that cannot be called from outside their module.

The **#define** statements following the prototypes are used by the *Styles* dialog box in the DIALOG.C module. They are placed in this include file instead of being lexically included in DIALOG.C. They are placed here because they must also be read by SKELETON.RC, the resource script file.

The header file concludes with a few more function prototypes. They describe functions from the HELP.C module. If you derive a control from Skeleton that does not include support for Visual Basic, these prototypes can be omitted.

## SKELETON.H

SKELETON.H is our prototype for a public header file. This is the file you'll need to **#include** in standard applications in order to communicate with the control. In the case of our Skeleton, no messages are defined; so, except for the comment, the file is empty:

```
// This file should contain message ID #defines and data structures
// used by applications to communicate with this control.
```

Later on, we'll be adding to this file when we create our custom controls.

# Creating the Source Files

Now that we've gotten the two simple header files out of the way, we're ready to code up the five main source files. The first three files, MAIN.C, PAINT.C, and DIALOG.C, are required to create controls for standard (non-visual) environments. The other two files, VISUAL.C and HELP.C, are provided so that you can easily hook into the visual environments. If you are creating a control that is not to be used in a visual environment, you won't need VISUAL.C or HELP.C.

## MAIN.C

MAIN.C has two important functions: It houses the *LibMain()* function so that our control can later be set up as a DLL, and it includes the "message dispatcher"—also known as the window procedure or *WndProc()*. You can think of the dispatcher as a 911 operator: When a call comes in, the operator jumps on the radio and passes the message on to the squad car, ambulance, or fire engine, as appropriate. When the *WndProc()* receives a message from the Windows god, it passes it on to the appropriate function.

Many books present window procedures in which all the code is inline, making for a truly unwieldy function. We shy away from large functions because they make it too hard to find anything. Therefore, the Skeleton *WndProc()* is designed to be a true dispatcher: It simply identifies a message and calls a local function to handle that message. Here is the complete

MAIN.C file:

```
#define MAIN
#include "Internal.H"

static Registered = FALSE;

#define GWL_MYDATA 0
#define GWW_EXTRA 4

static BOOL near pascal wm_NcCreate (HWND Window, LPCREATESTRUCT Create)
   {
   LPMYDATA MyData = (LPMYDATA) calloc (1, sizeof (MYDATA));
   SetWindowLong (Window, GWL_MYDATA, (long) MyData);
   return (MyData != NULL);
   }

static void near pascal wm_Create
     (HWND Window, LPCREATESTRUCT Create)
   {
   }

static void near pascal wm_Destroy (HWND Window)
   {
   }

static void near pascal wm_NcDestroy (HWND Window)
   {
   free ((LPMYDATA) GetWindowLong (Window, GWL_MYDATA));
   }

static HFONT near pascal wm_GetFont (HWND Window)
   {
   LPMYDATA MyData = (LPMYDATA) GetWindowLong (Window, GWL_MYDATA);
   HFONT Result = MyData->Font;
   if (! Result)
     Result = GetStockObject (SYSTEM_FONT);
   return Result;
   }

static void near pascal wm_SetFont (HWND Window, HFONT NewFont, BOOL Repaint)
   {
   LPMYDATA MyData = (LPMYDATA) GetWindowLong (Window, GWL_MYDATA);
   if (NewFont != MyData->Font)
     {
     MyData->Font = NewFont;
     if (Repaint)
       {
```

```
         InvalidateRect (Window, NULL, TRUE);
         UpdateWindow (Window);
         }
      }
   }

static void near pascal wm_Paint (HWND Window)
   {
   LPMYDATA MyData = (LPMYDATA) GetWindowLong (Window, GWL_MYDATA);
   PAINTSTRUCT ps;
   HDC dc = BeginPaint (Window, &ps);
   HBRUSH OldBrush;
   HBRUSH NewBrush = (HBRUSH) SendMessage (GetParent (Window),
      WM_CTLCOLOR,
      dc,
      MAKELONG (Window, CTLCOLOR_BTN));
   HFONT OldFont;
   HFONT NewFont = MyData->Font;
   if (NewBrush)
      OldBrush = SelectObject (dc, NewBrush);
   if (NewFont)
      OldFont = SelectObject (dc, NewFont);
   PaintMe (Window, dc, MyData);
   if (NewBrush)
      SelectObject (dc, OldBrush);
   if (NewFont)
      SelectObject (dc, OldFont);
   EndPaint (Window, &ps);
   }

LRESULT far pascal _export FAR PASCAL WndProc
      (
      HWND Window,
      UINT Msg,
      WPARAM wParam,
      LPARAM lParam
      )
   {
   LRESULT Result = 0;
   switch (Msg)
      {
      case WM_NCCREATE:
         Result = wm_NcCreate (Window,
            (LPCREATESTRUCT) lParam);
         break;
      case WM_CREATE:
         wm_Create (Window,
            (LPCREATESTRUCT) lParam);
         break;
```

```
      case WM_DESTROY:
        wm_Destroy (Window);
        break;
      case WM_NCDESTROY:
        wm_NcDestroy (Window);
        break;
      case WM_UNDO:
      case WM_CLEAR:
      case WM_COPY:
      case WM_CUT:
      case WM_PASTE:
        break;
      case WM_GETDLGCODE:
        Result = DLGC_STATIC;
        break;
      case WM_GETFONT:
        Result = wm_GetFont (Window);
        break;
      case WM_SETFONT:
        wm_SetFont (Window,
          wParam, LOWORD (lParam));
        break;
      case WM_PAINT:
        wm_Paint (Window);
        break;
      case WM_SETTEXT:
        Result = DefWindowProc (Window,
          Msg, wParam, lParam);
        InvalidateRect (Window, NULL, TRUE);
        break;
      default:
        Result = DefWindowProc (Window,
          Msg, wParam, lParam);
      }
    return Result;
    }

static WNDCLASS Class =
   {
   CS_HREDRAW | CS_VREDRAW | CS_DBLCLKS | CS_GLOBALCLASS,
   WndProc,
   0,
   GWW_EXTRA,
   0,
   NULL,
   NULL,
   COLOR_WINDOW + 1,
   NULL,
   NULL
```

```
    };

#pragma argsused
int far pascal LibMain
    (
    HINSTANCE hInstance,
    WORD DataSeg,
    WORD HeapSize,
    LPSTR CommandLine
    )
    {
    if (HeapSize > 0)
      UnlockData (0);
    LibInstance = hInstance;
    Class.hInstance = hInstance;
    Class.lpszClassName = ClassName;
    return RegisterClass (&Class) ? TRUE : FALSE;
    }
```

Let's take a close look at each function.

At the top of the module are several **static near** functions, *wm_NcCreate()*, *wm_Create()*, *wm_Destroy()*, and so on. Each of these functions handles a specific Windows message. The **static near** keywords used to define the functions are as close as the C language lets us get to nesting functions within other functions. You can easily nest functions in other languages, such as PL/I, Pascal, and Modula-2. Like a local variable, a nested function is visible only to the function in which it is defined. These languages allow an indefinite level of nesting. We can simulate one level, at least, by using the **static near** keywords, making the function so identified invisible to any other module in the project. Even though a DLL should be compiled as large model code, intrasegment calls can be **near** and thus incur less overhead than a **far** call. Also, the **static** keyword keeps the function name from being published. The linker won't even know that the function exists, making it possible to have **static near** functions of the same name in different modules.

The calling sequences for each of these **near** functions are designed to convert the generic parameters of a generalized Windows message into the specific parameters of an individual message. For example, the *WM_NCCREATE* and *WM_CREATE* messages do not use the *wParam* parameter; their *lParam* is actually a **far** pointer to a *CREATESTRUCT*. The calling sequences of *wm_NcCreate()* and *wm_Create()* accommodate this.

*wm_NcCreate()* processes the very first message a window receives. If internal resources (such as space for the *MYDATA* structure) are required for the window, this function should allocate those resources in response to this message. This is a window's only chance to refuse to be created; it does so by returning *FALSE* instead of *TRUE*. To maintain the create/destroy balance that Windows requires, any memory allocated while processing *WM_NCCREATE* should be freed while processing *WM_NCDESTROY*—the very *last* message a window receives.

The *wm_GetFont()* and *wm_SetFont()* functions support the corresponding Windows messages. Many dialog boxes specify a font other than the default System font. Such a dialog box sends each of its controls a *WM_SETFONT* message. The visual environments also set the font of each control on a form. However, the control must also be smart enough to know when a specific font has *not* been set, and to return the default System font in response to the *WM_GETFONT* message if necessary.

Incidentally, the code in *wm_SetFont()* that only invalidates the control window if the new font is not the same as the old, is needed for Visual Basic 3.0 support. Standard applications and earlier versions of VB do not need it, but VB 3.0 hurls *WM_SETFONT* messages, one after the other, at its controls—*even after sending a WM_DESTROY message.* There's no need to invalidate a window that's already received a *WM_DESTROY* message.

The *wm_Paint()* function performs the adjustments required by a custom control, then invokes the *PaintMe()* function located in the PAINT.C module. Besides possibly changing the font, a custom control should also send its parent a *WM_CTLCOLOR* message before it paints itself. The parent responds to the message by changing the foreground and background colors, if desired. It can also supply a new background brush.

The most important thing to note in *wm_Paint()*, however, is that the device context *dc* is restored to its original condition after it's been used. This is important. The objects selected into a device context are GDI (graphics device interface) objects. Because they *belong* to GDI and not to your application, they won't go away when your application closes. The parent window that created them must destroy them when it is done. Later, when we fill out the *PaintMe()* function, we'll have to follow the same discipline.

## The Message Dispatcher

Now that we've explored the Windows support functions, we're ready to examine the heart of MAIN.C—the dispatcher *WndProc()*. This function takes its job as message dispatcher very seriously. Notice that it does no actual processing; it only makes calls to other functions.

The clipboard messages, *WM_UNDO* through *WM_PASTE*, are provided as placeholders. You can add your own versions of the clipboard-related functions here. Moving on, the *WM_GETDLGCODE* message is sent by a parent dialog box to ask what keystrokes the control would like to receive. The value we return is appropriate for a static-type child window; most likely you'll want to return one or more of the standard constants (logically "or'ed" with the | operator) defined for this message. The standard constants are listed in Table 3.2.

The *WM_SETTEXT* message must be processed by the default window proc. There is, however, one important detail to consider: the default procedure does not redraw the window if the text changes. By adding a call to *InvalidateWindow()*, we can make sure this happens.

## Wrapping Up MAIN.C

As you're exploring the code in MAIN.C, you'll probably get the urge to add support for other messages so that you can process a "real" custom control. We've tried to resist this temptation to keep the code "lean and mean" and as general as possible.

Before we leave MAIN.C, let's examine the last function—*LibMain()*. Remember that this function is needed so that we can implement a control as a DLL. It is invoked automatically when the DLL is first loaded, just as *WinMain()* is invoked when an application is first loaded. Since the pur-

### Table 3.2  Keystrokes Wanted by a Control

| Message | Description |
| --- | --- |
| DLGC_BUTTON | Button (generic) |
| DLGC_DEFPUSHBUTTON | Default push button |
| DLGC_HASSETSEL | EM_SETSEL messages |
| DLGC_UNDEFPUSHBUTTON | No default push button processing. (A control can use this flag with DLGC_BUTTON to indicate that it processes button input but relies on the system for default push-button processing.) |
| DLGC_RADIOBUTTON | Radio button |
| DLGC_STATIC | Static control |
| DLGC_WANTALLKEYS | All keyboard input |
| DLGC_WANTARROWS | Arrow keys |
| DLGC_WANTCHARS | WM_CHAR messages |
| DLGC_WANTMESSAGE | All keyboard input (the application passes this message on to the control) |
| DLGC_WANTTAB | TAB key |

pose of the DLL is to provide a new global window class to Windows, this *LibMain()* registers the class when the DLL is loaded.

Most examples of *RegisterClass()* (including Microsoft's) use a *WNDCLASS* pointer and memory obtained by *GlobalAlloc()*—locked, used, unlocked, and then freed. Fortunately, we can use a better method—we'll just put it in the data segment. Then, most of the fields can be initialized by the compiler, and you'll save the execution time otherwise eaten by initialization code.

Every window in Windows has a data structure associated with it. We can specify that we'd like it to be a little *bigger* so it can hold more data than the stuff Windows keeps there. This will give us a place to keep our own data. At the top of the file we use the **#define** *GWW_EXTRA* statement to specify the number of bytes we want. We can use this extra memory any way we would like. We've defined enough space for a pointer to the *MYDATA* structure. We could append the whole *MYDATA* structure to the window structure, but the Windows API provides no easy way to get to it.

# PAINT.C

Now we get to the challenging, but fun part. Painting a custom control can be a complex and daunting task; on the other hand, sometimes it can be easy. Because our Skeleton control mimics a static control and simply paints text, it isn't very complicated.

If we are creating a control whose appearance is more involved (as most are), we'll definitely need a separate paint function—*PaintMe()*. The logical place to put this function is in its own file, PAINT.C. Here's the template for such a module:

```
#include "Internal.H"

static void near pascal PaintBorder
    (HWND Window, HDC dc)
  {
  DWORD dwStyle = GetWindowLong (Window, GWL_STYLE);
  LPSTYLEBITS Styles = (LPSTYLEBITS) &dwStyle;
  if (Styles->StdStyles.Border)
    {
    HBRUSH OldBrush =
      SelectObject (dc,
        GetStockObject (HOLLOW_BRUSH));
    RECT Rect;
    GetClientRect (Window, &Rect);
    Rectangle (dc,
      Rect.left, Rect.top,
```

```
          Rect.right,  Rect.bottom);
      SelectObject (dc, OldBrush);
      }
  }

#pragma argsused
void far pascal PaintMe (HWND Window, HDC dc, LPMYDATA MyData)
    {
    char Buffer[256];
    WORD Count;
    Count = (WORD)
      SendMessage (Window, WM_GETTEXT,
        sizeof Buffer, (long)(LPSTR) Buffer);
    TextOut (dc, 0, 0, Buffer, Count);
    PaintBorder (Window, dc);
    }
```

Notice that PAINT.C actually contains two functions—*PaintBorder()* and *PaintMe()*. The **static near** *PaintBorder()* function uses the window's style bits to determine if a border should be drawn around the window. Surprisingly, Windows does not draw borders automatically, perhaps because many possible styles of border are supported. Dialog boxes, for example, may use any of three border styles. Unless your custom control needs a special border, you'll be able to use *PaintBorder()* just as it is.

*PaintMe()*, on the other hand, will need to be changed. This simple version is provided so that you'll be able to compile and test the custom control Skeleton.

## DIALOG.C

DIALOG.C contains the set of functions that hook into the various standard resource editors. A partial list includes the original Dialog Editor from the Microsoft SDK and Borland's Resource Workshop. Any of these editors can work with your custom control if the following two conditions are met:

• The control resides in a DLL.

• The control has exported certain functions.

These conditions are easy to meet. The Skeleton DIALOG.C module will give you a real head start. We'd better warn you, though—it's a pretty meaty Skeleton. Don't worry, however, we'll take it a section at a time.

Perhaps the most important function used is *Info()*. This function must (using *GlobalAlloc()*) allocate a block of memory, set it to certain values, and return the handle to it.

## Working with Dialog Editors

The structure that Dialog Editor and most other resource editors require is *CTLINFO*, which is declared in the supplied header file CUSTCNTL.H. Other resource editors, such as Borland's Resource Workshop, have defined an extension to this structure. This can be accomplished because Dialog Editor doesn't look past the data it requires. The extended declaration for Resource Workshop is RWCTLINFO; it can only be found in Borland's version of CUSTCNTL.H. If you aren't using Borland's compiler you won't have access to this; so we've created our own variant, CONTROLINFO, which places the data items in the correct places but uses straightforward names uncluttered by those obfuscating Hungarian prefixes.

Keep in mind that the function name *Info()* isn't important because it is exported ordinally (for Dialog Editor) and by address (for Resource Workshop). *Info()* can report on just one control class. Although you can have as many styles for your custom control as you wish, they must all be variants of a single class. (Remember that radio buttons, check boxes, push buttons, and even group boxes are all different styles of the "Button" class.)

Here's the Skeleton *Info()* function from DIALOG.C:

```
#include "Internal.h"

HGLOBAL far pascal _export Info (void)
   {
   typedef struct
      {
      UINT TypeStyle;
      UINT SuggestedWidth: 15;
      UINT WidthPixels: 1;
      UINT SuggestedHeight: 15;
      UINT HeightPixels: 1;
      DWORD DefaultStyle;
      char Description[22];
      HBITMAP ToolboxBitmap;
      HCURSOR DropCursor;
      } TYPEINFO;
```

```
typedef struct
  {
  UINT Version;
  UINT TypeCount;
  char ClassName[CTLCLASS];
  char Title[94];
  char Reserved[10];
  TYPEINFO Type[1];
  } CONTROLINFO, FAR * LPCONTROLINFO;

HGLOBAL hCtlInfo;
LPCONTROLINFO CtlInfo;

hCtlInfo =
  GlobalAlloc (GHND, sizeof (CONTROLINFO));
if (hCtlInfo)
  {
  CtlInfo =
    (LPCONTROLINFO) GlobalLock (hCtlInfo);
  CtlInfo->Version = 100;
  CtlInfo->TypeCount = 1;
  lstrcpy (CtlInfo->ClassName, ClassName);
  lstrcpy (CtlInfo->Title, ClassName);
  CtlInfo->Type[0].SuggestedWidth = 50;
  CtlInfo->Type[0].SuggestedHeight = 40;
  CtlInfo->Type[0].DefaultStyle =
    WS_BORDER | WS_CHILD;
  lstrcpy (CtlInfo->Type[0].Description,
    ClassName);
  CtlInfo->Type[0].ToolboxBitmap =
    LoadBitmap (LibInstance,
      MAKEINTRESOURCE (100));
  CtlInfo->Type[0].DropCursor =
    LoadCursor (LibInstance,
      MAKEINTRESOURCE (100));
  GlobalUnlock (hCtlInfo);
  }
return hCtlInfo;
}
```

Because only one control style is supplied in this Skeleton, the *Type* member of *CONTROLINFO* is defined as an array with just one element. An advantage of defining this structure locally is that you can make it exactly the size you need. (The structure as defined in CUSTCNTL.H has space pre-allocated for 12 styles.)

The *GHND* parameter tells *GlobalAlloc()* to initialize the memory it allocates with zeros. Thus, we don't have to worry about the *Reserved* member, which must be zeroed out, or the *WidthPixels* and *HeightPixels* bits. These last two components don't exist as discrete members in the original structure. If they are set to 1, the *SuggestedWidth* and *SuggestedHeight* values refer to pixels rather than dialog units. If you use the original structure and want pixel values, you must perform a bitwise AND: *value & 0x8000*. Taking advantage of the bit-field feature of ANSI C produces clearer code.

The *DefaultStyle* member should be set to the style bits appropriate to the style you're defining. For example, the radio button type of "Button" would include the *BS_RADIOBUTTON* style, but the other types would not.

Because the components *ClassName*, *Title*, and *Description* are all set to *ClassName* (a pointer to the string "Skeleton"), you might be confused what each is for. *ClassName* is the name of the class; it will be used in dialog templates and in the *lpszClassName* parameter to *CreateWindow()*. The *Title* member was intended by Microsoft to hold copyright or author information. However, some resource editors use this value as a "suggested caption" for the control. *Description* is used by most resource editors to construct menu items that provide access to the control. For example, the *BS_PUSHBUTTON* style of the "Button" class might have a description of "Push Button."

The *ToolboxBitmap* and *DropCursor* members are extensions for Resource Workshop. *ToolboxBitmap* supplies the image used to represent the control in the Resource Workshop toolbox, and *DropCursor* is a handle to the cursor used when you are dragging one of these controls from the toolbox to a dialog form. In SKELETON.RC, we'll see "blanks"—a bare button for the bitmap and a similar cursor. The button bitmap must be 24x24 (not 22x22 as stated by Borland's documentation).

○   ○   ○

*Since cursors are always 32x32, there's room in the button bitmap for an image of the bitmap plus a hotspot "+" to show where the control will be dropped.*

○   ○   ○

## Supporting the Styles Dialog Box

The next component of DIALOG.C provides support for the Styles dialog box. This is the dialog box that appears when you double-click a control you've dropped on a dialog form. The dialog box template is included in SKELETON.RC. Figure 3.2 provides a picture of it in action.

**Figure 3.2  The dialog box template in action.**

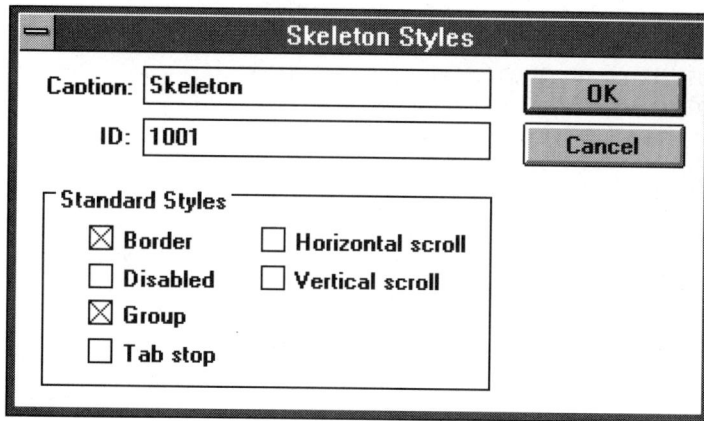

Although the physical appearance of the dialog box is defined in the resource script, its *behavior* is governed by the dialog procedure. First, the following structure is needed for us to communicate with the dialog:

```
typedef struct
    {
    LPCTLSTYLE Style;
    LPFNSTRTOID String2ID;
    LPFNIDTOSTR ID2String;
    } STYLEDATA, FAR * LPSTYLEDATA;
```

Next, we'll need a local function to handle the *WM_INITDIALOG* message:

```
static void near pascal wm_InitDialog
    (HWND Dialog, LPSTYLEDATA StyleData)
    {
    LPSTYLEBITS Styles =
      (LPSTYLEBITS) &StyleData->Style->dwStyle;
    char Buffer[64];
    if (Styles->StdStyles.TabStop)
      CheckDlgButton (Dialog, IDC_TABSTOP, 1);
    if (Styles->StdStyles.Group)
      CheckDlgButton (Dialog, IDC_GROUP, 1);
    if (Styles->StdStyles.HScroll)
      CheckDlgButton (Dialog, IDC_HSCROLL, 1);
    if (Styles->StdStyles.VScroll)
      CheckDlgButton (Dialog, IDC_VSCROLL, 1);
    if (Styles->StdStyles.Border)
      CheckDlgButton (Dialog, IDC_BORDER, 1);
```

```
if (Styles->StdStyles.Disabled)
   CheckDlgButton (Dialog, IDC_DISABLED, 1);
StyleData->ID2String (StyleData->Style->wId,
   Buffer, sizeof Buffer);
SetDlgItemText (Dialog, IDC_ID, Buffer);
SetDlgItemText (Dialog, IDC_CAPTION,
   StyleData->Style->szTitle);
}
```

Here we simply check each style bit; if it's on, we check the corresponding checkbox. The *ID2String()* function is supplied by the resource editor. It allows us to use symbolic constants for control IDs.

○　　○　　○

*When modifying the* wm_InitDialog() *function for a real control, you'll need to add checks for whatever additional styles you support.*

○　　○　　○

The next **static near** function handles the OK button event. This is accomplished by retrieving the data from the dialog box and putting it back into the structure:

```
static void near pascal wm_Command_OK
    (HWND Dialog, LPSTYLEDATA StyleData)
  {
LPSTYLEBITS Styles =
   (LPSTYLEBITS) &StyleData->Style->dwStyle;
char Buffer[64];
Styles->StdStyles.TabStop =
   IsDlgButtonChecked (Dialog, IDC_TABSTOP);
Styles->StdStyles.Group =
   IsDlgButtonChecked (Dialog, IDC_GROUP);
Styles->StdStyles.HScroll =
   IsDlgButtonChecked (Dialog, IDC_HSCROLL);
Styles->StdStyles.VScroll =
   IsDlgButtonChecked (Dialog, IDC_VSCROLL);
Styles->StdStyles.Border =
   IsDlgButtonChecked (Dialog, IDC_BORDER);
Styles->StdStyles.Disabled =
   IsDlgButtonChecked (Dialog, IDC_DISABLED);
GetDlgItemText (Dialog, IDC_ID,
   Buffer, sizeof Buffer);
StyleData->Style->wId =
   StyleData->String2ID (Buffer);
GetDlgItemText (Dialog, IDC_CAPTION,
   StyleData->Style->szTitle,
   sizeof StyleData->Style->szTitle);
}
```

As you might expect, this function is the inverse of *wm_InitDialog()*. Since *IsDlgButtonChecked()* conveniently returns 1 for TRUE and 0 for FALSE, we can use its value as a direct assignment to the *Styles* structure. *String2ID()* is the inverse of *ID2String()*; it allows us to store the true numeric ID of the control by translating from whatever the user typed.

By moving the bulk of processing into these local functions, the actual dialog procedure becomes more manageable:

```
BOOL far pascal _export StyleProc
    (
    HWND Dialog,
    UINT Msg,
    WPARAM wParam,
    LPARAM lParam
    )
  {
  static LPSTYLEDATA StyleData;
  switch (Msg)
    {
    case WM_INITDIALOG:
      StyleData = (LPSTYLEDATA) lParam;
      wm_InitDialog (Dialog, StyleData);
      return TRUE;
    case WM_COMMAND:
      switch (wParam)
        {
        case IDOK:
          wm_Command_OK (Dialog, StyleData);
          EndDialog (Dialog, TRUE);
          break;
        case IDCANCEL:
          EndDialog (Dialog, FALSE);
          break;
        default:
          return FALSE;
        }
      break;
    default:
      return FALSE;
    }
  return TRUE;
  }
```

When the *WM_INITDIALOG* message arrives, *lParam* will point to the *STYLEDATA* struct we declared earlier. Since pointers remain valid in Windows 3.1 even if memory should be shuffled, we can store this pointer in a local static variable so we'll have it when we need it—exactly once, when and if the user clicks the OK button.

The dialog itself is kicked off by the *Style()* function, the second of the required exports. Since most of the work is done by the dialog procedure, *Style()* itself is simple:

```
BOOL far pascal _export Style
    (
    HWND Window,
    HGLOBAL hCtlStyle,
    LPFNSTRTOID aString2ID,
    LPFNIDTOSTR aID2String
    )
{
BOOL Result;
STYLEDATA StyleData;
StyleData.Style =
    (LPCTLSTYLE) GlobalLock (hCtlStyle);
StyleData.String2ID = aString2ID;
StyleData.ID2String = aID2String;
Result = DialogBoxParam (LibInstance,
    "Styles", Window, DlgProc,
    (long) (LPSTYLEDATA) &StyleData);
GlobalUnlock (hCtlStyle);
return Result;
}
```

Here we allocate the *StyleData* structure (on the stack) and give it the information the dialog procedure will need. Since the resource editor will supply a handle to the global block that contains the *CTLSTYLE* structure, we invoke *GlobalLock()* to obtain a real pointer to the structure first. (After the dialog box is closed, we unlock the handle.)

◦ ◦ ◦

*This method of passing data was required by earlier versions of Windows that could run in Real Mode; now we're stuck with it.*

◦ ◦ ◦

Finally, we activate the dialog box by calling *DialogBoxParam()*. This function not only starts the dialog but allows us to pass it initial data—a big improvement over the older method which required a raft of static variables to temporarily hold the data.

The last of the three functions required by Dialog Editor is *Flags()*. This function provides the text string by which your custom styles can be represented. Internal to Dialog Editor, for example, is a *Flags()* function which converts 0x40000000L to *WS_CHILD*. If more than one custom style is set, *Flags()* should produce a string that includes the bitwise *or* operator

("|") between constants. On the other hand, if there are no custom styles (as is the case with the *Skeleton* class), this function doesn't have to do anything but NULL-terminate the string:

```
UINT far pascal _export Flags
    (
    DWORD Flags,
    LPSTR Buffer,
    UINT BufferSize
    )
    {
    LPSTYLEBITS Styles = (LPSTYLEBITS) &Flags;
    Buffer[0] = 0;
    return lstrlen (Buffer);
    }
```

## Supporting the Resource Workshop

What we've seen so far satisfies the needs of the Dialog Editor and any resource editor that follows its standards exactly. However, Resource Workshop, being a superset of Dialog Editor, requires one more function—*ListClasses()*. This function is exported by name rather than ordinally, so it *must* be named exactly "*ListClasses*."

One of the extensions of Resource Workshop allows more than one class to be defined in a single DLL. *ListClasses()* is intended to advise Resource Workshop what classes this DLL contains. This is the only extension that is not backwards compatible. We can maintain backward compatibility, however, by simply restricting ourselves to a single class per DLL; *ListClasses()* can report one class as easily as it can report many.

Before coding the *ListClasses()* function, we need to provide a few **typedefs**. These supply definitions that Microsoft omitted in their version of CUSTCNTL.H. (They are supplied in Borland's version; if you are using a Borland compiler, you won't need to add these to DIALOG.C):

```
typedef HGLOBAL (CALLBACK *LPFNINFO)( void );
typedef BOOL (CALLBACK *LPFNSTYLE)
    (
    HWND hWnd,
    HGLOBAL hCntlStyle,
    LPFNSTRTOID lpfnSID,
    LPFNIDTOSTR lpfnIDS
    );
typedef UINT (CALLBACK *LPFNFLAGS)
    (
    DWORD dwStyle,
```

```
    LPSTR lpBuff,
    UINT wBuffLength
    );

typedef HGLOBAL (CALLBACK *LPFNLOADRES)
    (LPSTR szType, LPSTR szId);
typedef BOOL (CALLBACK *LPFNEDITRES)
    (LPSTR szType, LPSTR szId);
```

The *ListClasses()* function provides a hook for you to add more features. For example, it is called with a pointer to an edit function. By invoking this function, your Styles dialog could start up any of the Resource Workshop editors. This might be handy for some kind of compound control, perhaps, but it's not a feature typically needed. That means we only need concern ourselves with the *ListClasses()* function's major task: to return a list of the classes in SKELETON.DLL, with pointers to the other three required functions:

```
#pragma argsused
HGLOBAL far pascal _export ListClasses
    (
    LPSTR CallingClass,
    UINT Version,
    LPFNLOADRES Load,
    LPFNEDITRES Edit
    )
{
typedef struct
    {
    LPFNINFO   fnRWInfo;
    LPFNSTYLE  fnRWStyle;
    LPFNFLAGS  fnFlags;
    char   ClassName[20];
    } RWCTLCLASS, FAR *LPRWCTLCLASS;

typedef struct {
    short   ClassCount;
    RWCTLCLASS  Class[1];
    } CTLCLASSLIST, FAR *LPCTLCLASSLIST;

HGLOBAL hClassList =
    GlobalAlloc (GHND, sizeof (CTLCLASSLIST));
LPCTLCLASSLIST ClassList =
    (LPCTLCLASSLIST) GlobalLock (hClassList);

ClassList->ClassCount = 1;
ClassList->Class[0].fnRWInfo = Info;
```

```
ClassList->Class[0].fnRWStyle = Style;
ClassList->Class[0].fnFlags = Flags;
_fstrcpy (ClassList->Class[0].ClassName,
  ClassName);

GlobalUnlock (hClassList);
return hClassList;
}
```

Again, the local **typedefs** define structures found in Borland's CUSTCNTL.H, except that we've allowed room for only one class. Now that this is done, we can allocate the global block, set the values, and return the handle.

# Supporting Visual Environments

Now that we've created MAIN.C, PAINT.C, and DIALOG.C, you could compile these modules and link them with SKELETON.RC and SKELETON.DEF to produce the SKELETON.DLL. The Skeleton custom control could then be used by Dialog Editor, Resource Workshop, or any other compliant resource editor. You would not, however, be able to use the control in a visual environment, such as Visual Basic.

Let's now add the additional layer required to meet the needs of the visual environments in the next section.

## VISUAL.C

The process of creating a dialog template was once a real pain. It had to be done entirely by writing a script. When Windows 3.0 emerged, Microsoft provided a useful dialog editor as part of the SDK. The editor defined the hooks we gave the Skeleton control DLL in the previous section. With this editor, you could select a custom control almost as easily as a standard control and place it on a dialog design. Borland's Resource Workshop extended the standard a little and provided an even more useful tool.

Then Visual Basic appeared and changed the rules. Visual controls (especially those designed for Visual Basic) don't present the same face to the programmer as standard controls. Although they are internally set up as child windows, receiving and sending messages, their API works in terms of properties, methods, and events. Visual Basic controls are stored in DLLs, but the hooks aren't the same as Dialog Editor's; so you can't usually use the same custom controls in Visual Basic and standard applications.

○　○　○

*However,* the hooks don't conflict. *It is possible to create a* dual-environment custom control *by adding the functionality we'll present in the VISUAL.C module.*

○　○　○

To create VISUAL.C, you'll need access to the Visual Basic Professional Edition. To interface to the visual environments, you need the **#include** file and import library from the CDK which comes only with Visual Basic Professional Edition. (It is not currently included with Visual C++.)

Once you have the CDK, you must add the following line to INTERNAL.H:

```
#include <vbapi.h>
```

Visual Basic controls reside in DLLs, although they have file extensions of .VBX. The extension helps to distinguish the VB controls from other DLLs. However, if you have a DLL with the proper VB hooks, you can add it to a Visual Basic project; just as a standard application can pass the name of a .VBX to *LoadLibrary()*. Therefore, the naming of the resulting DLL is up to you.

The hooks that Visual Basic requires are numerous and complex, and the size of VISUAL.C reflects this. We'll make it more manageable by inspecting it in reasonably sized chunks. Let's start at the top:

```
#include "internal.h"

#define _segment(p) \
   ((unsigned int) \
   (((unsigned long) (void far *) (p)) >> 16L))
#define _offsetin(struc, fld) \
   ((USHORT)&(((struc *)0)->fld))
#define VBERR_BADINDEX 381

extern HANDLE LibInstance;
static long Boolean[2] = { 0, -1 };

typedef struct
   {
   UINT : 16;
   } VBDATA;
typedef VBDATA far * LPVBDATA;
```

The *_segment* **#define** is used with Visual Basic strings (which are nothing like C strings). *_offsetin* is a handy way to determine the offset of a field within its structure. And *VBERR_BADINDEX*, although not used in the Skeleton, will prove useful to many controls derived from it.

The *Boolean* array helps convert between C TRUE (value 1) and Visual Basic True (value -1). (As a language, C is case sensitive. *TRUE*, *True*, and *true* are the names of three different entities in C. "TRUE" is the constant used in Boolean operations. Visual Basic, on the other hand, is case insensitive, and the Boolean value is commonly entered as "True".) Finally, the *VBDATA* structure (with a placeholder member) will be used to store control-specific data.

## Working with Properties

Visual controls are controlled primarily through the use of *properties*. Properties are generally data items, but you can program an action to correspond to the setting or retrieving of a property value. First, though, the properties have to be defined.

Prior to the introduction of Visual Basic, great emphasis was always placed on keeping Windows display text language-independent; but the strings that identify properties are almost always inline literals. You can create a language-independent Visual control by storing the name strings in the application's resource pool and loading them during control initialization. However, Visual Basic applications (and Visual C++ Foundation Class applications) load slowly, so you won't want to add any more initialization overhead then absolutely necessary.

A better strategy will be to set up properties during compile time. Considering the number of properties some controls have, the savings in time over run-time initialization is definitely noticeable. The properties are set up by initializing a set of data structures:

```
PROPINFO Property_About =
  {
  "(About)",
  DT_HSZ | PF_fGetMsg | PF_fNoRuntimeW |
    PF_fGetHszMsg,
  0, 0, 0, NULL, 0
  };

PPROPINFO Properties[] =
  {
  PPROPINFO_STD_NAME,
  PPROPINFO_STD_INDEX,
  PPROPINFO_STD_BACKCOLOR,
  PPROPINFO_STD_FORECOLOR,
  PPROPINFO_STD_LEFT,
  PPROPINFO_STD_TOP,
  PPROPINFO_STD_WIDTH,
```

```
      PPROPINFO_STD_HEIGHT,
      PPROPINFO_STD_FONTNAME,
      PPROPINFO_STD_FONTSIZE,
      PPROPINFO_STD_FONTBOLD,
      PPROPINFO_STD_FONTITALIC,
      PPROPINFO_STD_TABINDEX,
      PPROPINFO_STD_TABSTOP,
      PPROPINFO_STD_BORDERSTYLEON,
      PPROPINFO_STD_ENABLED,
      PPROPINFO_STD_PARENT,
      PPROPINFO_STD_TAG,
      PPROPINFO_STD_VISIBLE,
      PPROPINFO_STD_HELPCONTEXTID,
      PPROPINFO_STD_LAST,
      &Property_About,
      NULL
      };

  typedef enum
      {
      IPROPINFO_STD_NAME,
      IPROPINFO_STD_INDEX,
      IPROPINFO_STD_BACKCOLOR,
      IPROPINFO_STD_FORECOLOR,
      IPROPINFO_STD_LEFT,
      IPROPINFO_STD_TOP,
      IPROPINFO_STD_WIDTH,
      IPROPINFO_STD_HEIGHT,
      IPROPINFO_STD_FONTNAME,
      IPROPINFO_STD_FONTSIZE,
      IPROPINFO_STD_FONTBOLD,
      IPROPINFO_STD_FONTITALIC,
      IPROPINFO_STD_TABINDEX,
      IPROPINFO_STD_TABSTOP,
      IPROPINFO_STD_BORDERSTYLEON,
      IPROPINFO_STD_ENABLED,
      IPROPINFO_STD_PARENT,
      IPROPINFO_STD_TAG,
      IPROPINFO_STD_VISIBLE,
      IPROPINFO_STD_HELPCONTEXTID,
      IPROPINFO_STD_LAST,
      IPROPINFO_About,
      IPROPINFO_End
      } PROPSIX;
```

As a convention, all the "standard" properties are listed first. This is partly a requirement; the *PPROPINFO_STD_NAME* property must come first, and *PPROPINFO_STD_INDEX* must be second. After that, you're on your own; you can include or exclude properties as you see fit. Incidentally, if you encounter code where the first property listed is the property *PPROPINFO_STD_CTLNAME*, don't let it throw you. This was the property name first used by Visual Basic. VPAPI.H continues to supply the older term as an alias, but *PPROPINFO_STD_NAME* is preferred for new projects.

Another interesting standard property is *PPROPINFO_STD_LAST.* This isn't a "real" property; it serves as a placeholder separating the standard from the custom properties. It is not required, but we will be using it in HELP.C to process help requests.

In the Skeleton, we support one custom property, "(About)", and the usual standard properties. The *PROPINFO* structure is used to describe custom properties. The *PPROPINFO* array is then initialized to the standard and custom properties supported by this control. Finally, the *PROPSIX enum* is created. The entries correspond sequentially to the entries in the *PPROPINFO* array; they will be used later to identify messages regarding each property.

You'll find *IPROPINFO_End* useful, even though it isn't referred to anywhere else. The problem is that each entry in an enumerated list like this ends in a comma, except the last one. In a control with many properties, you can cut and paste similarly spelled property names to save some work. Unfortunately, it's easy to forget to remove the trailing comma from the last one and waste a compile. *IPROPINFO_End* is a good solution.

## Never Change the Order of Properties!

A software product usually goes through many stages of refinement during the course of its life. Often you'll want to remove a property, perhaps to replace it with another one that does more. Don't remove the old one! A property's values are stored on disk with an ID equivalent to its *PROPSIX enum.* If you add or delete an entry from the middle of the list, you'll throw off the values of all subsequent properties and never be able to load a form using the older version of the control.

## Handling Events

Events are handled like properties, except that events are not stored, so you can add or remove them as it suits you. This is fortunate because events *must* be listed in alphabetical order (except for *PEVENTINFO_STD_LAST*), which is another reason why language-independent controls are hard to create.

Events are easy to initialize:

```
PEVENTINFO Events[] =
  {
  PEVENTINFO_STD_CLICK,
  PEVENTINFO_STD_DBLCLICK,
  PEVENTINFO_STD_DRAGDROP,
  PEVENTINFO_STD_DRAGOVER,
  PEVENTINFO_STD_GOTFOCUS,
  PEVENTINFO_STD_LOSTFOCUS,
  PEVENTINFO_STD_MOUSEDOWN,
  PEVENTINFO_STD_MOUSEMOVE,
  PEVENTINFO_STD_MOUSEUP,
  PEVENTINFO_STD_LAST,
  NULL
  };

typedef enum
  {
  IPEVENTINFO_STD_CLICK,
  IPEVENTINFO_STD_DBLCLK,
  IPEVENTINFO_STD_DRAGDROP,
  IPEVENTINFO_STD_DRAGOVER,
  IPEVENTINFO_STD_GOTFOCUS,
  IPEVENTINFO_STD_LOSTFOCUS,
  IPEVENTINFO_STD_MOUSEDOWN,
  IPEVENTINFO_STD_MOUSEMOVE,
  IPEVENTINFO_STD_MOUSEUP
  IPEVENTINFO_STD_LAST,
  IPEVENTINFO_END
  } EVENTSIX;
```

All of the events used in the Skeleton control are standard ones. We'll show you how to add a custom event in Chapter 6.

## Handling Messages and Methods

A VB control is based on a Control Procedure just as a standard window is based on a Window Procedure. In fact, many of the messages are the same. As usual, we've kept the control proc small by invoking local functions to do the major work:

```
static void near pascal wm_NcCreate
     (
     HCTL Control,
     LPCREATESTRUCT Create
```

```
    )
    {
    LPVBDATA VbData =
      (LPVBDATA) VBDerefControl (Control);
    }

static void near pascal wm_NcDestroy
      (
      HCTL Control
      )
    {
    LPVBDATA VbData =
      (LPVBDATA) VBDerefControl (Control);
    }
```

The first function handles the *WM_NCCREATE* message that arrives
when a control first comes into existence. The second function handles the
*WM_NCDESTROY* message which is the last message the control receives
before it is destroyed. In the Skeleton, each function only does one thing—
dereference the *MYDATA* structure. In a real control, *wm_NcCreate()* would
allocate any memory needed by the *VbData* structure elements, and
*wm_NcDestroy()* would free this memory.

Just to remind you, there is no conflict between the *wm_NcCreate()*
function in this module and the function of the same name in MAIN.C
because each one is declared to be **static** and, therefore, is not "published"
by the linker.

We defined the Skeleton control's properties and events, but not its
methods. Why? A control's methods are pre-defined. There's a limited
number of them, and for most methods, the default behavior is adequate.
We will add a couple of structures to aid in handling the methods most
often overridden:

```
typedef struct
    {
    long Count;
    HSZ Item;
    long Index;
    } ADDITEM;
typedef ADDITEM far * LPADDITEM;

typedef struct
    {
    long Count;
    long Index;
    } REMOVEITEM;
typedef REMOVEITEM far * LPREMOVEITEM;
```

```
static long near pascal vbm_Method
    (
    HCTL Control,
    HWND Window,
    USHORT Method,
    void far * Args
    )
{
LPSTR Text;
LPADDITEM AddItem = Args;
LPREMOVEITEM RemoveItem = Args;
switch (Method)
    {
    default:
       return VBDefControlProc (Control,
          Window, VBM_METHOD,
          Method, (long) Args);
    }
}
```

For controls that rely only on default method handling, this whole block can be omitted. (To see it in action, see the Pagelist control in Chapter 7.)

## Handling Properties

There are two ways properties can be set and two ways their values can be retrieved. For simple properties, you just specify (in the *PROPINFO* structure) where in *MYDATA* the data is offset, and what data type it is. (The offset can be supplied with the *_offsetin* **#define** found in the beginning of VISUAL.C.) The visual environment then maintains these properties automatically. For more complex properties, you supply the *pf_GetData* and *pf_SetData* flags, which cause messages to be sent in order to set and retrieve property values:

```
static BOOL near pascal vbm_SetProperty
    (
    HCTL Control,
    HWND Window,
    USHORT Property,
    long Value,
    long far * Error
    )
{
LPVBDATA VbData =
    (LPVBDATA) VBDerefControl (Control);
switch (Property)
    {
```

```
    default:
    return FALSE;
    }
  }

static BOOL near pascal vbm_GetProperty
    (
    HCTL Control,
    HWND Window,
    USHORT Property,
    LPVOID Value,
    long far * Error
    )
  {
  LPVBDATA VbData =
    (LPVBDATA) VBDerefControl (Control);
  switch (Property)
    {
    default:
    return FALSE;
    }
  }
```

By the same token, design-time properties must retain their values until the application runs. This is done by storing the properties on disk as part of the project (or the .EXE, if the project has been compiled). Then, when the application runs, the values are loaded from disk. (That's why Visual Basic apps take so long to load. Well, one reason, anyway.) The following operations also take place in response to messages:

```
static BOOL near pascal vbm_LoadProperty
    (
    HCTL Control,
    HWND Window,
    USHORT Property,
    HFORMFILE FormFile,
    long far * Error
    )
  {
  LPVBDATA VbData =
    (LPVBDATA) VBDerefControl (Control);
  switch (Property)
    {
    default:
    return FALSE;
    }
  }
```

```
static BOOL near pascal vbm_SaveProperty
    (
    HCTL Control,
    HWND Window,
    USHORT Property,
    HFORMFILE FormFile,
    long far * Error
    )
{
LPVBDATA VbData =
    (LPVBDATA) VBDerefControl (Control);
switch (Property)
    {
    default:
    return FALSE;
    }
}
```

We're now ready to examine the Control Procedure itself:

```
long far pascal _export CtlProc
    (
    HCTL Control,
    HWND Window,
    USHORT Msg,
    USHORT wParam,
    long lParam
    )
{
long Error = 0;
switch (Msg)
    {
    case WM_NCCREATE:
      wm_NcCreate (Control, (LPCREATESTRUCT) lParam);
      break;
    case VBM_METHOD:
      return vbm_Method (Control, Window, wParam, (void far *) lParam);
    case VBN_COMMAND:
      switch (HIWORD (lParam))
        {
        default:
          break;
        }
      break;
    case VBM_SETPROPERTY:
      if (vbm_SetProperty (Control, Window, wParam, lParam, &Error))
        return Error;
      break;
    case VBM_GETPROPERTY:
```

```
        if (vbm_GetProperty (Control, Window, wParam, (LPVOID) lParam, &Error))
          return Error;
        break;
      case VBM_LOADPROPERTY:
        if (vbm_LoadProperty (Control, Window, wParam, (HFORMFILE) lParam,
          &Error))
          return Error;
        break;
      case VBM_SAVEPROPERTY:
        if (vbm_SaveProperty (Control, Window, wParam, (HFORMFILE) lParam,
          &Error))
          return Error;
        break;
      case VBM_GETPROPERTYHSZ:
        switch (wParam)
          {
          case IPROPINFO_About:
            *((HSZ far *) lParam) = GetAboutPropertyString (Control);
            break;
          }
        return 0;
      case VBM_INITPROPPOPUP:
        switch (wParam)
          {
          case IPROPINFO_About:
            return PopupAbout (Window);
          }
        break;
      case VBM_HELP:
        if (vbm_Help (Window,
            LOBYTE (wParam),
            HIBYTE (wParam),
            Properties, Events))
          return 0;
        break;
      case WM_DESTROY:
        WinHelp (Window, HelpFileName (), HELP_QUIT, 0);
        break;
      case WM_NCDESTROY:
        wm_NcDestroy (Control);
        break;
    return VBDefControlProc (Control, Window, Msg, wParam, lParam);
    }
```

Some properties must be displayed in a way that has little to do with the property's value. For example, *(About)* doesn't *have* a value, but it is represented by a string advising the user to click to see the About box. When the user clicks, the *VBM_INITPROPPOPUP* message is used to display the About box. The code that actually implements this feature is in HELP.C, which we'll look at shortly. HELP.C also contains the *vbm_Help()* and *HelpFileName()* functions.

You'll notice that *WinHelp()* is called to close down the Windows Help Engine during processing of the *WM_DESTROY* message, rather than *WM_NCDESTROY*. The *Window* parameter must be the same as the value passed when the Help Engine was started (if, indeed, it has been started), and it must apply to a valid window. By the time *WM_NCDESTROY* arrives, the window itself no longer exists, and the window handle is invalid.

## Providing the Visual Environment Hook

When a visual environment loads a custom control DLL (or VBX), it automatically invokes a certain exported function, just as Resource Workshop does. In the case of a visual environment, the function invoked is *VBINITCC()*. This function returns the address of a master structure that points to all the other structures we've defined:

```
MODEL Model =
   {
   VB_VERSION,
   MODEL_fFocusOk | MODEL_fArrows,
   (PCTLPROC) CtlProc,
   CS_VREDRAW | CS_HREDRAW,
   WS_BORDER,
   sizeof (MYDATA),
   8000,
   NULL,
   NULL,
   NULL,
   Properties,
   Events,
   IPROPINFO_STD_NAME,
   IPEVENTINFO_STD_CLICK,
   -1
   };

BOOL far pascal _export VBINITCC
      (
      USHORT Version,
      BOOL Runtime
      )
   {
   if (! Runtime)
      RegisterVbPopups ();
   Model.npszDefCtlName =
```

```
Model.npszClassName =
Model.npszParentClassName = ClassName;
return VBRegisterModel (LibInstance, &Model);
}
```

Finally, we close off the module with the function a visual environment automatically invokes when unloading the DLL:

```
VOID FAR PASCAL _export VBTERMCC (void)
  {
  UnregisterVbPopups ();
  }
```

The functions *RegisterVbPopups()* and *UnregisterVbPopups()* are located in HELP.C; we'll look at them in a moment.

The number "8000" in the *Model* structure specifies the starting number of a set of bitmaps in the DLL's resource pool. Like Resource Workshop, the visual environments require that bitmaps of a specific size represent the control in the environment's toolbox. These bitmaps are numbered, not named, and their numbers are offsets from the value specified in the *Model* structure. The bitmap that represents the control for a color VGA display must be located at offset zero (number 8000 for the Skeleton control). At offset one is the same bitmap in "pressed" condition; at offset 3 is a monochrome version; at offset 6 is an EGA version. We've supplied blanks for each of these on the program disk, named 8000.BMP, 8001.BMP, and so on. They are also referenced in SKELETON.RC.

## HELP.C

HELP.C is the last code module needed for our Skeleton control. It contains the functions that access the Windows Help Engine as well as the code for displaying the About box. The bad news is that the visual environments require a rather indirect method of displaying an About box. Thus, most of the code in this module is needed to support the About box.

◦   ◦   ◦

*The good news is that HELP.C can be used, unchanged, in every visual custom control project we'll create from now on.*

◦   ◦   ◦

Before we dissect HELP.C, you'll need to understand a little background on how the visual environments operate. Whenever a visual programmer selects a control property, the environment sends a *VBM_INITPROPPOPUP* message. Most of the time this message is ignored; when the visual environment receives a zero in response, it allows the visual programmer to simply type in a new value for the property. On the other hand, if a non-zero value is returned, the small combo-box arrow is replaced by an ellipsis button (...). When clicked, this button will usually display some kind of dialog box, like the color-pick dialog that appears when you want to change a control's foreground or background color.

The problem is that a dialog must not be displayed if the visual programmer *doesn't* select the ellipsis—simply clicking once on the property name doesn't necessarily mean the programmer intends to change the value. In addition, if you were to start a modal dialog directly in response to the *VBM_INITPROPPOPUP* message, it wouldn't *be* modal—because Visual Basic isn't written like most Windows apps, and the various windows actually behave in some respects as several different, concurrently running applications.

The solution is to respond to the *VBM_INITPROPPOPUP* message by creating a popup window—*not* a dialog box! The window is created, but will not be displayed unless the visual programmer clicks on the ellipsis. Then, and only then, will the popup window receive a *WM_SHOWWINDOW* message.

You could let the popup window itself *be* the About box. This approach is a hassle, however, because you'll need to place text, add an icon, manage the OK button, and so on. It's easier to use a conventional dialog box—we'll just use the *VBDialogBoxParam()* function to start it.

Now that you know why the functions in HELP.C can't be as simple as we'd have liked, let's look at the module itself:

```
#include "internal.h"

#define _segment(p) ((unsigned int) (((unsigned long) (void far *) (p))
                     >> 16L))

HSZ far pascal GetAboutPropertyString (HCTL Control)
   {
   return VBCreateHsz (_segment (Control), "Click here for About->");
   }
```

The first function is invoked in response to the *VBM_GETPROPERTYHSZ* message. *VBCreateHsz()* creates a NULL-terminated string in the visual data space and returns its handle. You should never leave handles lying around without knowing how they will be released; but in this case, the visual environment will release the string when it's done with it.

The dialog procedure for the About dialog is a textbook example of such code. The only command it expects is from the OK button:

```
#pragma argsused
BOOL _export FAR PASCAL AboutDlgProc
    (
    HWND    Dialog,
    WORD    msg,
    WORD    wParam,
    long    lParam
    )
  {
  switch (msg)
    {
    case WM_INITDIALOG:
      break;
    case WM_COMMAND:
      switch (wParam)
        {
        case IDOK:
          EndDialog (Dialog, IDOK);
          break;
        default:
          return FALSE;
        }
      break;
    default:
      return FALSE;
    }
  return TRUE;
  }
```

The About dialog procedure, of course, is distinct from the About *popup*
procedure. The word "popup" here refers only to the kind of window
because this window will never actually appear—its only job is to trigger
the About dialog when it receives a *WM_SHOWWINDOW* message:

```
LONG _export FAR PASCAL AboutPopupWndProc
    (
    HWND    Window,
    USHORT  Message,
    USHORT  wParam,
    LONG    lParam
    )
  {
  switch (Message)
    {
    case WM_SHOWWINDOW:
      if (wParam)
```

```
            {
            VBDialogBoxParam (LibInstance, "About", AboutDlgProc, NULL);
            return 0L;
            }
        break;
    }
    return DefWindowProc (Window, Message, wParam, lParam);
    }
```

Likewise, the *PopupAbout()* function creates an instance of the About popup window class:

```
static char AboutPopupClass[] = "AboutPopup";

HWND far pascal PopupAbout (HWND Window)
    {
    return CreateWindow
        (
        AboutPopupClass,
        NULL,
        WS_POPUP,
        0, 0, 0, 0,
        Window,
        NULL,
        LibInstance,
        NULL
        );
    }
```

Just to make sure the sequence is clear in your mind, let's go over it once more:

1.  When the visual message dispatcher receives a *VBM_INITPOPUP* message for the *(About)* property, it calls *PopupAbout()*.

2.  *PopupAbout()* creates a window of the "AboutPopup" Class.

3.  The window procedure for the AboutPopup window waits for a *WM_SHOWWINDOW* message; when it arrives, it calls *VBDialogBoxParam()* to create the About box.

## Supporting the Windows Help Engine

Activating the Windows Help Engine and displaying an About box are related only because both tasks appear on the *Help* menu. Although generating the name of a help file has nothing to do with the About box, we've slipped the *HelpFileName()* function into HELP.C for two reasons. First, VISUAL.C is about as large as we'd like to make it. And second, like the other functions in HELP.C, this one will not need any modifications when used in a derived control.

Rather than hard-code a help filename, we can derive the name of the help file from the name of the DLL. *HelpFileName()* does this just once; on subsequent invocations it simply returns the result of its original calculations:

```
static LPSTR near pascal HelpFileName (void)
    {
    static char Pathname[MAXPATH] = { 0 };
    if (! Pathname[0])
        {
        char Drive[MAXDRIVE];
        char Dir[MAXDIR];
        char FName[MAXFILE];
        char Ext[MAXEXT];
        GetModuleFileName (LibInstance, Pathname, MAXPATH);
        _splitpath (Pathname, Drive, Dir, FName, Ext);
        _makepath (Pathname, Drive, Dir, FName, ".HLP");
        }
    return Pathname;
    }
```

The **static** keyword places the *Pathname* variable in the data segment, not the stack; it will retain whatever value it is given between calls.

Visual Basic supports on-line help for controls during design time. You can implement this by responding to the *VBM_HELP* message:

```
BOOL far pascal vbm_Help
    (
    HWND Window,
    BYTE HelpType,
    BYTE i,
    PPROPINFO Properties[],
    PEVENTINFO Events[]
    )
    {
    BOOL Result = FALSE;
    switch (HelpType)
        {
        case VBHELP_PROP:
            if (Properties[i] < PPROPINFO_STD_LAST)
                {
                WinHelp (Window, HelpFileName (), HELP_KEY,
                    (DWORD) (LPSTR) Properties[i]->npszName);
                Result = TRUE;
                }
            break;
```

```
      case VBHELP_EVT:
        if (Events[i] < PEVENTINFO_STD_LAST)
          {
          WinHelp (Window, HelpFileName (), HELP_KEY,
            (DWORD) (LPSTR) Events[i]->npszName);
          Result = TRUE;
          }
        break;
      case VBHELP_CTL:
        WinHelp (Window, HelpFileName (), HELP_CONTENTS, 0);
        Result = TRUE;
        break;
      }
    return Result;
    }
```

This function provides context-sensitive help as long as a keyword is provided in the help file for each of the control's unique properties and events. If a request comes in for a standard property or event, the function returns FALSE, signifying that default handling is appropriate.

Finally, we're left with the twin jobs of registering and unregistering the popup window classes. Recall that we called the *RegisterVbPopups()* and *UnregisterVbPopups()* functions during initialization and termination of the visual layer (in VISUAL.C). Here are their definitions:

```
static HANDLE IdeTask = FALSE;

static WNDCLASS Class =
    {
    0,
    (WNDPROC) AboutPopupWndProc,
    0,
    0,
    0,
    NULL,
    NULL,
    NULL,
    NULL,
    NULL
    };

void far pascal RegisterVbPopups (void)
    {
    Class.hInstance      = LibInstance;
    Class.lpszClassName = AboutPopupClass;
    RegisterClass (&Class);
    }

void far pascal UnregisterVbPopups (void)
```

```
    {
    if (IdeTask == GetCurrentTask())
        {
        UnregisterClass (AboutPopupClass, LibInstance);
        IdeTask = NULL;
        }
    }
```

The *IdeTask* variable is used to detect the difference between the visual development environment and the simple running of a Visual Basic or Visual C++ application. There can be only one instance of Visual Basic or App Studio at a time, but you could run any number of visual applications at the same time. In VISUAL.C we made sure the popups were only registered at design time (in other words, by the IDE):

```
    Y
    Y
    if (! Runtime)
        RegisterVbPopups ();
    Y
    Y
```

By saving the task handle when the popups are registered, we can be sure we don't unregister them until the IDE terminates.

# Wrapping Up the Skeleton Control

We have now covered each of the header files and main code modules for our Skeleton control. In order to complete the control and compile and link it, we'll need to build a module definition file, SKELETON.DEF, and a resource file, SKELETON.RC.

## SKELETON.DEF

We mentioned that the Dialog Editor exports the three required functions ordinally. That means that the function *name* will not be exported; instead, it will be exported by number—and you get to specify the number. The *_export* directive is inadequate for that; ordinal functions must be listed in the module definition file. Here's SKELETON.DEF:

```
LIBRARY          Skeleton
EXETYPE   WINDOWS
CODE    PRELOAD MOVEABLE DISCARDABLE
DATA    PRELOAD MOVEABLE SINGLE
HEAPSIZE 4096
```

```
EXPORTS
        WEP PRIVATE
        Info        @2
        Style       @3
        Flags       @4
        WndProc     @5
        StyleProc   @6
        ListClasses
```

The *WEP PRIVATE* line generates a warning by the Borland compilers but is required by Visual C++. If you intend to compile under Borland, you should replace *PRIVATE* with *RESIDENTNAME*. The functions *Info()*, *Style()*, and *Flags()* must be exported ordinally as 2, 3, and 4, respectively. Likewise, the control's window procedure (defined in MAIN.C) must be exported as ordinal 5. Microsoft's documentation claims that the Style dialog procedure must be exported as ordinal 6, although we don't think it's really necessary since the Styles dialog is invoked by the *Style()* function. Still, there's no reason not to go along with the gag. Finally, *ListClasses()* must *not* be exported ordinally.

## SKELETON.RC

The *resource script* file contains all the resources your control will need: the bitmaps and cursors, the Styles and About dialog boxes. This file, like a source code module, is compiled; but instead of producing a .OBJ file, it produces a *resource* file with a .RES extension. The contents of the .RES file are appended to the finished DLL by the linker.

The first component of the .RC file is the Styles dialog box template. As we mentioned while describing DIALOG.C, this dialog box is used by the dialog

**Figure 3.2  The Skeleton dialog.**

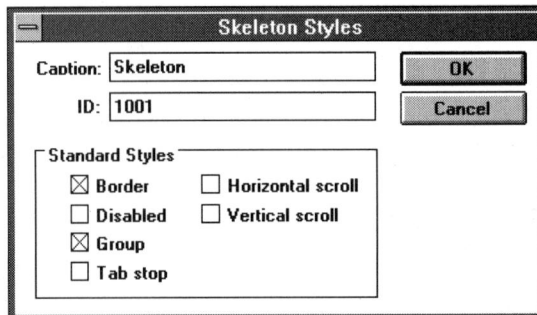

editor to allow manipulation of the styles supported by your custom control. A picture of the dialog is shown in Figure 3.2. Here's the template itself:

```
Styles DIALOG DISCARDABLE  0, 0, 210, 114
STYLE DS_MODALFRAME | WS_POPUP | WS_VISIBLE |
  WS_CAPTION | WS_SYSMENU
CAPTION "Skeleton Styles"
FONT 8, "MS Sans Serif"
BEGIN
    RTEXT    "Caption:",IDC_STATIC,5,7,31,7
    EDITTEXT  IDC_CAPTION,38,4,106,12,ES_AUTOHSCROLL
    RTEXT    "ID:",IDC_STATIC,5,23,30,7
    EDITTEXT  IDC_ID,38,21,106,12,ES_AUTOHSCROLL
    GROUPBOX  "Standard  Styles",IDC_STATIC,8,41,137,66
    CONTROL"Border", IDC_BORDER, "Button", BS_AUTOCHECKBOX | WS_TABSTOP,
22,55,34,10
    CONTROL"Disabled", IDC_DISABLED, "Button", BS_AUTOCHECKBOX |
WS_TABSTOP, 22,67,44,10
    CONTROL"Group", IDC_GROUP, "Button", BS_AUTOCHECKBOX | WS_TABSTOP,
22,79,34,10
    CONTROL"Tab stop", IDC_TABSTOP, "Button", BS_AUTOCHECKBOX | WS_TABSTOP,
22,91,46,10
    CONTROL"Horizontal scroll", IDC_HSCROLL, "Button", BS_AUTOCHECKBOX |
WS_TABSTOP, 75,55,66,10
    CONTROL"Vertical scroll", IDC_VSCROLL, "Button", BS_AUTOCHECKBOX |
WS_TABSTOP, 75,67,61,10
    DEFPUSHBUTTON "OK", IDOK, 154,4,50,14
    PUSHBUTTON "Cancel", IDCANCEL, 154,21,50,14
END
```

Additional resources for the Borland Resource Workshop are simply the bitmap that represents the control in the toolbox, and a cursor that tells the user that he or she is about to drop one of those controls on his or her dialog. These are shown in Figure 3.3. They are stored in TBX.BMP and TBX.CUR, and are made part of the .RC file via an *RCINCLUDE* statement:

```
// For Resource Workshop
100 BITMAP MOVEABLE PURE "TBX.BMP"
100 CURSOR DISCARDABLE "TBX.CUR"
```

**Figure 3.3  The Skeleton toolbox bitmap and cursor.**

Likewise the visual development environments require a set of bitmaps for toolboxes of different display resolutions, and our implementation of VISUAL.C and HELP.C needs an About box template:

```
// For Visual Basic
8000 BITMAP MOVEABLE PURE "8000.BMP"
8001 BITMAP MOVEABLE PURE "8001.BMP"
8003 BITMAP MOVEABLE PURE "8003.BMP"
8006 BITMAP MOVEABLE PURE "8006.BMP"

ABOUT DIALOG 41, 45, 192, 125
STYLE DS_MODALFRAME | WS_POPUP | WS_CAPTION
CAPTION "About Skeleton Custom Control"
FONT 8, "MS Sans Serif"
BEGIN
   CONTROL "Skeleton Custom Control", 0, "STATIC", SS_CENTER | WS_CHILD |
WS_VISIBLE, 0, 8, 190, 8
   CONTROL "by Paul S. Cilwa", 0, "STATIC", SS_CENTER | WS_CHILD |
WS_VISIBLE, 0, 16, 190, 8
   CONTROL "MAIN", 0, "STATIC", SS_ICON | WS_CHILD | WS_VISIBLE, 87, 29,
18, 20
   CONTROL "Version 1.0", 0, "STATIC", SS_CENTER | WS_CHILD | WS_VISIBLE,
0, 59, 190, 8
   CONTROL "©1993 by Paul S. Cilwa", 0, "STATIC", SS_CENTER | WS_CHILD |
WS_VISIBLE, 0, 79, 190, 8
   CONTROL "All Rights Reserved", 0, "STATIC", SS_CENTER | WS_CHILD |
WS_VISIBLE, 0, 88, 190, 8
   CONTROL "OK", IDOK, "BUTTON", BS_PUSHBUTTON | WS_CHILD | WS_VISIBLE |
WS_TABSTOP, 74, 102, 45, 15
END

MAIN ICON "SKELETON.ICO"
```

The set of bitmaps—admittedly a rather plain bunch—is shown in Figure 3.4. You can take these "blank" bitmaps and add whatever artwork makes the bitmap appropriately suggestive of your custom control. You can also modify the About box (shown in Figure 3.5) as needed. Since the About box displays an icon that is also supposed to represent the control, that's included as well (see Figure 3.6).

---

**Figure 3.4  The Visual environment Skeleton bitmaps from right to left: 8000, 8001, 8003, 8006.**

---

**Figure 3.5  The Skeleton About box for the visual environment.**

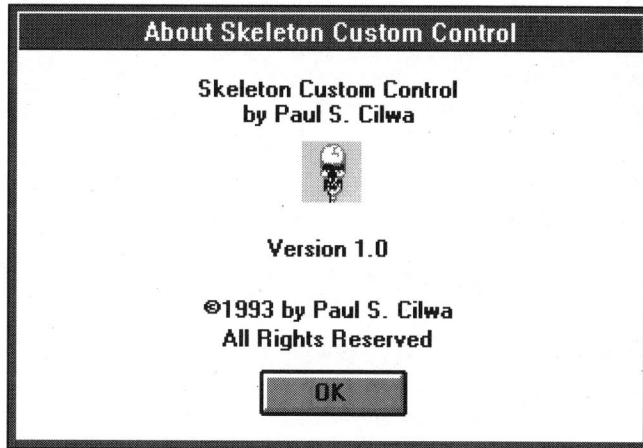

**Figure 3.6  The Skeleton MAIN icon.**

The last element in the .RC file is one you may never have seen before, but it is nevertheless important—more important, perhaps, for DLLs than any other Windows module. It is the *VersionInfo* resource. This resource type was introduced at about the same time as Windows 3.1 and is accessed by functions in VER.DLL. Although you'll probably never access it directly, it is used by setup applications to avoid overwriting a newer version of your DLL with an older version. Here's the Skeleton *VersionInfo* resource:

```
1 VERSIONINFO LOADONCALL MOVEABLE DISCARDABLE
FILEVERSION 1, 0, 0, 0
PRODUCTVERSION 1, 0, 0, 0
FILEOS VOS__WINDOWS16
FILETYPE VFT_DLL
BEGIN
  BLOCK "StringFileInfo"
  BEGIN
    BLOCK "040904E4"
    BEGIN
      VALUE "CompanyName", "Coriolis Group\000"
      VALUE "FileDescription", "Skeleton Custom Control for Visual Basic
```

```
and Windows\000"
        VALUE  "FileVersion",  "1.0.0.0\000"
        VALUE  "InternalName",  "SKELETON\000"
        VALUE  "LegalCopyright",  "Copyright © Paul S. Cilwa 1993\000"
        VALUE  "OriginalFilename",  "Skeleton.vbx\000"
        VALUE  "ProductName",  "Windows Programming Power\000"
        VALUE  "ProductVersion",  "1.0.0.0\000"
        VALUE  "Comments",  "\000"
     END
   END
END
```

# Renaming the Skeleton Control

A standard (non-visual) Windows app must load a custom control DLL by using the *LoadLibrary()* function. The application calls *LoadLibrary()* with the name of the DLL to be loaded. *LoadLibrary()* doesn't care what extension is used to name the DLL.

If you are using the control with Visual Basic, on the other hand, you should use the extension .VBX to name the DLL. With Visual Basic, the *File..Add to Project* dialog box is preset to display files with .VBX extensions (as well as the other Visual Basic module extensions). Therefore it seems reasonable to rename any custom control DLL to give it a .VBX extension if it can be used in a visual environment, even if it can be used by non-visual applications as well.

This means that, after compiling and linking the Skeleton project and obtaining a SKELETON.DLL file, that file should be renamed SKELETON.VBX.

### An Easy Way to Rename Files

We've provided a utility named DLL2VBX on the listings diskette to help you rename your DLLs as .VBXs. Use this little utility to quickly rename files with an extension of .DLL so that they have an extension of .VBX instead. If a file with the target name already exists in that directory, it will be deleted before the file is renamed.

## Taking the Skeleton Control for a Test Drive

Now that we've completed all of our development work, you might be interested in taking the Skeleton control for a test drive. Here are the steps you'll need to follow:

1. Compile all of the C source files presented in this chapter. These files are stored in the \SKELETON directory in the code diskette and include MAIN.C, PAINT.C, DIALOG.C, VISUAL.C, and DIALOG.C. (If you plan to test the Skeleton with a non-visual environment, you won't need VISUAL.C or HELP.C. You will, however, need to define NONVISUAL, to turn off the **#include** of VBAPI.H.) When you compile the C source files, make sure that the two header files, INTERNAL.H and SKELETON.H, are available.

2. Compile the resource script file, SKELETON.RC.

3. Link all of the compiled source files and create the DLL, SKELETON.DLL. If you are creating a visual control, make sure your linker can find VBAPI.LIB.

4. Use the DLL2VBX utility provided on disk to rename the DLL as SKELETON.VBX.

At this point, you'll have a DLL (VBX) that you can use with a visual environment (Visual Basic) or a non-visual environment (Borland C++, and so on). We'll quickly show you how to use the Skeleton with Visual Basic. If you don't have access to Visual Basic, you'll still be able to use the Skeleton as a "standard control." The details for using the control in a standard Windows application are provided in the next chapter.

---

**Figure 3.7 Using the Skeleton control with Visual Basic. The "blank" button on the bottom left is the one used.**

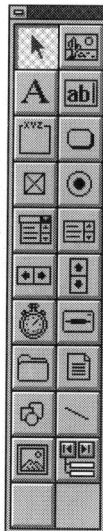

## Using the Control with Visual Basic

You should now be able to start Visual Basic and add SKELETON.VBX to the project using the *File..Add to Project* menu command. A "blank" button will be added to the toolbox as shown in Figure 3.7; you'll be able to display the About box and, if you copy SKELETON.HLP from the program disk, you'll be able to view the online help as well. (Of course, SKELETON.HLP is just a, er, Skeleton of a help file.)

# Summary

We've now completed the custom control template—Skeleton. Unlike some templates, the code we've developed represents a major portion of the work—more than half the code for simpler controls, as you'll see in later chapters.

We'll be moving on and showing you, step-by-step, how to derive much more powerful controls from the Skeleton control. But first we'll take time out to discuss a number of important strategies for using custom controls with Windows apps.

# 4

# Using Custom Controls

The finest custom control in the world is useless by itself. But as soon as it is made part of an application, its value becomes evident. A DLL-based custom control offers flexibility while a custom control that's part of a standard library offers installation benefits that are hard to ignore.

n this chapter we'll look at the different options for using controls so you can choose, in advance, the best strategy for your new control. We'll also look at the requirements of different programming languages and environments, so you can use your new custom controls anywhere.

# Using a DLL Control in a Standard Windows App

A DLL-based custom control can be used by any standard application—even one that's already written and for which you have no source code! In the previous chapter we showed you how to package the Skeleton control as a DLL. When the DLL is loaded, the Skeleton class gets registered automatically. Of course, not all custom controls do this.

⚬   ⚬   ⚬

*A custom control doesn't have to reside in a DLL.*

⚬   ⚬   ⚬

Normally, when you create a DLL, you also create an import library. This is a standard (static) library of modules that is made part of your application by the linker. For example, if you call function *MyFunc()* in MYFUNC.DLL, you would probably tell the linker to include the MYFUNC.LIB import library. The linker would fix up references to *MyFunc()* so they would point to the function having the name supplied by the library.

Now, if MYFUNC.LIB were a standard library, the code for *MyFunc()* would actually be there; and, after linking, calls to *MyFunc()* would simply transfer control to the function, which would execute, and return. However, in an import library, each "function" is really just a stub which checks to see if the DLL is loaded, loads it if it is not, and *then* transfers control to the correct entry point of the DLL.

Unfortunately, this entire scheme doesn't work with a DLL-based custom control because you don't create a custom control by invoking a function in its DLL. You have to explicitly load the library, usually during initialization of your application. This is done with the *LoadLibrary()* function:

```
LibInst = LoadLibrary ("MYFUNC.DLL");
```

A library is *not* automatically freed when your application closes, so you should call *FreeLibrary()* before your application terminates:

```
FreeLibrary (LibInst);
```

If you must register a control in the DLL, do it after the library has been loaded. (The control's documentation should tell you whether, and how, to do this.) As mentioned, our custom controls register themselves.

Once the DLL is loaded and the control class is registered, your application is free to create controls of that class as often as it wishes. Later in this chapter we'll explain how you can use controls as parts of dialog boxes, and as dynamically created child windows.

○   ○   ○

*If you distribute an application that uses a custom control stored in a DLL, you must also distribute the DLL.*

○   ○   ○

Although this may seem obvious, many programmers create Windows apps using controls and don't realize what they are getting into. Here are some important issues to think about:

• Where will you put the DLL?

• What if a DLL from some other vendor already exists with the same name as the one you are using?

• What if the user is installing a new version of the application?

• What should the app do if the DLL is accidentally erased?

We'll actually consider solutions to these issues later in the chapter, but some programmers solve these problems by avoiding them altogether. Instead, they place the custom control code in a standard, static library, rather than a DLL.

# Including and Registering a Control from a Standard Library

To prepare our Skeleton class for a static library, you simply alter the control project in the following ways:

1.  Change the name of the *LibMain()* function in the Skeleton (MAIN.C) to something like *RegisterSkeleton()*. The parameter list can also be simplified, but don't forget to pass the application instance handle in place of the library instance handle.

2. Remove the *CS_GLOBALCLASS* flag from the control's style bits (MAIN.C). By default, the control will be local to the application.

3. Omit DIALOG.C, VISUAL.C, and HELP.C, and remove the **#include** of VBAPI.H from INTERNAL.H. A static library-based control cannot hook into any dialog editors or visual environments.

4. Compile the code for the medium, not large model. (Windows applications should almost always be compiled for medium model.)

5. In your main application code, invoke *RegisterSkeleton()* instead of *LoadLibrary()*.

○   ○   ○

*You may want to consider preparing your control in both static and dynamic libraries. You can then use the DLL version for application design in Dialog Editor or Resource Workshop but then link to a static library to create the actual product release.*

○   ○   ○

# Using a Custom Control in a Dialog Template

Ideally, your custom control will reside in a DLL that can hook to Dialog Editor, Resource Workshop, or another resource editor you may use. In this case, once your control has been added to the editor's menu or toolbox (you'll have to read your editor's documentation to find out how), the rest is automatic. Select the control from the menu or toolbox, place it where you want it, then use the control's Style dialog to fine-tune it.

Alternatively, you can place a static control on the dialog, then edit the resulting resource script. Look for "STATIC" (including the quotes), and change it to Skeleton (or whatever class name is appropriate). For a control that resides *only* in a static library, this technique is your only option.

This is also the only way to add a standard custom control to a Visual C++ Version 1.0 application. For some reason, this version does not support the hooks Microsoft defined for the older Dialog Editor.

# Creating a Custom Control Dynamically

Because a custom control is just a child window, you can create one anywhere that you can create a child window. Once the control has been registered (we described this earlier), you can use the *CreateWindow()* function for each copy of the control you want. If the control does not include the *WS_VISIBLE* style, you'll also have to invoke *ShowWindow()*. Using *WS_VISIBLE* is simpler.

You can dynamically add a control to a dialog box. But remember that once a dialog box is created, it no longer uses "dialog units" for coordinates. Regular device coordinates, with (0,0) signifying the upper left corner of the client area, are in effect.

One way to deal with this is to make sure your new control is the same size as, and/or is lined up with, an existing control. You can get the location and size of the existing control with the *GetClientRect()* function, then pass the values you get (after suitable massaging) to *CreateWindow()*.

When working with dialog boxes, another method is to include all the controls you might ever want in the resource script, but omit the *WS_VISIBLE* style from any you might *not* want. Then your dialog procedure can call *ShowWindow()* to "create" previously hidden controls. (*ShowWindow()* can also be used to hide visible controls.) Dialog controls can also be rearranged on-screen by calling *MoveWindow()*.

# Adding a Custom Control to Your "Visual" Project

In Visual Basic, visual-compliant controls are added to a project by using the *File..Add File* command. In Visual C++ App Studio, the *File..Install Control* command does the same thing (but remember, Visual C++ Version 1.0 is restricted to Visual Basic 1.0 controls). Once added to the project, the control is included in the toolbox and can be selected and added to a form (dialog) like any other control. When selected, its properties can be accessed from the properties window normally, as well.

However, be aware that Visual C++ App Studio has an additional requirement: .VBX controls may only be used on a Foundation Classes form. If you intend to write a standard C application, or are writing C++ but not with the Foundation Classes, you cannot use a visual-compliant control.

# Installing Custom Controls

Earlier in this chapter we brought up some issues concerning DLLs and product installation. Let's look at each of these issues and consider possible solutions.

## Where Should a DLL Be Stored?

Microsoft has recommended that *all* DLLs be placed in the \WINDOWS \SYSTEM subdirectory. Of course, not all vendors follow this recommendation—not even Microsoft is totally compliant. There are, however, advantages to placing your DLLs in this subdirectory.

One advantage is that your application can easily find the DLL without your needing to make changes to the PATH environment variable.

The PATH variable was useful in the DOS world. Unfortunately, it is limited to 128 characters, and most users find that they often run out of space when adding directories to the PATH.

In Windows, where any application might be running at the same time as any other, and where the PATH environment variable cannot be changed, the situation is even more troublesome. Fortunately, you don't have to type pathnames in Windows. Any application file can be fully qualified; you just click on an icon or a filename in File Manager and the program runs, even if it is not in the "current" directory.

But if an application's directory is not in the PATH, how can it find its DLLs? Windows searches the application's default directory, then the \WINDOWS directory, then \WINDOWS\SYSTEM, and finally the PATH. By putting all DLLs—or, at least, yours—in \WINDOWS\SYSTEM, you accommodate Windows' requirements and abilities, without having to strain the PATH variable any further.

You could *derive* a fully qualified DLL pathname from the application's own pathname (obtainable by calling *GetModuleFileName()*). But there is another reason to keep all DLLs in a single directory; Windows cannot load two different DLLs with the same name at the same time. If your user wants to maintain two versions of your application—for testing, say—and one crashes, leaving its DLL loaded, then the newer version will be unable to load its DLL. If you want to keep DLLs with the applications that reference them, be sure to rename them with each new version, as Microsoft does with the Visual Basic run-time DLL. (VBRUN100.DLL was distributed with Visual Basic 1.0; VBRUN300.DLL is distributed with version 3.0.)

## What If a DLL Exists with the Same Name?

As mentioned, two different DLLs cannot have the same module name and be run at the same time. (This same restriction applies to application files.) The module name is supplied by the module definition file, but it almost always matches the physical filename; and, unfortunately, filenames are limited to eight characters. Ordinarily, it is a good idea to make your filenames as descriptive as possible, but a DLL named CLOCK.DLL, DATE.DLL, or FORMAT.DLL is likely to be used by someone else. PSCCLK10.DLL is safer. (For those of you in the back of the classroom, those are its author's initials, followed by a three-letter abbreviation of the control, followed by a version number.)

## What If the User Is Installing a New Version of the Application?

In most cases, a duplicate module name occurs when a user is installing another one of your products or a new version of an old one. For that reason, you should always use the VERSIONINFO resource to identify your DLLs, and, if you find a duplicate, check it as a standard part of your installation routine. After all, you wouldn't want a user to write over a more recent, but compatible version of your DLL just because he or she bought an older copy of another product from a dealer's shelf.

This brings up a variant of the naming problem. By using VERSIONINFO, you can avoid suffering from minor release inconsistencies. But any time you put out a DLL, be sure that it is compatible with older versions. It's okay to fix bugs and add features, but never remove old features without renaming the DLL.

○   ○   ○

*By renaming the DLL, you can ensure that a DLL upgrade to one of your products doesn't interfere with the running of another one of them.*

○   ○   ○

## What Should an App Do If a DLL Is Erased?

This is a tough one because there's really nothing an application *can* do. It certainly can't create a replacement DLL out of the ether—if it had the code stored internally, it wouldn't *need* a DLL.

An app could, however, use the *OpenFile()* function to search for a DLL's existence. *OpenFile()* uses the same search order to find a file that Windows uses to locate a DLL. (This is because Windows uses *OpenFile()* to access the DLL.) If you want to have the most user-friendly application on the planet, you can search for any required file as part of your application initialization. If the file cannot be found, advise the user before quitting—or, maybe, kick off the application's installation program with a parameter that will tell it to install just the missing file(s).

# 5

# Creating a
# Panel Control

It's pretty easy to spot an application created by a visual environment such as Visual C++ or Visual Basic. Few visual programmers can resist adding useful features like 3-D panels, toolbars, and sophisticated and highly decorated dialogs to their applications. Fortunately, you can easily add these types of features in your own apps by using custom controls.

n this chapter we'll build our first powerful and useful software component—a custom Panel control. This control will help bring your programs into the modern age by giving them a high-tech, component look and feel. Along the way, you'll learn how to use the Skeleton control we created in Chapter 3.

# A Look at the Panel Control

Our Panel control creates the effect of a 3-D panel having one or two bevels, each of which can be either "raised above" or "sunken into" the plane of an application's window. It basically duplicates the functionality of the ThreeD control that comes with Visual Basic. You can use the panel to group related controls. In addition, you can place text on the control, as with a standard group box control—except that the text can be aligned vertically at the top, middle, or bottom; and horizontally to the left, center, or right. The ThreeD control also supports multi-line text, which a group box does not.

In addition, the Panel control also supports "flood fills"—a technique of partially (or completely) filling with color the area within the bevels. Since the amount of fill can be changed during run time, this effect can be used to create a progress bar. An example of the Panel control we'll be developing is shown in Figure 5.1.

# Designing the Panel Control

We'll be designing the Panel control to work with standard Windows apps. This means that we won't need to provide the unique visual hooks required to support Visual Basic. After all, VB already provides a ThreeD control.

○ ○ ○

*To implement our first working control, we'll need to concentrate on the standard Windows-support aspects—the window procedure, and the messages that will allow us to access the control's features.*

○ ○ ○

**Figure 5.1  A sample Panel control.**

To recap, here are the requirements of the Panel control:

- It is similar to a static control in that it sends no notification messages to its parent.
- It displays two bevels, either raised or sunken, of a specified width.
- It displays text using a specified alignment.
- It supports flood fills in an appropriate portion of the rectangle as directed.

# Using the Panel Control

We'll set up the Panel control so that it can be completely controlled through its initial style bits and the messages the parent application sends it. The complete details for using the control are presented in Appendix A.

# Creating the Panel Control

To create the Panel control, we'll only need to write two source files: MAIN.C and DIALOG.C. In addition, two header files are required: PANEL.H and INTERNAL.H. Each of these files can be copied from the Skeleton project. (PANEL.H is copied from SKELETON.H.) In addition, SKELETON.RC and SKELETON.DEF should be copied as PANEL.RC and PANEL.DEF, respectively.

We'll examine each of the files that are required for the Panel control, and we'll point out how these files have been changed from the versions used with the Skeleton control we created in Chapter 3.

## PANEL.H

This header file contains the styles and message definitions that will be needed by the Windows apps that use our Panel control. Here is the complete header file:

```
#define PNLS_TOP 0x00000000L
#define PNLS_MIDDLE 0x00000001L
#define PNLS_BOTTOM 0x00000002L
#define PNLS_LEFT 0x00000000L
#define PNLS_CENTER 0x00000004L
#define PNLS_RIGHT 0x00000008L
#define PNLS_INNERBEVELRAISED 0x00000010L
```

```
#define  PNLS_INNERBEVELSUNK  0x00000000L
#define  PNLS_INNERBEVELWIDTH(n) (n << 5)
#define  PNLS_OUTERBEVELRAISED  0x00000100L
#define  PNLS_OUTERBEVELSUNK  0x00000000L
#define  PNLS_OUTERBEVELWIDTH(n) (n << 9)
#define  PNLS_INTERBEVELWIDTH(n) (n << 12)
#define  PNLS_BEVELTEXTWIDTH(n) (n << 14)

#define  PNLM_SETUPPERRANGE  (WM_USER+1)
#define  PNLM_SETLOWERRANGE  (WM_USER+2)
#define  PNLM_SETPOS  (WM_USER+3)
#define  PNLM_SETFILLCOLOR  (WM_USER+4)
```

The first block of **#define** directives, those beginning with *PNLS_*, are style bits. *PNLS_TOP*, for example, indicates that the text should be displayed at the top of the panel. It can be combined with *PNLS_CENTER* to display text at the top center of the panel, or *PNLS_RIGHT* to display text at the top right. (Details on these and the other style bits can be found in Appendix A.)

Several of the **#define** directives illustrate an interesting technique. Usually, styles consist of a single bit or, at most, a set of bits. But this is not a requirement. The resource compiler can handle any ANSI C pre-processor construct. *PNLS_INNERBEVELWIDTH* can accept any value from 0-7 and produce an appropriate bit pattern for combining with the other values.

The block of **#define** directives that begins with *PNLM_* consists of Panel-specific message definitions.

◦   ◦   ◦

*The complete set of Panel messages is described in detail in Appendix A.*

◦   ◦   ◦

## INTERNAL.H

This header file is intended for use only within the Panel project. It contains the **#include** directives, data structures, and **#define** directives used internally by the control:

```
#include  <windows.h>
#include  "Panel.H"
#include  <custcntl.h>
#include  <string.h>
#include  <stdlib.h>

#ifdef MAIN
HINSTANCE LibInstance = 0;
```

```c
char far * ClassName = "Panel";
#else
extern HINSTANCE LibInstance;
extern char far * ClassName;
#endif

typedef enum
    {
    PNL_TOP,
    PNL_MIDDLE,
    PNL_BOTTOM
    } PNL_VALIGNMENT;

typedef enum
    {
    PNL_LEFT,
    PNL_CENTER,
    PNL_RIGHT
    } PNL_HALIGNMENT;

typedef struct
    {
    struct
        {
        UINT VAlign: 2;
        UINT HAlign: 2;
        UINT InnerBevelRaised: 1;
        UINT InnerBevelWidth: 3;
        UINT OuterBevelRaised: 1;
        UINT OuterBevelWidth: 3;
        UINT InterBevelWidth: 2;
        UINT BevelTextBorder: 2;
        } CustomStyles;
    struct
        {
        UINT TabStop: 1;
        UINT Group: 1;
        UINT Thickframe: 1;
        UINT SysMenu: 1;
        UINT HScroll: 1;
        UINT VScroll: 1;
        UINT DlgFrame: 1;
        UINT Border: 1;
        UINT Maximize: 1;
        UINT ChipChildren: 1;
        UINT ClipSiblings: 1;
        UINT Disabled: 1;
        UINT Visible: 1;
```

```
      UINT Minimize: 1;
      UINT Child: 1;
      UINT Popup: 1;
      } StdStyles;
  } STYLEBITS, FAR * LPSTYLEBITS;

typedef struct
  {
  HFONT Font;
  PNL_VALIGNMENT VAlign;
  PNL_HALIGNMENT HAlign;
  int cx, cy;
  RECT TextRect;
  COLORREF BackColor, TextColor, HiliteColor, ShadowColor;
  HBRUSH HiliteBrush, ShadowBrush;
  POINT OuterBevelTopLeft[7], OuterBevelBottomRight[7];
  POINT InnerBevelTopLeft[7], InnerBevelBottomRight[7];
  WORD InnerBevelWidth;
  WORD OuterBevelWidth;
  WORD UpperRange, LowerRange, Percentage;
  COLORREF FillColor;
  } MYDATA, far * LPMYDATA;

void far pascal PaintMe (HWND Window, HDC dc, LPMYDATA MyData);

#define IDC_STATIC 0
#define IDC_CAPTION 101
#define IDC_ID 102
#define IDC_BORDER 103
#define IDC_DISABLED 104
#define IDC_GROUP 105
#define IDC_TABSTOP 106
#define IDC_INTERBEVELWIDTH107
#define IDC_BEVELTEXTWIDTH 108
#define IDC_INNERBEVELRAISED 109
#define IDC_INNERBEVELSUNK 110
#define IDC_INNERBEVELWIDTH111
#define IDC_OUTERBEVELRAISED 112
#define IDC_OUTERBEVELSUNK 113
#define IDC_OUTERBEVELWIDTH114
#define IDC_TOP  115
#define IDC_MIDDLE 116
#define IDC_BOTTOM 117
#define IDC_LEFT 118
#define IDC_CENTER 119
#define IDC_RIGHT120
```

After becoming familiar with the INTERNAL.H file used in the Skeleton control (see Chapter 3), the only part of this file that is likely to be of interest is the definition of the *MYDATA* structure template. This is the place where all of the key data components that help define the Panel control are stored. Some of these components include:

- text color
- shadow color
- background color
- highlight color
- inner and outer bevel widths
- fill color
- vertical and horizontal text alignment
- text font

You should familiarize yourself with these variables, but we won't discuss them until they are actually used—mostly during the paint operation.

## MAIN.C

When we examined Skeleton's MAIN.C module, we did so from the top down. Let's take the Panel MAIN.C module from the bottom up. The last function is *LibMain()*. This function is called automatically when the DLL is first loaded, and refers to the static *WndClass* variable declared just before it:

```
static WNDCLASS Class =
   {
   CS_HREDRAW | CS_VREDRAW | CS_DBLCLKS | CS_GLOBALCLASS,
   WndProc,
   0,
   GWW_EXTRA,
   0,
   NULL,
   NULL,
   COLOR_BTNFACE + 1,
   NULL,
   NULL
   };

#pragma argsused
int far pascal LibMain
```

```
    (
    HINSTANCE hInstance,
    WORD DataSeg,
    WORD HeapSize,
    LPSTR CommandLine
    )
{
if (HeapSize > 0)
    UnlockData (0);
LibInstance = hInstance;
Class.hInstance = hInstance;
Class.lpszClassName = ClassName;
return RegisterClass (&Class) ? TRUE : FALSE;
}
```

The code is unchanged from Skeleton except for the window's background color. Setting the background color of any custom control is easy. You just specify the desired color when registering the window. Most windows (including Skeleton) use the *COLOR_WINDOW* constant; in this case we'll use *COLOR_BTNFACE*. Later, we'll use the *COLOR_BTNHIGHLIGHT* and *COLOR_BTNSHADOW* constants for painting the bevels, and *COLOR_BTNTEXT* for displaying the text. These colors are chosen by the user from Control Panel; we neither know nor care what they are.

Next up from *LibMain()* is the main window procedure, *WndProc()*:

```
LRESULT far pascal _export FAR PASCAL WndProc
    (
    HWND Window,
    UINT Msg,
    WPARAM wParam,
    LPARAM lParam
    )
{
LRESULT Result = 0;
switch (Msg)
    {
    case WM_NCCREATE:
        Result = wm_NcCreate (Window, (LPCREATESTRUCT) lParam);
        break;
    case WM_CREATE:
        wm_Create (Window, (LPCREATESTRUCT) lParam);
        break;
    case WM_DESTROY:
        wm_Destroy (Window);
        break;
    case WM_NCDESTROY:
        wm_NcDestroy (Window);
        break;
```

```
        case WM_SIZE:
          wm_Size (Window, LOWORD (lParam), HIWORD (lParam));
          break;
        case WM_GETDLGCODE:
          Result = DLGC_STATIC;
          break;
        case WM_GETFONT:
          Result = wm_GetFont (Window);
          break;
        case WM_SETFONT:
          wm_SetFont (Window, wParam, LOWORD (lParam));
          break;
        case WM_PAINT:
          wm_Paint (Window);
          break;
        case WM_SETTEXT:
          Result = DefWindowProc (Window, Msg, wParam, lParam);
          CalcMetrics (Window, (LPMYDATA) GetWindowLong (Window, GWL_MYDATA));
          break;
        case PNLM_SETUPPERRANGE:
          ((LPMYDATA) GetWindowLong (Window, GWL_MYDATA))->UpperRange = wParam;
          break;
        case PNLM_SETLOWERRANGE:
          ((LPMYDATA) GetWindowLong (Window, GWL_MYDATA))->LowerRange = wParam;
          break;
        case PNLM_SETPOS:
          pnlm_SetPos (Window, wParam);
          break;
        case PNLM_SETFILLCOLOR:
          ((LPMYDATA) GetWindowLong (Window, GWL_MYDATA))->FillColor = lParam;
          break;
        default:
          Result = DefWindowProc (Window, Msg, wParam, lParam);
        }
    return Result;
    }
```

## Handling Messages

In addition to the messages handled by the MAIN.C module from the
Skeleton control, we've added support for the *WM_SIZE* message and
additional handling for the *WM_SETTEXT* message. We've added this support because either message requires that we recalculate text positions. This
is done by the *CalcMetrics()* function, which we'll examine shortly.

The only other messages handled are the Panel-specific messages, as
defined in PANEL.H and described in Appendix A. In every case but one, a
one-line assignment is made of the new value to the *MyData* structure. The
exception is *PNLM_SETPOS*, which sets a new value used to calculate the

amount of flood fill. Calculating the percentage to be filled takes more than one line, so we'll move this code into its own helper function:

```
static void near pascal pnlm_SetPos (HWND Window, WORD Value)
  {
  LPMYDATA MyData = (LPMYDATA) GetWindowLong (Window, GWL_MYDATA);
  register WORD Upper = MyData->UpperRange - MyData->LowerRange;
  if (Upper)
    {
    register WORD aPercentage;
    Value -= MyData->LowerRange;
    aPercentage = ((Value * 100L) / Upper);
    if (aPercentage != MyData->Percentage)
      {
      MyData->Percentage = aPercentage;
      InvalidateRect (Window, &MyData->TextRect, FALSE);
      UpdateWindow (Window);
      }
    }
  }
```

Nothing happens unless *UpperRange* has already been set to some value greater than zero. This helps avoid divide-by-zero errors. If *UpperRange* is valid, this function normalizes the new *Value* by canceling out the effect of a non-zero *LowerRange* (if there is one), and calculates the percentage the new *Value* represents. It then invalidates the text rectangle of the control and demands an instant update of the invalidated portion of the window. Only the text rectangle is invalidated because it is the only portion which is, in fact, invalid. The bevels are still fine, and if the entire window were invalidated, the constant repainting of the bevels would be quite distracting to the user.

The *wm_Paint()* function is unchanged from the Skeleton control:

```
static void near pascal wm_Paint (HWND Window)
  {
  LPMYDATA MyData = (LPMYDATA) GetWindowLong (Window, GWL_MYDATA);
  PAINTSTRUCT ps;
  HDC dc = BeginPaint (Window, &ps);
  HBRUSH OldBrush;
  HBRUSH NewBrush = (HBRUSH) SendMessage (GetParent (Window),
    WM_CTLCOLOR,
    dc,
    MAKELONG (Window, CTLCOLOR_BTN));
  HFONT OldFont;
  HFONT NewFont = MyData->Font;
  if (NewBrush)
```

```
   OldBrush = SelectObject (dc, NewBrush);
if (NewFont)
   OldFont = SelectObject (dc, NewFont);
PaintMe (Window, dc, MyData);
if (NewBrush)
   SelectObject (dc, OldBrush);
if (NewFont)
   SelectObject (dc, OldFont);
EndPaint (Window, &ps);
}
```

This function is the same because the actual *work* of painting is done by the *PaintMe()* function provided in the PAINT.C module.

The *wm_SetFont()* function must add yet another invocation of *CalcMetrics()*, since changing the font also potentially changes the coordinates of the text:

```
static void near pascal wm_SetFont (HWND Window, HFONT NewFont, BOOL Repaint)
   {
   LPMYDATA MyData = (LPMYDATA) GetWindowLong (Window, GWL_MYDATA);
   if (NewFont != MyData->Font)
      {
      MyData->Font = NewFont;
      if (Repaint)
         {
         InvalidateRect (Window, NULL, TRUE);
         UpdateWindow (Window);
         }
      CalcMetrics (Window, MyData);
      }
   }
```

*wm_GetFont()* is unchanged from Skeleton:

```
static HFONT near pascal wm_GetFont (HWND Window)
   {
   LPMYDATA MyData = (LPMYDATA) GetWindowLong (Window, GWL_MYDATA);
   HFONT Result = MyData->Font;
   if (! Result)
      Result = GetStockObject (SYSTEM_FONT);
   return Result;
   }
```

Receipt of the *WM_SIZE* message is simply a signal for the Panel control to recalculate its polygons and text placements. *wm_Size()* first stores the control's width and height so *CalcMetrics()* can do its job:

```
static void near pascal wm_Size (HWND Window, int Width, int Height)
  {
  LPMYDATA MyData = (LPMYDATA) GetWindowLong (Window, GWL_MYDATA);
  MyData->cx = Width;
  MyData->cy = Height;
  CalcMetrics (Window, MyData);
  InvalidateRect (Window, NULL, TRUE);
  }
```

As you can see, *wm_NcDestroy()* is unchanged from the Skeleton control:

```
static void near pascal wm_NcDestroy (HWND Window)
  {
  free ((LPMYDATA) GetWindowLong (Window, GWL_MYDATA));
  }
```

However, *wm_NcDestroy()* is filled out now; it deletes two GDI objects:

```
static void near pascal wm_Destroy (HWND Window)
  {
  LPMYDATA MyData = (LPMYDATA) GetWindowLong (Window, GWL_MYDATA);
  DeleteObject (MyData->HiliteBrush);
  DeleteObject (MyData->ShadowBrush);
  }
```

These objects were created while processing the *WM_CREATE* message, at the same time that the other fields of the *MyData* structure were filled:

```
static void near pascal wm_Create (HWND Window, LPCREATESTRUCT Create)
  {
  LPSTYLEBITS Styles = (LPSTYLEBITS) &Create->style;
  LPMYDATA MyData = (LPMYDATA) GetWindowLong (Window, GWL_MYDATA);
  MyData->VAlign    = Styles->CustomStyles.VAlign;
  MyData->HAlign    = Styles->CustomStyles.HAlign;
  MyData->BackColor = GetSysColor (COLOR_BTNFACE);
  MyData->TextColor = GetSysColor (COLOR_BTNTEXT);
  MyData->HiliteColor = GetSysColor (COLOR_BTNHIGHLIGHT);
  MyData->ShadowColor = GetSysColor (COLOR_BTNSHADOW);
  MyData->HiliteBrush = CreateSolidBrush (MyData->HiliteColor);
  MyData->ShadowBrush = CreateSolidBrush (MyData->ShadowColor);
  }
```

## Supporting Bevels

The primary helper function, called from several other places, is *CalcMetrics()*. This function builds the bevel polygons, based on the size of the control and the various bevel and border widths. It also calculates the placement of the text itself:

```
static void near pascal CalcMetrics (HWND Window, LPMYDATA MyData)
   {
   DWORD Style = GetWindowLong (Window, GWL_STYLE);
   LPSTYLEBITS Styles = (LPSTYLEBITS) &Style;
   register Width;
   char Buffer[256];
   WORD Length, TextHeight;
   HDC dc;
   RECT Client, Temp;
   HFONT OldFont, NewFont = MyData->Font;

   Length = GetWindowText (Window, Buffer, sizeof Buffer);
   dc = GetDC (Window);
   if (NewFont)
      OldFont = SelectObject (dc, NewFont);
   GetClientRect (Window, &Client);

   Width = Styles->CustomStyles.OuterBevelWidth;
   MyData->OuterBevelBottomRight[0].x = Client.left;
   MyData->OuterBevelBottomRight[0].y = Client.bottom;
   MyData->OuterBevelBottomRight[1].x = Client.right;
   MyData->OuterBevelBottomRight[1].y = Client.bottom;
   MyData->OuterBevelBottomRight[2].x = Client.right;
   MyData->OuterBevelBottomRight[2].y = Client.top;
   MyData->OuterBevelBottomRight[3].x = Client.right - Width;
   MyData->OuterBevelBottomRight[3].y = Client.top + Width;
   MyData->OuterBevelBottomRight[4].x = Client.right - Width;
   MyData->OuterBevelBottomRight[4].y = Client.bottom - Width;
   MyData->OuterBevelBottomRight[5].x = Client.left + Width;
   MyData->OuterBevelBottomRight[5].y = Client.bottom - Width;
   MyData->OuterBevelBottomRight[6].x = Client.left;
   MyData->OuterBevelBottomRight[6].y = Client.bottom;

   MyData->OuterBevelTopLeft[0].x = Client.left;
   MyData->OuterBevelTopLeft[0].y = Client.bottom;
   MyData->OuterBevelTopLeft[1].x = Client.left;
   MyData->OuterBevelTopLeft[1].y = Client.top;
   MyData->OuterBevelTopLeft[2].x = Client.right;
   MyData->OuterBevelTopLeft[2].y = Client.top;
   MyData->OuterBevelTopLeft[3].x = Client.right - Width;
   MyData->OuterBevelTopLeft[3].y = Client.top + Width;
   MyData->OuterBevelTopLeft[4].x = Client.left + Width;
   MyData->OuterBevelTopLeft[4].y = Client.top + Width;
   MyData->OuterBevelTopLeft[5].x = Client.left + Width;
```

```
MyData->OuterBevelTopLeft[5].y = Client.bottom - Width;
MyData->OuterBevelTopLeft[6].x = Client.left;
MyData->OuterBevelTopLeft[6].y = Client.bottom;

Width += Styles->CustomStyles.InterBevelWidth;
Client.left += Width;
Client.top += Width;
Client.right -= Width;
Client.bottom -= Width;

Width = Styles->CustomStyles.InnerBevelWidth;
MyData->InnerBevelBottomRight[0].x = Client.left;
MyData->InnerBevelBottomRight[0].y = Client.bottom;
MyData->InnerBevelBottomRight[1].x = Client.right;
MyData->InnerBevelBottomRight[1].y = Client.bottom;
MyData->InnerBevelBottomRight[2].x = Client.right;
MyData->InnerBevelBottomRight[2].y = Client.top;
MyData->InnerBevelBottomRight[3].x = Client.right - Width;
MyData->InnerBevelBottomRight[3].y = Client.top + Width;
MyData->InnerBevelBottomRight[4].x = Client.right - Width;
MyData->InnerBevelBottomRight[4].y = Client.bottom - Width;
MyData->InnerBevelBottomRight[5].x = Client.left + Width;
MyData->InnerBevelBottomRight[5].y = Client.bottom - Width;
MyData->InnerBevelBottomRight[6].x = Client.left;
MyData->InnerBevelBottomRight[6].y = Client.bottom;

MyData->InnerBevelTopLeft[0].x = Client.left;
MyData->InnerBevelTopLeft[0].y = Client.bottom;
MyData->InnerBevelTopLeft[1].x = Client.left;
MyData->InnerBevelTopLeft[1].y = Client.top;
MyData->InnerBevelTopLeft[2].x = Client.right;
MyData->InnerBevelTopLeft[2].y = Client.top;
MyData->InnerBevelTopLeft[3].x = Client.right - Width;
MyData->InnerBevelTopLeft[3].y = Client.top + Width;
MyData->InnerBevelTopLeft[4].x = Client.left + Width;
MyData->InnerBevelTopLeft[4].y = Client.top + Width;
MyData->InnerBevelTopLeft[5].x = Client.left + Width;
MyData->InnerBevelTopLeft[5].y = Client.bottom - Width;
MyData->InnerBevelTopLeft[6].x = Client.left;
MyData->InnerBevelTopLeft[6].y = Client.bottom;

Width += Styles->CustomStyles.BevelTextBorder;
Client.left += Width;
Client.top += Width;
Client.right -= Width;
Client.bottom -= Width;
```

```
CopyRect (&Temp, &Client);
TextHeight =
   DrawText (dc, Buffer, Length, &Temp, DT_CALCRECT);
switch (MyData->VAlign)
   {
   case PNL_TOP:
      MyData->TextRect.top = Client.top;
      MyData->TextRect.bottom = TextHeight;
      break;
   case PNL_MIDDLE:
      MyData->TextRect.top = (Client.top + Client.bottom - TextHeight) / 2;
      MyData->TextRect.bottom = Client.bottom;
      break;
   case PNL_BOTTOM:
      MyData->TextRect.top = Client.bottom - TextHeight;
      MyData->TextRect.bottom = Client.bottom;
      break;
   };
MyData->TextRect.left = Client.left;
MyData->TextRect.right = Client.right;
if (NewFont)
   SelectObject (dc, OldFont);
ReleaseDC (Window, dc);
}
```

The bulk of the code in this function is devoted to building the polygons for the bevels. A polygon is represented as an array of points. The points are determined by referencing the size of the control and the various widths and borders specified in the style bits. Likewise, the size of the text and its position are calculated. Doing this requires a device context. Don't forget to select the same font into the device context that you intend to use when actually painting the text; otherwise the calculations will be (understandably) irrelevant. This may seem obvious, but it is a common mistake many programmers make.

The bevels are interesting because of their shape. In Windows the "light source" is assumed to be coming from the upper left, so if all bevels were to be one pixel thick, a raised bevel can be achieved by simply drawing lines of *COLOR_BTNHIGHLIGHT* on the left and top edges of the control, and lines of *COLOR_BTNSHADOW* on the right and bottom edges. (A sunken bevel reverses the colors.)

But a bevel thicker than one pixel should display diagonal edges. Generically, a beveled edge is shaped like the one shown in Figure 5.2.

The same shape, inverted, is used for the lower right bevel. The points are calculated from the size of the control and the width of the bevel, but the basic shape is always the same.

**Figure 5.2  A sample beveled edge.**

## Wrapping Up MAIN.C

Finally, the top of the MAIN.C module features the *wm_NcCreate()* function, which is unchanged from Skeleton:

```
#define MAIN
#include "Internal.H"

#define GWL_MYDATA 0
#define GWW_EXTRA 4

#pragma argsused
static BOOL near pascal wm_NcCreate (HWND Window, LPCREATESTRUCT Create)
  {
  LPMYDATA MyData = (LPMYDATA) calloc (1, sizeof (MYDATA));
  SetWindowLong (Window, GWL_MYDATA, (long) MyData);
  return (MyData != NULL);
  }
```

## PAINT.C

As with the Skeleton control, the PAINT.C module contains the code for actually painting the control. The main functions used in this module include *PaintMe()*, *PaintBorder()*, *PaintStandardText()*, and *PaintFloodFill()*. We'll explore each of these functions so that you can see how the components of the Panel control are displayed.

The *PaintMe()* function of this module is invoked to paint the Panel's border, text, and (optional) flood fill. We've implemented it mainly as a management function which delegates these three aspects of its work to helper functions:

```
void far pascal PaintMe (HWND Window, HDC dc, LPMYDATA MyData)
  {
```

```
DWORD dwStyle = GetWindowLong (Window, GWL_STYLE);
LPSTYLEBITS Styles = (LPSTYLEBITS) &dwStyle;
COLORREF OldColor = SetTextColor (dc, GetSysColor (COLOR_BTNTEXT));
int OldMode = SetBkMode (dc, TRANSPARENT);
PaintBorder (dc, MyData, Styles);
if (! MyData->UpperRange)
   PaintStandardText (Window, dc, MyData, Styles);
else
   PaintFloodFill (dc, MyData);
SetTextColor (dc, OldColor);
SetBkMode (dc, OldMode);
}
```

## Painting Bevels and Text

The *PaintBorder()* function actually paints the bevels. These are best drawn using the *Polygon()* GDI function, which is part of the Windows SDK. This function draws a shape and fills it all at once; you only have to supply an appropriate pen and brush. We recommend using the stock *HOLLOW_BRUSH* so that the shape is achieved solely by a brush fill:

```
static void near pascal PaintBorder
    (
    HDC dc,
    LPMYDATA MyData,
    LPSTYLEBITS Styles
    )
{
HPEN OldPen = SelectObject (dc, GetStockObject (NULL_PEN));
HBRUSH OldBrush;

if (Styles->CustomStyles.OuterBevelWidth)
   {
   OldBrush = SelectObject (dc, MyData->HiliteBrush);
   if (Styles->CustomStyles.OuterBevelRaised)
     Polygon (dc, MyData->OuterBevelTopLeft, 7);
   else
     Polygon (dc, MyData->OuterBevelBottomRight, 7);
   SelectObject (dc, MyData->ShadowBrush);
   if (Styles->CustomStyles.OuterBevelRaised)
     Polygon (dc, MyData->OuterBevelBottomRight, 7);
   else
     Polygon (dc, MyData->OuterBevelTopLeft, 7);
   }
if (Styles->CustomStyles.InnerBevelWidth)
   {
   SelectObject (dc, MyData->HiliteBrush);
```

```
    if (Styles->CustomStyles.InnerBevelRaised)
      Polygon (dc, MyData->InnerBevelTopLeft, 7);
    else
      Polygon (dc, MyData->InnerBevelBottomRight, 7);
    SelectObject (dc, MyData->ShadowBrush);
    if (Styles->CustomStyles.InnerBevelRaised)
      Polygon (dc, MyData->InnerBevelBottomRight, 7);
    else
      Polygon (dc, MyData->InnerBevelTopLeft, 7);
    }
  SelectObject (dc, OldBrush);
  SelectObject (dc, OldPen);
  }
```

Don't be intimidated by the number of lines of code here. Each block is quite similar to the other. In each case, an appropriate brush is selected based on whether the bevel is to appear raised or sunken. Then the *Polygon()* function does the work, again, using the appropriate set of points that we calculated in the *CalcMetrics()* function.

The *PaintStandardText()* function will be invoked if the Panel is *not* being used as a percentage bar. A static array of styles allows efficient mapping of Panel alignments to *DrawText()* flags:

```
static UINT HAlignFlag[3] = { DT_LEFT, DT CENTER, DT RIGHT };

static void near pascal PaintStandardText
    (
    HWND Window,
    HDC dc,
    LPMYDATA MyData,
    LPSTYLEBITS Styles
    )
  {
  char Buffer[256];
  int Length = (int) SendMessage (Window, WM_GETTEXT,
    sizeof Buffer, (long)(LPSTR) Buffer);
  DrawText (dc, Buffer, Length, &MyData->TextRect,
    HAlignFlag[Styles->CustomStyles.HAlign] | DT_NOCLIP);
  }
```

## Supporting Flood Fills

The *PaintFloodFill()* function is the most complex of the bunch because it has to:

• Paint text (the percentage value) in (possibly) two colors.

- Calculate the size of the percentage-complete *and* the percentage-incomplete rectangles.
- Paint both the complete and incomplete areas.

Calculating the percentage area is easy, even if you hate math. The only tricky part is that we'd like to paint this control as smoothly and efficiently as possible. Consider the following situation. Suppose the control represents a value that is 40 percent full, as shown in Figure 5.3.

The next value will probably be 41 percent. If we called *InvalidateRect()* with *TRUE* as the Repaint Background parameter when the new value arrives, the percent-filled area would blink as the underlying gray background is repainted.

Worse yet, only two choices of "text mode" are available to us—*TRANSPARENT* and *OPAQUE*. In *OPAQUE* mode, Windows will clear the area beneath the text being written, but only to the nearest "solid" (non-dithered) color available. Because the light gray button face is *not* a solid color, a darker (or lighter) rectangle will appear beneath the text.

We can use the *TRANSPARENT* mode, however, but if we do, Windows won't erase the old text from beneath the new text. The result is a dark blotch where a percentage should be.

The best solution is to use the *TRANSPARENT* mode, but to erase the background ourselves—exactly enough of it, but no more, so that the completion bar won't flicker.

Here's the code that meets all of these requirements:

```
static void near pascal PaintFloodFill (HDC dc, LPMYDATA MyData)
   {
   char Buffer[8];
   RECT FloodRect, BareRect;
   HBRUSH FillBrush = CreateSolidBrush (MyData->FillColor);
   HBRUSH BareBrush = CreateSolidBrush (GetSysColor (COLOR_BTNFACE));
   int Length = wsprintf (Buffer, "%d%c", MyData->Percentage, '%');
   HRGN ClippingRegion;

   FloodRect.top =
   FloodRect.left = MyData->OuterBevelWidth + MyData->InnerBevelWidth;
   FloodRect.bottom = MyData->cy - FloodRect.top;
```

**Figure 5.3  A percentage bar showing 40 percent completion.**

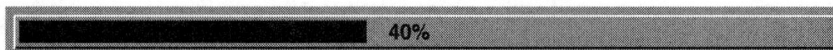

```
    FloodRect.right = MyData->cx - FloodRect.left;
    if (MyData->Percentage < 100)
      {
      register long Width = FloodRect.right - FloodRect.left;
      Width = ((Width * MyData->Percentage) / 100L);
      FloodRect.right = FloodRect.left + (int) Width;
      }

    BareRect.top = FloodRect.top;
    BareRect.left = FloodRect.right;
    BareRect.bottom = FloodRect.bottom;
    BareRect.right = MyData->cx - FloodRect.left;
    FillRect (dc, &BareRect, BareBrush);
    DrawText (dc, Buffer, Length, &MyData->TextRect, DT_CENTER | DT_NOCLIP);

    if (MyData->Percentage > 0)
      {
      FillRect (dc, &FloodRect, FillBrush);
      LPtoDP (dc, (LPPOINT) &FloodRect, 2);
      ClippingRegion = CreateRectRgn (FloodRect.left,
        FloodRect.top,
        FloodRect.right,
        FloodRect.bottom);
      SelectClipRgn (dc, ClippingRegion);
      if (MyData->FillColor == GetSysColor (COLOR_BTNTEXT))
        SetTextColor (dc, RGB (255 - GetRValue (MyData->FillColor),
          255 - GetGValue (MyData->FillColor),
          255 - GetBValue (MyData->FillColor)));
      DrawText (dc, Buffer, Length, &MyData->TextRect, DT_CENTER);
      }

    DeleteObject (FillBrush);
    DeleteObject (BareBrush);
    DeleteObject (ClippingRegion);
    }
```

In the first section of the code, space is allocated for the various brushes and rectangles, and for a *clipping region*. We'll study this more closely in just a moment.

In the next block, the *FloodRect* dimensions are calculated. Next, *BareRect* is initialized. You can see that *BareRect* will occupy exactly the portion of the panel that complements the *FloodFill* portion. At this point, the *FillRect()* function fills the "uncompleted" side of the panel, incidentally erasing any text that may have previously been written there. *DrawText()* is then able to place the new text on a clean slate, so to speak.

The next block will only be executed if the percentage completed is greater than zero. *FillRect()* is used again, this time with the dimensions stored in *FloodRect,* and using the *FloodBrush.* If the percentage is approximately 50 percent, this may partially erase the display text just written.

We have to rewrite the text, then, in exactly the same position, but in a color which will contrast legibly with the progress bar. On the other hand, we must *not* overwrite any portion of the text which resides in the *uncompleted* area.

How can this be done? If we give *DrawText()* the *FloodFill* rectangle in which to center the text, instead of the *TextRect* rectangle, the display text will wind up being centered in the flooded area, not the panel; this is not what we want at all. We could backtrack and calculate the text position in every detail instead of using *DrawText()* to do the centering for us, but who wants to do that? Fortunately, there is an answer: We can manipulate the ·aforementioned *Clipping Region.*

Whenever a window receives a *WM_PAINT* message, the *PAINTSTRUCT* returned by the *BeginPaint()* function details exactly what areas are invalid and need to be repainted. The invalid area is called the clipping region because any attempt to paint outside this area will be "clipped" (ignored— and, no, we don't know why they didn't call it the Ignore Region). Usually Windows' job of painting is more complex than our job of figuring which pieces are in the clipping area and which are out, so we generally ignore the boundaries, letting Windows do the clipping for us.

But we can manipulate the clipping region to our own advantage if we want. In this case, we want to tell *DrawText()* to center and write using the entire *TextRect*, but only want Windows to *actually* allow drawing in the flooded area. Clipping regions use device coordinates rather than logical ones, but a quick call to *LPtoDP()* makes that conversion for us. We then use *FloodRect* to create a rectangular region. (The main difference between a rectangle and a region is that a region can contain *many* rectangles, some of which may overlap.) A region is a GDI object like a pen or brush, so once we select it into the device context, we're ready to go.

However, unlike most GDI objects, you needn't—in fact, *can't*—replace the new clipping region with an "old" one before releasing the device context.

Before drawing the text, we set the text color to an arithmetic "reverse" of the color used to draw the flood fill. This guarantees that the text will be visible (as long as the flood fill isn't a 50 percent gray).

○   ○   ○

*The end result is that, even when the flood fill partially overlays the text, the entire text will be visible, even if in two colors; and the operation will proceed smoothly with almost no visible flicker.*

○   ○   ○

# PANEL.RC

The resource script file for the Panel control provides the same components as the Skeleton resource script file. Of course, the components have been modified for the occasion. To see how the Styles dialog box looks in action, check out Figure 5.4.

The text of the entire resource script is shown here:

```
#include "internal.h"

// For Dialog Editor
Styles DIALOG -2, 1, 210, 212
STYLE DS_MODALFRAME | WS_POPUP | WS_VISIBLE | WS_CAPTION | WS_SYSMENU
CAPTION "Panel Styles"
FONT 8, "MS Sans Serif"
BEGIN
  RTEXT "Caption:", IDC_STATIC, 5,7,31,7
  EDITTEXT IDC_CAPTION, 38, 4, 107, 12, ES_AUTOHSCROLL
  RTEXT "ID:", IDC_STATIC, 5,23,30,7
  EDITTEXT IDC_ID, 38, 21, 107, 12, ES_AUTOHSCROLL
  CONTROL "Standard Styles", IDC_STATIC, "BUTTON",
    BS_GROUPBOX | WS_CHILD | WS_VISIBLE | WS_GROUP, 8, 41, 138, 26
  CONTROL "Disabled", IDC_DISABLED, "Button",
    BS_AUTOCHECKBOX | WS_CHILD | WS_VISIBLE | WS_TABSTOP, 19, 52, 40, 10
```

**Figure 5.4  The Panel Styles dialog box for Dialog Editor.**

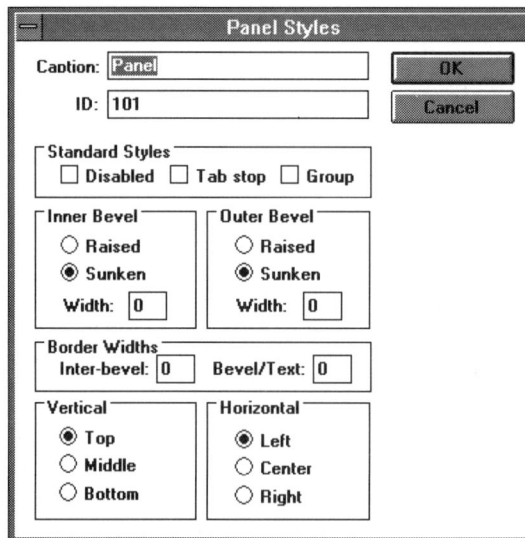

```
CONTROL "Tab stop", IDC_TABSTOP, "Button",
   BS_AUTOCHECKBOX | WS_CHILD | WS_VISIBLE | WS_TABSTOP, 64, 52, 41, 10
CONTROL "Group", IDC_GROUP, "Button",
   BS_AUTOCHECKBOX | WS_CHILD | WS_VISIBLE | WS_TABSTOP, 109, 52, 32, 10
CONTROL "Inner Bevel", IDC_STATIC, "button",
   BS_GROUPBOX | WS_CHILD | WS_VISIBLE | WS_GROUP, 8, 69, 67, 54
CONTROL "Raised", IDC_INNERBEVELRAISED, "BUTTON",
   BS_AUTORADIOBUTTON | WS_CHILD | WS_VISIBLE | WS_TABSTOP, 19, 81, 47, 12
CONTROL "Sunken", IDC_INNERBEVELSUNK, "BUTTON",
   BS_AUTORADIOBUTTON | WS_CHILD | WS_VISIBLE, 19, 93, 41, 12
CONTROL "Width:", IDC_STATIC, "STATIC",
   SS_LEFT | WS_CHILD | WS_VISIBLE | WS_GROUP, 20, 109, 23, 8
CONTROL "", IDC_INNERBEVELWIDTH, "EDIT",
   ES_LEFT | WS_CHILD | WS_VISIBLE | WS_BORDER | WS_TABSTOP, 47, 107, 16, 12
CONTROL "Outer Bevel", IDC_STATIC, "button",
   BS_GROUPBOX | WS_CHILD | WS_VISIBLE | WS_GROUP, 79, 69, 67, 54
CONTROL "Raised", IDC_OUTERBEVELRAISED, "BUTTON",
   BS_AUTORADIOBUTTON | WS_CHILD | WS_VISIBLE | WS_TABSTOP, 90, 81, 47, 12
CONTROL "Sunken", IDC_OUTERBEVELSUNK, "BUTTON",
   BS_AUTORADIOBUTTON | WS_CHILD | WS_VISIBLE, 90, 93, 41, 12
CONTROL "Width:", IDC_STATIC, "STATIC",
   SS_LEFT | WS_CHILD | WS_VISIBLE | WS_GROUP, 91, 109, 23, 8
CONTROL "", IDC_OUTERBEVELWIDTH, "EDIT",
   ES_LEFT | WS_CHILD | WS_VISIBLE | WS_BORDER | WS_TABSTOP, 118, 107, 16, 12
CONTROL "Border Widths", 103, "button",
   BS_GROUPBOX | WS_CHILD | WS_VISIBLE, 8, 125, 138, 25
CONTROL "Inter-bevel:", -1, "STATIC",
   SS_LEFT | WS_CHILD | WS_VISIBLE | WS_GROUP, 18, 136, 39, 8
CONTROL "", IDC_INTERBEVELWIDTH, "EDIT",
   ES_LEFT | WS_CHILD | WS_VISIBLE | WS_BORDER | WS_TABSTOP, 58, 134, 16, 12
CONTROL "Bevel/Text:", -1, "STATIC",
   SS_LEFT | WS_CHILD | WS_VISIBLE | WS_GROUP, 81, 136, 38, 8
CONTROL "", IDC_BEVELTEXTWIDTH, "EDIT",
   ES_LEFT | WS_CHILD | WS_VISIBLE | WS_BORDER | WS_TABSTOP, 122, 134, 16, 12
CONTROL "Vertical", IDC_STATIC, "button",
   BS_GROUPBOX | WS_CHILD | WS_VISIBLE | WS_GROUP, 8, 151, 67, 54
CONTROL "Top", IDC_TOP, "BUTTON",
   BS_AUTORADIOBUTTON | WS_CHILD | WS_VISIBLE | WS_TABSTOP, 18, 163, 28, 12
CONTROL "Middle", IDC_MIDDLE, "BUTTON",
   BS_AUTORADIOBUTTON | WS_CHILD | WS_VISIBLE, 18, 175, 41, 12
CONTROL "Bottom", IDC_BOTTOM, "BUTTON",
   BS_AUTORADIOBUTTON | WS_CHILD | WS_VISIBLE, 18, 187, 37, 12
CONTROL "Horizontal", IDC_STATIC, "button",
   BS_GROUPBOX | WS_CHILD | WS_VISIBLE | WS_GROUP, 79, 151, 67, 54
CONTROL "Left", IDC_LEFT, "BUTTON",
   BS_AUTORADIOBUTTON | WS_CHILD | WS_VISIBLE | WS_TABSTOP, 90, 164, 28, 12
CONTROL "Center", IDC_CENTER, "BUTTON",
   BS_AUTORADIOBUTTON | WS_CHILD | WS_VISIBLE, 90, 176, 41, 12
CONTROL "Right", IDC_RIGHT, "BUTTON",
```

```
        BS_AUTORADIOBUTTON | WS_CHILD | WS_VISIBLE, 90, 188, 37, 12
    CONTROL "OK", IDOK, "BUTTON",
        BS_DEFPUSHBUTTON | WS_CHILD | WS_VISIBLE | WS_GROUP | WS_TABSTOP,
        154,4,50,14
    PUSHBUTTON "Cancel", IDCANCEL, 154,21,50,14,
        WS_CHILD | WS_VISIBLE
END


// For Resource Workshop
100 BITMAP "tbx.bmp"
100 CURSOR "tbx.cur"


1 VERSIONINFO
FILEVERSION 1, 0, 0, 0
PRODUCTVERSION 1, 0, 0, 0
FILEFLAGSMASK VS_FF_DEBUG | VS_FF_PRERELEASE | VS_FF_PRIVATEBUILD |
VS_FF_INFOINFERRED | VS_FF_SPECIALBUILD
FILEOS VOS__WINDOWS16
FILETYPE VFT_APP
BEGIN
    BLOCK "StringFileInfo"
    BEGIN
        BLOCK "04090000"
        BEGIN
            VALUE "CompanyName", "Paul S. Cilwa\000"
            VALUE "FileDescription", "Panel Custom Control\000"
            VALUE "FileVersion", "0.9\000"
            VALUE "InternalName", "PANEL\000"
            VALUE "LegalCopyright", "©1993 Paul S. Cilwa\000"
            VALUE "OriginalFilename", "PANEL.DLL\000"
            VALUE "ProductName", "Panel Custom Control\000"
            VALUE "ProductVersion", "1.0\000"
        END

    END

END
```

The bitmap and cursor are used by Resource Workshop; they are variants of the same basic theme: a simplified 3-D panel. Bitmap 100 is for the Resource Workshop toolbar; Cursor 100 is the Resource Workshop drag cursor. You can see them in Figure 5.5.

○   ○   ○

*Since the Panel control will not be used in a visual environment, the visual bitmaps, About box, and icon have been omitted.*

○   ○   ○

**Figure 5.5   The Panel bitmap and cursor for Resource Workshop.**

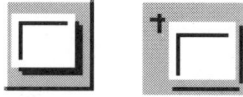

# DIALOG.C

This module provides the Dialog Editor/Resource Workshop-style hooks. The basic framework comes straight from the Skeleton version of this file. The *Info()* function, for example, didn't have to be changed at all:

```c
#include "Internal.h"

#pragma argsused
HGLOBAL far pascal _export Info (void)
   {
   typedef struct
     {
     UINT TypeStyle;
     UINT SuggestedWidth: 15;
     UINT WidthPixels: 1;
     UINT SuggestedHeight: 15;
     UINT HeightPixels: 1;
     DWORD DefaultStyle;
     char Description[22];
     HBITMAP ToolboxBitmap;
     HCURSOR DropCursor;
     } TYPEINFO;

   typedef struct
     {
        UINT Version;
        UINT TypeCount;
        char ClassName[CTLCLASS];
     char Title[94];
     char Reserved[10];
        TYPEINFO Type[1];
     } CONTROLINFO, FAR * LPCONTROLINFO;

   HGLOBAL hCtlInfo;
   LPCONTROLINFO CtlInfo;

   hCtlInfo = GlobalAlloc (GHND, sizeof (CONTROLINFO));
   if (hCtlInfo)
     {
```

```
   CtlInfo = (LPCONTROLINFO) GlobalLock (hCtlInfo);
   CtlInfo->Version = 100;
   CtlInfo->TypeCount = 1;
   lstrcpy (CtlInfo->ClassName, ClassName);
   lstrcpy (CtlInfo->Title, ClassName);
   CtlInfo->Type[0].SuggestedWidth = 40;
   CtlInfo->Type[0].SuggestedHeight = 50;
   CtlInfo->Type[0].DefaultStyle = 0;
   lstrcpy (CtlInfo->Type[0].Description, ClassName);
   CtlInfo->Type[0].ToolboxBitmap =
      LoadBitmap (LibInstance, MAKEINTRESOURCE (100));
   CtlInfo->Type[0].DropCursor =
      LoadCursor (LibInstance, MAKEINTRESOURCE (100));
   GlobalUnlock (hCtlInfo);
   }
 return hCtlInfo;
 }
```

The only components you might consider altering are *SuggestedWidth* and *SuggestedHeight*. We didn't because—after all—what is the ideal size for a "panel"? Likewise, we've left the default style at zero, which will provide no bevels and text aligned at the top left—much like a standard static control, except that it will be button-colored instead of window-colored. (In most setups, that's *gray* instead of *white*.)

The next functions are those that drive the Style dialog box. As in Skeleton, helper functions devoted to each message precede the dialog proc itself. For example, the *wm_InitDialog()* function processes the message of that name, using the information supplied it to set the various dialog controls to appropriate starting values:

```
typedef struct
   {
   LPCTLSTYLE Style;
   LPFNSTRTOID String2ID;
   LPFNIDTOSTR ID2String;
   } STYLEDATA, FAR * LPSTYLEDATA;

static void near pascal wm_InitDialog
      (HWND Dialog, LPSTYLEDATA StyleData)
   {
   LPSTYLEBITS Styles =
      (LPSTYLEBITS) &StyleData->Style->dwStyle;
   char Buffer[64];
   if (Styles->StdStyles.TabStop)
      CheckDlgButton (Dialog, IDC_TABSTOP, 1);
   if (Styles->StdStyles.Group)
      CheckDlgButton (Dialog, IDC_GROUP, 1);
```

```
if (Styles->StdStyles.Disabled)
  CheckDlgButton (Dialog, IDC_DISABLED, 1);
switch (Styles->CustomStyles.VAlign)
  {
  case PNL_TOP:
    CheckDlgButton (Dialog, IDC_TOP, 1);
    break;
  case PNL_MIDDLE:
    CheckDlgButton (Dialog, IDC_MIDDLE, 1);
    break;
  case PNL_BOTTOM:
    CheckDlgButton (Dialog, IDC_BOTTOM, 1);
    break;
  }
switch (Styles->CustomStyles.HAlign)
  {
  case PNL_LEFT:
    CheckDlgButton (Dialog, IDC_LEFT, 1);
    break;
  case PNL_CENTER:
    CheckDlgButton (Dialog, IDC_CENTER, 1);
    break;
  case PNL_RIGHT:
    CheckDlgButton (Dialog, IDC_RIGHT, 1);
    break;
  }
if (Styles->CustomStyles.InnerBevelRaised)
  CheckDlgButton (Dialog, IDC_INNERBEVELRAISED, 1);
else
  CheckDlgButton (Dialog, IDC_INNERBEVELSUNK, 1);
SetDlgItemInt (Dialog, IDC_INNERBEVELWIDTH,
  Styles->CustomStyles.InnerBevelWidth, FALSE);
if (Styles->CustomStyles.OuterBevelRaised)
  CheckDlgButton (Dialog, IDC_OUTERBEVELRAISED, 1);
else
  CheckDlgButton (Dialog, IDC_OUTERBEVELSUNK, 1);
SetDlgItemInt (Dialog, IDC_OUTERBEVELWIDTH,
  Styles->CustomStyles.OuterBevelWidth, FALSE);
StyleData->ID2String (StyleData->Style->wId,
  Buffer, sizeof Buffer);
SetDlgItemText (Dialog, IDC_ID, Buffer);
SetDlgItemText (Dialog, IDC_CAPTION,
  StyleData->Style->szTitle);
SetDlgItemInt (Dialog, IDC_INTERBEVELWIDTH,
  Styles->CustomStyles.InterBevelWidth, FALSE);
SetDlgItemInt (Dialog, IDC_BEVELTEXTWIDTH,
  Styles->CustomStyles.BevelTextBorder, FALSE);
}
```

Likewise, the *wm_Command_OK()* function plucks the values *from* those controls and places them back into the *StyleData* structure:

```
static void near pascal wm_Command_OK
    (HWND Dialog, LPSTYLEDATA StyleData)
  {
  LPSTYLEBITS Styles =
    (LPSTYLEBITS) &StyleData->Style->dwStyle;
  BOOL Code;
  char Buffer[64];
  Styles->StdStyles.TabStop =
    IsDlgButtonChecked (Dialog, IDC_TABSTOP);
  Styles->StdStyles.Group =
    IsDlgButtonChecked (Dialog, IDC_GROUP);
  Styles->StdStyles.Disabled =
    IsDlgButtonChecked (Dialog, IDC_DISABLED);
  if (IsDlgButtonChecked (Dialog, IDC_TOP))
    Styles->CustomStyles.VAlign = PNL_TOP;
  else if (IsDlgButtonChecked (Dialog, IDC_MIDDLE))
    Styles->CustomStyles.VAlign = PNL_MIDDLE;
  else
    Styles->CustomStyles.VAlign = PNL_BOTTOM;
  if (IsDlgButtonChecked (Dialog, IDC_LEFT))
    Styles->CustomStyles.HAlign = PNL_LEFT;
  else if (IsDlgButtonChecked (Dialog, IDC_CENTER))
    Styles->CustomStyles.HAlign = PNL_CENTER;
  else
    Styles->CustomStyles.HAlign = PNL_RIGHT;
  Styles->CustomStyles.InnerBevelRaised =
    IsDlgButtonChecked (Dialog, IDC_INNERBEVELRAISED);
  Styles->CustomStyles.InnerBevelWidth =
    GetDlgItemInt (Dialog, IDC_INNERBEVELWIDTH, &Code, FALSE);
  Styles->CustomStyles.OuterBevelRaised =
    IsDlgButtonChecked (Dialog, IDC_OUTERBEVELRAISED);
  Styles->CustomStyles.OuterBevelWidth =
    GetDlgItemInt (Dialog, IDC_OUTERBEVELWIDTH, &Code, FALSE);
  GetDlgItemText (Dialog, IDC_ID, Buffer, sizeof Buffer);
  StyleData->Style->wId = StyleData->String2ID (Buffer);
  GetDlgItemText (Dialog, IDC_CAPTION,
    StyleData->Style->szTitle,
    sizeof StyleData->Style->szTitle);
  Styles->CustomStyles.InterBevelWidth =
    GetDlgItemInt (Dialog, IDC_INTERBEVELWIDTH, &Code, FALSE);
  Styles->CustomStyles.BevelTextBorder =
    GetDlgItemInt (Dialog, IDC_BEVELTEXTWIDTH, &Code, FALSE);
  }
```

Next up is the dialog proc itself. The best part is that this code is unchanged from Skeleton:

```
#pragma argsused
BOOL far pascal _export StyleProc
    (
    HWND Dialog,
    UINT Msg,
    WPARAM wParam,
    LPARAM lParam
    )
{
static LPSTYLEDATA StyleData;
switch (Msg)
    {
    case WM_INITDIALOG:
      StyleData = (LPSTYLEDATA) lParam;
      wm_InitDialog (Dialog, StyleData);
      return TRUE;
    case WM_COMMAND:
      switch (wParam)
        {
        case IDOK:
          wm_Command_OK (Dialog, StyleData);
          EndDialog (Dialog, TRUE);
          break;
        case IDCANCEL:
          EndDialog (Dialog, FALSE);
          break;
        default:
          return FALSE;
        }
      break;
    default:
      return FALSE;
    }
return TRUE;
}
```

Likewise, the *Style()* function, which the resource editor will invoke when it needs the Style dialog to be displayed, is unaltered from Skeleton:

```
BOOL far pascal _export Style
    (
    HWND Window,
    HGLOBAL hCtlStyle,
```

```
     LPFNSTRTOID aString2ID,
     LPFNIDTOSTR aID2String
     )
{
BOOL Result;
static char far DlgName[] = "Styles";
STYLEDATA StyleData;
StyleData.Style = (LPCTLSTYLE) GlobalLock (hCtlStyle);
StyleData.String2ID = aString2ID;
StyleData.ID2String = aID2String;
Result = DialogBoxParam (LibInstance,
   DlgName, Window, (FARPROC) StyleProc,
   (long) (LPSTYLEDATA) &StyleData);
GlobalUnlock (hCtlStyle);
return (Result == IDOK);
}
```

The *Flags()* function, on the other hand, has grown enormously. Each possible custom style bit must produce a specific **#define** name. Of course, we could take the easy way out and just generate a number. But in spite of the work up front, the *real* easy way is the way that will make it easier for you, as a programmer, to *use* the resource scripts that are generated; and that means meaningful constant names. So, we wind up with the following function:

```
#pragma argsused
UINT far pascal _export Flags
     (
     DWORD Flags,
     LPSTR Buffer,
     UINT BufferSize
     )
{
static LPSTR VAlign[3] =
     {
     "PNLS_TOP",
     "PNLS_MIDDLE",
     "PNLS_BOTTOM"
     };
static LPSTR HAlign[3] =
     {
     " | PNLS_LEFT",
     " | PNLS_CENTER",
     " | PNLS_RIGHT"
     };
static LPSTR InnerBevel[2] =
     {
     " | PNLS_INNERBEVELSUNK",
     " | PNLS_INNERBEVELRAISED"
     };
```

```
static LPSTR InnerBevelWidth = " | PNLS_INNERBEVELWIDTH(%d)";
static LPSTR OuterBevel[2] =
   {
   " | PNLS_OUTERBEVELSUNK",
   " | PNLS_OUTERBEVELRAISED"
   };
static LPSTR OuterBevelWidth = " | PNLS_OUTERBEVELWIDTH(%d)";
static LPSTR InterBevelWidth = " | PNLS_INTERBEVELWIDTH(%d)";
static LPSTR BevelTextBorder = " | PNLS_BEVELTEXTWIDTH(%d)";
char Temp[32];
LPSTYLEBITS Styles = (LPSTYLEBITS) &Flags;
Buffer[0] = 0;
lstrcat (Buffer, VAlign[Styles->CustomStyles.VAlign]);
lstrcat (Buffer, HAlign[Styles->CustomStyles.HAlign]);
lstrcat (Buffer, InnerBevel[Styles->CustomStyles.InnerBevelRaised]);
wsprintf (Temp, InnerBevelWidth, Styles->CustomStyles.InnerBevelWidth);
lstrcat (Buffer, Temp);
lstrcat (Buffer, OuterBevel[Styles->CustomStyles.OuterBevelRaised]);
wsprintf (Temp, OuterBevelWidth, Styles->CustomStyles.OuterBevelWidth);
lstrcat (Buffer, Temp);
wsprintf (Temp, InterBevelWidth, Styles->CustomStyles.InterBevelWidth);
lstrcat (Buffer, Temp);
wsprintf (Temp, BevelTextBorder, Styles->CustomStyles.BevelTextBorder);
lstrcat (Buffer, Temp);
return lstrlen (Buffer);
}
```

We chose to create static arrays of strings which could then be simply referenced by index. The obvious alternative is to use stacks of **switch** statements. Either way, the end result is the same: The incoming style bits are converted to a string which, when run through a C compiler with the proper header file, will produce the same bits.

The file concludes unchanged from Skeleton:

```
typedef HGLOBAL (CALLBACK *LPFNINFO)( void );
typedef BOOL (CALLBACK *LPFNSTYLE)
   (
   HWND hWnd,
   HGLOBAL hCntlStyle,
   LPFNSTRTOID lpfnSID,
   LPFNIDTOSTR lpfnIDS
   );
typedef UINT (CALLBACK *LPFNFLAGS)
   (
   DWORD dwStyle,
   LPSTR lpBuff,
   UINT wBuffLength
   );
```

```
typedef HGLOBAL (CALLBACK *LPFNLOADRES) (LPSTR szType, LPSTR szId);
typedef BOOL (CALLBACK *LPFNEDITRES) (LPSTR szType, LPSTR szId);

#pragma argsused
HGLOBAL far pascal _export ListClasses
    (
    LPSTR CallingClass,
    UINT Version,
    LPFNLOADRES Load,
    LPFNEDITRES Edit
    )
  {
  typedef struct
    {
    LPFNINFO   fnRWInfo;
    LPFNSTYLE  fnRWStyle;
    LPFNFLAGS  fnFlags;
    char   ClassName[20];
    } RWCTLCLASS, FAR *LPRWCTLCLASS;

  typedef struct {
    short  ClassCount;
    RWCTLCLASS Class[1];
    } CTLCLASSLIST, FAR *LPCTLCLASSLIST;

  HGLOBAL hClassList = GlobalAlloc (GHND, sizeof (CTLCLASSLIST));
  LPCTLCLASSLIST ClassList = (LPCTLCLASSLIST) GlobalLock (hClassList);

  ClassList->ClassCount = 1;
  ClassList->Class[0].fnRWInfo = Info;
  ClassList->Class[0].fnRWStyle = Style;
  ClassList->Class[0].fnFlags = Flags;
  _fstrcpy (ClassList->Class[0].ClassName, ClassName);

  GlobalUnlock (hClassList);
  return hClassList;
  }
```

## PANEL.DEF

This last component required by the project DLL is customized as follows:

```
LIBRARY    Panel
EXETYPE    WINDOWS
CODE    MOVEABLE DISCARDABLE
```

```
DATA    SINGLE
HEAPSIZE  4096
EXPORTS
   WEP        RESIDENTNAME
   Info      @2
   Style       @3
   Flags       @4
   WndProc     @5
   StyleProc   @6
   ListClasses
```

# PANEL.PAS

As a bonus, and as the only non-C module, is this Borland Pascal unit that will allow the Panel control to be used in Borland Pascal for Windows applications as easily as in any C app. Since Pascal units suffer no artificial division between the data definitions and implementations—that is, there are no separate "header" and "code" files—the constants which describe Panel style bits and messages, and the class definitions are contained in this single module:

```
Unit Panel;

   (**********************************************)
               Interface
   (**********************************************)

   Uses
      Objects,
      WinTypes,
      WinProcs,
      ODialogs,
      OString;

   Const
      pnls_Top = $00;
      pnls_Middle = $01;
      pnls_Bottom = $02;
      pnls_Left = $00;
      pnls_Center = $04;
      pnls_Right = $08;
      pnls_InnerBevelRaised = $10;
      pnls_InnerBevelSunk = $00;
      pnls_OuterBevelRaised = $100;
      pnls_OuterBevelSunk = $000;
```

```
Type
  tPanelBevelWidth = 0..7;

Function pnls_InnerBevelWidth (n: tPanelBevelWidth): LongInt;
Function pnls_OuterBevelWidth (n: tPanelBevelWidth): LongInt;
Function pnls_InterBevelWidth (n: tPanelBevelWidth): LongInt;
Function pnls_BevelTextWidth (n: tPanelBevelWidth): LongInt;

Const
  pnlm_SetUpperRange = wm_User + 1;
  pnlm_SetLowerRange = wm_User + 2;
  pnlm_SetPosition = wm_User + 3;
  pnlm_SetFillColor = wm_User + 4;

Type
  pPanel = ^tPanel;
  tPanel = Object (tStatic)
    Function GetClassName: pChar; Virtual;
    Procedure SetUpperRange (Value: Word);
    Procedure SetLowerRange (Value: Word);
    Procedure SetPosition (Value: Word);
    Procedure SetFillColor (const aFillColor: tColorRef);
    End;

(***********************************************)
        Implementation
(***********************************************)

Function pnls_InnerBevelWidth (n: tPanelBevelWidth): LongInt;
  Begin
  pnls_InnerBevelWidth := n shl 5;
  End;

Function pnls_OuterBevelWidth (n: tPanelBevelWidth): LongInt;
  Begin
  pnls_OuterBevelWidth := n shl 9;
  End;

Function pnls_InterBevelWidth (n: tPanelBevelWidth): LongInt;
  Begin
  pnls_InterBevelWidth := n shl 12;
  End;

Function pnls_BevelTextWidth (n: tPanelBevelWidth): LongInt;
  Begin
  pnls_BevelTextWidth := n shl 14;
  End;
```

```
Function tPanel.GetClassName: pChar;
  Begin
  GetClassName := 'Panel';
  End;

Procedure tPanel.SetUpperRange (Value: Word);
  Begin
  SendMessage (hWindow, pnlm_SetUpperRange, Value, 0);
  End;

Procedure tPanel.SetLowerRange (Value: Word);
  Begin
  SendMessage (hWindow, pnlm_SetLowerRange, Value, 0);
  End;

Procedure tPanel.SetPosition (Value: Word);
  Begin
  SendMessage (hWindow, pnlm_SetPosition, Value, 0);
  End;

Procedure tPanel.SetFillColor (const aFillColor: tColorRef);
  Begin
  SendMessage (hWindow, pnlm_SetFillColor, 0, aFillColor);
  End;

Const
  rPanel: tStreamRec =
    (
    ObjType: 10;
    VmtLink: Ofs (TypeOf (tPanel)^);
    Load: @tPanel.Load;
    Store: @tPanel.Store
    );

Var
  DLL: tHandle;
  PrevExitProc: Pointer;

Procedure MyExitProc; Far;
  Begin
  ExitProc := PrevExitProc;
  FreeLibrary (DLL);
  End;

Begin
RegisterType (rPanel);
DLL := LoadLibrary ('Panel.DLL');
```

```
PrevExitProc := ExitProc;
ExitProc := @MyExitProc;
End.
```

In Pascal, the four **#define** statements from PANEL.H that use bit-shifting to insert numeric values into the style doubleword are rendered as callable functions. There's no real loss of efficiency, however, since a typical app will probably not invoke these functions more than once—certainly, not more than once per panel! And Borland Pascal's "smart linker" won't even include the machine code for these functions in an application that doesn't invoke them.

# Enhancing the Panel Control

Now that we've designed and implemented Panel, what enhancements could be made? Certainly a list of things will occur to you through time, as you have a chance to use it. Here's a short list to get you started:

- Messages could be added to allow customized colors for the panel background, highlight and shadow, and text colors.

- You might provide an alternate means of setting percents, where you send the percentage directly to the Panel instead of making it calculate the amount.

- When Panel is being used to display a graphic percentage bar, why not use the text value as input to *wsprintf()*? Then, instead of a display that reads "41%," you could make the display read, "41% Done."

- If you make that enhancement, then how about an option where the flood fill shows percentage, but the text gives a straight value, like "526 of 1,000 Records Processed"?

- It might be nice for the percentage text to be placed like regular text is, not always in the middle of the panel.

- You could add messages that would allow dynamic adjustment of styles such as bevel width, or determine whether a bevel is raised or sunken.

Obviously, the sky's the limit. You could easily spend the next few years of your life creating the ultimate Panel control—but don't do it! Because our next control, a "Virtual Listbox," is going to be even more fun.

# 6

# The Virtual
# Listbox Control

nyone who has ever used a Windows program is certainly familiar with listbox controls. As you know, they are especially useful for presenting a list of options, such as filenames, preferences, or special pre-defined values to the user of an application.

The basic listbox control that Windows provides cannot "hold" more than 32K of data. Although this is enough data for most applications, you may need a more powerful and flexible listbox for storing more data. In this chapter, we are going to build a better one.

**W**hile 32K of data may sound like a lot at first—it's certainly adequate for a list of available fonts, or files in a directory, or honest congressmen—as soon as you get into database applications this limitation begins to hurt. Even a county-wide mailing list can have thousands of entries.

To get around this limitation, we'll adapt our flexible Skeleton control to create what we call a *Virtual Listbox*. This unique control will appear and behave like the standard Windows single-selection listbox. However, using our virtual technique, we'll be able to get much more storage space out of the standard listbox. In fact, our Virtual Listbox will be able to hold up to 32K *items*—enough for most applications. (And we'll give you a hint as to how its capacity can be made even larger.) Even better, the listbox will load instantly, and it will be easy to use and adapt to your own needs.

## Designing a Virtual Listbox

In a perfect world, what features would you want in a listbox? How about the following two:

• Stores and displays an unlimited number of items

• Loads quickly

Let's look at each item on our "wish list." First, we'd like to display an "unlimited" number of items. A listbox that can support an unlimited number of items may sound like overkill. However, many applications must present a rather large list of data fields or values. Still, "unlimited" is a pretty tall order. Not only would we have to find a place to keep all of the items, we would have to write a new scroll bar to appear at the listbox's side. (The standard Windows scroll bar is itself limited to a 32K upper limit.)

o    o    o

*To avoid having to create a new "super scroll bar," we'll cut back on our first requirement and design the listbox to hold 32K items.*

o    o    o

Even 32,000 (approximately) items of indeterminate length can take up a lot of storage space. Conventional listboxes are limited because they must store the text of the items they display.

Suppose we don't store the items at all? Suppose we let the *owner* of the listbox—the entity that already has the items to be displayed—just *keep* them? The listbox could notify the parent application when each item must be displayed, and the parent could then supply the text for the desired item. With this approach, the Virtual Listbox would never need to actually *store* anything.

Fortunately, a version of a listbox that works this way is already available. It's called an *Ownerdraw* listbox. Instead of putting text into the listbox, you send *addresses* to it. When the listbox needs to display an item, it notifies the parent, which uses the address to find and render that text at the proper location. But an Ownerdraw listbox still has to store addresses. What if the items could be identified by *number*? Then all you'd have to do to load a Virtual Listbox is to tell it how many items it "owned." It would then notify its parent, as an Ownerdraw listbox does, when an item needed to be drawn. But instead of requiring an address, the parent would just need the *index* of the item to render it.

Using this technique, we'll easily be able to satisfy the second item on the wish list and load the listbox quickly. With the Virtual Listbox, you can send one simple message, like the following, to set up its list of items:

```
SendMessage (Listbox, VL_SETCOUNT, 8000, 0);
```

Then, as the user brings each item into view, the Virtual Listbox would notify its parent dialog or window that the item in question needs to be displayed.

## Managing and Displaying Data

An Ownerdraw listbox requires its parent not only to render each item (choose the text with which it will be displayed), but to draw it as well. That's nice if you want to include pictures with each item, but it's an unnecessary hassle when each item is plain text, as most are. Therefore, we can simplify the parent's job somewhat. We'll notify the parent as each item needs displaying, and the parent will have to render it.

○   ○   ○
*The Virtual Listbox will take care of the actual painting of the text.*
○   ○   ○

This gives us an unexpected benefit that will make the Virtual Listbox even more valuable. In some cases, you'll want to display your data as columnar text. If the Virtual Listbox is going to notify the parent for each item anyway, why not notify it for each *column* for each item, as well? Each column could then be formatted and even aligned within its column separately.

## Adding Special Virtual Listbox Messages

As with all Windows-based controls, the Virtual Listbox will be message-driven. Several messages serve purposes identical to analogous listbox messages. Is there any reason why we can't just use the standard listbox messages? After all, why should we create new messages when adequate ones already exist?

But, when designing, you should look at how Microsoft has handled a similar situation. (After all, we are playing in their field.) The Combobox, another standard control, is also physically similar to the listbox and uses many similar messages. Did Microsoft re-use the listbox messages? No. Listbox messages start with *LB_*, and Combobox messages begin with *CB_*. More to the point, the actual binary values of the analogous messages (for example, *LB_ADDSTRING* and *CB_ADDSTRING*) are not the same. Following their lead, we'll begin Virtual Listbox message names with *VL_*.

We only have to support three pairs of messages: one to set and get the number of items in the listbox, one to set and get the current selection, and one to set and get the list of tab stops that identify the different columns. There is also one special message, *VL_QUERYITEM*. We'll hold back on describing this message until after we've presented the messages that the Virtual Listbox returns to its parent.

*VL_SETCOUNT* is the message that specifies how many "entries" the listbox needs to store. Standard listboxes use the *wParam* parameter, which for standard Windows is 16 bits wide, to specify an item index. (Under Windows NT, both *wParam* and *lParam* are 32 bits.) This would give you a maximum list of 65,536 items, except that the standard listbox also reserves the value -1 to indicate that an item has not been selected. This means *wParam* must be interpreted as a *signed*, not an unsigned, value. Therefore, only 32,768 items can be referenced. That's okay, because it matches the limits of the standard Windows scroll bar.

Whenever possible, you should provide a means to get any value you can set. We'll use the *VL_GETCOUNT* message for this purpose.

Just like a standard Listbox, the application must be able to determine which item is selected, and to select an item programmatically. That's the job of the *VL_GETCURSEL* and *VL_SETCURSEL* messages, respectively.

The *VL_SETTABSTOPS* message will parallel the *LB_SETTABSTOPS* message; there should also be a matching *VL_GETTABSTOPS* message.

## Using Notifications

The Virtual Listbox will communicate with its parent application using *notification messages*. These are simply *WM_COMMAND* messages sent by the control to its parent. Notification messages advise the parent that an event has taken place; they do not provide any details. If details are required, the parent can, as part of its notification handling, send another message to the control. For example, suppose the user selects an item in the Virtual Listbox. The parent will receive a *VLN_SELCHANGE* notification to indicate that an item has been selected. To determine which item has been selected, the application can send a *VL_GETCURSEL* message to the control—even while it is still processing the *VLN_SELCHANGE* notification. Although this kind of "recursive programming" may cause your head to spin, it will only make you dizzy if you think about it too much.

We'll need to support the same notification messages that a standard listbox does (with a *VLN_* prefix instead of *LB_*, of course). That is, the Virtual Listbox will need to report selection changes, mouse double-clicks, and keyboard focus changes. These are handled by the *VLN_SELCHANGE*, *VLN_DBLCLK*, *VLN_SETFOCUS*, and *VLN_KILLFOCUS* notifications, respectively. These notifications are quite easy to implement.

## The VLN_READYITEM Notification and the VL_QUERYITEM Message

The magic of the Virtual Listbox is pretty well wrapped up in the *VLN_READYITEM* notification and the *VL_QUERYITEM* message, and the *pas de deux* they perform. The *VLN_READYITEM* notification is sent by the Virtual Listbox to notify its parent whenever an item needs to be displayed.

When the parent dialog or window receives the *VLN_READYITEM* notification, it will have to find out *which* item needs to be drawn. It does this by sending a *VL_QUERYITEM* message back to the Virtual Listbox.

The Virtual Listbox must return a pointer to a structure to the parent window. This structure must identify the requested item, and provide space for the display string, the number of the columns being rendered, and a place for an alignment indicator.

Now, we'd like to allow the application to supply either the entire item at once (tab delimited), or one column at a time. We'll have the Virtual Listbox first send a *VLN_READYITEM* with a column ID of zero; if the application supplies a string we'll use it. If not, we'll send *VLN_READYITEM*s for each column (and be ready to handle a *VL_QUERYITEM* for each notification). The Virtual Listbox can deduce how many columns there are by the number of tab stops that were specified.

We'll illustrate the conversation graphically. Figure 6.1 shows the dance of the messages.

**Figure 6.1 The notifications and messages used to display an item.**

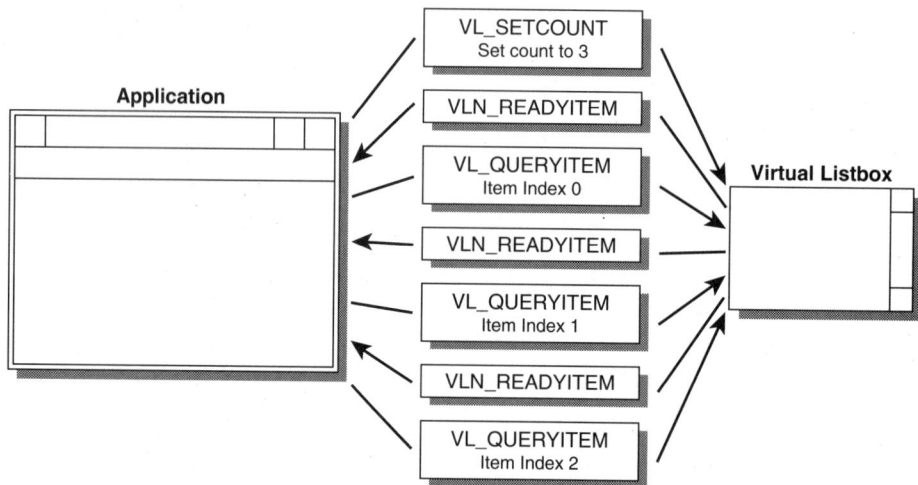

In this example, the application sends the Virtual Listbox a *VL_SETCOUNT* message to set the item count to 3. Each time the listbox needs to be displayed, it will send a *VLN_READYITEM* notification for each visible item—in this case, all three. The application will process each message by sending the Virtual Listbox a *VL_QUERYITEM* message. The listbox processes this message by returning a pointer to a *QUERYITEM* structure, which we'll have to define. The application then modifies the structure, adding text and, perhaps, alignment instructions. The Virtual Listbox can then display the item.

The sequence is only slightly more complex when each column is treated separately. Figure 6.2 shows how this sequence works.

Now the question arises: How will the Virtual Listbox know whether to display the whole item at once, or to query for each column separately? If we initialize the text buffer in the *QUERYSTRUCT* to a zero-length string and the application places something in the buffer, the Virtual Listbox will know not to query column by column.

We now have enough of a design to document how the Visual Listbox works. Remember, the final design of a custom control should *be* the documentation.

**Figure 6.2 The sequence of messages and notifications when a single item is rendered one column at a time.**

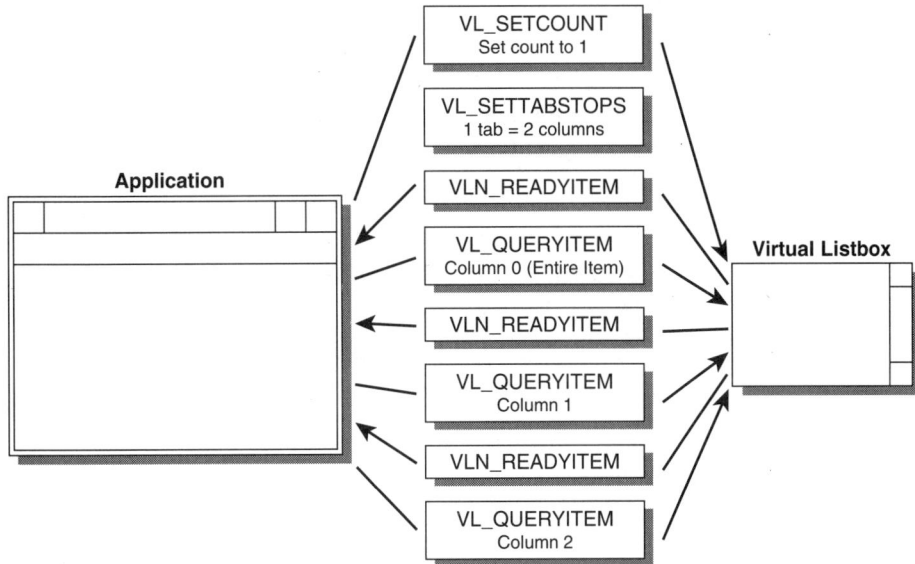

⚬ ⚬ ⚬

*If you understand how a control will work well enough to tell someone else how to use it, you have a design clear enough to code from.*

⚬ ⚬ ⚬

By designing for the user—and, in this case, the user is a programmer—you'll turn up any weaknesses in time to avoid them. (The instructions for using the Virtual Listbox control can be found in Appendix A.)

# Creating the Virtual Listbox Control

To create the Virtual Listbox, we'll need the nine files listed in Table 6.1.

Because this control is designed to work with both visual and non-visual environments, it needs more support than the Panel control we created in the previous chapter. In particular, we need to develop the VISUAL.C and HELP.C source files for this control.

## Table 6.1   Files Needed for the Virtual Listbox Control

| File | Description |
|------|-------------|
| VLISTBOX.H | Contains the message and data structure definitions for the Virtual Listbox control. You'll need to include this file in your Windows app if you are using the control in a non-visual environment. |
| INTERNAL.H | Contains the internal IDs used to support the control as well as needed function prototypes. |
| MAIN.C | Contains the base code for the Virtual Listbox control. |
| PAINT.C | Contains the code for painting the Virtual Listbox control. |
| DIALOG.C | Provides the hooks needed by the standard resource editors. |
| VISUAL.C | Provides all the hooks needed to make the Virtual Listbox accessible to a visual programming environment. |
| HELP.C | Provides the support code to access the Windows Help Engine. |
| VLISTBOX.RC | Provides the code for the module definition file to create the Virtual Listbox. |
| VLISTBOX.DEF | Provides the resources for the Virtual Listbox. |

*Special note:* You'll need to include VBAPI.LIB in the list of libraries to be linked into the end-product DLL. This library comes with Visual Basic 3.0 Professional Edition, and is required to create a visual-style (VBX) custom control. Since the Virtual Listbox is implemented as both a standard and a visual custom control, the linker needs this library in order to create the desired DLL.

### A Note on Naming DLLs

There is currently no standard filename extension for DLLs which support both standard and visual custom controls. If the DLL has a .VBX extension, it will show up in the Visual Basic *File..Add to Project File* dialog box. Therefore, we recommend renaming the resulting DLL to VLISTBOX.VBX.

## VLISTBOX.H

This **#include** file is the only one which must be referenced by a programmer using the Virtual Listbox in a standard (non-visual) Windows application. It provides the **#define** statements for the messages, notifications, and styles, as well as the definition of the *QUERYITEM* struct:

```
#define  VL_SETCOUNT  (WM_USER+1)
#define  VL_GETCOUNT  (WM_USER+2)
#define  VL_SETCURSEL  (WM_USER+3)
#define  VL_GETCURSEL  (WM_USER+4)
#define  VL_SETTABSTOPS  (WM_USER+5)
#define  VL_GETTABSTOPS  (WM_USER+6)
#define  VL_QUERYITEM  (WM_USER+7)

#define  VLN_SELCHANGE  (LBN_SELCHANGE)
#define  VLN_DBLCLK  (LBN_DBLCLK)
#define  VLN_KILLFOCUS  (LBN_KILLFOCUS)
#define  VLN_SETFOCUS  (LBN_SETFOCUS)
#define  VLN_READYITEM  (100)

#define  VLS_INTEGRALHEIGHT  0x00000001L

typedef struct
   {
   int Index;
   char Buffer[128];
   BYTE Column;
   BYTE Align;
   } QUERYITEM, far * LPQUERYITEM;
```

This listing presents the complete VLISTBOX.H file. Notice that, where possible, we've defined the Virtual Listbox notifications to mirror their standard listbox counterparts. Although this is not necessary, it helps to simplify our code.

A few pages back, while designing the Virtual Listbox, we described how the *VLN_READYITEM* notification would cause the parent window to send a *VL_QUERYITEM* message back to the Virtual Listbox, to find out which item needed rendering. The *QUERYITEM* structure is what *VL_QUERYITEM* actually returns. By giving the parent the index of the item and column to be rendered, the parent can copy the rendering into *Buffer* and even adjust *Align* if desired. We'll see this process in action when we describe the PAINT.C module a few pages from now.

## INTERNAL.H

This header file, used by all the code modules, contains all the function prototypes. It also provides IDs for the controls in the dialog boxes referenced by the DIALOG.C module. Here is the complete header file:

```
#ifdef MAIN
#define VLMAIN
#endif
```

```
#include <windows.h>
#include "vlistbox.h"
#include <vbapi.h>
#include <custcntl.h>
#include <string.h>
#include <direct.h>
#include <stdlib.h>

#ifdef MAIN
HINSTANCE LibInstance = 0;
char far * ClassName = "VListbox";
#else
extern HINSTANCE LibInstance;
extern char far * ClassName;
#endif

typedef struct
   {
   struct
     {
     UINT IntegralHeight: 1;
     UINT : 15;
     } CustomStyles;
   struct
     {
     UINT TabStop: 1;
     UINT Group: 1;
     UINT Thickframe: 1;
     UINT SysMenu: 1;
     UINT HScroll: 1;
     UINT VScroll: 1;
     UINT DlgFrame: 1;
     UINT Border: 1;
     UINT Maximize: 1;
     UINT ChipChildren: 1;
     UINT ClipSiblings: 1;
     UINT Disabled: 1;
     UINT Visible: 1;
     UINT Minimize: 1;
     UINT Child: 1;
     UINT Popup: 1;
     } StdStyles;
   } STYLEBITS, FAR * LPSTYLEBITS;

#define MAXTABS 16

typedef struct
   {
   HFONT   Font;
```

```
int     Count;
int     cxChar,
        cyChar;
int     LinesPerWindow,
        ColumnsPerWindow;
int     x, y;
int     TopRecord;
int     Selection;
BOOL HasFocus;
int     TabCount;
int     Tabs[MAXTABS];
} MYDATA, far * LPMYDATA;

void far pascal PaintMe (HWND Window, HDC dc, LPMYDATA MyData);
LPQUERYITEM far pascal vl_QueryItem (void);

#define IDC_STATIC 0
#define IDC_GROUPBOX 0
#define IDC_CAPTION 101
#define IDC_ID 102
#define IDC_DEFINITION 103
#define IDC_BORDER 104
#define IDC_DISABLED 105
#define IDC_GROUP 106
#define IDC_TABSTOP 107
#define IDC_VISIBLE 108
#define IDC_INTEGRALHEIGHT 109

HSZ far pascal GetAboutPropertyString (HCTL Control);
HWND far pascal PopupAbout (void);
void far pascal RegisterVbPopups (void);
void far pascal UnregisterVbPopups (void);
LPSTR far pascal HelpFileName (void);
BOOL far pascal vbm_Help
    (
    HWND Window,
    BYTE HelpType,
    BYTE i,
    PPROPINFO Properties[],
    PEVENTINFO Events[]
    );
```

Again this file follows the same format as the INTERNAL.H file we created for the Skeleton. Thus, its contents should be self-explanatory. (For a quick review, see the section on INTERNAL.H in Chapter 3.) We would, however, like to point out the *Tabs* array in the *MYDATA* structure. In the C programming tradition, *Tabs* would be a *pointer* to an array, allocated via a call to *malloc()*. Such an implementation frees us from deciding the maximum number of tab stops at compile time. However, this approach needlessly complicates the code. Instead, we've pre-allocated the *Tabs* array within the *MYDATA* struct to hold just 16 elements. After all, this allocation doesn't take an inordinate amount of space.

# MAIN.C

This module contains the base code for the Virtual Listbox control. It is based on the MAIN.C Skeleton module described in Chapter 4. We'll step through the different sections of this file so you can see how it works.

Like the MAIN.C module we developed for the Skeleton control, our Virtual Listbox MAIN.C begins by defining space for its "extra bytes":

```
#define MAIN
#include "Internal.H"

#define GWL_MYDATA 0
#define GWW_EXTRA  4
```

Recall that we are defining this extra space so that we can store a pointer to the *MYDATA* structure.

Next, the file includes its function definitions. The *wm_NcCreate()* function in this section is unchanged from the Skeleton control:

```
static BOOL near pascal wm_NcCreate (HWND Window, LPCREATESTRUCT Create)
  {
  LPMYDATA MyData = (LPMYDATA) calloc (1, sizeof (MYDATA));
  SetWindowLong (Window, GWL_MYDATA, (long) MyData);
  return (MyData != NULL);
  }
```

The following *wm_Create()* function will be invoked when the main window procedure receives the *WM_CREATE* message:

```
static void near pascal wm_Create (HWND Window, LPCREATESTRUCT Create)
  {
  LPMYDATA MyData = (LPMYDATA) GetWindowLong (Window, GWL_MYDATA);
  TEXTMETRIC tm;
  HDC dc = CreateIC ("DISPLAY", NULL, NULL, NULL);
  GetTextMetrics (dc, &tm);
  MyData->x = Create->x;
  MyData->y = Create->y;
  MyData->cxChar = tm.tmAveCharWidth;
```

```
MyData->cyChar = tm.tmHeight + tm.tmExternalLeading;
MyData->Selection = -1;
DeleteDC (dc);
}
```

The *CreateIC()* function used here is from the Windows API. It creates an *information context* which is similar to a device context. An information context cannot be used to draw with, but it is well-suited for obtaining information, such as the average size of a font character, and it is less taxing on system resources than a device context.

The *wm_Destroy()* and *wm_NcDestroy()* functions used in the Virtual Listbox's MAIN.C are unchanged from those used in the Skeleton control. Since *wm_Destroy()* doesn't actually do anything, you can remove it if you want to. We like to include it in our controls in case we need to enhance the code at a later point. Usually, *wm_Destroy()* ends up being one of the functions that needs to be updated. So we think it is a good idea to keep it around, empty or not:

```
static void near pascal wm_Destroy (HWND Window)
  {
  }

static void near pascal wm_NcDestroy (HWND Window)
  {
  free ((LPMYDATA) GetWindowLong (Window, GWL_MYDATA));
  }
```

If a window needs to know its location in screen coordinates, there's no easier way than to intercept the *WM_MOVE* message. When this message arrives, we simply store the *x* and *y* coordinates that the message provides:

```
static void near pascal wm_Move (HWND Window, int x, int y)
  {
  LPMYDATA MyData = (LPMYDATA) GetWindowLong (Window, GWL_MYDATA);
  MyData->x = x;
  MyData->y = y;
  }
```

Likewise, we need to store sizing data from the *WM_SIZE* message. In addition, if the *VLS_INTEGRALHEIGHT* style has been set, we need to re-size the window so that it encloses no partial lines:

```
.static void near pascal wm_Size (HWND Window, int Width, int Height)
  {
```

```
LPMYDATA MyData = (LPMYDATA) GetWindowLong (Window, GWL_MYDATA);
DWORD dwStyle = GetWindowLong (Window, GWL_STYLE);
LPSTYLEBITS Styles = (LPSTYLEBITS) &dwStyle;
MyData->LinesPerWindow = Height / MyData->cyChar;
MyData->ColumnsPerWindow = Width / MyData->cxChar;
if (Styles->CustomStyles.IntegralHeight &&
    ((MyData->LinesPerWindow * MyData->cyChar) != Height))
  {
  register cy = MyData->LinesPerWindow * MyData->cyChar;
  if (Styles->StdStyles.Border)
    cy += (GetSystemMetrics (SM_CYBORDER) << 1);
  if (Styles->StdStyles.VScroll)
    Width += GetSystemMetrics (SM_CXVSCROLL);
  MoveWindow (Window, MyData->x, MyData->y, Width, cy, TRUE);
  }
}
```

Finally, the *wm_SetFont()*, *wm_GetFont()*, and *wm_Paint()* functions are unchanged from the Skeleton control:

```
static HFONT near pascal wm_GetFont (HWND Window)
  {
  LPMYDATA MyData = (LPMYDATA) GetWindowLong (Window, GWL_MYDATA);
  HFONT Result = MyData->Font;
  if (! Result)
    Result = GetStockObject (SYSTEM_FONT);
  return Result;
  }

static void near pascal wm_SetFont (HWND Window, HFONT NewFont, BOOL Repaint)
  {
  LPMYDATA MyData = (LPMYDATA) GetWindowLong (Window, GWL_MYDATA);
  if (NewFont != MyData->Font)
    {
    MyData->Font = NewFont;
    if (Repaint)
      {
      InvalidateRect (Window, NULL, TRUE);
      UpdateWindow (Window);
      }
    }
  }

static void near pascal wm_Paint (HWND Window)
  {
  LPMYDATA MyData = (LPMYDATA) GetWindowLong (Window, GWL_MYDATA);
  PAINTSTRUCT ps;
  HDC dc = BeginPaint (Window, &ps);
```

```
    HBRUSH OldBrush;
    HBRUSH NewBrush = (HBRUSH) SendMessage (GetParent (Window),
      WM_CTLCOLOR,
      dc,
      MAKELONG (Window, CTLCOLOR_BTN));
    HFONT OldFont;
    HFONT NewFont = MyData->Font;
    LPMYDATA MyData = (LPMYDATA) GetWindowLong (Window, GWL_MYDATA);
    if (NewBrush)
      OldBrush = SelectObject (dc, NewBrush);
    if (NewFont)
      OldFont = SelectObject (dc, NewFont);
    PaintMe (Window, dc, MyData);
    if (NewBrush)
      SelectObject (dc, OldBrush);
    if (NewFont)
      SelectObject (dc, OldFont);
    EndPaint (Window, &ps);
    }
```

If you don't remember how these functions operate, you may want to review their descriptions in Chapter 3.

## Supporting Scrolling

The Virtual Listbox has a vertical scroll bar. We haven't used scrolling features in the Skeleton or Panel controls, but don't worry; scrolling is easy to support. All we have to do is provide handling for two standard messages, *WM_VSCROLL* and *WM_KEYDOWN*.

Any scroll bar is actually a mouse-only control. The keyboard control that you, as a user, associate with a scroll bar actually doesn't require a scroll bar at all. By applying a mouse to a vertical scroll bar, *WM_VSCROLL* messages are produced. Here's the function we'll use to process these messages:

```
static void near pascal wm_VScroll (HWND Window, WORD Code, int Position)
  {
  LPMYDATA MyData = (LPMYDATA) GetWindowLong (Window, GWL_MYDATA);
  register Adjust = 0;
  switch (Code)
    {
    case SB_TOP:
      Adjust = -MyData->TopRecord;
      break;
    case SB_BOTTOM:
      Adjust = MyData->Count - MyData->TopRecord;
```

```
        break;
    case SB_LINEUP:
      Adjust = -1;
      break;
    case SB_LINEDOWN:
      Adjust = 1;
      break;
    case SB_PAGEUP:
      Adjust = -MyData->LinesPerWindow;
      break;
    case SB_PAGEDOWN:
      Adjust = MyData->LinesPerWindow;
      break;
    case SB_THUMBTRACK:
      Adjust = Position - MyData->TopRecord;
      break;
    }
  if ((MyData->TopRecord + Adjust) < 0)
    Adjust = -MyData->TopRecord;
  if ((MyData->TopRecord + Adjust) >= MyData->Count)
    Adjust = MyData->Count - MyData->TopRecord - 1;
  if (Adjust)
    {
    MyData->TopRecord += Adjust;
    SetScrollPos (Window, SB_VERT, MyData->TopRecord, TRUE);
    InvalidateRect (Window, NULL, TRUE);
    UpdateWindow (Window);
    }
  }
```

We're using a standard technique for handling scroll bars here. In fact, the basic algorithm was first published by Charles Petzold in the classic *Programming Windows*. Notice that we are using very descriptive variable names here.

The keyboard behavior you may associate with scroll bars actually belongs to the *window* containing the scroll bar. For example, pressing the down arrow key is the equivalent to clicking the little arrow button on the bottom of the vertical scroll bar. We provide this behavior by responding to the *WM_KEYDOWN* message:

```
static void near pascal wm_KeyDown (HWND Window, WORD Key)
  {
  LPMYDATA MyData = (LPMYDATA) GetWindowLong (Window, GWL_MYDATA);
  switch (Key)
    {
    case VK_HOME:
      MyData->Selection = 0;
```

```
        break;
      case VK_END:
        MyData->Selection = MyData->Count - 1;
        break;
      case VK_UP:
        MyData->Selection-;
        break;
      case VK_DOWN:
        MyData->Selection++;
        break;
      case VK_PRIOR:
        MyData->Selection -= MyData->LinesPerWindow;
        break;
      case VK_NEXT:
        MyData->Selection += MyData->LinesPerWindow;
        break;
    }
  if (MyData->Selection < 0)
    MyData->Selection = 0;
  if (MyData->Selection >= MyData->Count)
    MyData->Selection = MyData->Count - 1;
  if (MyData->Selection < MyData->TopRecord)
    MyData->TopRecord = MyData->Selection;
  if (MyData->Selection > (MyData->TopRecord + MyData->LinesPerWindow))
    MyData->TopRecord = MyData->Selection - MyData->LinesPerWindow + 1;
  SetScrollPos (Window, SB_VERT, MyData->TopRecord, TRUE);
  InvalidateRect (Window, NULL, TRUE);
  UpdateWindow (Window);
  }
```

## Supporting Notification Messages

All notification messages are actually *WM_COMMAND* messages, constructed identically except for the actual notification code. To simplify sending these messages, we've included the following little function:

```
static void near pascal NotifyParent
    (
    HWND Window,
    WORD Notification
    )
  {
  SendMessage (GetParent (Window),
    WM_COMMAND,
    GetWindowWord (Window, GWW_ID),
    MAKELONG (Window, Notification));
  }
```

By definition, all notification messages are sent to the parent window. The *wParam* parameter always contains the child window ID of the control; the low-order word of the *lParam* parameter contains the control's window handle. That leaves the high-order word of *lParam* for the notification code itself.

## Tracking Listbox Selections

When the user clicks the left mouse button while the mouse cursor is positioned over an entry in the Virtual Listbox, a *WM_LBUTTONDOWN* message is generated. What the user wants to do, of course, is select that item. The next function, *wm_LButtonDown()*, handles this. (If the cursor is not positioned on an item, nothing happens.) Here is the complete function:

```
static void near pascal wm_LButtonDown (HWND Window, POINT Point)
  {
  LPMYDATA MyData = (LPMYDATA) GetWindowLong (Window, GWL_MYDATA);
  register Index = Point.y / MyData->cyChar;
  if (Index < 0)
    Index = 0;
  Index += MyData->TopRecord;
  if (Index < MyData->Count)
    SendMessage (Window, VL_SETCURSEL, Index, 0);
  NotifyParent (Window, VLN_SELCHANGE);
  SetFocus (Window);
  }
```

If the user *double*-clicks, the Virtual Listbox just notifies its parent. (The parent may or may not choose to react.)

```
static void near pascal wm_LButtonDblClk (HWND Window)
  {
  NotifyParent (Window, VLN_DBLCLK);
  }
```

## Formatting Listboxes

Earlier, we defined the *VL_SETTABSTOPS* and *VL_GETTABSTOPS* messages to manage an array of tab stops. The tab stops support a multi-column Virtual Listbox by indicating where each column begins. They also imply the number of columns, which is one greater than the number of tab stops.

*vl_SetTabStops()* is a simple function that copies as many as *MAXTABS* (16) elements from the *Tab* array parameter into the *Tabs* array member of *MYDATA*. *vl_GetTabStops()* does the opposite, returning the stored tab stops to the caller. By checking for *Tabs* to be a NULL pointer, *vl_GetTabStops()* can serve double duty, able to return just the tab count if that's all that's wanted:

```
static void near pascal vl_SetTabStops (HWND Window, WORD Count, LPWORD Tabs)
   {
   LPMYDATA MyData = (LPMYDATA) GetWindowLong (Window, GWL_MYDATA);
   register t;
   MyData->TabCount = (Count > MAXTABS) ? MAXTABS : Count;
   for (t = 0; t < Count; t++)
      MyData->Tabs[t] = Tabs[t];
   }

static WORD near pascal vl_GetTabStops (HWND Window, WORD SuppliedCount,
LPWORD Tabs)
   {
   LPMYDATA MyData = (LPMYDATA) GetWindowLong (Window, GWL_MYDATA);
   register t, Count = MyData->TabCount;
   if (Count > SuppliedCount)
     Count = SuppliedCount;
    if (Tabs)
     for (t = 0; t < Count; t++)
        Tabs[t] = MyData->Tabs[t];
   return Count;
   }
```

## Concluding the Main Module

This brings us to the main window procedure for the Virtual Listbox control:

```
LRESULT far pascal _export FAR PASCAL WndProc
     (
     HWND Window,
     UINT Msg,
     WPARAM wParam,
     LPARAM lParam
     )
   {
   LRESULT Result = 0;
   switch (Msg)
      {
      case WM_NCCREATE:
         Result = wm_NcCreate (Window, (LPCREATESTRUCT) lParam);
         break;
      case WM_CREATE:
         wm_Create (Window, (LPCREATESTRUCT) lParam);
         break;
      case WM_DESTROY:
```

```
    wm_Destroy (Window);
    break;
case WM_NCDESTROY:
  wm_NcDestroy (Window);
  break;
case WM_MOVE:
  wm_Move (Window, LOWORD (lParam), HIWORD (lParam));
  break;
case WM_SIZE:
  wm_Size (Window, LOWORD (lParam), HIWORD (lParam));
  break;
case WM_GETFONT:
  Result = wm_GetFont (Window);
  break;
case WM_SETFONT:
  wm_SetFont (Window, wParam, LOWORD (lParam));
  break;
case WM_PAINT:
  wm_Paint (Window);
  break;
case WM_VSCROLL:
  wm_VScroll (Window, wParam, LOWORD (lParam));
  break;
case WM_KEYDOWN:
  wm_KeyDown (Window, wParam);
  break;
case WM_LBUTTONDOWN:
  wm_LButtonDown (Window, MAKEPOINT (lParam));
  break;
case WM_LBUTTONDBLCLK:
  wm_LButtonDblClk (Window);
  break;
case WM_SETFOCUS:
  ((LPMYDATA) GetWindowLong (Window, GWL_MYDATA))->HasFocus = TRUE;
  InvalidateRect (Window, NULL, TRUE);
  NotifyParent (Window, VLN_SETFOCUS);
  break;
case WM_KILLFOCUS:
  ((LPMYDATA) GetWindowLong (Window, GWL_MYDATA))->HasFocus = FALSE;
  InvalidateRect (Window, NULL, TRUE);
  NotifyParent (Window, VLN_KILLFOCUS);
  break;
case WM_GETDLGCODE:
  Result = DLGC_WANTARROWS;
  break;
case VL_SETCOUNT:
  ((LPMYDATA) GetWindowLong (Window, GWL_MYDATA))->Count = wParam;
  SetScrollRange (Window, SB_VERT, 0, wParam, FALSE);
```

```
        InvalidateRect (Window, NULL, TRUE);
        break;
    case VL_GETCOUNT:
        Result = ((LPMYDATA) GetWindowLong (Window, GWL_MYDATA))->Count;
        break;
    case VL_SETCURSEL:
        ((LPMYDATA) GetWindowLong (Window, GWL_MYDATA))->Selection = wParam;
        InvalidateRect (Window, NULL, TRUE);
        UpdateWindow (Window);
        break;
    case VL_GETCURSEL:
        Result = ((LPMYDATA) GetWindowLong (Window, GWL_MYDATA))->Selection;
        break;
    case VL_SETTABSTOPS:
        vl_SetTabStops (Window, wParam, (LPWORD) lParam);
        break;
    case VL_GETTABSTOPS:
        Result = vl_GetTabStops (Window, wParam, (LPWORD) lParam);
        break;
    case VL_QUERYITEM:
        Result = (long) vl_QueryItem ();
        break;
    default:
        Result = DefWindowProc (Window, Msg, wParam, lParam);
    }
return Result;
}
```

A number of messages, such as *VL_GETCOUNT* and *VL_SETCOUNT*,
only get or set values from *MyData* and can be implemented in a couple of
lines of code (plus the *break* statement). Because the code is very simple,
we didn't bother moving it into separate handlers. Also, not *every* message
handler is in MAIN.C. For example, *vl_QueryItem()* is placed in PAINT.C for
a reason that will become evident shortly.

We can finish up MAIN.C with the *LibMain()* function, which is used to
register the Virtual Listbox control class:

```
static WNDCLASS Class =
    {
    CS_HREDRAW | CS_VREDRAW | CS_DBLCLKS | CS_GLOBALCLASS,
    WndProc,
    0,
    GWW_EXTRA,
    0,
    NULL,
    NULL,
    COLOR_WINDOW + 1,
```

```
    NULL,
    NULL
    };

#pragma argsused
int far pascal LibMain
    (
    HINSTANCE hInstance,
    WORD DataSeg,
    WORD HeapSize,
    LPSTR CommandLine
    )
    {
    if (HeapSize > 0)
      UnlockData (0);
    LibInstance = hInstance;
    Class.hInstance = hInstance;
    Class.lpszClassName = ClassName;
    return RegisterClass (&Class) ? TRUE : FALSE;
    }
```

## PAINT.C

As in the Skeleton control, the PAINT.C module is responsible for the physical appearance of the control. Unlike the Skeleton, however, painting the Virtual Listbox is actually interesting. Let's take a close look at each section of PAINT.C. We'll start at the top:

```
#include "Internal.H"

static volatile QUERYITEM QueryItem;

LPQUERYITEM far pascal vl_QueryItem (void)
    {
    return (LPQUERYITEM) &QueryItem;
    }
```

These first few lines of the module, in addition to including INTERNAL.H, allocate space for one *QueryItem* structure. The *vl_QueryItem()* function simply returns this structure's address. Don't worry about the **volatile** keyword; we'll explain it next, when we look at the *PaintMe()* function:

```
void far pascal PaintMe (HWND Window, HDC dc, LPMYDATA MyData)
    {
    register Index, Line = 0, t;
    RECT Rect;
```

```
HBRUSH NewBrush;
UINT OldAlign = GetTextAlign (dc);

SetWindowOrg (dc, 0, MyData->cyChar * MyData->TopRecord);
SetBkMode (dc, TRANSPARENT);
GetClientRect (Window, &Rect);

Index = MyData->TopRecord;
while ((Line <= MyData->LinesPerWindow) &&
    (Index < MyData->Count))
  {
  Rect.top = MyData->cyChar * Index;
  Rect.bottom = Rect.top + MyData->cyChar;

  if (Index == MyData->Selection)
    {
    NewBrush = CreateSolidBrush (GetSysColor (COLOR_HIGHLIGHT));
    SetTextColor (dc, GetSysColor (COLOR_HIGHLIGHTTEXT));
    }
  else
    {
    NewBrush = CreateSolidBrush (GetSysColor (COLOR_WINDOW));
    SetTextColor (dc, GetSysColor (COLOR_WINDOWTEXT));
    }
  FillRect (dc, &Rect, NewBrush);
  DeleteObject (NewBrush);

  QueryItem.Index = Index;
  QueryItem.Column = 0;
  QueryItem.Align = DT_LEFT;
  QueryItem.Buffer[0] = 0;
  SendMessage (GetParent (Window),
    WM_COMMAND,
    GetWindowWord (Window, GWW_ID),
    MAKELONG (Window, VLN_READYITEM));

  if (QueryItem.Buffer[0])
    {
    SetTextAlign (dc, QueryItem.Align);
    TabbedTextOut (dc, 0, MyData->cyChar * Index,
      (LPSTR) QueryItem.Buffer,
      lstrlen ((LPSTR) QueryItem.Buffer),
      MyData->TabCount, MyData->Tabs, 0);
    }
  else for (t = 0; t <= MyData->TabCount; t++)
    {
    QueryItem.Column = t + 1;
    QueryItem.Align = DT_LEFT;
    QueryItem.Buffer[0] = 0;
```

```
        SendMessage (GetParent (Window),
          WM_COMMAND,
          GetWindowWord (Window, GWW_ID),
          MAKELONG (Window, VLN_READYITEM));
      if (QueryItem.Buffer[0])
          {
          int x = (t == 0) ? 0 : MyData->Tabs[t-1];
          SetTextAlign (dc, QueryItem.Align);
          TextOut (dc, x, MyData->cyChar * Index,
            (LPSTR) QueryItem.Buffer,
            lstrlen ((LPSTR) QueryItem.Buffer));
          }
        }

    if (MyData->HasFocus)
      if ((Index == MyData->Selection) ||
          ((MyData->Selection == -1) && (Index == MyData->TopRecord)))
        DrawFocusRect (dc, &Rect);

    Index++;
    Line++;
    }
  SetTextAlign (dc, OldAlign);
  }
```

This function is a little longer than we generally like them to be. Unfortunately, it needs to cover a lot of territory. Don't worry, though; it's easy to follow. In the first few lines, *SetWindowOrg()* is used to set the window coordinates so that *MyData->TopRecord* falls naturally at the top of the listbox. This allows us to easily calculate the *y* coordinate of each line from the line number itself.

The **while** loop allows most of the remaining code to operate on each visible line displayed in the Virtual Listbox. It calculates a rectangle for displaying the text and sets the text color and rectangle background color. These colors depend on whether this particular line happens to be selected.

In the next block of code, the *QueryItem* struct is initialized: *Column* is set to zero, the *Buffer* is NULL-terminated so that its "string length" will be zero, and *Align* is set to *DT_LEFT*. (This flag is used by the Windows API function *TextOut()* for left-justified strings.) Then, the *VLN_READYITEM* notification is sent to the parent window.

Here's where a bit of magic occurs. When *SendMessage()* transmits a message, it actually performs something like a function call to the target window's window procedure. (This is as opposed to *PostMessage()*, which places the message in the target window's queue and immediately returns.) The parent window, in processing the *VLN_READYITEM* notification, is supposed to send a *VL_QUERYITEM* message back to the Virtual Listbox control. This will occur *while* the Virtual Listbox is still waiting for the *VLN_READYITEM* notification to complete, resulting in a *recursive operation*. The handling of the *VL_QUERYITEM* message is simple; the Virtual Listbox returns the address of the *QueryItem* structure. The parent window then makes whatever alterations to the structure it deems appropriate (like copying text into it, and perhaps changing the *Align* member to some other value) and returns. Thus, when execution resumes with the next line, *QueryItem* will *already have been changed* by the parent window.

Some optimizing compilers, not realizing that an indirect recursive call has been made, might assume that *QueryItem* has not been changed. If the contents of one of *QueryItem*'s fields were still in a register, such a compiler might not reload it. This could lead to strange and elusive bugs. Nevertheless, you shouldn't be afraid of using recursive functions. In our case, the **volatile** keyword notifies the compiler that the contents of the *QueryItem* structure are likely to change at any time, for no apparent reason. The compiler will therefore make sure that no shortcuts are taken when referencing this structure.

Once a structure is defined as **volatile**, its fields are also **volatile** by association. Therefore, we need to cast each of *QueryItem*'s pointers. When we write the following statement:

```
(LPSTR) QueryItem.Buffer
```

we are not being redundant. We are casting a **volatile** *LPSTR* to a *non-volatile LPSTR*. We can do this safely because we know that *QueryItem* will not change while *TextOut()* is executing. The compiler likes to be reassured, and it will display a warning if we forget to add the cast.

We want the Virtual Listbox's parent to be able to render an item in its entirety, or a column at a time. You'll remember that the Virtual Listbox accommodates this by sending a *VLN_READYITEM* notification once for an entire item, and then once for each column if the parent doesn't supply text for that item on the first attempt. The **if** statement implements this. If text was supplied for *Column==0*, it is painted with the *TabbedTextOut()* API function. This function will use the tab stop array stored in the *MYDATA* structure to align columns. That takes care of displaying an item that is rendered all at once.

If, on the other hand, the first notification was ignored, *VLN_READYITEM* notifications will be sent for each column. At this point, some columns can be left blank without harm. Items that *are* supplied are aligned individually, allowing for left, center, and right justification of each column, independent of the others. Since tabbing is not done within the column, the faster *TextOut()* is used instead of *TabbedTextOut()*.

Finally, if the window has the input focus, the focus rectangle is drawn around the item before moving on to the next line. And, at the conclusion of the loop, the original alignment is restored to the device context.

 o    o    o

*Remember to always restore a device context to its original condition before releasing it.*

o    o    o

## DIALOG.C

The DIALOG.C module provides the hooks needed by the standard resource editors, such as Borland Resource Workshop and Microsoft's Dialog Editor. The first function in this file, *Info()*, provides information about the control when asked by the resource editor:

```c
#include "Internal.h"

#pragma argsused
HGLOBAL far pascal _export Info (void)
    {
    typedef struct
        {
        UINT TypeStyle;
        UINT SuggestedWidth: 15;
        UINT WidthPixels: 1;
        UINT SuggestedHeight: 15;
        UINT HeightPixels: 1;
        DWORD DefaultStyle;
        char Description[22];
        HBITMAP ToolboxBitmap;
        HCURSOR DropCursor;
        } TYPEINFO;

    typedef struct
        {
        UINT Version;
        UINT TypeCount;
        char ClassName[CTLCLASS];
        char Title[94];
        char Reserved[10];
        TYPEINFO Type[1];
        } CONTROLINFO, FAR * LPCONTROLINFO;
```

```
HGLOBAL hCtlInfo;
LPCONTROLINFO CtlInfo;

hCtlInfo = GlobalAlloc (GHND, sizeof (CONTROLINFO));
if (hCtlInfo)
    {
    CtlInfo = (LPCONTROLINFO) GlobalLock (hCtlInfo);
    CtlInfo->Version = 100;
    CtlInfo->TypeCount = 1;
    lstrcpy (CtlInfo->ClassName, ClassName);
    lstrcpy (CtlInfo->Title, ClassName);
    CtlInfo->Type[0].SuggestedWidth = 50;
    CtlInfo->Type[0].SuggestedHeight = 40;
    CtlInfo->Type[0].DefaultStyle =
        WS_BORDER | WS_CHILD | WS_VSCROLL |
        VLS_INTEGRALHEIGHT;
    lstrcpy (CtlInfo->Type[0].Description, ClassName);
    CtlInfo->Type[0].ToolboxBitmap =
        LoadBitmap (LibInstance, MAKEINTRESOURCE (100));
    CtlInfo->Type[0].DropCursor =
        LoadCursor (LibInstance, MAKEINTRESOURCE (100));
    GlobalUnlock (hCtlInfo);
    }
return hCtlInfo;
}
```

Notice that *Info()* adds only Virtual Listbox specifics to the values we inherited from the Skeleton version of DIALOG.C. Of course, this is true of all the functions in this module. For example, the style dialog proc is almost unchanged from the Skeleton:

```
typedef struct
    {
    LPCTLSTYLE Style;
    LPFNSTRTOID String2ID;
    LPFNIDTOSTR ID2String;
    } STYLEDATA, FAR * LPSTYLEDATA;

static void near pascal wm_InitDialog
    (HWND Dialog, LPSTYLEDATA StyleData)
    {
    LPSTYLEBITS Styles =
        (LPSTYLEBITS) &StyleData->Style->dwStyle;
    char Buffer[64];
    if (Styles->StdStyles.TabStop)
        CheckDlgButton (Dialog, IDC_TABSTOP, 1);
    if (Styles->StdStyles.Group)
        CheckDlgButton (Dialog, IDC_GROUP, 1);
```

```
   if (Styles->StdStyles.Border)
      CheckDlgButton (Dialog, IDC_BORDER, 1);
   if (Styles->StdStyles.Disabled)
      CheckDlgButton (Dialog, IDC_DISABLED, 1);
   if (Styles->StdStyles.Visible)
      CheckDlgButton (Dialog, IDC_VISIBLE, 1);
   if (Styles->CustomStyles.IntegralHeight)
      CheckDlgButton (Dialog, IDC_INTEGRALHEIGHT, 1);
   StyleData->ID2String (StyleData->Style->wId,
      Buffer, sizeof Buffer);
   SetDlgItemText (Dialog, IDC_ID, Buffer);
   SetDlgItemText (Dialog, IDC_CAPTION,
      StyleData->Style->szTitle);
   }

static void near pascal wm_Command_OK
   (HWND Dialog, LPSTYLEDATA StyleData)
   {
   LPSTYLEBITS Styles =
      (LPSTYLEBITS) &StyleData->Style->dwStyle;
   char Buffer[64];
   Styles->StdStyles.TabStop =
      IsDlgButtonChecked (Dialog, IDC_TABSTOP);
   Styles->StdStyles.Group =
      IsDlgButtonChecked (Dialog, IDC_GROUP);
   Styles->StdStyles.Border =
      IsDlgButtonChecked (Dialog, IDC_BORDER);
   Styles->StdStyles.Disabled =
      IsDlgButtonChecked (Dialog, IDC_DISABLED);
   Styles->StdStyles.Visible =
      IsDlgButtonChecked (Dialog, IDC_VISIBLE);
   Styles->CustomStyles.IntegralHeight =
      IsDlgButtonChecked (Dialog, IDC_INTEGRALHEIGHT);
   GetDlgItemText (Dialog, IDC_ID,
      Buffer, sizeof Buffer);
   StyleData->Style->wId = StyleData->String2ID (Buffer);
   GetDlgItemText (Dialog, IDC_CAPTION,
      StyleData->Style->szTitle,
      sizeof StyleData->Style->szTitle);
   }

#pragma argsused
BOOL far pascal _export StyleProc
   (
   HWND Dialog,
   UINT Msg,
   WPARAM wParam,
   LPARAM lParam
   )
```

```
   {
   static LPSTYLEDATA StyleData;
   switch (Msg)
      {
      case WM_INITDIALOG:
         StyleData = (LPSTYLEDATA) lParam;
         wm_InitDialog (Dialog, StyleData);
         return TRUE;
      case WM_COMMAND:
         switch (wParam)
            {
            case IDOK:
               wm_Command_OK (Dialog, StyleData);
               EndDialog (Dialog, TRUE);
               break;
            case IDCANCEL:
               EndDialog (Dialog, FALSE);
               break;
            default:
               return FALSE;
            }
         break;
      default:
         return FALSE;
      }
   return TRUE;
   }

BOOL far pascal _export Style
      (
      HWND Window,
      HGLOBAL hCtlStyle,
      LPFNSTRTOID aString2ID,
      LPFNIDTOSTR aID2String
      )
   {
   BOOL Result;
   static char far DlgName[] = "Styles";
   STYLEDATA StyleData;
   StyleData.Style = (LPCTLSTYLE) GlobalLock (hCtlStyle);
   StyleData.String2ID = aString2ID;
   StyleData.ID2String = aID2String;
   Result = DialogBoxParam (LibInstance,
      DlgName, Window, (FARPROC) StyleProc,
      (long) (LPSTYLEDATA) &StyleData);
   GlobalUnlock (hCtlStyle);
   return (Result == IDOK);
   }
```

## Supporting Custom Styles

A couple of style components have changed, however. For example, horizontal and vertical scroll bars are not considered options by the Virtual Listbox.

The one custom style that the Virtual Listbox does support is *VLS_INTEGRALHEIGHT*. The opposite of the standard listbox's *LBS_NOINTEGRALHEIGHT* style, it should be specified if you do not want to see a partial item at the bottom of the Virtual Listbox. The *Flags()* function must be able to deal with this string:

```
UINT far pascal _export Flags
    (
    DWORD Flags,
    LPSTR Buffer,
    UINT BufferSize
    )
    {
    LPSTYLEBITS Styles = (LPSTYLEBITS) &Flags;
    if (Styles->CustomStyles.IntegralHeight)
        {
        if (Buffer[0])
          lstrcat (Buffer, " | ");
        lstrcat (Buffer, "VLS_INTEGRALHEIGHT");
        }
    return lstrlen (Buffer);
    }
```

## Supporting the Borland Workshop

We close out the module with the *ListClasses()* function, which, you'll recall, provides the hook required by the Borland Resource Workshop:

```
typedef HGLOBAL (CALLBACK *LPFNINFO)( void );
typedef BOOL (CALLBACK *LPFNSTYLE)
    (
    HWND hWnd,
    HGLOBAL hCntlStyle,
    LPFNSTRTOID lpfnSID,
    LPFNIDTOSTR lpfnIDS
    );
typedef UINT (CALLBACK *LPFNFLAGS)
    (
    DWORD   dwStyle,
    LPSTR   lpBuff,
    UINT    wBuffLength
    );
```

```
typedef HGLOBAL (CALLBACK *LPFNLOADRES) (LPSTR szType, LPSTR szId);
typedef BOOL (CALLBACK *LPFNEDITRES) (LPSTR szType, LPSTR szId);

#pragma argsused
HGLOBAL far pascal _export ListClasses
    (
    LPSTR CallingClass,
    UINT Version,
    LPFNLOADRES Load,
    LPFNEDITRES Edit
    )
{
typedef struct
    {
    LPFNINFO   fnRWInfo;
    LPFNSTYLE  fnRWStyle;
    LPFNFLAGS  fnFlags;
    char   ClassName[20];
    } RWCTLCLASS, FAR *LPRWCTLCLASS;

typedef struct {
    short   ClassCount;
    RWCTLCLASS Class[1];
    } CTLCLASSLIST, FAR *LPCTLCLASSLIST;

HGLOBAL hClassList = GlobalAlloc (GHND, sizeof (CTLCLASSLIST));
LPCTLCLASSLIST ClassList = (LPCTLCLASSLIST) GlobalLock (hClassList);

ClassList->ClassCount = 1;
ClassList->Class[0].fnRWInfo = Info;
ClassList->Class[0].fnRWStyle = Style;
ClassList->Class[0].fnFlags = Flags;
_fstrcpy (ClassList->Class[0].ClassName, ClassName);

GlobalUnlock (hClassList);
return hClassList;
}
```

Because the only information that is unique to the Virtual Listbox class, the class name itself, is supplied via the *ClassName* variable, this function remains unchanged from the Skeleton. If you had any doubts about the usefulness of the Skeleton, they should have been dispelled by now.

# VISUAL.C

The VISUAL.C module provides all the hooks needed to make the Virtual Listbox accessible to a visual programming environment, such as Visual Basic.

● ● ●

*If you plan to use the Virtual Listbox control with a visual environment,*
*you'll need to include VISUAL.C and HELP.C when you compile and*
*link the control.*

● ● ●

As we discuss VISUAL.C, you'll notice that it follows the basic framework of the VISUAL.C file we created for the Skeleton control. Let's start at
the top and work our way through the file. At the beginning, the key
properties are defined using *PROPINFO* initialized variables:

```
#include "internal.h"

#define _segment(p) ((unsigned int) (((unsigned long) (void far *) (p)) >> 16L))
#define _offsetin(struc, fld) ((USHORT)&(((struc *)0)->fld))
#define VBERR_BADINDEX 381

static long Boolean[2] = { 0, -1 };

typedef struct
    {
    UINT : 16;
    } VBDATA;
typedef VBDATA far * LPVBDATA;

PROPINFO Property_About =
    {
    "(About)",
    DT_HSZ | PF_fGetMsg | PF_fNoRuntimeW | PF_fGetHszMsg,
    0, 0, 0, NULL, 0
    };

PROPINFO Property_ListCount =
    {
    "ListCount",
    DT_LONG | PF_fGetMsg | PF_fSetMsg | PF_fSaveMsg,
    0, 0, 0, NULL, 0
    };

PROPINFO Property_ListIndex =
    {
    "ListIndex",
    DT_LONG | PF_fGetMsg | PF_fSetMsg | PF_fNoShow,
    0, 0, 0, NULL, 0
    };
```

```
PROPINFO Property_TabStops =
   {
   "TabStops",
   DT_SHORT | PF_fGetMsg | PF_fSetMsg | PF_fSaveMsg | PF_fPropArray |
PF_fNoShow,
   0, 0, 0, NULL, 0
   };

PROPINFO Property_TabCount =
   {
   "TabCount",
   DT_SHORT | PF_fGetMsg | PF_fSetMsg | PF_fNoShow,
   0, 0, 0, NULL, 0
   };

PPROPINFO Properties[] =
   {
   PPROPINFO_STD_CTLNAME,
   PPROPINFO_STD_INDEX,
   PPROPINFO_STD_BACKCOLOR,
   PPROPINFO_STD_FORECOLOR,
   PPROPINFO_STD_LEFT,
   PPROPINFO_STD_TOP,
   PPROPINFO_STD_WIDTH,
   PPROPINFO_STD_HEIGHT,
   PPROPINFO_STD_FONTNAME,
   PPROPINFO_STD_FONTSIZE,
   PPROPINFO_STD_FONTBOLD,
   PPROPINFO_STD_FONTITALIC,
   PPROPINFO_STD_TABINDEX,
   PPROPINFO_STD_TABSTOP,
   PPROPINFO_STD_BORDERSTYLEON,
   PPROPINFO_STD_ENABLED,
   PPROPINFO_STD_PARENT,
   PPROPINFO_STD_TAG,
   PPROPINFO_STD_VISIBLE,
   PPROPINFO_STD_HELPCONTEXTID,
   PPROPINFO_STD_LAST,
   &Property_About,
   &Property_ListCount,
   &Property_ListIndex,
   &Property_TabStops,
   &Property_TabCount,
   NULL
   };
```

```
typedef enum
  {
  IPROPINFO_STD_CTLNAME,
  IPROPINFO_STD_INDEX,
  IPROPINFO_STD_BACKCOLOR,
  IPROPINFO_STD_FORECOLOR,
  IPROPINFO_STD_LEFT,
  IPROPINFO_STD_TOP,
  IPROPINFO_STD_WIDTH,
  IPROPINFO_STD_HEIGHT,
  IPROPINFO_STD_FONTNAME,
  IPROPINFO_STD_FONTSIZE,
  IPROPINFO_STD_FONTBOLD,
  IPROPINFO_STD_FONTITALIC,
  IPROPINFO_STD_TABINDEX,
  IPROPINFO_STD_TABSTOP,
  IPROPINFO_STD_BORDERSTYLEON,
  IPROPINFO_STD_ENABLED,
  IPROPINFO_STD_PARENT,
  IPROPINFO_STD_TAG,
  IPROPINFO_STD_VISIBLE,
  IPROPINFO_STD_HELPCONTEXTID,
  IPROPINFO_STD_LAST,
  IPROPINFO_About,
  IPROPINFO_ListCount,
  IPROPINFO_ListIndex,
  IPROPINFO_TabStops,
  IPROPINFO_TabCount,
  IPROPINFO_End
  } PROPSIX;
```

In addition to the *(About)* property, we've defined *ListCount*, *ListIndex*, *TabStops*, and *TabCount* properties. Where possible, these names correspond to standard Listbox property names. Because we specified the *PF_fPropArray* flag in its description, *TabStops* is an array property. Several items use the *PF_fNoShow* flag to prevent their showing up in the development environment's property window. We do this to avoid confusion with a property that can neither be given nor provide a meaningful value at design time, like *ListIndex*.

○  ○  ○

*Complete descriptions of how to use the Virtual Listbox properties are provided in Appendix A.*

○  ○  ○

## Adding New Events

The only Virtual Listbox event we must add is *GetText*. This event encapsulates the *VLN_READYITEM* notification/*VL_QUERYITEM* message ballet you saw described for the PAINT.C module:

```
WORD Event_GetText_Params[] = { ET_I2, ET_I2, ET_HLSTR, ET_I2 };
EVENTINFO Event_GetText =
   {
   "GetText",
   4, 8,
   (PWORD) Event_GetText_Params,
   "ListIndex as Integer, Column as Integer, Text as String, Alignment as
         Integer",
   EF_fNoUnload
   };

PEVENTINFO Events[] =
   {
   PEVENTINFO_STD_CLICK,
   PEVENTINFO_STD_DBLCLICK,
   PEVENTINFO_STD_DRAGDROP,
   PEVENTINFO_STD_DRAGOVER,
   PEVENTINFO_STD_GOTFOCUS,
   PEVENTINFO_STD_LOSTFOCUS,
   PEVENTINFO_STD_MOUSEDOWN,
   PEVENTINFO_STD_MOUSEMOVE,
   PEVENTINFO_STD_MOUSEUP,
   PEVENTINFO_STD_LAST,
   &Event_GetText,
   NULL
   };

typedef enum
   {
   IPEVENTINFO_STD_CLICK,
   IPEVENTINFO_STD_DBLCLK,
   IPEVENTINFO_STD_DRAGDROP,
   IPEVENTINFO_STD_DRAGOVER,
   IPEVENTINFO_STD_GOTFOCUS,
   IPEVENTINFO_STD_LOSTFOCUS,
   IPEVENTINFO_STD_MOUSEDOWN,
   IPEVENTINFO_STD_MOUSEMOVE,
   IPEVENTINFO_STD_MOUSEUP,
   IPEVENTINFO_STD_LAST,
   IPEVENTINFO_GetText,
   IPEVENTINFO_END
   } EVENTSIX;
```

Here's the trick to adding custom events: The *EVENTINFO* structure is similar in concept to the *PROPINFO* structure. It supplies the event name and its argument list, in both machine and user languages.

In the documentation for the VB 1.0 CDK, we were told that, unlike properties, events must be arranged alphabetically. This is no longer so. Events are arranged like properties, with the standard events first, followed by *PEVENTINFO_STD_LAST* and then any custom events.

The *GetText* event handler, when triggered, will be passed a number of parameters, which we must describe. The array *Event_GetText_Params* describes these parameters by data type for the development environment. The *EVENTINFO* structure provides the same information in the Visual Basic language for the programmer.

The *wm_NcCreate()* and *wm_NcDestroy()* functions in VISUAL.C are not used by the Virtual Listbox control, so we've deleted the code from the Skeleton. Since the Virtual Listbox implements none of the standard methods, we can also omit *vbm_Method()*.

## Supporting Tab Stops

Although many visual controls must maintain some internal data—that's what the *VbData* structure is for, after all—the Virtual Listbox control is not one of them. The visual layer of the Virtual Listbox can rely on its underlying standard layer to maintain the list of tab stops. However, when the control is used in a visual environment, the visual layer must *pass* tab stop values to and from the standard layer. This is done in response to the *VLM_SETPROPERTY, VLM_GETPROPERTY, VLM_SETDATA,* and *VLM_GETDATA* messages.

Setting a tab stop means retrieving the current list of tab stops from the underlying standard layer, adding the new tab to it, and sending the modified list back. This is done in the *SetTabStop()* function, which returns *TRUE* if it succeeds, and *FALSE* if the index is out of range. According to our programmer's documentation as presented in Appendix A, the first tab array element is one, not zero:

```
static BOOL near pascal SetTabStop (HWND Window, int Index, int Tab)
    {
    register TabCount;
    int Tabs[MAXTABS];

    if ((Index < 1) || (Index > MAXTABS))
        return FALSE;

    TabCount = (int) SendMessage (Window, VL_GETTABSTOPS,
```

```
      MAXTABS, (long) (LPWORD) Tabs);
  if (Index > TabCount)
    TabCount += 1;
  Tabs[Index - 1] =VBXTwipsToPixels (Tab);
  SendMessage (Window, VL_SETTABSTOPS,
    TabCount, (long) (LPWORD) Tabs);

  return TRUE;
  }
```

Note that the tab stop itself must be converted from "twips"—the unit of measurement used by Visual Basic—into pixels, Windows' default unit of measurement.

Tab stops, as well as the other properties, are actually set in the *vbm_SetProperty()* function:

```
static BOOL near pascal vbm_SetProperty
    (
    HCTL Control,
    HWND Window,
    USHORT Property,
    long Value,
    long far * Error
    )
{
LPDATASTRUCT Data = (LPDATASTRUCT) Value;
switch (Property)
    {
    case IPROPINFO_ListCount:
      SendMessage (Window, VL_SETCOUNT, (WORD) Value, 0);
      break;
    case IPROPINFO_ListIndex:
      SendMessage (Window, VL_SETCURSEL, (WORD) Value, 0);
      break;
    case IPROPINFO_TabStops:
      if (! SetTabStop (Window, Data->index[0].data, Data->data))
        *Error = VBERR_BADINDEX;
      break;
    case IPROPINFO_TabCount:
      if (Value == 0)
        SendMessage (Window, VL_SETTABSTOPS, 0, 0);
      break;
    default:
      return FALSE;
    }
  return TRUE;
  }
```

The *ListCount* and *ListIndex* properties are also set by simply passing the new values on to the underlying Visual Basic window itself.

The *TabStops* property is special in another way: As an array property, it cannot use the *Value* parameter directly as most other properties do. Instead, the *Value* parameter is used as a pointer to a *Data* structure that includes the index of the array element being set.

Assigning a value to *TabCount* is only useful if the tab stops are being cleared. Thus, *vbm_SetProperty()* does nothing unless the new value is zero.

Just as we wrote a special function to set tab stops, we'll supply a function for retrieving them from the underlying layer:

```
static BOOL near pascal GetTabStop (HWND Window, int Index, LPLONG Tab)
  {
  register TabCount;
  int Tabs[MAXTABS];

  TabCount = (int) SendMessage (Window, VL_GETTABSTOPS,
    MAXTABS, (long) (LPWORD) Tabs);

  if ((Index < 1) || (Index > TabCount))
    return FALSE;
  else
    {
    *Tab = VBXPixelsToTwips (Tabs[Index-1]);
    return TRUE;
    }
  }
```

This function makes the *vbm_GetProperty()* function slightly simpler:

```
static BOOL near pascal vbm_GetProperty
    (
    HCTL Control,
    HWND Window,
    USHORT Property,
    LPVOID Value,
    long far * Error
    )
  {
  LPDATASTRUCT Data = (LPDATASTRUCT) Value;
  switch (Property)
    {
    case IPROPINFO_ListCount:
      *(long far *)Value = SendMessage (Window, VL_GETCOUNT, 0, 0);
      break;
    case IPROPINFO_ListIndex:
      *(long far *)Value = SendMessage (Window, VL_GETCURSEL, 0, 0);
```

```
      break;
    case IPROPINFO_TabStops:
      if (! GetTabStop (Window, Data->index[0].data, &Data->data))
        *Error = VBERR_BADINDEX;
      break;
    case IPROPINFO_TabCount:
      *(long far *)Value = (int) SendMessage (Window,
        VL_GETTABSTOPS, MAXTABS, NULL);
      break;
    default:
      return FALSE;
    }
  return TRUE;
  }
```

Incidentally, note the use of the *VBERR_BADINDEX* **#define**. In Chapter 3 we said that it would prove useful for most controls. This value is predefined by Visual Basic for an array index error, but we have to supply the **#define** statement ourselves, since it was inexplicably omitted from VBAPI.H.

## Loading and Saving Properties

The *vbm_LoadProperty()* function is invoked when a Virtual Listbox is being loaded from disk. The function is called once for each property described with a *PF_fSaveMsg* flag. For the Virtual Listbox, these properties include *ListCount* and *TabStop*.

Although the helper functions are defined first in the source file, let's look at *vbm_LoadProperty()* before we examine the helpers:

```
static BOOL near pascal vbm_LoadProperty
    (
    HCTL Control,
    HWND Window,
    USHORT Property,
    HFORMFILE FormFile,
    long far * Error
    )
  {
  switch (Property)
    {
    case IPROPINFO_ListCount:
      LoadListCount (Window, FormFile);
      return TRUE;
    case IPROPINFO_TabStops:
      LoadTabStops (Window, FormFile);
      return TRUE;
```

```
    default:
    return FALSE;
    }
  }
```

In the parameter list you'll find *FormFile*. This is a handle to the file containing the Visual "form" (dialog box) being loaded. The stored properties of each control on the form are available with this handle. Now look at *vbm_SaveProperty()*, the counterpart function:

```
static BOOL near pascal vbm_SaveProperty
    (
    HCTL Control,
    HWND Window,
    USHORT Property,
    HFORMFILE FormFile,
    long far * Error
    )
  {
  switch (Property)
    {
    case IPROPINFO_ListCount:
      SaveListCount (Window, FormFile);
      return TRUE;
    case IPROPINFO_TabStops:
      SaveTabStops (Window, FormFile);
      return TRUE;
    default:
      return FALSE;
    }
  }
```

As you can see, the two functions are perfect parallels; one loads the control properties and the other saves them. This extends to the helper functions as well. Let's look at *LoadListCount()* and *SaveListCount()* together:

```
static void near pascal LoadListCount (HWND Window, HFORMFILE FormFile)
  {
  int ListCount;
  VBReadFormFile (FormFile, &ListCount, sizeof ListCount);
  SendMessage (Window, VL_SETCOUNT, ListCount, 0);
  }

static void near pascal SaveListCount (HWND Window, HFORMFILE FormFile)
  {
  int ListCount = (int) SendMessage (Window, VL_GETCOUNT, 0, 0);
  VBWriteFormFile (FormFile, &ListCount, sizeof ListCount);
  }
```

Here we call two functions from the Visual Basic CDK, *VBReadFormFile()* and *VBWriteFormFile()*. These functions take as parameters the form file handle, a pointer to the *PROPINFO* structure of the property being loaded or saved, and a count of bytes to be transferred. That's all. The visual environment takes care of all the other housekeeping tasks including making sure the form file handle is valid and that the next byte read or written will wind up in the right place. All you have to promise is that, whatever you write, you will read in the same order and the same amount. That's easy with the *ListCount* property; it's a little more effort (not much!) with the *TabStops* property.

```
static void near pascal LoadTabStops (HWND Window, HFORMFILE FormFile)
  {
  int TabCount;
  int Tabs[MAXTABS];
  VBReadFormFile (FormFile, &TabCount, sizeof TabCount);
  VBReadFormFile (FormFile, Tabs, TabCount * sizeof Tabs[0]);
  SendMessage (Window, VL_SETTABSTOPS,
    TabCount, (long) (LPWORD) Tabs);
  }

static void near pascal SaveTabStops (HWND Window, HFORMFILE FormFile)
  {
  int TabCount;
  int Tabs[MAXTABS];
  TabCount = (int) SendMessage (Window, VL_GETTABSTOPS,
    MAXTABS, (long) (LPWORD) Tabs);
  VBWriteFormFile (FormFile, &TabCount, sizeof TabCount);
  VBWriteFormFile (FormFile, Tabs, TabCount * sizeof Tabs[0]);
  }
```

As you can see, to load the *TabStops* property we read it from the form file, then pass what we've read to the underlying standard layer. To save the property, we retrieve it from the underlying layer, then write it to the form file in exactly the same order.

## Triggering the GetText Event

We're ready to move on to the *vln_QueryItem()* function. This routine is called in response to the *VLN_READYITEM* notification from the underlying layer:

```
static void near vln_QueryItem (HCTL Control, HWND Window)
  {
  LPQUERYITEM Query = (LPQUERYITEM) SendMessage (Window, VL_QUERYITEM, 0, 0);
```

```
int Alignment, Column, ListIndex;
struct
   {
   LPINT Alignment;
   HLSTR Text;
   LPINT Column;
   LPINT ListIndex;
   LPINT Index;
   } Params;

Alignment = Query->Align;
Column = Query->Column;
ListIndex = Query->Index;

Params.Alignment = &Alignment;
Params.Text = VBCreateHlstr (Query->Buffer, lstrlen (Query->Buffer));
Params.Column = &Column;
Params.ListIndex = &ListIndex;

VBFireEvent (Control, IPEVENTINFO_GetText, &Params);

Query->Align = Alignment;
if (VBGetHlstrLen (Params.Text))
   lstrcpy (Query->Buffer, VBDerefZeroTermHlstr (Params.Text));
else
   Query->Buffer[0] = 0;
VBDestroyHlstr (Params.Text);
}
```

The *GetText* event is triggered in this function. Prior to triggering the event, we obtain the *QueryItem* structure from the underlying window, then package its components into the set of parameters the event expects. The visual programmer can examine these values and respond (or not), much as the standard programmer would deal with *VLN_READYITEM*. Upon returning from the triggered event, the parameters (which may have been changed) are copied back into *Query*.

## Wrapping Up VISUAL.C

The *CtlProc()* function is also very similar to the Skeleton version; the only changes are the removal of references to the Skeleton routines we deleted because they did nothing (such as *vbm_Method()* and *wm_NcDestroy()*) and the addition of a dispatch to the *vln_QueryItem()* routine:

```
long far pascal _export CtlProc
   (
```

```
    HCTL Control,
    HWND Window,
    USHORT Msg,
    USHORT wParam,
    long lParam
    )
{
long Error = 0;
switch (Msg)
    {
    case VBN_COMMAND:
      switch (HIWORD (lParam))
        {
        case  VLN_READYITEM:
          vln_QueryItem (Control, Window);
          break;
        default:
          break;
        }
      break;
    case VBM_SETPROPERTY:
      if (vbm_SetProperty (Control, Window,
          wParam, lParam, &Error))
        return Error;
      break;
    case VBM_GETPROPERTY:
      if (vbm_GetProperty (Control, Window,
          wParam, (LPVOID) lParam, &Error))
        return Error;
      break;
    case VBM_LOADPROPERTY:
      if (vbm_LoadProperty (Control, Window,
          wParam, (HFORMFILE) lParam, &Error))
        return Error;
      break;
    case VBM_SAVEPROPERTY:
      if (vbm_SaveProperty (Control, Window,
          wParam, (HFORMFILE) lParam, &Error))
        return Error;
      break;
    case VBM_GETPROPERTYHSZ:
      switch (wParam)
        {
        case  IPROPINFO_About:
          *((HSZ far *) lParam) = GetAboutPropertyString (Control);
          break;
        }
      return 0;
    case VBM_INITPROPPOPUP:
```

```
        switch (wParam)
            {
            case IPROPINFO_About:
               return PopupAbout (Window);
            }
         break;
      case VBM_HELP:
         if (vbm_Help (Window,
              LOBYTE (wParam),
              HIBYTE (wParam),
              Properties, Events))
            return 0;
         break;
      case WM_NCDESTROY:
         WinHelp (Window, HelpFileName (), HELP_QUIT, 0);
         break;
      }
   return VBDefControlProc (Control, Window, Msg, wParam, lParam);
   }
```

The module closes with *VBINITCCO* and *VBTERMCCO,* the functions
that provide the primary hooks into the visual environment:

```
MODEL Model =
   {
   VB_VERSION,
   MODEL_fFocusOk | MODEL_fArrows,
   (PCTLPROC) CtlProc,
   0,
   WS_BORDER | WS_CHILD | WS_VSCROLL | VLS_INTEGRALHEIGHT,
   sizeof (VBDATA),
   8000,
   NULL,
   NULL,
   NULL,
   Properties,
   Events,
   IPROPINFO_STD_CTLNAME,
   IPEVENTINFO_STD_CLICK,
   -1
   };

#pragma argsused
BOOL far pascal _export VBINITCC
     (
     USHORT Version,
```

```
    BOOL Runtime
    )
{
if(! Runtime)
    Register VbPopups ();
Model.npszDefCtlName =
Model.npszClassName =
Model.npszParentClassName = (PSTR) ClassName;
return VBRegisterModel (LibInstance, &Model);
}

VOID FAR PASCAL _export VBTERMCC (void)
  {
  UnregisterVbPopups ();
  }
```

## HELP.C

Recall that this module provides the support code so that we can access the Windows Help Engine. Fortunately, we can use the same exact file that we developed for the Skeleton control. All you need to do is copy it to the Virtual Listbox project.

## VLISTBOX.DEF

The Virtual Listbox's module definition file comes directly from Skeleton, with (of course) the module name changed:

```
LIBRARY    VListbox
EXETYPE    WINDOWS
CODE       PRELOAD MOVEABLE DISCARDABLE
DATA       PRELOAD MOVEABLE SINGLE
HEAPSIZE  0
EXPORTS
           WEP          RESIDENTNAME
           Info         @2
           Style        @3
           Flags        @4
           WndProc      @5
           StyleProc    @6
           ListClasses
```

Remember that **WEP** should be marked **PRIVATE** instead of **RESIDENTNAME** if you are using the newer Microsoft linker.

**Figure 6.3  The Virtual Listbox Styles dialog box for Dialog Editor.**

# VLISTBOX.RC

The Virtual Listbox resources are derived from the Skeleton resources, as well. To support the Dialog Editor, we supply a Styles dialog (shown in Figure 6.3). Here is the complete listing for VLISTBOX.RC:

```
#include "internal.h"

// For Dialog Editor

Styles DIALOG PRELOAD MOVEABLE DISCARDABLE 20, 20, 200, 177
STYLE DS_MODALFRAME | WS_POPUP | WS_CAPTION | WS_SYSMENU
CAPTION "Virtual Listbox Style"
FONT 8, "Helv"
BEGIN
  CONTROL "Caption", IDC_GROUPBOX, "Button", BS_GROUPBOX | WS_CHILD |
WS_VISIBLE, 6, 4, 140, 41
  CONTROL "", IDC_CAPTION, "EDIT", ES_LEFT | ES_AUTOHSCROLL | WS_CHILD |
WS_VISIBLE | WS_BORDER | WS_TABSTOP, 10, 23, 130, 12
  CONTROL "Control ID", IDC_GROUPBOX, "Button", BS_GROUPBOX | WS_CHILD |
WS_VISIBLE, 6, 51, 140, 31
  CONTROL "", IDC_ID, "EDIT", ES_LEFT | ES_AUTOHSCROLL | WS_CHILD |
WS_VISIBLE | WS_BORDER | WS_TABSTOP, 10, 66, 90, 12
  CONTROL "Id definition", IDC_STATIC, "STATIC", SS_GRAYFRAME | WS_CHILD
| WS_VISIBLE | WS_GROUP, 101, 66, 42, 12
  CONTROL "", IDC_DEFINITION, "STATIC", SS_LEFT | WS_CHILD | WS_VISIBLE |
WS_GROUP, 102, 67, 40, 9
```

```
   CONTROL "Attributes", IDC_GROUPBOX, "Button", BS_GROUPBOX | WS_CHILD |
WS_VISIBLE, 6, 88, 140, 41
   CONTROL "&Tab stop", IDC_TABSTOP, "Button", BS_AUTOCHECKBOX | WS_CHILD
| WS_VISIBLE | WS_TABSTOP, 10, 101, 45, 10
   CONTROL "&Disabled", IDC_DISABLED, "Button", BS_AUTOCHECKBOX | WS_CHILD
| WS_VISIBLE | WS_TABSTOP, 10, 113, 45, 10
   CONTROL "&Group", IDC_GROUP, "Button", BS_AUTOCHECKBOX | WS_CHILD |
WS_VISIBLE | WS_TABSTOP, 59, 101, 36, 10
   CONTROL "&Border", IDC_BORDER, "Button", BS_AUTOCHECKBOX | WS_CHILD |
WS_VISIBLE | WS_TABSTOP, 59, 113, 36, 10
   CONTROL "&Visible", IDC_VISIBLE, "Button", BS_AUTOCHECKBOX | WS_CHILD |
WS_VISIBLE | WS_TABSTOP, 98, 101, 45, 10
   CONTROL "Listbox", IDC_GROUPBOX, "Button", BS_GROUPBOX | WS_CHILD |
WS_VISIBLE, 6, 131, 140, 39
   CONTROL "Integr&al height", IDC_INTEGRALHEIGHT, "Button",
BS_AUTOCHECKBOX | WS_CHILD | WS_VISIBLE | WS_TABSTOP, 10, 155, 66, 10
   CONTROL "OK", IDOK, "Button", BS_DEFPUSHBUTTON | WS_CHILD | WS_VISIBLE
| WS_GROUP | WS_TABSTOP, 153, 8, 40, 14
   CONTROL "Cancel", IDCANCEL, "Button", BS_PUSHBUTTON | WS_CHILD |
WS_VISIBLE | WS_TABSTOP, 153, 25, 40, 14
   CONTROL "Help", IDHELP, "Button", BS_PUSHBUTTON | WS_CHILD | WS_VISIBLE
| WS_TABSTOP, 153, 156, 40, 14
END
```

To support Borland's Resource Workshop, we need to add a toolbox bitmap and a cursor. The bitmap and cursor are shown in Figure 6.4. The statements that include them in the application's resource pool are as follows:

```
// For Resource Workshop
100 BITMAP "tbx.bmp"
100 CURSOR "tbx.cur"
```

---

**Figure 6.4   The Virtual Listbox bitmap and cursor for Resource Workshop.**

---

**Figure 6.5   The Virtual Listbox toolbar bitmaps for Visual Basic.**

---

**Figure 6.6  The Virtual Listbox About box for Visual Basic.**

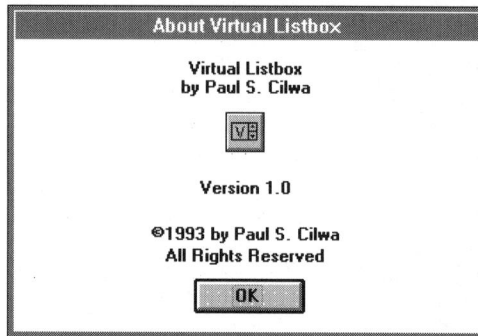

**Figure 6.7  The Virtual Listbox icon for Visual Basic.**

Visual Basic requires the set of toolbox bitmaps shown in Figure 6.5; an About box and program icon are also needed. These are shown in Figures 6.6 and 6.7, respectively. Here are the .RC script statements:

```
// For Visual Basic
8000 BITMAP "8000.bmp"
8001 BITMAP "8001.bmp"
8003 BITMAP "8003.bmp"
8006 BITMAP "8006.bmp"

ABOUT DIALOG 41, 45, 192, 125
STYLE DS_MODALFRAME | WS_POPUP | WS_CAPTION
CAPTION "About Virtual Listbox"
FONT 8, "MS Sans Serif"
BEGIN
  CONTROL "Virtual Listbox", 0, "STATIC", SS_CENTER | WS_CHILD |
WS_VISIBLE, 0, 8, 190, 8
  CONTROL "by Paul S. Cilwa", 0, "STATIC", SS_CENTER | WS_CHILD |
WS_VISIBLE, 0, 16, 190, 8
  CONTROL "MAIN", 0, "STATIC", SS_ICON | WS_CHILD | WS_VISIBLE, 87, 29,
18, 20
  CONTROL "Version 1.0", 0, "STATIC", SS_CENTER | WS_CHILD | WS_VISIBLE,
0, 59, 190, 8
  CONTROL "©1993 by Paul S. Cilwa", 0, "STATIC", SS_CENTER | WS_CHILD |
WS_VISIBLE, 0, 79, 190, 8
```

```
   CONTROL "All Rights Reserved", 0, "STATIC", SS_CENTER | WS_CHILD |
WS_VISIBLE, 0, 88, 190, 8
   CONTROL "OK", IDOK, "BUTTON", BS_PUSHBUTTON | WS_CHILD | WS_VISIBLE |
WS_TABSTOP, 74, 102, 45, 15
END

MAIN ICON "vlistbox.ico"
```

The final entry in the .RC file is the version control structure:

```
// Version control

1 VERSIONINFO LOADONCALL MOVEABLE DISCARDABLE
FILEVERSION 0, 0, 0, 0
PRODUCTVERSION 0, 0, 0, 0
FILEOS VOS__WINDOWS16
FILETYPE VFT_DLL
BEGIN
   BLOCK "StringFileInfo"
   BEGIN
      BLOCK "040904E4"
      BEGIN
         VALUE "CompanyName", "Coriolis Group\000"
         VALUE "FileDescription", "Virtual Listbox Custom Control for
                  Visual Basic and Windows\000"
         VALUE "FileVersion", "0.0.0.0\000"
         VALUE "InternalName", "VLISTBOX\000"
         VALUE "LegalCopyright", "Copyright © Paul S. Cilwa 1993\000"
         VALUE "OriginalFilename", "vlistbox.vbx\000"
         VALUE "ProductName", "Windows Programming Power \000"
         VALUE "ProductVersion", "0.0.0.0\000"
         VALUE "Comments", "\000"
      END
   END
END
```

# Enhancing the Virtual Listbox Control

While documenting the Virtual Listbox code, we thought of several enhancements that could be made. For example, you could make a point of
implementing a *List* property array for the visual environment that would
correspond to the standard listbox property. Of course, the only way to
implement it would be to trigger a *GetText* event for the requested item; but
it would provide a further level of correspondence between the two kinds
of listboxes. Another, more useful improvement would be support for a

multiple selection style. To parallel the standard listbox, you'd have to supply a *Selected* property array. Requests of this array would translate to *VB_GETSEL* and *VB_SETSEL* messages, depending on whether the selection status of an item was being read or set.

Another improvement would be to allow more than 32K items in the Virtual Listbox. To implement this, you'd have to use the *lParam* parameter for the item counts and indexes instead of the *wParam* message. You'd also have to write a new, wider-range scroll bar. We used *wParam* to maintain consistency with the standard listbox messages. Although this isn't a big issue with *VB/LB_GETCURSEL* and so on, it would require complete remapping of the parameters of a *VB_SETSEL* message. Remember, if one word and one long parameter are not enough, you can always pack as much information into a message as needed by making *lParam* point to a data structure.

The keyboard interface can also be improved. For example, standard listboxes will advance the selection to the next item beginning with a letter you type. Probably the best way to implement this feature would be to invent a new event, perhaps called *SearchText*. Its parameters would include the starting index and the letter the user had typed; the event handler would reset the index to the item that should now be selected, and the Virtual Listbox would do the rest.

We would also like to see *any* listbox pay attention to the Del and Ins keys. We don't expect the listbox to do anything with such keystrokes directly, but it would be nice to have notifications/events triggered where you could program an appropriate response if you wanted to.

Of course, all these enhancements should be implemented first at the level of the underlying window, using a message-based API. The implementation of the visual layer on top of that then becomes a trivial task of finding the best, most consistent names for the properties, events, and event parameters.

# The Pagelist Control

Nearly all Windows applications are file- or document-oriented. The user selects the file to be operated on with the *File..Open* command, and the file is opened in a standard document window. Once the file is opened, it can then be scrolled for viewing. Sometimes, however, it's desirable to select "pages" *within* a document, such as in a presentation program or a desktop publishing app.

n this chapter we'll build on the multiple-column listbox that Windows provides to create a useful Pagelist control. The Pagelist control allows the user to easily access any specific page in a document by clicking on the control. We'll create the control by modifying the core group of files (such as MAIN.C, DIALOG.C, VISUAL.C, and so on) that we've been working with in earlier chapters.

# A Look at the Pagelist Control

If you have ever used a Windows application like Aldus PageMaker, you already know how useful a Pagelist control can be. In PageMaker, page icons are displayed below a document window. Each page icon is displayed as a small rectangle containing a page number and a turned-down corner. If you click on one of the rectangles, you'll be taken to the selected page number. The rectangle that is currently highlighted indicates which page is currently selected in the document window. The real advantage of this "document paging" technique is that complex documents can be viewed one page at a time, and the scroll bars in the active window can be used to scroll within the displayed page.

A example of the Pagelist control that we'll be creating is shown in Figure 7.1. Aldus wrote their Pagelist control from scratch, but ours will be easier because we can cheat.

◌   ◌   ◌

*To create the Pagelist control, we'll be using an encapsulated version of an "Ownerdraw" multiple-column listbox that Windows already provides for us.*

◌   ◌   ◌

**Figure 7.1   A sample Pagelist control.**

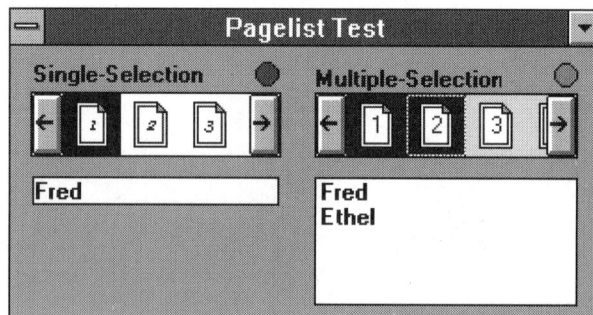

# Building on Existing Controls— The Ownerdraw Type Listbox

Multiple-column listboxes are created from regular Windows listboxes. To set up a multiple-column listbox, you simply use the *LBS_MULTICOLUMN* style. To see an example, check out the directory window of the File Manager when the *View..Name* option is selected from the menu, as shown in Figure 7.2. Notice the little icons displayed next to the filenames. A standard listbox displays plain text, period. Only in an "Ownerdraw" listbox does an application have the freedom to display items any way it likes.

Normal listboxes display only text because they do their own drawing as, indeed, most windows do. Instead, an Ownerdraw listbox sends a message to its parent window each time an entry must be displayed. The parent then renders the item using any combination of text, colors, and graphics that it deems appropriate.

◦   ◦   ◦

*The big advantage of an "Ownerdraw" type listbox is that you can take full control over how the listbox items are displayed.*

◦   ◦   ◦

You might ask what good a window is that doesn't draw itself? After all, drawing a window's contents might seem like the hard part; why should we bother writing the code needed to support such a task? With a listbox, the

---

**Figure 7.2  An example of an Ownerdraw listbox**

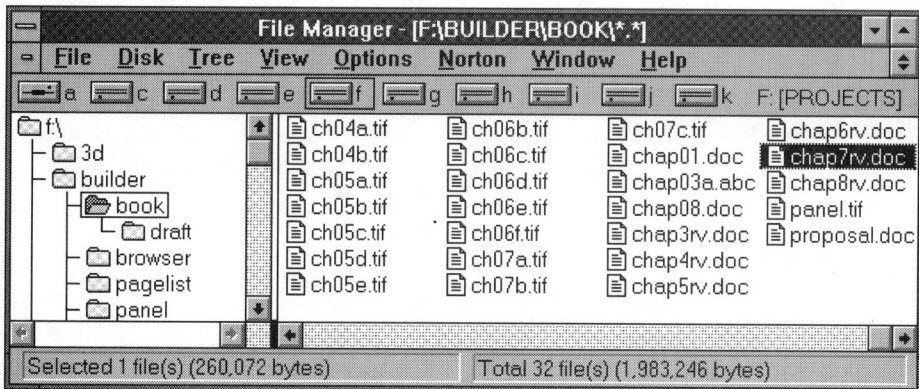

non-drawing tasks can become quite involved since they include storing the items the listbox "contains," responding to mouse clicks and keystrokes, and keeping track of which item or items are currently selected.

Because an Ownerdraw listbox is a regular listbox at heart, its physical behavior is already defined for us. We can support single, multiple, and extended selection styles. We can also store strings or data pointers.

# Designing the Pagelist Control

As we've discussed, an Ownerdraw listbox is an excellent starting point for a Pagelist control. The only difference between a standard listbox and a Pagelist is that, instead of displaying the actual text, each item will be represented by an icon image of a document page, with the page number superimposed upon it. Let's take a closer look at some of the other design issues involved in creating the control.

As you know, one of the parameters to the *CreateWindow()* function is a handle to the new window's parent window. When it needs to be painted, an Ownerdraw listbox sends *WM_DRAWITEM* messages to the parent. In order to hide the drawing details from *its* parent, a Pagelist control must "insert" itself between that Ownerdraw listbox and the window or dialog that wants to use it.

Now, in the previous chapter we created a standard Windows control, then wrapped a Visual Basic layer around it. We *could* insert the Pagelist behavior at this point, but a better way to encapsulate an Ownerdraw control is to make it a *child window* of a parent control. This is not as unusual as it sounds. Aren't the buttons at the extremities of a scroll bar ordinary command buttons? Isn't a combo box a chimera of an edit or static control and a listbox?

❍   ❍   ❍

*The Pagelist control, then, will merely be a child control that has three child controls of its own: two command buttons and one Ownerdraw listbox.*

❍   ❍   ❍

Again, you might ask, what's the point? Anyone can easily place two direction buttons and an Ownerdraw listbox directly on a dialog box. Of course, the drawing code, as well as the code that ties the three pieces together, would have to be copied each time such a combination was used. The Pagelist control is useful, not because it does something that couldn't be done with the component controls, but because it formalizes a specific relationship between those controls, providing a consistent interface whenever a Pagelist control is used. In short, it makes a Pagelist just another tool in the old toolbox, instead of a technique. And tools are always more accessible than techniques.

Figure 7.3 shows how the Pagelist control is implemented using other controls. Notice the arrangement of the child windows within the Pagelist control.

## Drawing Items in the Control

Remember that we can draw items in an Ownerdraw listbox any way we wish. Thus, we could use Windows GDI calls to actually draw the Pagelist controls' page icons, folded-down corners and all. Alternatively, we could use bitmaps.

Our approach is to use an icon. By doing so we'll gain three major advantages: First, we're required to distinguish items that are selected, unselected, items having an input focus, or items without an input focus; and we'll be able to do that easily with icons. (Standard listboxes display selected items by highlighting them, usually in a color. An input focus is typically displayed with a dotted line around an item.) Because icons are essentially bitmaps with an additional transparency layer, we can paint a background—highlighted if the item is selected—then put the icon on top of the background. Any color used will bleed through the transparent portions of the image, making for a much more attractive display.

**Figure 7.3  Creating the Pagelist control from other controls.**

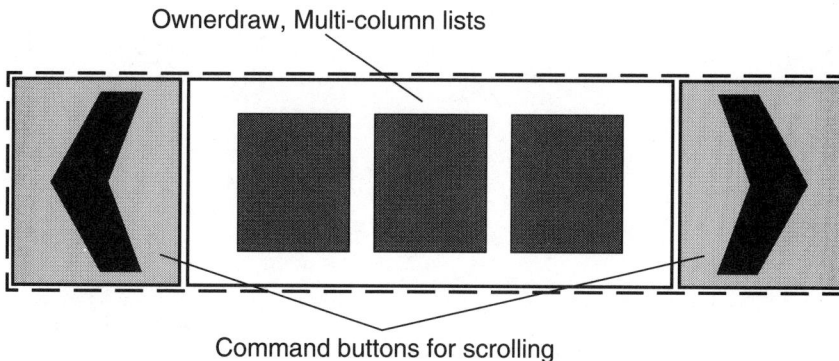

Ownerdraw, Multi-column lists

Command buttons for scrolling

Second, icons are device-independent by nature. We can supply icons for both VGA and EGA displays, and in color and monochrome; Windows will select the most appropriate one to be drawn without any further effort on our part. Finally, icons can be drawn with a single function call; bitmaps and drawing functions take more effort (and device-independent bitmaps take a *lot* more effort).

## The Pagelist Control's Interface

In spite of its unique appearance, the Pagelist control will appear to the programmer as a specialized listbox. The messages it receives will be based on the messages used with a standard listbox. The Pagelist notifications will also be based on a listbox's notifications.

Many of the standard listbox's styles will also be accommodated. Some make no sense, however, and can be omitted. For example, the Pagelist displays only page numbers and they are always in order. Therefore it would be silly to try and support the *LBS_SORT* style (or rather, the omission of it).

Even though the message set is a subset of the listbox's messages, and the values of the messages are identical, we'll change the *LB_* prefix to *PL_*. (Recall that we followed this philosophy in Chapter 5 when we created the Panel control.)

(The buttons that flank the listbox in Pagelist are used internally and do not communicate with the parent window at all; thus we needn't worry about an interface between them and the parent window.)

# Creating the Pagelist Control

The Pagelist control is implemented in C using the following modules:

PAGELIST.H
INTERNAL.H
MAIN.C
PAINT.C
DIALOG.C
VISUAL.C
HELP.C
PAGELIST.RC
PAGELIST.DEF

We'll also need to link in VBAPI.LIB since the Pagelist control is implemented as both a standard and a visual custom control. When you build (compile and link) the control, make sure you include this file in your list of library files. Your linker will then link the necessary code into the final DLL that is created. (As with the Virtual Listbox, the DLL will be assigned an extension of .VBX.) In the remainder of this chapter, we'll explore each of the files that make up the Pagelist control. We'll start with the header files.

## PAGELIST.H

This **#include** file is the only one which must be referenced by a programmer using the Pagelist control in a standard (non-Visual) Windows app. It provides the **#define** directives for the messages and notifications that the control requires. Here is the complete file:

```
#define  PL_ADDITEM        LB_ADDSTRING
#define  PL_DELETEITEM     LB_DELETESTRING
#define  PL_GETCARETINDEX  LB_GETCARETINDEX
#define  PL_GETCOUNT       LB_GETCOUNT
#define  PL_GETCURSEL      LB_GETCURSEL
#define  PL_GETSEL         LB_GETSEL
#define  PL_GETSELCOUNT    LB_GETSELCOUNT
#define  PL_GETSELITEMS    LB_GETSELITEMS
#define  PL_GETTEXT        LB_GETTEXT
#define  PL_GETTEXTLEN     LB_GETTEXTLEN
#define  PL_GETTOPINDEX    LB_GETTOPINDEX
#define  PL_INSERTITEM     LB_INSERTSTRING
#define  PL_RESETCONTENT   LB_RESETCONTENT
#define  PL_SELITEMRANGE   LB_SELITEMRANGE
#define  PL_SETCARETINDEX  LB_SETCARETINDEX
#define  PL_SETCURSEL      LB_SETCURSEL
#define  PL_SETSEL         LB_SETSEL
#define  PL_SETTOPINDEX    LB_SETTOPINDEX

#define  PLN_SELCHANGE     LBN_SELCHANGE
#define  PLN_DBLCLK        LBN_DBLCLK
#define  PLN_SETFOCUS      LBN_SETFOCUS
#define  PLN_KILLFOCUS     LBN_KILLFOCUS

#define  PLS_MULTIPLESEL   1
#define  PLS_EXTENDEDSEL   2

#define  PL_ERR            LB_ERR
```

The messages are placed at the beginning of the file and assigned the prefix *PL_*. The four notifications follow the messages and are assigned the prefix *PLN_*.

Notice that *all* of the Pagelist messages equate to their listbox message counterparts. Hey, why not? The Pagelist messages and notifications are a subset of the standard listbox API.

The messages, notifications, and styles that are defined in this file are explained in much more detail in Appendix A. Before you move on to the other modules, you might want to read up on each of the messages and notifications.

# INTERNAL.H

This header file, used by all the code modules, contains all of the function prototypes. It also provides IDs for the controls in the dialog boxes referenced by DIALOG.C:

```
#include <windows.h>
#include "Pagelist.H"
#include <vbapi.h>
#include <custcntl.h>
#include <string.h>
#include <dir.h>
#include <stdlib.h>

#ifdef MAIN
HINSTANCE LibInstance = 0;
char far * ClassName = "Pagelist";
#else
extern HINSTANCE LibInstance;
extern char far * ClassName;
#endif

typedef struct
   {
   struct
      {
      UINT MultipleSel: 1;
      UINT ExtendedSel: 1;
      UINT : 14;
      } CustomStyles;
   struct
      {
      UINT TabStop: 1;
      UINT Group: 1;
      UINT Thickframe: 1;
      UINT SysMenu: 1;
      UINT HScroll: 1;
      UINT VScroll: 1;
```

```
        UINT DlgFrame: 1;
        UINT Border: 1;
        UINT Maximize: 1;
        UINT ChipChildren: 1;
        UINT ClipSiblings: 1;
        UINT Disabled: 1;
        UINT Visible: 1;
        UINT Minimize: 1;
        UINT Child: 1;
        UINT Popup: 1;
        } StdStyles;
    } STYLEBITS, FAR * LPSTYLEBITS;

typedef struct
    {
    HFONT   Font;
    HWND Listbox;
    HWND LeftButton;
    HWND RightButton;
    BOOL MultiSelect;
    HICON   Icon;
    HFONT   ButtonFont;
    HBRUSH DefaultBrush;
    HBRUSH SelectedBrush;
    } MYDATA, far * LPMYDATA;

void far pascal wm_MeasureItem
        (
        LPMEASUREITEMSTRUCT  MeasureItem
        );
void far pascal wm_DrawItem
        (
        HWND  Window,
        LPMYDATA MyData,
        LPDRAWITEMSTRUCT  DrawItem
        );

#define IDC_STATIC 0
#define IDC_CAPTION 101
#define IDC_ID 102
#define IDC_BORDER 103
#define IDC_DISABLED 104
#define IDC_GROUP 105
#define IDC_TABSTOP 106
#define IDC_HSCROLL 107
#define IDC_VSCROLL 108
#define IDC_SORTED 109
#define IDC_MULTISELECTION 110
```

```
HSZ far pascal GetAboutPropertyString (HCTL Control);
HWND far pascal PopupAbout (HWND Window);
void far pascal RegisterVbPopups (void);
void far pascal UnregisterVbPopups (void);
LPSTR far pascal HelpFileName (void);
BOOL far pascal vbm_Help
    (
    HWND Window,
    BYTE HelpType,
    BYTE i,
    PPROPINFO Properties[],
    PEVENTINFO Events[]
    );


#define ID_LISTBOX 1
#define ID_LEFTBUTTON 2
#define ID_RIGHTBUTTON 3
```

The three **#define** directives at the bottom of the file will be used by Pagelist to keep track of its three subsidiary child windows.

## MAIN.C

This module contains the base code for the Pagelist control. The opening directives and the *wm_NcCreate()* function are unchanged from the Skeleton MAIN.C module:

```
#define MAIN
#include "Internal.H"

#define GWL_MYDATA 0
#define GWW_EXTRA 4

#pragma argsused
static BOOL near pascal wm_NcCreate (HWND Window, LPCREATESTRUCT Create)
    {
    LPMYDATA MyData = (LPMYDATA) calloc (1, sizeof (MYDATA));
    SetWindowLong (Window, GWL_MYDATA, (long) MyData);
    return (MyData != NULL);
    }
```

The *wm_Create()* function, however, has been changed. Because the Pagelist control is a child window that contains three controls of its own, it needs to create each of these windows as part of its own initialization:

```
static void near pascal wm_Create (HWND Window, LPCREATESTRUCT Create)
  {
  LPMYDATA MyData = (LPMYDATA) GetWindowLong (Window, GWL_MYDATA);
  DWORD ListBoxStyle =
    WS_CHILD | WS_VISIBLE | LBS_NOTIFY |
    LBS_OWNERDRAWFIXED | LBS_MULTICOLUMN | LBS_HASSTRINGS;
  LPSTYLEBITS Styles = (LPSTYLEBITS) &Create->style;
    LOGFONT LogFont;

  if (Styles->CustomStyles.ExtendedSel)
    {
    ListBoxStyle |= LBS_EXTENDEDSEL;
    MyData->MultiSelect = TRUE;
    }
  else if (Styles->CustomStyles.MultipleSel)
    {
    ListBoxStyle |= LBS_MULTIPLESEL;
    MyData->MultiSelect = TRUE;
    }
  MyData->Listbox = CreateWindow
    (
    "Listbox",
    NULL,
    ListBoxStyle,
    0, 0, 0, 0,
    Window,
    ID_LISTBOX,
    LibInstance,
    NULL
    );
  SendMessage (MyData->Listbox, LB_SETCOLUMNWIDTH,
      GetSystemMetrics (SM_CXICON), OL);

  MyData->LeftButton = CreateWindow
    (
    "Button",
    "ç",
    WS_CHILD | WS_VISIBLE | BS_PUSHBUTTON,
    0, 0, 0, 0,
    Window,
    ID_LEFTBUTTON,
    LibInstance,
    NULL
    );

  MyData->RightButton = CreateWindow
    (
    "Button",
```

```
    "è",
    WS_CHILD | WS_VISIBLE | BS_PUSHBUTTON,
    0, 0, 0, 0,
    Window,
    ID_RIGHTBUTTON,
    LibInstance,
    NULL
    );

MyData->Icon = LoadIcon (LibInstance, "MAIN");

MyData->ButtonFont = CreateFont (12, 0, 0, 0, 400, 0, 0, 0,
    SYMBOL_CHARSET, OUT_DEFAULT_PRECIS, CLIP_DEFAULT_PRECIS,
    DEFAULT_QUALITY, DEFAULT_PITCH | FF_DONTCARE,
    "WingDings");
SendMessage (MyData->LeftButton, WM_SETFONT, MyData->ButtonFont, 0);
SendMessage (MyData->RightButton, WM_SETFONT, MyData->ButtonFont, 0);

MyData->DefaultBrush = CreateSolidBrush (GetSysColor (COLOR_WINDOW));
MyData->SelectedBrush = CreateSolidBrush (GetSysColor (COLOR_HIGHLIGHT));
}
```

The first part of the function translates the style bits with which the
Pagelist was created into the appropriate bits for the Ownerdraw listbox
child. Next, the *CreateWindow()* function is called to create each of the
subsidiary child windows: the listbox and the two buttons.

If you look closely at the code that initializes the two buttons
(*MyData>LeftButton* and *MyData->RightButton*), you'll see a few odd-look-
ing characters. What are they used for? These characters represent right and
left arrow symbols in the "Wingdings" font. Wingdings, a TrueType font that
comes with Windows 3.1, is a collection of little pictographs, such as arrows
and bullets.

The code that actually accesses the Wingdings font is the following
*CreateFont()* function found in the code above:

```
MyData->ButtonFont = CreateFont (12, 0, 0, 0, 400, 0, 0, 0,
    SYMBOL_CHARSET, OUT_DEFAULT_PRECIS, CLIP_DEFAULT_PRECIS,
    DEFAULT_QUALITY, DEFAULT_PITCH | FF_DONTCARE,
    "WingDings");
```

In *wm_Create()* we also need to load the icon that we'll use to represent
each page. The two *CreateSolidBrush()* functions are used to create brushes for
both unselected and selected items. The colors used here are obtained from the
system palette; they are the colors the user previously selected using Control
Panel (or the original defaults, if the user was particularly timid).

Since anything we create we must also destroy, the *wm_Destroy()* function proves useful:

```
static void near pascal wm_Destroy (HWND Window)
  {
  LPMYDATA MyData = (LPMYDATA) GetWindowLong (Window, GWL_MYDATA);
  DestroyIcon (MyData->Icon);
  DeleteObject (MyData->ButtonFont);
  DeleteObject (MyData->DefaultBrush);
  DeleteObject (MyData->SelectedBrush);
  }
```

The *wm_NcDestroy()* function is unchanged from the Skeleton, as are *wm_GetFont()* and *wm_SetFont()*:

```
static void near pascal wm_NcDestroy (HWND Window)
  {
  free ((LPMYDATA) GetWindowLong (Window, GWL_MYDATA));
  }

static HFONT near pascal wm_GetFont (HWND Window)
  {
  LPMYDATA MyData = (LPMYDATA) GetWindowLong (Window, GWL_MYDATA);
  HFONT Result = MyData->Font;
  if (! Result)
    Result = GetStockObject (SYSTEM_FONT);
  return Result;
  }

static void near pascal wm_SetFont (HWND Window, HFONT NewFont, BOOL Repaint)
  {
  LPMYDATA MyData = (LPMYDATA) GetWindowLong (Window, GWL_MYDATA);
  if (NewFont != MyData->Font)
    {
    MyData->Font = NewFont;
    if (Repaint)
      {
      InvalidateRect (Window, NULL, TRUE);
      UpdateWindow (Window);
      }
    }
  }
```

*wm_Size()* makes sure the relative positions of the child controls remain appropriate in case the control is resized. When a window is first created, it also receives a *WM_SIZE message*, so all of our child window position and size adjustments are made right here:

```
static void near pascal wm_Size (HWND Window, int Width, int Height)
  {
  LPMYDATA MyData = (LPMYDATA) GetWindowLong (Window, GWL_MYDATA);
  int cx = GetSystemMetrics (SM_CXICON) / 2;
  MoveWindow
    (
    MyData->LeftButton,
    0, 0, cx, Height, TRUE
    );
  MoveWindow
    (
    MyData->RightButton,
    Width-cx, 0, cx, Height, TRUE
    );
  MoveWindow
    (
    MyData->Listbox,
    cx, 0, Width-(cx*2), Height, TRUE
    );
  }
```

## Processing Notifications

Next comes the little helper routine, *NotifyParent()*. We've explored this function before in other controls that we've built. Recall that its main function is to simplify the work of sending notification messages to the parent window:

```
static void near pascal NotifyParent
    (
    HWND  Window,
    WORD  Notification
    )
  {
  SendMessage (GetParent (Window), WM_COMMAND,
    GetWindowWord (Window, GWW_ID),
    MAKELONG (Window, Notification));
  }
```

Speaking of notifications, the Pagelist control will *itself* receive notifications—from *its* child windows. For example, when either of the command buttons is pressed, a *BN_CLICKED* notification will arrive. The *bn_Clicked()* function processes these:

```
static void near pascal bn_Clicked
    (
```

```
      HWND  Window,
      WORD  ButtonID
      )
  {
  LPMYDATA MyData = (LPMYDATA) GetWindowLong (Window, GWL_MYDATA);
  int TopItem = (int) SendMessage (MyData->Listbox, LB_GETTOPINDEX, 0, 0L);
  switch (ButtonID)
      {
      case ID_LEFTBUTTON:
        if (TopItem > 0)
          TopItem-;
        break;
      case ID_RIGHTBUTTON:
        TopItem++;
        break;
      }
  SendMessage (MyData->Listbox, LB_SETTOPINDEX, (WORD) TopItem, 0L);
  SetFocus (MyData->Listbox);
  }
```

Notification messages, you may recall, are specialized *WM_COMMAND* messages. These are dispatched by *wm_Command()*:

```
static void near pascal wm_Command
      (
      HWND     Window,
      WORD     wParam,
      long     lParam
      )
  {
  switch (wParam)
      {
      case ID_LISTBOX:
        NotifyParent (Window, HIWORD (lParam));
        break;
      case ID_LEFTBUTTON:
      case ID_RIGHTBUTTON:
        bn_Clicked (Window, wParam);
        break;
      }
  }
```

Notifications from the listbox are simply passed, unchanged, to the parent window. Therefore, they will appear to have been generated by the Pagelist itself. We can do this because the notification values are identical to the corresponding listbox values.

## Concluding the Main Module

The remaining lines in this module tie together all the helper functions that preceded them. The *WndProc()* function is the usual combination of Skeleton and original code:

```
LRESULT far pascal _export FAR PASCAL WndProc
    (
    HWND Window,
    UINT Msg,
    WPARAM wParam,
    LPARAM lParam
    )
{
LRESULT Result = 0;
switch (Msg)
    {
    case WM_NCCREATE:
        Result = wm_NcCreate (Window, (LPCREATESTRUCT) lParam);
        break;
    case WM_CREATE:
        wm_Create (Window, (LPCREATESTRUCT) lParam);
        break;
    case WM_DESTROY:
        wm_Destroy (Window);
        break;
    case WM_NCDESTROY:
        wm_NcDestroy (Window);
        break;
    case WM_GETDLGCODE:
        Result = DLGC_STATIC;
        break;
    case WM_GETFONT:
        Result = wm_GetFont (Window);
        break;
    case WM_SETFONT:
        wm_SetFont (Window, wParam, LOWORD (lParam));
        break;
    case WM_SETTEXT:
        Result = DefWindowProc (Window, Msg, wParam, lParam);
        InvalidateRect (Window, NULL, TRUE);
        break;
    case WM_SIZE:
        wm_Size (Window, LOWORD (lParam), HIWORD (lParam));
        break;
    case WM_MEASUREITEM:
        wm_MeasureItem ((LPMEASUREITEMSTRUCT) lParam);
        Result = TRUE;
```

```
      break;
   case WM_DRAWITEM:
      wm_DrawItem (Window,
         (LPMYDATA) GetWindowLong (Window, GWL_MYDATA),
            (LPDRAWITEMSTRUCT) lParam);
      Result = TRUE;
      break;
   case WM_COMMAND:
      wm_Command (Window, wParam, lParam);
      break;
   case WM_SETFOCUS:
      SetFocus (((LPMYDATA) GetWindowLong (Window, GWL_MYDATA))->Listbox);
      break;
   case WM_SETREDRAW:
   case PL_ADDITEM:
   case PL_DELETEITEM:
   case PL_GETCARETINDEX:
   case PL_GETCOUNT:
   case PL_GETCURSEL:
   case PL_GETSEL:
   case PL_GETSELCOUNT:
   case PL_GETSELITEMS:
   case PL_GETTEXT:
   case PL_GETTEXTLEN:
   case PL_GETTOPINDEX:
   case PL_INSERTITEM:
   case PL_RESETCONTENT:
   case PL_SELITEMRANGE:
   case PL_SETCARETINDEX:
   case PL_SETCURSEL:
   case PL_SETSEL:
   case PL_SETTOPINDEX:
      Result =
         SendMessage (((LPMYDATA) GetWindowLong (Window, GWL_MYDATA))->Listbox,
            Msg, wParam, lParam);
      break;
   default:
      Result = DefWindowProc (Window, Msg, wParam, lParam);
   }
 return Result;
 }
```

Just as notifications from the listbox were passed on up to Pagelist's parent, messages sent to the Pagelist are passed directly down to the underlying listbox.

You may realize that we don't need to process the *WM_PAINT* message because each and every pixel of Pagelist's client area is occupied by one of the three children. On the other hand, the child listbox will send

*WM_MEASUREITEM* and *WM_DRAWITEM* messages to Pagelist in order to implement the listbox's Ownerdraw feature. The functions that handle these messages are located in PAINT.C, and we'll get to them shortly. Meanwhile, here's the *LibMain()* for the DLL:

```
static WNDCLASS Class =
  {
  CS_HREDRAW | CS_VREDRAW | CS_DBLCLKS | CS_GLOBALCLASS,
  WndProc,
  0,
  GWW_EXTRA,
  0,
  NULL,
  NULL,
  COLOR_WINDOW + 1,
  NULL,
  NULL
  };

#pragma argsused
int CALLBACK LibMain
    (
    HINSTANCE hInstance,
    WORD DataSeg,
    WORD HeapSize,
    LPSTR CommandLine
    )
  {
  if (HeapSize > 0)
    UnlockData (0);
  LibInstance = hInstance;
  Class.hInstance = hInstance;
  Class.lpsz ClassName = ClassName;
  Class.hCursor = LoadCursor (NULL, IDC_ARROW);
  return RegisterClass (&Class) ? TRUE : FALSE;
  }
```

## PAINT.C

Even though the Pagelist control does not process *WM_PAINT* messages, it still has to draw each item of the underlying Ownerdraw listbox. We support the painting operations by responding to *WM_MEASUREITEM* and *WM_DRAWITEM* messages. Since they perform a conceptually similar function, we decided to put them both in the PAINT.C module. The first function you'll encounter in PAINT.C is *wm_MeasureItem()*:

```
#include "Internal.H"

void far pascal wm_MeasureItem
    (
    LPMEASUREITEMSTRUCT  MeasureItem
    )
  {
  MeasureItem->itemHeight = GetSystemMetrics (SM_CYICON);
  }
```

There are actually two kinds of Ownerdraw listboxes: those with the *LBS_OWNERDRAWFIXED* style, and those with the *LBS_OWNERDRAW-VARIABLE* style. The latter type supports items of varying sizes; it sends *WM_MEASUREITEM* messages for each item. Fixed-size listboxes, on the other hand, send this message only once; only one message is required because all items are assumed to be the same size. For the Pagelist control, items are the size of a standard icon, so that's the value we'll return.

The *WM_DRAWITEM* message requires more elaborate processing. First of all, like the *WM_MEASUREITEM* message, data is exchanged via a specialized structure (rather than the simple returning of a **long** like most messages do). The *DRAWITEMSTRUCT* contains any number of fields; together they supply a device context, and detail exactly where and how large the item is to appear. The structure also indicates whether the item being painted is selected or not, and whether or not it should be painted with the focus caret—the dotted line that indicates the Pagelist has the focus:

```
void far pascal wm_DrawItem
    (
    HWND Window,
    LPMYDATA MyData,
    LPDRAWITEMSTRUCT DrawItem
    )
  {
  HANDLE NewBrush, OldPen;
  int OldBkMode;

  NewBrush = (HBRUSH) SendMessage (GetParent (Window),
    WM_CTLCOLOR, DrawItem->hDC,
    MAKELONG (Window, CTLCOLOR_LISTBOX));
  if (! NewBrush)
    {
    if (DrawItem->itemState & ODS_SELECTED)
      FillRect (DrawItem->hDC, &DrawItem->rcItem, MyData->SelectedBrush);
    else
      FillRect (DrawItem->hDC, &DrawItem->rcItem, MyData->DefaultBrush);
    }
```

```
    else
      {
      FillRect (DrawItem->hDC, &DrawItem->rcItem, NewBrush);
      if (DrawItem->itemState & ODS_SELECTED)
        InvertRect (DrawItem->hDC, &DrawItem->rcItem);
      }

  if (DrawItem->itemState & ODS_FOCUS)
    DrawFocusRect (DrawItem->hDC, &DrawItem->rcItem);

  if (DrawItem->itemID != (WORD) -1)
      {
      HFONT OldFont;
      char Buffer[32];
      DrawIcon (DrawItem->hDC,
        DrawItem->rcItem.left,
        DrawItem->rcItem.top,
        MyData->Icon);
      OldBkMode = SetBkMode (DrawItem->hDC, TRANSPARENT);
      OldFont = SelectObject (DrawItem->hDC, MyData->Font);
      itoa (DrawItem->itemID + 1, Buffer, 10);
      DrawText
        (
        DrawItem->hDC,
        Buffer,
        -1,
        &DrawItem->rcItem,
        DT_CENTER | DT_VCENTER | DT_NOCLIP | DT_SINGLELINE
        );
      SetBkMode (DrawItem->hDC, OldBkMode);
      SelectObject (DrawItem->hDC, OldFont);
      }
  }
```

Thanks to *FillRect()* and *DrawFocusRect()*, and the fact that we've already been handed a rectangle with the appropriate coordinates, these jobs are all handled easily. The icon is drawn with a single function call. Adding the page number only takes a couple more calls, depending on whether you count the functions that set the text color in the device context, and later replace the original values.

## DIALOG.C

The DIALOG.C module used with the Pagelist control is similar to the other DIALOG.C modules we have created before. Let's explore its main components, and along the way we'll point out the new features that have been added. Let's start at the top:

```
#include "Internal.h"

#pragma argsused
HGLOBAL far pascal _export Info (void)
   {
   typedef struct
      {
      UINT TypeStyle;
      UINT SuggestedWidth: 15;
      UINT WidthPixels: 1;
      UINT SuggestedHeight: 15;
      UINT HeightPixels: 1;
      DWORD DefaultStyle;
      char Description[22];
      HBITMAP ToolboxBitmap;
      HCURSOR DropCursor;
      } TYPEINFO;

   typedef struct
      {
      UINT Version;
      UINT TypeCount;
      char ClassName[CTLCLASS];
      char Title[94];
      char Reserved[10];
      TYPEINFO Type[1];
      } CONTROLINFO, FAR * LPCONTROLINFO;

   HGLOBAL hCtlInfo;
   LPCONTROLINFO CtlInfo;

   hCtlInfo = GlobalAlloc (GHND, sizeof (CONTROLINFO));
   if (hCtlInfo)
      {
      CtlInfo = (LPCONTROLINFO) GlobalLock (hCtlInfo);
      CtlInfo->Version = 100;
      CtlInfo->TypeCount = 1;
      lstrcpy (CtlInfo->ClassName, ClassName);
      lstrcpy (CtlInfo->Title, ClassName);
      CtlInfo->Type[0].SuggestedWidth =
         GetSystemMetrics (SM_CXICON) * 5;
      CtlInfo->Type[0].WidthPixels = TRUE;
      CtlInfo->Type[0].SuggestedHeight =
         GetSystemMetrics (SM_CYICON);
      CtlInfo->Type[0].HeightPixels = TRUE;
      CtlInfo->Type[0].DefaultStyle = WS_BORDER | WS_CHILD;
      lstrcpy (CtlInfo->Type[0].Description, ClassName);
      CtlInfo->Type[0].ToolboxBitmap =
         LoadBitmap (LibInstance, MAKEINTRESOURCE (100));
```

```
CtlInfo->Type[0].DropCursor =
    LoadCursor (LibInstance, MAKEINTRESOURCE (100));
GlobalUnlock (hCtlInfo);
  }
return hCtlInfo;
}
```

As usual, *Info()* is responsible for initializing the control settings, such as the control's size (height and width), default border style, title, version number, and so on. Notice that all of these settings are stored in the *CtlInfo* structure.

One small, easy-to-miss enhancement is that the suggested size of a newly created control is made to be one icon high, five icons wide. The size of a standard icon is easily obtained via the *GetSystemMetrics()* function, but the measurement is given in pixels, not dialog units. Therefore, we must also set the *WidthPixels* and *HeightPixels* flags in the *CtlInfo* structure to advise the Resource Editor that this is so.

Next up are the *wm_InitDialog()* and *wm_Command_OK()* functions. Again, you won't find any big surprises here. But note that we have added support for the *ExtendedSelection* and *MutlipleSelection* styles:

```
typedef struct
  {
  LPCTLSTYLE Style;
  LPFNSTRTOID String2ID;
  LPFNIDTOSTR ID2String;
  } STYLEDATA, FAR * LPSTYLEDATA;

static void near pascal wm_InitDialog
    (HWND Dialog, LPSTYLEDATA StyleData)
  {
  LPSTYLEBITS Styles =
    (LPSTYLEBITS) &StyleData->Style->dwStyle;
  char Buffer[64];
  if (Styles->StdStyles.TabStop)
    CheckDlgButton (Dialog, IDC_TABSTOP, 1);
  if (Styles->StdStyles.Group)
    CheckDlgButton (Dialog, IDC_GROUP, 1);
  if (Styles->StdStyles.HScroll)
    CheckDlgButton (Dialog, IDC_HSCROLL, 1);
  if (Styles->StdStyles.VScroll)
    CheckDlgButton (Dialog, IDC_VSCROLL, 1);
  if (Styles->StdStyles.Border)
    CheckDlgButton (Dialog, IDC_BORDER, 1);
  if (Styles->StdStyles.Disabled)
    CheckDlgButton (Dialog, IDC_DISABLED, 1);
```

```
  if (Styles->CustomStyles.MultipleSel)
    CheckDlgButton (Dialog, IDC_MULTISELECTION, 1);
  if (Styles->CustomStyles.ExtendedSel)
    CheckDlgButton (Dialog, IDC_EXTENDEDSELECTION, 1);
  StyleData->ID2String (StyleData->Style->wId,
    Buffer, sizeof Buffer);
  SetDlgItemText (Dialog, IDC_ID, Buffer);
  SetDlgItemText (Dialog, IDC_CAPTION,
    StyleData->Style->szTitle);
  }

static void near pascal wm_Command_OK
    (HWND Dialog, LPSTYLEDATA StyleData)
  {
  LPSTYLEBITS Styles =
    (LPSTYLEBITS) &StyleData->Style->dwStyle;
  char Buffer[64];
  Styles->StdStyles.TabStop =
    IsDlgButtonChecked (Dialog, IDC_TABSTOP);
  Styles->StdStyles.Group =
    IsDlgButtonChecked (Dialog, IDC_GROUP);
  Styles->StdStyles.HScroll =
    IsDlgButtonChecked (Dialog, IDC_HSCROLL);
  Styles->StdStyles.VScroll =
    IsDlgButtonChecked (Dialog, IDC_VSCROLL);
  Styles->StdStyles.Border =
    IsDlgButtonChecked (Dialog, IDC_BORDER);
  Styles->StdStyles.Disabled =
    IsDlgButtonChecked (Dialog, IDC_DISABLED);
  Styles->CustomStyles.MultipleSel =
    IsDlgButtonChecked (Dialog, IDC_MULTISELECTION);
  Styles->CustomStyles.ExtendedSel =
    IsDlgButtonChecked (Dialog, IDC_EXTENDEDSELECTION);
  GetDlgItemText (Dialog, IDC_ID,
    Buffer, sizeof Buffer);
  StyleData->Style->wId = StyleData->String2ID (Buffer);
  GetDlgItemText (Dialog, IDC_CAPTION,
    StyleData->Style->szTitle,
    sizeof StyleData->Style->szTitle);
  }
```

The actual dialog procedure adds extra handling for the multiple and extended selection checkboxes. The problem is that either one, but not both, can be checked. One way to handle this would be to include, on the dialog, a group box labeled, "Selection" with three option buttons: "Single," "Multiple," and "Extended." The alternative, which we chose, was to monitor changes to the check state of those two checkboxes, and to uncheck the other checkbox whenever one is checked:

```
#pragma argsused
BOOL far pascal _export StyleProc
    (
    HWND Dialog,
    UINT Msg,
    WPARAM wParam,
    LPARAM lParam
    )
    {
    static LPSTYLEDATA StyleData;
    switch (Msg)
        {
        case WM_INITDIALOG:
            StyleData = (LPSTYLEDATA) lParam;
            wm_InitDialog (Dialog, StyleData);
            return TRUE;
        case WM_COMMAND:
            switch (wParam)
                {
                case IDOK:
                    wm_Command_OK (Dialog, StyleData);
                    EndDialog (Dialog, TRUE);
                    break;
                case IDCANCEL:
                    EndDialog (Dialog, FALSE);
                    break;
                case IDC_MULTISELECTION:
                    if (IsDlgButtonChecked (Dialog, IDC_MULTISELECTION))
                        CheckDlgButton (Dialog, IDC_EXTENDEDSELECTION, 0);
                    break;
                case IDC_EXTENDEDSELECTION:
                    if (IsDlgButtonChecked (Dialog, IDC_EXTENDEDSELECTION))
                        CheckDlgButton (Dialog, IDC_MULTISELECTION, 0);
                    break;
                default:
                    return FALSE;
                }
            break;
        default:
            return FALSE;
        }
    return TRUE;
    }

BOOL far pascal _export Style
    (
    HWND Window,
    HGLOBAL hCtlStyle,
    LPFNSTRTOID aString2ID,
```

```
        LPFNIDTOSTR aID2String
        )
  {
  FARPROC DlgProc;
  BOOL Result;
  STYLEDATA StyleData;
  StyleData.Style = (LPCTLSTYLE) GlobalLock (hCtlStyle);
  StyleData.String2ID = aString2ID;
  StyleData.ID2String = aID2String;
  DlgProc =
    MakeProcInstance ((FARPROC) StyleProc, LibInstance);
  Result = DialogBoxParam (LibInstance,
    "Styles", Window, DlgProc,
    (long) (LPSTYLEDATA) &StyleData);
  FreeProcInstance (DlgProc);
  GlobalUnlock (hCtlStyle);
  return Result;
  }
```

The *Flags()* function is also affected by the two custom styles Pagelist supports. Since a Pagelist can be either *PLS_MULTIPLESEL* or *PLS_EXTENDEDSEL*, but not both, we don't have to worry about returning a series of custom flags:

```
#pragma argsused
UINT far pascal _export Flags
     (
     DWORD Flags,
     LPSTR Buffer,
     UINT BufferSize
     )
  {
  LPSTYLEBITS Styles = (LPSTYLEBITS) &Flags;
  Buffer[0] = 0;
  if (Styles->CustomStyles.MultipleSel)
    lstrcat (Buffer, "PLS_MULTIPLESEL");
  else if (Styles->CustomStyles.ExtendedSel)
    lstrcat (Buffer, "PLS_EXTENDEDSEL");
  return lstrlen (Buffer);
  }
```

The module concludes without changes from Skeleton:

```
typedef HGLOBAL (CALLBACK *LPFNINFO)( void );
typedef BOOL (CALLBACK *LPFNSTYLE)
  (
  HWND hWnd,
```

```
    HGLOBAL  hCntlStyle,
    LPFNSTRTOID  lpfnSID,
    LPFNIDTOSTR  lpfnIDS
    );
typedef UINT (CALLBACK *LPFNFLAGS)
    (
    DWORD    dwStyle,
    LPSTR    lpBuff,
    UINT     wBuffLength
    );

typedef HGLOBAL (CALLBACK *LPFNLOADRES) (LPSTR szType, LPSTR szId);
typedef BOOL (CALLBACK *LPFNEDITRES) (LPSTR szType, LPSTR szId);

#pragma argsused
HGLOBAL far pascal _export ListClasses
    (
    LPSTR CallingClass,
    UINT Version,
    LPFNLOADRES Load,
    LPFNEDITRES Edit
    )
    {
    typedef struct
        {
        LPFNINFO   fnRWInfo;
        LPFNSTYLE  fnRWStyle;
        LPFNFLAGS  fnFlags;
        char   ClassName[20];
        } RWCTLCLASS, FAR *LPRWCTLCLASS;

    typedef struct {
        short  ClassCount;
        RWCTLCLASS  Class[1];
        } CTLCLASSLIST, FAR *LPCTLCLASSLIST;

    HGLOBAL hClassList = GlobalAlloc (GHND, sizeof (CTLCLASSLIST));
    LPCTLCLASSLIST ClassList = (LPCTLCLASSLIST) GlobalLock (hClassList);

    ClassList->ClassCount = 1;
    ClassList->Class[0].fnRWInfo = Info;
    ClassList->Class[0].fnRWStyle = Style;
    ClassList->Class[0].fnFlags = Flags;
    _fstrcpy (ClassList->Class[0].ClassName, ClassName);

    GlobalUnlock (hClassList);
    return hClassList;
    }
```

# VISUAL.C

After having implemented the Virtual Listbox control in the previous chapter, you'll find few, if any, surprises in the Pagelist VISUAL.C module. The property list, for example, adds only the listbox properties that the Virtual Listbox omitted, but there are no other properties used that you've never seen before. We also did not need to use any custom events. Here's the complete set of properties and events defined in this file:

```c
#include "internal.h"

#define _segment(p) ((unsigned intX((unsigned long) (void far *) (p)) >> 16L))
#define _offsetin(struc, fld) ((USHORT)&(((struc *)0)->fld))
#define VBERR_BADINDEX 381

static long Boolean[2] = { 0, -1 };
static int DefaultWidth;
static int RequiredHeight, RequiredClientHeight;

typedef struct
    {
    int Top, Left;
    enum
        {
        MS_Single,
        MS_Multiple,
        MS_Extended
        } MultiSelect;
    } VBDATA;
typedef VBDATA far * LPVBDATA;

PROPINFO Property_About =
    {
    "(About)",
    DT_HSZ | PF_fGetMsg | PF_fNoRuntimeW | PF_fGetHszMsg,
    0, 0, 0, NULL, 0
    };

PROPINFO Property_ListCount =
    {
    "ListCount",
    DT_LONG | PF_fGetMsg | PF_fNoRuntimeW | PF_fNoShow,
    0, 0, 0, NULL, 0
    };

PROPINFO Property_ListIndex =
    {
```

```
   "ListIndex",
   DT_LONG | PF_fGetMsg | PF_fSetMsg | PF_fNoShow,
   0, 0, 0, NULL, 0
   };

PROPINFO Property_List =
   {
   "List",
   DT_HSZ | PF_fGetMsg | PF_fSetMsg | PF_fNoShow |
     PF_fPropArray | PF_fNoRuntimeW,
   0, 0, 0, NULL, 0
   };

PROPINFO Property_TopIndex =
   {
   "TopIndex",
   DT_LONG | PF_fGetMsg | PF_fSetMsg | PF_fNoShow,
   0, 0, 0, NULL, 0
   };

PROPINFO Property_MultiSelect =
   {
   "MultiSelect",
   DT_ENUM | PF_fSetData | PF_fGetData | PF_fSaveData | PF_fNoRuntimeW |
     PF_fPreHwnd | PF_fDefVal,
   _offsetin (VBDATA, MultiSelect),
   0, 0,
   (LPSTR) "None\0Simple\0Extended\0\0", 0
   };

PROPINFO Property_Selected =
   {
   "Selected",
   DT_BOOL | PF_fSetMsg | PF_fGetMsg | PF_fNoShow | PF_fPropArray,
   0, 0, 0, NULL, 0
   };

PPROPINFO Properties[] =
   {
   PPROPINFO_STD_NAME,
   PPROPINFO_STD_INDEX,
   PPROPINFO_STD_BACKCOLOR,
   PPROPINFO_STD_FORECOLOR,
   PPROPINFO_STD_LEFT,
   PPROPINFO_STD_TOP,
   PPROPINFO_STD_WIDTH,
   PPROPINFO_STD_HEIGHT,
   PPROPINFO_STD_FONTNAME,
   PPROPINFO_STD_FONTSIZE,
```

```
            PPROPINFO_STD_FONTBOLD,
            PPROPINFO_STD_FONTITALIC,
            PPROPINFO_STD_TABINDEX,
            PPROPINFO_STD_TABSTOP,
            PPROPINFO_STD_BORDERSTYLEON,
            PPROPINFO_STD_ENABLED,
            PPROPINFO_STD_PARENT,
            PPROPINFO_STD_TAG,
            PPROPINFO_STD_VISIBLE,
            PPROPINFO_STD_HELPCONTEXTID,
            PPROPINFO_STD_LAST,
            &Property_About,
            &Property_ListCount,
            &Property_ListIndex,
            &Property_List,
            &Property_TopIndex,
            &Property_MultiSelect,
            &Property_Selected,
            NULL
            };

        typedef enum
            {
            IPROPINFO_STD_NAME,
            IPROPINFO_STD_INDEX,
            IPROPINFO_STD_BACKCOLOR,
            IPROPINFO_STD_FORECOLOR,
            IPROPINFO_STD_LEFT,
            IPROPINFO_STD_TOP,
            IPROPINFO_STD_WIDTH,
            IPROPINFO_STD_HEIGHT,
            IPROPINFO_STD_FONTNAME,
            IPROPINFO_STD_FONTSIZE,
            IPROPINFO_STD_FONTBOLD,
            IPROPINFO_STD_FONTITALIC,
            IPROPINFO_STD_TABINDEX,
            IPROPINFO_STD_TABSTOP,
            IPROPINFO_STD_BORDERSTYLEON,
            IPROPINFO_STD_ENABLED,
            IPROPINFO_STD_PARENT,
            IPROPINFO_STD_TAG,
            IPROPINFO_STD_VISIBLE,
            IPROPINFO_STD_HELPCONTEXTID,
            IPROPINFO_STD_LAST,
            IPROPINFO_About,
            IPROPINFO_ListCount,
            IPROPINFO_ListIndex,
            IPROPINFO_List,
            IPROPINFO_TopIndex,
```

```
         IPROPINFO_MultiSelect,
         IPROPINFO_Selected,
         IPROPINFO_End
         } PROPSIX;

PEVENTINFO Events[] =
         {
         PEVENTINFO_STD_CLICK,
         PEVENTINFO_STD_DBLCLICK,
         PEVENTINFO_STD_DRAGDROP,
         PEVENTINFO_STD_DRAGOVER,
         PEVENTINFO_STD_GOTFOCUS,
         PEVENTINFO_STD_LOSTFOCUS,
         PEVENTINFO_STD_MOUSEDOWN,
         PEVENTINFO_STD_MOUSEMOVE,
         PEVENTINFO_STD_MOUSEUP,
         PEVENTINFO_STD_LAST,
         NULL
         };

typedef enum
         {
         IEVENTINFO_STD_CLICK,
         IEVENTINFO_STD_DBLCLK,
         IEVENTINFO_STD_DRAGDROP,
         IEVENTINFO_STD_DRAGOVER,
         IEVENTINFO_STD_GOTFOCUS,
         IEVENTINFO_STD_LOSTFOCUS,
         IEVENTINFO_STD_MOUSEDOWN,
         IEVENTINFO_STD_MOUSEMOVE,
         IEVENTINFO_STD_MOUSEUP,
         IEVENTINFO_STD_LAST,
         IEVENTINFO_End
         } EVENTSIX;
```

If you need a refresher course in how this file is put together, you may want to review VISUAL.C in the chapter on the Skeleton Control.

The use of the properties that are defined in this new VISUAL.C module is described in detail in Appendix A.

Actually, the only interesting feature of the property list is the *PF_fPreHwnd* flag, used to describe the *MultiSelect* property. The only time you can tell a listbox whether it should support single, multiple, or extended selection is when the listbox is created. This is done using style bits supplied to the *CreateWindow()* function. To support this kind of feature, the kind that can only be set prior to a window's creation, Visual Basic has given us the *PF_fPreHwnd* flag. This flag tells Visual Basic, "If I change this style, you must destroy and re-create the control."

Recognizing and applying these style bits is *wm_NcCreate()*'s job:

```
static void near pascal wm_NcCreate
    (
    HCTL Control,
    LPCREATESTRUCT Create
    )
{
    LPVBDATA VbData = (LPVBDATA) VBDerefControl (Control);
    switch (VbData->MultiSelect)
    {
    case MS_Multiple:
        Create->style |= PLS_MULTIPLESEL;
        break;
    case MS_Extended:
        Create->style |= PLS_EXTENDEDSEL;
        break;
    }
}
```

The *Create* structure, which is passed to *wm_NcCreate()* from the *WM_CREATE* message itself, is built by Visual Basic before *CreateWindow()* is actually invoked to create the control. Thus we can modify it before the actual window is created.

In the Virtual Listbox control, we provided support for messages that actually set properties. Now we'll get to implement control methods as well:

```
typedef struct
    {
    long Count;
    HSZ Item;
    long Index;
    } ADDITEM;
typedef ADDITEM far * LPADDITEM;

typedef struct
    {
    long Count;
    long Index;
    } REMOVEITEM;
typedef REMOVEITEM far * LPREMOVEITEM;

static long near pascal vbm_Method
    (
    HCTL Control,
    HWND Window,
    USHORT Method,
```

```
    void far * Args
    )
{
LPSTR Text;
LPADDITEM AddItem = Args;
LPREMOVEITEM RemoveItem = Args;
switch (Method)
    {
    case METH_ADDITEM:
        Text = VBDerefHsz (AddItem->Item);
        if (AddItem->Count == 3)
            SendMessage (Window, PL_INSERTITEM,
                (WORD) AddItem->Index, (long) Text);
        else
            SendMessage (Window, PL_ADDITEM, 0, (long) Text);
        return 0;
    case METH_CLEAR:
        SendMessage (Window, PL_RESETCONTENT, 0, 0);
        return 0;
    case METH_REMOVEITEM:
        SendMessage (Window, PL_DELETEITEM, (WORD) RemoveItem->Index, 0);
        return 0;
    default:
        return VBDefControlProc (Control, Window, VBM_METHOD, Method,
                                (long) Args);
    }
}
```

First, note the *ADDITEM* and *REMOVEITEM* structures. The arguments passed (via the *Args* parameter) are different for each method being processed. For these two methods, an argument count and an index are received. *AddItem* also holds the text of the item, which is conveniently rendered as a C-style string—all we have to do is dereference the handle. Other than this, processing methods is just like handling property messages; we convert them to the appropriate messages for the underlying window and then pass them on.

*vbm_SetProperty()* and *vbm_GetProperty()* are similar to the other examples you've seen. We've mimicked the behavior of the standard listbox, particularly in the way the *ListIndex* property acts differently for single and multiple-selection listboxes. Specifically, where *ListIndex* returns the selected item index from a single-selection listbox, it instead returns the index of the item with the focus caret when the listbox supports multiple selection:

```
#pragma argsused
static BOOL near pascal vbm_SetProperty
    (
```

```
            HCTL Control,
            HWND Window,
            USHORT Property,
            long Value,
            long far * Error
            )
        {
        LPVBDATA VbData = (LPVBDATA) VBDerefControl (Control);
        switch (Property)
            {
            case IPROPINFO_ListIndex:
                if (SendMessage (Window, PL_SETCARETINDEX, (WORD) Value, TRUE) ==
                    PL_ERR)
                    *Error = VBERR_BADINDEX;
                else if (! VbData->MultiSelect)
                    SendMessage (Window, PL_SETCURSEL, (WORD) Value, 0);
                return TRUE;
            case IPROPINFO_TopIndex:
                if (SendMessage (Window, PL_SETTOPINDEX, (WORD) Value, 0) == PL_ERR)
                    *Error = VBERR_BADINDEX;
                return TRUE;
            case IPROPINFO_Selected:
                {
                LPDATASTRUCT Data = (LPDATASTRUCT) Value;
                if (! VbData->MultiSelect)
                    {
                    if (SendMessage (Window, PL_SETCURSEL,
                     Data->data ? Data->index[0].data : -1, 0) == PL_ERR)
                        *Error = VBERR_BADINDEX;
                    }
                else
                    {
                    if (SendMessage (Window, PL_SETSEL, (WORD) Data->data,
                     Data->index[0].data) == PL_ERR)
                        *Error = VBERR_BADINDEX;
                    }
                }
                return TRUE;
            default:
                return FALSE;
            }
        }

#pragma argsused
static BOOL near pascal vbm_GetProperty
        (
        HCTL Control,
        HWND Window,
```

```
      USHORT  Property,
      LPVOID  Value,
      long far *  Error
      )
{
LPVBDATA  VbData  =  (LPVBDATA)  VBDerefControl  (Control);
switch  (Property)
   {
   case  IPROPINFO_ListCount:
      *(long far *)Value  =  SendMessage  (Window,  PL_GETCOUNT,  0,  0);
      return  TRUE;
   case  IPROPINFO_ListIndex:
      if  (!  VbData->MultiSelect)
         *(long far *)Value  =  SendMessage  (Window,  PL_GETCURSEL,  0,  0);
      else
         *(long far *)Value  =  SendMessage  (Window,  PL_GETCARETINDEX,  0,  0);
      return  TRUE;
   case  IPROPINFO_List:
      {
      LPDATASTRUCT  Data  =  (LPDATASTRUCT)  Value;
      char  Buffer[255];
      if  (SendMessage  (Window,  PL_GETTEXT,
         (WORD)  Data->index[0].data,  (long)(LPSTR)  Buffer)  ==  PL_ERR)
         *Error  =  VBERR_BADINDEX;
      else
         Data->data  =  (long)  VBCreateHsz  (_segment(Control),  Buffer);
      }
      return  TRUE;
   case  IPROPINFO_TopIndex:
      *(long far *)Value  =  SendMessage  (Window,  PL_GETTOPINDEX,  0,  0);
      return  TRUE;
   case  IPROPINFO_Selected:
      {
      LPDATASTRUCT  Data  =  (LPDATASTRUCT)  Value;
      if  (!  VbData->MultiSelect)
         Data->data  =  Boolean[(SendMessage  (Window,  PL_GETCURSEL,  0,  0)
                              ==  Data->index[0].data)];
      else
         {
         register  Result;
         Result  =  SendMessage  (Window,  PL_GETSEL,
          (WORD)  Data->index[0].data,  0);
         if  (Result  ==  PL_ERR)
            *Error  =  VBERR_BADINDEX;
         else
            Data->data  =  Boolean[Result];
         }
      }
      return  TRUE;
```

```
    default:
      return FALSE;
    }
  }
```

Now let's look at a special feature of the Visual Basic Pagelist control. This feature shows how capabilities missing from the underlying standard control can be added. For example, assume we want to limit the height of a Pagelist control to that of a standard icon. It's OK if the programmer makes it wider or narrower; we just want to police its height. We can do this by intercepting the *WM_MOVE* and *WM_SIZE* messages before the standard control gets them:

```
static void near pascal wm_Move (HCTL Control, int Left, int Top)
  {
  LPVBDATA VbData = (LPVBDATA) VBDerefControl (Control);
  VbData->Left = Left;
  VbData->Top = Top;
  }

static BOOL near pascal wm_Size (HCTL Control, HWND Window, int Width, int
Height)
  {
  LPVBDATA VbData = (LPVBDATA) VBDerefControl (Control);
  if (Height != RequiredClientHeight)
    {
    MoveWindow (Window, VbData->Left, VbData->Top,
      Width, RequiredHeight, TRUE);
    return TRUE;
    }
  return FALSE;
  }
```

The *wm_Move()* function simply stores the coordinates of the control so they'll be handy when processing the *WM_SIZE* message. In *wm_Size()*, we check to see if the new height matches the height we want; if it doesn't, we call *MoveWindow()* to change the size.

There's a potential gotcha here: Calling *MoveWindow()* will cause another *WM_MOVE* message to arrive before we've even finished processing this one! To avoid an infinite recursion situation, be sure you only invoke *MoveWindow()* when a test has failed—and make sure the test can fail. If you are developing code like this and your test bed crashes when it tries to display your control, odds are that *wm_Move()* has been called recursively until the stack blew out.

The control procedure itself adds code to handle the *VBN_COMMAND* messages generated by the underlying control. These are the usual *WM_COMMAND* notification messages sent to the Pagelist's parent window; Visual Basic "reflects" them back as *VBN_COMMAND* messages. We use the notifications to trigger the standard events for selection change, lost and gained focus, and so on:

```
long far pascal _export CtlProc
    (
    HCTL Control,
    HWND Window,
    USHORT Msg,
    USHORT wParam,
    long lParam
    )
{
long Error = 0;
switch (Msg)
    {
    case WM_NCCREATE:
        wm_NcCreate (Control, (LPCREATESTRUCT) lParam);
        break;
    case VBM_METHOD:
        return vbm_Method (Control, Window, wParam, (void far *) lParam);
    case VBN_COMMAND:
        switch (HIWORD (lParam))
            {
            case PLN_SELCHANGE:
                VBFireEvent (Control, IEVENTINFO_STD_CLICK, NULL);
                break;
            case PLN_DBLCLK:
                VBFireEvent (Control, IEVENTINFO_STD_DBLCLK, NULL);
                break;
            case PLN_SETFOCUS:
                VBFireEvent (Control, IEVENTINFO_STD_GOTFOCUS, NULL);
                break;
            case PLN_KILLFOCUS:
                VBFireEvent (Control, IEVENTINFO_STD_LOSTFOCUS, NULL);
                break;
            default:
                break;
            }
        break;
    case VBM_SETPROPERTY:
        if (vbm_SetProperty (Control, Window, wParam, lParam, &Error))
            return Error;
```

```
        break;
    case VBM_GETPROPERTY:
      if (vbm_GetProperty (Control, Window, wParam, (LPVOID) lParam, &Error))
        return Error;
      break;
    case VBM_GETPROPERTYHSZ:
      switch (wParam)
        {
        case IPROPINFO_About:
          *((HSZ far *) lParam) = GetAboutPropertyString (Control);
          break;
        }
      return 0;
    case VBM_INITPROPPOPUP:
      switch (wParam)
        {
        case IPROPINFO_About:
          return PopupAbout (Window);
        }
      break;
    case VBM_HELP:
      if (vbm_Help (Window,
          LOBYTE (wParam),
          HIBYTE (wParam),
          Properties, Events))
        return 0;
      break;
    case VBM_GETDEFSIZE:
      return MAKELONG (DefaultWidth, RequiredHeight);
    case WM_MOVE:
      wm_Move (Control, LOWORD (lParam), HIWORD (lParam));
      break;
    case WM_SIZE:
      if (wm_Size (Control, Window, LOWORD (lParam), HIWORD (lParam)))
        return 0;
      break;
    case WM_DESTROY:
      WinHelp (Window, HelpFileName (), HELP_QUIT, 0);
      break;
    }
  return VBDefControlProc (Control, Window, Msg, wParam, lParam);
  }
```

The module closes in the usual way. We also use *VBINITCC()* to calculate the required height and suggested width of a Pagelist control:

```
MODEL Model =
  {
```

```
        VB_VERSION,
        MODEL_fFocusOk | MODEL_fArrows,
        (PCTLPROC) CtlProc,
        CS_VREDRAW | CS_HREDRAW,
        WS_BORDER,
        sizeof (MYDATA),
        8000,
        NULL,
        NULL,
        NULL,
        Properties,
        Events
        };

#pragma argsused
BOOL far pascal _export VBINITCC
        (
        USHORT Version,
        BOOL Runtime
        )
    {
    if (! Runtime)
        RegisterVbPopups ();
    Model.npszDefCtlName =
    Model.npszClassName =
    Model.npszParentClassName = (PSTR) ClassName;
    DefaultWidth = (GetSystemMetrics (SM_CXICON) * 6) +
        (GetSystemMetrics (SM_CXBORDER) * 2);
    RequiredClientHeight = GetSystemMetrics (SM_CYICON);
    RequiredHeight = RequiredClientHeight + (GetSystemMetrics (SM_CYBORDER) * 2);
    return VBRegisterModel (LibInstance, &Model);
    }

VOID FAR PASCAL _export VBTERMCC (void)
    {
    UnregisterVbPopups ();
    }
```

# PAGELIST.RC

The entire contents of the PAGELIST.RC file is as follows:

```
#include "internal.h"

// For Dialog Editor
Styles DIALOG 0, 0, 210, 114
STYLE DS_MODALFRAME | WS_POPUP | WS_VISIBLE | WS_CAPTION | WS_SYSMENU
```

```
CAPTION "PageList Styles"
FONT 8, "MS Sans Serif"
BEGIN
   RTEXT "Caption:", IDC_STATIC, 5,7,31,7
   EDITTEXT IDC_CAPTION, 38,4,106,12, ES_AUTOHSCROLL
   RTEXT "ID:", IDC_STATIC, 5,23,30,7
   EDITTEXT IDC_ID, 38,21,106,12, ES_AUTOHSCROLL
   GROUPBOX "Standard Styles", IDC_STATIC, 8, 41, 149, 66
   CONTROL "Border", IDC_BORDER, "Button", BS_AUTOCHECKBOX | WS_TABSTOP,
22,55,34,10
   CONTROL "Disabled", IDC_DISABLED, "Button", BS_AUTOCHECKBOX |
WS_TABSTOP, 22,67,44,10
   CONTROL "Group", IDC_GROUP, "Button", BS_AUTOCHECKBOX | WS_TABSTOP,
22,79,34,10
   CONTROL "Tab stop", IDC_TABSTOP, "Button", BS_AUTOCHECKBOX |
WS_TABSTOP, 22, 91, 46, 10
   CONTROL "Horizontal scroll", IDC_HSCROLL, "Button", BS_AUTOCHECKBOX |
WS_TABSTOP, 75,55,66,10
   CONTROL "Vertical scroll", IDC_VSCROLL, "Button", BS_AUTOCHECKBOX |
WS_TABSTOP, 75, 67, 61, 10
   CONTROL "Multiple Selection", IDC_MULTISELECTION, "BUTTON",
BS_AUTOCHECKBOX | WS_CHILD | WS_VISIBLE | WS_TABSTOP, 75, 79, 79, 12
   CONTROL "Extended Selection", IDC_EXTENDEDSELECTION, "BUTTON",
BS_AUTOCHECKBOX | WS_CHILD | WS_VISIBLE | WS_TABSTOP, 75, 91, 79, 12
   DEFPUSHBUTTON "OK", IDOK, 154,4,50,14
   PUSHBUTTON "Cancel", IDCANCEL, 154,21,50,14
END

// For Resource Workshop
100 BITMAP "tbx.bmp"
100 CURSOR "tbx.cur"

// For Visual Basic
8000 BITMAP "8000.bmp"
8001 BITMAP "8001.bmp"
8003 BITMAP MOVEABLE PURE "8003.BMP"
8006 BITMAP MOVEABLE PURE "8006.BMP"

ABOUT DIALOG 41, 45, 192, 125
STYLE DS_MODALFRAME | WS_POPUP | WS_CAPTION
CAPTION "About PageList Custom Control"
FONT 8, "MS Sans Serif"
BEGIN
   CONTROL "PageList Custom Control", 0, "STATIC", SS_CENTER | WS_CHILD |
WS_VISIBLE, 0, 8, 190, 8
   CONTROL "by Paul S. Cilwa", 0, "STATIC", SS_CENTER | WS_CHILD |
WS_VISIBLE, 0, 16, 190, 8
```

```
   CONTROL "MAIN", 0, "STATIC", SS_ICON | WS_CHILD | WS_VISIBLE, 87, 29,
18, 20
   CONTROL "Version 1.0", 0, "STATIC", SS_CENTER | WS_CHILD | WS_VISIBLE,
0, 59, 190, 8
   CONTROL "©1993 by Paul S. Cilwa", 0, "STATIC", SS_CENTER | WS_CHILD |
WS_VISIBLE, 0, 79, 190, 8
   CONTROL "All Rights Reserved", 0, "STATIC", SS_CENTER | WS_CHILD |
WS_VISIBLE, 0, 88, 190, 8
   CONTROL "OK", IDOK, "BUTTON", BS_PUSHBUTTON | WS_CHILD | WS_VISIBLE |
WS_TABSTOP, 74, 102, 45, 15
END


Main ICON "document.ico"

1 VERSIONINFO LOADONCALL MOVEABLE DISCARDABLE
FILEVERSION 0, 0, 0, 0
PRODUCTVERSION 0, 0, 0, 0
FILEOS VOS__WINDOWS16
FILETYPE VFT_DLL
BEGIN
   BLOCK "StringFileInfo"
   BEGIN
     BLOCK "040904E4"
     BEGIN
        VALUE "CompanyName", "Coriolis Group\000"
        VALUE "FileDescription", "Pagelist Custom Control for Visual Basic
and Windows\000"
        VALUE "FileVersion", "0.0.0.0\000"
        VALUE "InternalName", "PAGELIST\000"
        VALUE "LegalCopyright", "Copyright © Paul S. Cilwa 1993\000"
        VALUE "OriginalFilename", "Pagelist.vbx\000"
        VALUE "ProductName", "Windows Programming Power\000"
        VALUE "ProductVersion", "0.0.0.0\000"
        VALUE "Comments", "\000"
     END
   END
END
```

The Style dialog box, shown in Figure 7.4, is a variant of the one we've been using all along. The bitmap and cursor for the Borland Resource Workshop are shown in Figure 7.5, while the bitmaps for the Visual Basic toolboxes are shown in Figure 7.6.

The About box, which displays the same icon used in the Pagelist control itself, is shown in 7.7. The icon itself is shown in 7.8.

**Figure 7.4   The Pagelist Styles dialog box for Dialog Editor.**

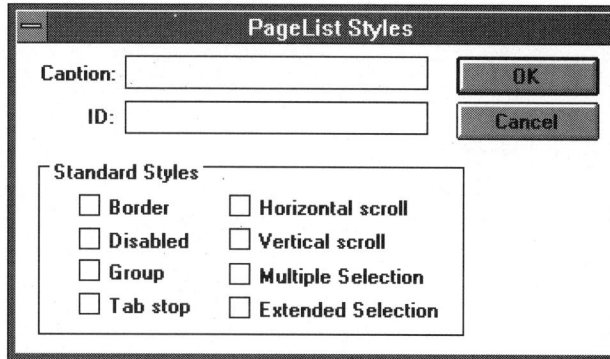

**Figure 7.5   The Pagelist bitmap and cursor for Borland Resource Workshop.**

**Figure 7.6   From left to right: Pagelist bitmaps 8000, 8001, 8003, and 8006 for Visual Basic.**

**Figure 7.7   The Pagelist About box for Visual Basic.**

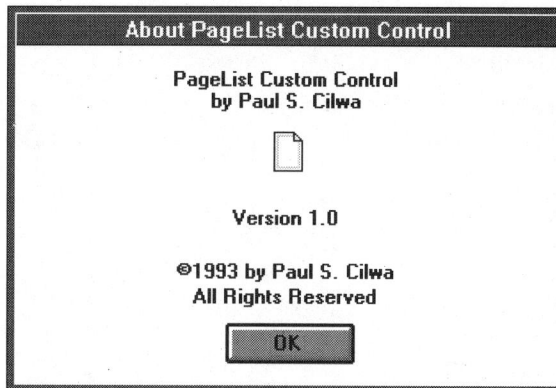

---

**Figure 7.8  The Pagelist icon for Visual Basic.**

---

## PAGELIST.DEF

Pagelist's module definition file is as follows:

```
LIBRARY    PageList
EXETYPE    WINDOWS
CODE       PRELOAD MOVEABLE DISCARDABLE
DATA       PRELOAD MOVEABLE SINGLE
HEAPSIZE 4096
EXPORTS
        WEP          RESIDENTNAME
        Info         @2
        Style        @3
        Flags        @4
        WndProc      @5
        StyleProc    @6
        ListClasses
```

# Enhancing Pagelist

The Pagelist control can be a handy control just as it is. But let's face it; anything can be improved. Here are a few enhancements to consider:

- Make the *standard* Pagelist (instead of just the Visual Basic version) impose a height requirement.
- Add a message (and property) that lets the programmer supply an icon, instead of using only the one provided.
- Allow the programmer to supply an *array* of icons, so that each page (up to some limit, of course) can be represented by a different icon.

We hope you're now beginning to appreciate the power of inheritance as a programming methodology. The Pagelist control was especially designed to show you how easily you can derive new controls from an existing one. If you are already proficient in object-oriented programming, you've known this for a while. As for the rest of you, *this* is what OOP programmers do all the time—and with *all* their data elements, not just controls.

In the next chapter, we'll take one last look at listboxes as we take advantage of Visual Basic 3.0's *data binding* feature to create a listbox that automatically links to a database.

# 8

# The Browser Control

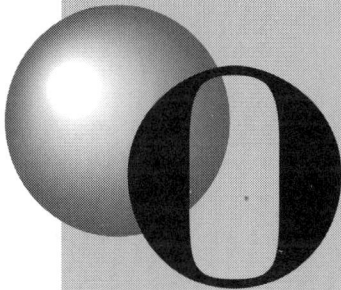

One of the amazing things about building controls as we've been building them is that you can start with an existing control and create an entirely new control—sometimes with a radically different appearance—with very little new code. Although the code is not, strictly speaking, object-oriented, the *idea* is object-oriented with a vengeance.

n this chapter we'll start with a standard listbox and use it to create a read-only browser to work in conjunction with Visual Basic's Data control. Visual Basic provides the means to examine one record at a time through its suite of "bound data" controls, but Visual Basic as delivered lacks any automated way of scanning more than one record at a glance.

Although this new control we'll build is specific to Visual Basic—it requires Visual Basic's Data control—creating it entails a number of lessons about control building, particularly about controls that internally resemble other controls.

# A Look at the Browser Control

Our new Browser control, shown in Figure 8.1, is designed to work in concert with Visual Basic's most powerful control—the Data control. While Visual Basic's "bound" controls allow the user to manipulate one record at a time, the Browser control created in this chapter will provide listbox-style access to one or more fields from an entire database table at once. But to fully understand how the Browser control works, you'll first need to see how VB's Data control works.

With the release of VB 3.0, Microsoft added powerful database support by providing the Microsoft Access Engine. Up until VB 3.0, Visual Basic had never really been suitable for developing real-world database apps. But the landscape has changed. Now you can use VB to create and view databases and perform a myriad of database processing tasks—often without any traditional programming at all.

---

**Figure 8.1  The Browser control looks and acts like a listbox, but it binds to Visual Basic's Data control shown below it.**

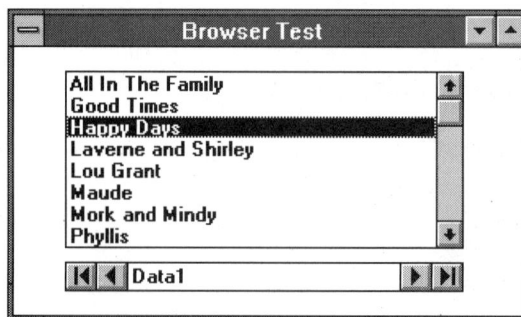

---

⊙   ⊙   ⊙

*The Data control does not, itself, allow viewing or editing of database fields. Rather, it provides control of the database to "data-aware" controls that are logically connected to it. Such a control is called a "bound" control.*

⊙   ⊙   ⊙

Visual Basic provides several types of bound controls. They are old favorites that have been enhanced including the checkbox, edit box, label (static control), and so on. Each of these controls can only display the value of a single field at a time. Although the Control Development Kit (CDK) gives instructions on creating a "multiple bound" control, Visual Basic itself doesn't provide one.

# Designing the Browser Control

We'll design the Browser control so that it will supply Visual Basic programs with a useful database "browse" capability. If you have programmed in a database development environment such as dBASE or Clipper, you already know how important it is to be able to easily view the rows of a database table in a listbox fashion.

Like the Pagelist control in Chapter 7, the Browser's function could be implemented at the Visual Basic level with standard components. This could be done using the following method:

1.  Create a standard listbox control and a Data control.
2.  Initialize the database.
3.  Display (enumerate) each row by sending it to the listbox.

Although this approach is easy to implement, it has several disadvantages:

- It's slow. The enumeration takes place at interpreted VB speed, instead of lightning-like C speed.
- It's awkward. It requires similar code to be placed in each VB application that needs a Browser.
- You must somehow associate each entry in the listbox with a database "bookmark," so that you can match up a whole row with any entry the user selects. (We'll explain what a bookmark is shortly.)

This last issue is particularly important. The Browser's sole mission in life is to display, in a condensed format, the database rows that the user is working on. The actual work of processing these rows (sorting, converting, appending, and so on) is done elsewhere, usually in a form (dialog) with a text box for each field. The only way to obtain a row in the database is to maintain a link between each Browser entry and the actual database where the row is from. This is done using *bookmarks*, which are strings the Data control supplies that uniquely identify each row. But the bookmarks—one for each row—have to be stored somewhere. If the Browser were implemented at the Visual Basic level, they would have to be stored in a parallel array.

○   ○   ○

*By implementing the Browser as a custom control, all of the "bookkeeping" required to support the Browser can be encapsulated within the Browser and kept hidden from the Visual Basic programmer.*

○   ○   ○

## Design Options

Our first major design decision is to determine which component the Browser control should be based on. We have three choices:

1. We could write a new listbox-like control from scratch.

2. We could modify the Virtual Listbox we wrote in Chapter 6.

3. We could build on the standard listbox.

Let's consider each of these options.

Should we build another listbox from scratch? Let's not if we can possibly avoid it. We've already done this once (in Chapter 6) and, as much fun as it was, it would be more fun to cover new ground.

Considering the second option, how could we use the Virtual Listbox we created? Because the Virtual Listbox does not actually store anything internally except a count of externally stored items, we would have to store the bookmarks in the *VbData* structure and manage them at the visual interface level. In fact, the only reason to use the Virtual Listbox would be that it can be "loaded" instantly with a count, rather than having to send it each row of a potentially large database. You can imagine querying the Data control for a count of records, sending that count to the Virtual Listbox, and then retrieving the records only as they are scrolled into view. Sounds great, and really efficient!

However, it turns out that this approach will not work: *The Data control cannot supply a count of rows.* At least not until *after* all its rows have been enumerated. Since we have to enumerate the rows to get the bookmarks anyway, we may as well load those bookmarks into a standard listbox, which is already set up to store string data. And that's exactly what we'll do—use the third option.

Of course, a *standard* listbox would be loaded with display strings, not database bookmarks. So, once more, we'll be using an Ownerdraw listbox. This time, however, we'll base the control directly on the listbox, rather than by creating a new composite control. That means our MAIN.C component will be very small.

## Using an Ownerdraw Listbox

An Ownerdraw type listbox, you may recall, stores 32-bit values for each item. As each item needs to be displayed, a *WM_DRAWITEM* message is received that includes the 32-bit value for the item. The processing of the *WM_DRAWITEM* message obviously must include decoding of that value into text (or a picture), in addition to doing the actual painting. Although a bookmark is a text string to the Visual Basic programmer, in the CDK, a Visual Basic string is represented by a 32-bit value. Thus, storing bookmarks as Ownerdraw items can be done without resorting to any further trickery.

Since the contents of the Browser are supposed to represent the contents of the database, we will not need to support the *AddItem, RemoveItem,* or *Clear* events. If the database changes, the Data control will notify all its bound controls including the Browser, which will then reload.

On the other hand, the Browser *is* intended to provide a means of navigating through the database. Since the Data control also provides this—however crudely—the Data control and the Browser are visually redundant. A form that uses a Browser, then, will probably make its Data control invisible.

To the Visual Basic programmer, the Browser control will actually seem simpler than a listbox control. For example, there is no need for a *Sorted* property; the database is already sorted. Multiple selection also doesn't need to be supported (although it could be—but we won't do it). And, since the Browser's job is to select records for the Data control, there is no need for a *List* property.

## Formatting Data

There is one feature that we implemented with the Virtual Listbox that we'd like to repeat here even if it does mean copying some code. Recall that the

Virtual Listbox allowed each field of a multi-column display to be formatted separately by the application. We'll also support this feature in the Browser control. However, we'll have to change the name of the event in which the application does the formatting, since the app will not be "getting the text." We'll call the event *FormatField*.

# Creating the Browser Control

The Browser control is implemented in C using the following modules:

```
INTERNAL.H
MAIN.C
VISUAL.C
HELP.C
BROWSER.RC
BROWSER.DEF
```

You might notice that this control requires three fewer files than the other controls we've developed. We don't need a public include file (BROWSER.H), the dialog support file (DIALOG.C), or the control painting module (PAINT.C) because the Browser control is only used as a Visual Basic control. The control will be "painted" by a *WM_DRAWITEM* message handler that we'll implement in the VISUAL.C module.

Since the Browser is implemented as a visual custom control, you'll need to include VBAPI.LIB in the list of libraries to be linked into the end-product DLL. This is the same technique required for compiling and linking the Panel and Virtual Listbox controls.

## INTERNAL.H

This header file, referenced by all the code modules, contains all the function prototypes. Since the Browser control can't be used as a standard control, the only functions come from the HELP.C module:

```
#include <windows.h>
#include <vbapi.h>
#include <custcntl.h>
#include <direct.h>
#include <stdlib.h>
#include <alloc.h>
#include <mem.h>
```

```
#ifdef MAIN
HINSTANCE LibInstance = 0;
char far * ClassName = "Browser";
#else
extern HINSTANCE LibInstance;
extern char far * ClassName;
#endif

HSZ far pascal GetAboutPropertyString (HCTL Control);
HWND far pascal PopupAbout (HWND Window);
void far pascal RegisterVbPopups (void);
void far pascal UnregisterVbPopups (void);
LPSTR far pascal HelpFileName (void);
BOOL far pascal vbm_Help
    (
    HWND Window,
    BYTE HelpType,
    BYTE i,
    PPROPINFO Properties[],
    PEVENTINFO Events[]
    );
```

This module is interesting more for its omissions than its inclusions. Namely, the *MYDATA* structure is absent. Recall that this data structure was used by our standard controls, and since Browser is derived from the existing listbox control, we do not have to write a standard component. Likewise, the usual functions from PAINT.C are missing.

## MAIN.C

This module contains the base code for the Browser control. Again, since the Browser is derived from the standard listbox control, we won't need as much code as was required for the other controls we've created. In fact, the only function needed in MAIN.C is *LibMain()*. Here is the complete file:

```
#define MAIN
#include "Internal.H"

#pragma argsused
int far pascal LibMain
    (
    HINSTANCE hInstance,
    WORD DataSeg,
    WORD HeapSize,
```

```
        LPSTR CommandLine
        )
    {
    if (HeapSize > 0)
        UnlockData (0);
    LibInstance = hInstance;
    return TRUE;
    }
```

## VISUAL.C

Nearly all of the code required to implement the Browser control is found in the VISUAL.C module. As always, this file implements the Visual Basic layer of the control. Since everything that makes a Browser different from the listbox on which it is based resides *in* the visual layer, we should take a close look at each section of the file.

### Supporting Tab Stops

At the start of the module we have, as always, the *VBDATA* structure definition:

```
#include "internal.h"

#define _segment(p) ((unsigned int) (((unsigned long) (void far *) (p)) >>16L))
#define _offsetin(struc, fld) ((USHORT)&(((struc *)0)->fld))
#define VBERR_BADINDEX 381

static long Boolean[2] = { 0, -1 };

#define MAXTABS 7

typedef struct
    {
    UINT AutoSelect: 1;
    UINT TabCount: 4;
    int TabStops[MAXTABS-1];
    HCTL DataSource;
    } VBDATA;
typedef VBDATA far * LPVBDATA;
```

Why have we set aside space for a *TabStops* array? After all, the Virtual Listbox control didn't need one.

Ah, but that's because we *wrote* the underlying Virtual Listbox window; we made sure it could return as well as accept a tab stops array. The standard listbox that underlies the Browser control allows tab stops to be set, but not to be read. To make the Browser's tab stops work the same for the VB programmer as the Virtual Listbox tab stops, we'll have to store the array here.

## Defining the Properties

The module continues by defining the properties:

```
PROPINFO Property_About =
   {
   "(About)",
   DT_HSZ | PF_fGetMsg | PF_fNoRuntimeW | PF_fGetHszMsg,
   0, 0, 0, NULL, 0
   };

PROPINFO Property_ListCount =
   {
   "ListCount",
   DT_LONG | PF_fGetMsg | PF_fSetMsg | PF_fNoRuntimeW | PF_fNoShow,
   0, 0, 0, NULL, 0
   };

PROPINFO Property_ListIndex =
   {
   "ListIndex",
   DT_LONG | PF_fGetMsg | PF_fSetMsg | PF_fNoShow,
   0, 0, 0, NULL, 0
   };

PROPINFO Property_TabStops =
   {
   "TabStops",
   DT_LONG | PF_fGetMsg | PF_fSetMsg | PF_fPropArray | PF_fNoShow,
   0, 0, 0, NULL, 0
   };

PROPINFO Property_TabCount =
   {
   "TabCount",
   DT_SHORT | PF_fGetMsg | PF_fSetMsg | PF_fNoShow,
   0, 0, 0, NULL, 0
   };

PROPINFO Property_AutoSelect =
   {
   "AutoSelect",
```

```
      DT_BOOL | PF_fGetData | PF_fSetData | PF_fSaveData | PF_fDefVal,
      0, 0x10,
      -1, 0, 0
      };

  PPROPINFO Properties[] =
      {
      PPROPINFO_STD_NAME,
      PPROPINFO_STD_INDEX,
      PPROPINFO_STD_BACKCOLOR,
      PPROPINFO_STD_FORECOLOR,
      PPROPINFO_STD_LEFT,
      PPROPINFO_STD_TOP,
      PPROPINFO_STD_WIDTH,
      PPROPINFO_STD_HEIGHT,
      PPROPINFO_STD_FONTNAME,
      PPROPINFO_STD_FONTSIZE,
      PPROPINFO_STD_FONTBOLD,
      PPROPINFO_STD_FONTITALIC,
      PPROPINFO_STD_TABINDEX,
      PPROPINFO_STD_TABSTOP,
      PPROPINFO_STD_BORDERSTYLEON,
      PPROPINFO_STD_ENABLED,
      PPROPINFO_STD_PARENT,
      PPROPINFO_STD_TAG,
      PPROPINFO_STD_VISIBLE,
      PPROPINFO_STD_HELPCONTEXTID,
      PPROPINFO_STD_DATAFIELD,
      PPROPINFO_STD_DATASOURCE,
      PPROPINFO_STD_ALIGN,
      PPROPINFO_STD_LAST,
      &Property_About,
      &Property_ListCount,
      &Property_ListIndex,
      &Property_TabStops,
      &Property_TabCount,
      &Property_AutoSelect,
      NULL
      };

  typedef enum
      {
      IPROPINFO_STD_NAME,
      IPROPINFO_STD_INDEX,
      IPROPINFO_STD_BACKCOLOR,
      IPROPINFO_STD_FORECOLOR,
      IPROPINFO_STD_LEFT,
      IPROPINFO_STD_TOP,
```

```
IPROPINFO_STD_WIDTH,
IPROPINFO_STD_HEIGHT,
IPROPINFO_STD_FONTNAME,
IPROPINFO_STD_FONTSIZE,
IPROPINFO_STD_FONTBOLD,
IPROPINFO_STD_FONTITALIC,
IPROPINFO_STD_TABINDEX,
IPROPINFO_STD_TABSTOP,
IPROPINFO_STD_BORDERSTYLEON,
IPROPINFO_STD_ENABLED,
IPROPINFO_STD_PARENT,
IPROPINFO_STD_TAG,
IPROPINFO_STD_VISIBLE,
IPROPINFO_STD_HELPCONTEXTID,
IPROPINFO_STD_DATAFIELD,
IPROPINFO_STD_DATASOURCE,
IROPINFO_STD_ALIGN,
IPROPINFO_STD_LAST,
IPROPINFO_About,
IPROPINFO_ListCount,
IPROPINFO_ListIndex,
IPROPINFO_TabStops,
IPROPINFO_TabCount,
IPROPINFO_AutoSelect,
IPROPINFO_End
} PROPSIX;
```

Of the custom properties used, we've already seen *ListCount, ListIndex, TabStops*, and *TabCount* in the Virtual Listbox control. We'll be implementing them similarly here. The *AutoSelect* property is brand new. Its use has to do with the fact that most bound controls only access the Data control's *current* record, while the Browser displays *all* of them. Without the Browser, the user's means of moving from record to record is the Data control. But the Browser is designed to display *all* the records in a Data control's current recordset. In effect, it *replaces* the Data control for the user. The user will click on a given item in the Browser as a signal to make that selection the new current record.

Still, in some applications a change of selection *might* have other interpretations. That's why the *AutoSelect* property exists. If its value is equal to *True*, then changing the Browser selection will automatically change the current record in the associated Data control. If *AutoSelect* is *False*, selecting a Browser item has no additional effect other than the standard Click event. (The Visual Basic programmer can still change the Data control's current record programmatically in response to that event.)

## Defining the Events

The Browser control will require one new event in its event list:

```
WORD Event_FormatField_Params[] = { ET_I2, ET_HLSTR, ET_I2 };
EVENTINFO Event_FormatField =
   {
   "FormatField",
   3, 6,
   (PWORD) Event_FormatField_Params,
   "Column as Integer, Text as String, Alignment as Integer",
   EF_fNoUnload
   };

PEVENTINFO Events[] =
   {
   PEVENTINFO_STD_CLICK,
   PEVENTINFO_STD_DBLCLICK,
   PEVENTINFO_STD_DRAGDROP,
   PEVENTINFO_STD_DRAGOVER,
   PEVENTINFO_STD_GOTFOCUS,
   PEVENTINFO_STD_LOSTFOCUS,
   PEVENTINFO_STD_MOUSEDOWN,
   PEVENTINFO_STD_MOUSEMOVE,
   PEVENTINFO_STD_MOUSEUP,
   PEVENTINFO_STD_LAST,
   &Event_FormatField,
     NULL
   };

typedef enum
   {
   IEVENTINFO_STD_CLICK,
   IEVENTINFO_STD_DBLCLK,
   IEVENTINFO_STD_DRAGDROP,
   IEVENTINFO_STD_DRAGOVER,
   IEVENTINFO_STD_GOTFOCUS,
   IEVENTINFO_STD_LOSTFOCUS,
   IEVENTINFO_STD_MOUSEDOWN,
   IEVENTINFO_STD_MOUSEMOVE,
   IEVENTINFO_STD_MOUSEUP,
   IEVENTINFO_STD_LAST,
   IPEVENTINFO_FormatField,
   IEVENTINFO_End
   } EVENTSIX;
```

We've previously seen the definition of a new event, *GetText*, in the Virtual Listbox control. The new Browser event, *FormatField*, is very similar to *GetText*—it has one less parameter, but the remaining parameters are the same. Whereas Virtual Listbox's *GetText* event gave the Visual Basic program a chance to supply the text of a field just before Virtual Listbox painted it, the *FormatField* event gives the Visual Basic program a chance to *reformat* text just before Browser paints it.

The *wm_NcCreate()* function has the usual job of initializing the *VbData* structure:

```
#pragma argsused
static void near pascal wm_NcCreate
    (
    HCTL Control,
    LPCREATESTRUCT Create
    )
    {
    LPVBDATA VbData = (LPVBDATA) VBDerefControl (Control);
    VbData->TabCount = 0;
    }
```

## Working with Properties

Although the property lists of the Virtual Listbox and Browser controls are so similar, the code is different because the visual layer of the Browser must manage the tab stops. (The standard window layer of the Virtual Listbox control did the job of managing the tab stops.) The *AutoSelect* property is not represented in these functions because it was described with the *pf_fSetData* and *pf_fGetData* flags. This means the visual environment takes care of managing that property value automatically. We have to work with the others, as the following code shows:

```
static BOOL near pascal vbm_SetProperty
    (
    HCTL Control,
    HWND Window,
    USHORT Property,
    long Value,
    long far * Error
    )
    {
    LPVBDATA VbData = (LPVBDATA) VBDerefControl (Control);
    LPDATASTRUCT Data = (LPDATASTRUCT) Value;
    switch (Property)
        {
        case IPROPINFO_ListIndex:
            SendMessage (Window, LB_SETCURSEL, (WORD) Value, 0);
```

```
        break;
      case IPROPINFO_TabStops:
        if ((Data->index[0].data >= 1) && (Data->index[0].data <= MAXTABS))
          {
          if (Data->index[0].data > VbData->TabCount)
            VbData->TabCount = Data->index[0].data;
          VbData->TabStops[Data->index[0].data - 1] =
            VBXTwipsToPixels (Data->data);
          SendMessage (Window,
            LB_SETTABSTOPS,
            VbData->TabCount,
            (long) (LPWORD) VbData->TabStops);
          }
        else
          *Error = VBERR_BADINDEX;
        break;
      case IPROPINFO_TabCount:
        if (Value == 0)
          VbData->TabCount = 0;
        break;
      default:
        return FALSE;
      }
    return TRUE;
    }

#pragma argsused
static BOOL near pascal vbm_GetProperty
    (
    HCTL Control,
    HWND Window,
    USHORT Property,
    LPVOID Value,
    long far * Error
    )
    {
    LPVBDATA VbData = (LPVBDATA) VBDerefControl (Control);
    LPDATASTRUCT Data = (LPDATASTRUCT) Value;
    switch (Property)
      {
      case IPROPINFO_ListCount:
        *(long far *)Value = SendMessage (Window, LB_GETCOUNT, 0, 0);
        break;
      case IPROPINFO_ListIndex:
        *(long far *)Value = SendMessage (Window, LB_GETCURSEL, 0, 0);
        break;
      case IPROPINFO_TabStops:
        if ((Data->index[0].data >= 1) && (Data->index[0].data <= MAXTABS))
```

```
      Data->data =
         VBXPixelsToTwips (VbData->TabStops[Data->index[0].data-1]);
      else
         *Error = VBERR_BADINDEX;
      break;
   case IPROPINFO_TabCount:
      *(long far *)Value = VbData->TabCount;
      break;
   default:
      return FALSE;
   }
   return TRUE;
}
```

Although we don't have to worry about *storing* the *AutoSelect* property, we do need to *read* it now and then. This will help us to determine what action must be taken if the user makes a selection from the Browser list:

```
static void near pascal lbn_SelChange (HCTL Control, HWND Window)
   {
   LPVBDATA VbData = (LPVBDATA) VBDerefControl (Control);
   if (VbData->AutoSelect)
      {
      int i = (int) SendMessage (Window, LB_GETCURSEL, 0, 0);
      if (i > -1)
         {
         DATAACCESS DataAccess;
         DataAccess.usVersion = VB_VERSION;
         DataAccess.hctlData = VbData->DataSource;
         DataAccess.hctlBound = Control;
         DataAccess.hlstrBookMark =
            (HSZ) SendMessage (Window, LB_GETITEMDATA, i, 0);
         DataAccess.sAction = DATA_BOOKMARK;
         VBSendControlMsg (DataAccess.hctlData,
            VBM_DATA_METHOD, 0, (long) &DataAccess);
         }
      }
   }
```

The code that executes "if *VbData->AutoSelect* is *True*" is the only code needed to convince the Data control to switch to another record. Remember that at any given time, the Data control has a *RecordSet* property which is a collection of all the records it has retrieved. That's what the Browser displays. But the Data control also has a pointer to a *current* record; and that's what the other bound controls are displaying. By changing the current record, we'll change the contents of those controls as well.

Whenever such a change is made to the Data control—or a more significant change, such as the Data control's having its *RecordSource* property changed—the Data control makes whatever calculations it has to make, then sends a *VBM_DATA_AVAILABLE* message to each of the controls that is bound to it. In Browser's case, any previous bookmarks must be released, the new recordset enumerated, and the bookmarks for each record stored in the underlying listbox:

```
static void near pascal ClearContents (HWND Window)
  {
  register i, Count = SendMessage (Window, LB_GETCOUNT, 0, 0);
  for (i = 0; i < Count; i++)
    VBDestroyHlstr ((HLSTR) SendMessage (Window, LB_GETITEMDATA, i, 0));
  SendMessage (Window, LB_RESETCONTENT, 0, 0);
  }

static void near pascal vbm_DataAvailable
    (
    HCTL Control,
    HWND Window,
    LPDATAACCESS DataAccess
    )
  {
  if ((DataAccess->sAction == DATA_ADDNEW) ||
      (DataAccess->sAction == DATA_CLOSE) ||
      (DataAccess->sAction == DATA_DELETE) ||
      (DataAccess->sAction == DATA_REFRESH) ||
      (DataAccess->sAction == DATA_ROLLBACK))
    {
    LPVBDATA VbData = (LPVBDATA) VBDerefControl (Control);
    long Error;
    VbData->DataSource = DataAccess->hctlData;
    ClearContents (Window);
    DataAccess->sAction = DATA_BOOKMARK;
    DataAccess->lData = DATA_BOOKMARKFIRST;
    Error = VBSendControlMsg (DataAccess->hctlData,
      VBM_DATA_GET, 0, (long) DataAccess);
    while ((! Error) && (! (DataAccess->fs & DA_fEOF)))
      {
      SendMessage (Window, LB_ADDSTRING, 0, DataAccess->lData);
      DataAccess->hlstrBookMark = (HLSTR) DataAccess->lData;
      DataAccess->lData = DATA_BOOKMARKNEXT;
      Error = VBSendControlMsg (DataAccess->hctlData,
        VBM_DATA_GET, 0, (long) DataAccess);
      }
    }
  VBSetControlFlags (Control, CTLFLG_DATACHANGED, FALSE);
  }
```

The method we use to enumerate the records in the recordset is basically the same as is detailed in the *Professional Features* manual that comes with Visual Basic. Note the *ClearContents()* function. Before loading the listbox with new bookmarks, we must destroy any that we've already stored; *ClearContents()* does this for us.

## Supporting Text

As you'll recall from our work with the Pagelist control in Chapter 7, the first message that the parent of a fixed-size Ownerdraw listbox must deal with is *WM_MEASUREITEM*. This is how we handle it:

```
static void near pascal wm_MeasureItem
    (
    HWND Window,
    LPMEASUREITEMSTRUCT  MeasureItem
    )
{
HDC DC = GetDC (Window);
HANDLE OldFont, NewFont = SendMessage (Window, WM_GETFONT, 0, 0);
TEXTMETRIC tm;
if (! NewFont)
   NewFont = GetStockObject (SYSTEM_FONT);
OldFont = SelectObject (DC, NewFont);
GetTextMetrics (DC, &tm);
SelectObject (DC, OldFont);
ReleaseDC (Window, DC);
MeasureItem->itemHeight =
   tm.tmHeight-tm.tmInternalLeading;
}
```

By grabbing a device context for the window and selecting the font we intend to use into it, we can get the text metrics—that is, the size information—and determine the height of a line. Note that we remember to restore the original font to the device context before releasing it, just as we do when we're painting on the screen.

The next several helper functions exist to break up the work of the *wm_DrawItem()* function. The first part of the job, preparing to retrieve the text from the Data control, is performed by the *GetFieldName()* function:

```
static int near pascal GetFieldName
    (
    HCTL Control,
    HLSTR Bookmark,
    LPDATAACCESS DataAccess
    )
```

```
    {
    LPVBDATA VbData = (LPVBDATA) VBDerefControl (Control);
    DataAccess->usVersion = VB_VERSION;
    DataAccess->hctlData = VbData->DataSource;
    DataAccess->hctlBound = Control;
    DataAccess->hlstrBookMark = Bookmark;
    DataAccess->fs = 0;
    DataAccess->usDataType = DT_HSZ;
    VBGetControlProperty (Control,
      IPROPINFO_STD_DATAFIELD,
      &DataAccess->hszDataField);
    if ((! DataAccess->hszDataField) ||
        *VBDerefHsz (DataAccess->hszDataField) == 0)
      {
      if (DataAccess->hszDataField)
        {
        VBDestroyHsz (DataAccess->hszDataField);
        DataAccess->hszDataField = NULL;
        }
      DataAccess->sAction = DATA_FIELDSCOUNT;
      VBSendControlMsg (VbData->DataSource,
        VBM_DATA_GET, NULL, (long) DataAccess);
      return (int) DataAccess->lData;
      }
    else
      return 1;
    }
```

In the first part of this function, a *DataAccess* structure (defined in
VBAPI.H), which is passed as a parameter to *GetFieldName()*, is initialized.
The Browser control itself is then queried for the value of the standard
*DataField* property. If this property has a blank value, all fields are to be
displayed by the Browser; so a count of those fields is obtained from the
Data control and returned to the caller. If the *DataField* property actually
specifies a field name, *GetFieldName()* returns 1—but the field name (or an
*HLSTR* representing it) remains in the *DataAccess* structure.

Actually, we don't like the fact that *GetFieldName()* returns a field *count*
to its caller. It does return a name, as well—sometimes—but it would be
cleaner to have two functions: one to return field counts, the other to set the
field name if it exists. It was tried this way, but the two functions wound up
repeating virtually the same code. Given a choice, we chose to err on the
side of smaller code.

*GetFieldName()* is called from *DrawFields()*:

```
static void near pascal DrawFields
    (
```

```
    HDC DC,
    int x, int y,
    HCTL Control,
    HLSTR Bookmark
    )
{
LPVBDATA VbData = (LPVBDATA) VBDerefControl (Control);
DATAACCESS DataAccess;
int FieldCount = GetFieldName (Control, Bookmark, &DataAccess);
DataAccess.sAction = DATA_FIELDVALUE;
for (DataAccess.sDataFieldIndex = 0;
    DataAccess.sDataFieldIndex < FieldCount;
    DataAccess.sDataFieldIndex++)
    {
    char Buffer[128];
    int Align = DT_LEFT;
    int Tab = (DataAccess.sDataFieldIndex == 0) ?
      0 : VbData->TabStops[DataAccess.sDataFieldIndex-1];
    VBSendControlMsg (VbData->DataSource, VBM_DATA_GET, NULL, (long)
        &DataAccess);
    lstrcpy (Buffer, (LPSTR) VBDerefHsz ((HSZ) DataAccess.lData));
    VBDestroyHsz ((HSZ) DataAccess.lData);
    FormatField (Control, DataAccess.sDataFieldIndex + 1, Buffer, &Align);
    SetTextAlign (DC, Align);
    TextOut (DC, Tab + x, y, (LPSTR) Buffer, lstrlen ((LPSTR) Buffer));
    }
if (DataAccess.hszDataField)
    VBDestroyHsz (DataAccess.hszDataField);
}
```

The **for** loop allows us to treat two different cases identically. We might be asking for a specific field, or we might be enumerating fields. Thanks to the field count returned by *GetFieldName()*, the loop may be executed once, or once for each field. If it is retrieving one specific field, the name of the field is already located in the structure. If we are enumerating, that structure member is *NULL*, as it should be.

For each field we retrieve—even if it's just one—we invoke a function called *FormatField()*. This function is actually placed ahead of *DrawFields()* in the module. We just didn't want to describe it until after we were done with the function that calls it. *FormatField()* encapsulates the event trigger which sends the text of this field to the Visual Basic program for last-minute formatting before it is actually painted:

```
static void near pascal FormatField
    (
    HCTL Control,
```

```
    int Column,
    LPSTR Buffer,
    LPINT Align
    )
{
struct
    {
    LPINT Alignment;
    HLSTR Text;
    LPINT Column;
    LPINT Index;
    } Params;

Params.Alignment = Align;
Params.Text = VBCreateHlstr (Buffer, lstrlen (Buffer));
Params.Column = &Column;

VBFireEvent (Control, IPEVENTINFO_FormatField, &Params);

if (VBGetHlstrLen (Params.Text))
    lstrcpy (Buffer, VBDerefZeroTermHlstr (Params.Text));
else
    Buffer[0] = 0;
VBDestroyHlstr (Params.Text);
}
```

This function is simpler than its counterpart in the Virtual Listbox control, mostly because there is no static structure involved that must retain its value between messages. In this case, we simply perform the necessary conversions to and from Visual Basic strings. Note that the event also allows the Visual Basic program to change the default alignment as well.

Why bother with this? After all, the Data control can *ask* for the data to be formatted, can't it? For example, the following SQL *Select* statement can be placed in the Data control's *RecordSource* property:

```
Select format(Account,'0-00000-0') from Accounts
```

This will, in fact, work. Unfortunately, the following will not (although it *should*):

```
Select format(Account,'0-00000-0'),
    Patient,
    format (Balance,'$#,###,##0.00')
from Accounts
```

We assume that there is a bug somewhere in the SQL engine that returns the formatted account field twice: once where it belongs, and once in place of the requested Balance field. Thus, the *FormatField* event is the only way for Browser to display data formatted on a field-by-field basis. Fortunately, it was easy to implement and easier still to use in the Visual Basic program.

## Wrapping Up VISUAL.C

The final function in this module is *wm_DrawItem()*, the actual handler for the message sent by an Ownerdraw listbox when an item needs to be painted. Don't be confused; while *DrawFields()* concentrates on obtaining, preparing, and painting the actual text of the item, *wm_DrawItem()* concentrates on the physical appearance of the item as a whole (whether it is selected or not, in focus or not, and so on). Much of the code is unchanged from the Pagelist control, which also made use of an Ownerdraw listbox:

```c
void far pascal wm_DrawItem
    (
    HCTL Control,
    HWND Window,
    LPDRAWITEMSTRUCT DrawItem
    )
{
HANDLE NewBrush, OldFont;
int OldBkMode;
DWORD NewTextColor;

OldFont = SelectObject (DrawItem->hDC, SendMessage (Window, WM_GETFONT,
    0, 0));

if (DrawItem->itemState & ODS_SELECTED)
    {
    NewBrush = CreateSolidBrush (GetSysColor (COLOR_HIGHLIGHT));
    NewTextColor = GetSysColor (COLOR_HIGHLIGHTTEXT);
    }
else
    {
    NewBrush = CreateSolidBrush (GetBkColor (DrawItem->hDC));
    NewTextColor = GetSysColor (COLOR_WINDOWTEXT);
    }
FillRect (DrawItem->hDC, &DrawItem->rcItem, NewBrush);
DeleteObject (NewBrush);

if (DrawItem->itemState & ODS_FOCUS)
    DrawFocusRect (DrawItem->hDC, &DrawItem->rcItem);
```

```
    if (DrawItem->itemData)
      {
      DWORD OldTxtColor;
      OldTxtColor = SetTextColor (DrawItem->hDC, NewTextColor);
      OldBkMode = SetBkMode (DrawItem->hDC, TRANSPARENT);
      DrawFields (DrawItem->hDC,
        DrawItem->rcItem.left, DrawItem->rcItem.top,
        Control,
        (HLSTR) DrawItem->itemData);
      SetTextColor (DrawItem->hDC, OldTxtColor);
      SetBkMode (DrawItem->hDC, OldBkMode);
      }
    SelectObject (DrawItem->hDC, OldFont);
    }
```

Next comes *CtlProc()*, which performs its usual job of dispatching the various messages a Browser might receive:

```
long far pascal _export CtlProc
    (
    HCTL Control,
    HWND Window,
    USHORT Msg,
    USHORT wParam,
    long lParam
    )
{
long Error = 0;
switch (Msg)
    {
    case WM_NCCREATE:
      wm_NcCreate (Control, (LPCREATESTRUCT) lParam);
      break;
    case VBN_COMMAND:
      switch (HIWORD (lParam))
        {
        case LBN_SELCHANGE:
          lbn_SelChange (Control, Window);
          VBFireEvent (Control, IEVENTINFO_STD_CLICK, NULL);
          break;
        case LBN_DBLCLK:
          VBFireEvent (Control, IEVENTINFO_STD_DBLCLK, NULL);
          break;
        case LBN_SETFOCUS:
          VBFireEvent (Control, IEVENTINFO_STD_GOTFOCUS, NULL);
          break;
        case LBN_KILLFOCUS:
          VBFireEvent (Control, IEVENTINFO_STD_LOSTFOCUS, NULL);
          break;
```

```
            default:
              break;
            }
        break;
      case VBM_SETPROPERTY:
        if (vbm_SetProperty (Control, Window, wParam, lParam, &Error))
          return Error;
        break;
      case VBM_GETPROPERTY:
        if (vbm_GetProperty (Control, Window, wParam, (LPVOID) lParam, &Error))
          return Error;
        break;
      case VBM_GETPROPERTYHSZ:
        switch (wParam)
            {
            case IPROPINFO_About:
              *((HSZ far *) lParam) = GetAboutPropertyString (Control);
              break;
            }
        return 0;
      case VBM_INITPROPPOPUP:
        switch (wParam)
            {
            case IPROPINFO_About:
              return PopupAbout (Window);
            }
        break;
      case VBM_HELP:
        if (vbm_Help (Window,
              LOBYTE (wParam),
              HIBYTE (wParam),
              Properties, Events))
          return 0;
        break;
      case WM_DESTROY:
        WinHelp (Window, HelpFileName (), HELP_QUIT, 0);
        ClearContents (Window);
        break;
      case VBN_MEASUREITEM:
        wm_MeasureItem (Window, (LPMEASUREITEMSTRUCT) lParam);
        return TRUE;
      case VBN_DRAWITEM:
        wm_DrawItem (Control, Window, (LPDRAWITEMSTRUCT) lParam);
        return TRUE;
      case VBM_DATA_AVAILABLE:
        vbm_DataAvailable (Control, Window, (LPDATAACCESS) lParam);
        return 0;
      }
  return VBDefControlProc (Control, Window, Msg, wParam, lParam);
  }
```

Note the standard events that are triggered in response to the various notification messages that arrive from the underlying listbox. This is the same method used internally by the various Visual Basic standard controls.

Finally, we're left with the *Model* structure, and the *VBINITCC()* and *VBTERMCC()* functions:

```
MODEL Model =
   {
   VB_VERSION,
   MODEL_fFocusOk | MODEL_fArrows | MODEL_fLoadMsg,
   (PCTLPROC) CtlProc,
   0,
   WS_BORDER | WS_CHILD | WS_VSCROLL | LBS_OWNERDRAWFIXED |
     LBS_NOTIFY | LBS_NOINTEGRALHEIGHT,
   sizeof (VBDATA),
   8000,
   NULL,
   NULL,
   NULL,
   Properties,
   Events,
   IPROPINFO_STD_NAME,
   IEVENTINFO_STD_CLICK,
   -1
   };

#pragma argsused
BOOL far pascal _export VBINITCC
     (
     USHORT Version,
     BOOL Runtime
     )
   {
   if (! Runtime)
     RegisterVbPopups ();
   Model.npszDefCtlName =
   Model.npszClassName = (PSTR) ClassName;
   Model.npszParentClassName = "Listbox";
   return VBRegisterModel (LibInstance, &Model);
   }

VOID FAR PASCAL _export VBTERMCC (void)
   {
   UnregisterVbPopups ();
   }
```

## HELP.C

This module is unchanged from the Skeleton control; simply copy it to this project.

## BROWSER.DEF

The Browser's module definition file comes directly from Skeleton with (of course) the module name changed:

```
LIBRARY    BROWSER
EXE TYPE   WINDOWS
CODE       PRELOAD MOVEABLE DISCARDABLE
DATA       PRELOAD MOVEABLE SINGLE
HEAPSIZE  0
EXPORTS
        WEP          RESIDENTNAME
        Info         @2
        Style        @3
        Flags        @4
        WndProc      @5
        StyleProc    @6
        ListClasses
```

Remember that *WEP* should be marked *PRIVATE* instead of *RESIDENTNAME* if you are using the newer Microsoft linker.

## BROWSER.RC

The Browser resources are derived from the Skeleton resources, as well. Because we don't have to support the Dialog Editor, the entries associated with Dialog Editor have been omitted:

```
#include "internal.h"

// For Visual Basic
8000 BITMAP "8000.bmp"
8001 BITMAP "8001.bmp"
8003 BITMAP "8003.BMP"
8006 BITMAP "8006.BMP"

ABOUT DIALOG 41, 45, 192, 125
STYLE DS_MODALFRAME | WS_POPUP | WS_CAPTION
```

```
CAPTION "About Browser Listbox"
FONT 8, "MS Sans Serif"
BEGIN
   CONTROL "Browser Listbox", 0, "STATIC", SS_CENTER | WS_CHILD |
WS_VISIBLE, 0, 8, 190, 8
   CONTROL "by Paul S. Cilwa", 0, "STATIC", SS_CENTER | WS_CHILD |
WS_VISIBLE, 0, 16, 190, 8
   ICON "MAIN", 0, 87, 29, 18, 20
   CONTROL "Version 1.0", 0, "STATIC", SS_CENTER | WS_CHILD | WS_VISIBLE,
0, 59, 190, 8
   CONTROL "\2511993 by Paul S. Cilwa", 0, "STATIC", SS_CENTER | WS_CHILD
| WS_VISIBLE, 0, 79, 190, 8
   CONTROL "All Rights Reserved", 0, "STATIC", SS_CENTER | WS_CHILD |
WS_VISIBLE, 0, 88, 190, 8
   PUSHBUTTON "OK", IDOK, 74, 102, 45, 15
END

MAIN ICON "BROWSER.ICO"
```

The four visual toolbox bitmaps are shown in Figure 8.2. The About box can be seen in Figure 8.3, and the Browser icon is shown in Figure 8.4.

**Figure 8.2  Browser bitmaps 8000, 8001, 8003, and 8006 for Visual Basic.**

**Figure 8.3  The Browser About box for Visual Basic.**

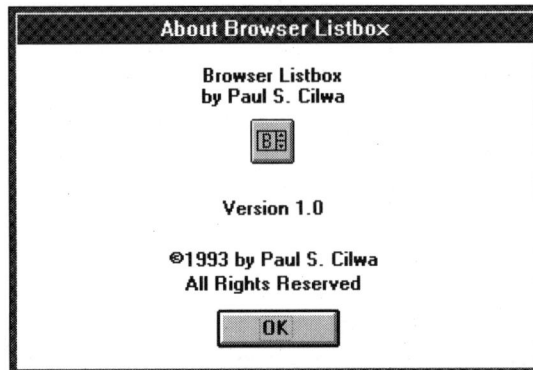

---

**Figure 8.4   The Browser icon.**

---

As always, don't forget the version control information;

```
VERSIONINFO LOADONCALL MOVEABLE DISCARDABLE
FILEVERSION 0, 0, 0, 0
PRODUCTVERSION 0, 0, 0, 0
FILEOS VOS__WINDOWS16
FILETYPE VFT_DLL
BEGIN
   BLOCK "StringFileInfo"
   BEGIN
     BLOCK "040904E4"
     BEGIN
       VALUE "CompanyName", "Coriolis Group\000"
       VALUE "FileDescription", "Browser Custom Control for Visual Basic
and Windows\000"
       VALUE "FileVersion", "0.0.0.0\000"
       VALUE "InternalName", "BROWSER\000"
       VALUE "LegalCopyright", "Copyright © Paul S. Cilwa 1993\000"
       VALUE "OriginalFilename", "browser.vbx\000"
       VALUE "ProductName", "Windows Programming Power\000"
       VALUE "ProductVersion", "0.0.0.0\000"
       VALUE "Comments", "\000"
     END
   END
END
```

# Enhancing the Browser Control

The Browser control is actually a very useful tool. It has already been used, as is, in a major project for a metropolitan hospital. Our data-based applications are usually MDI apps in which the first MDI child window consists of a list of the available records. If the user double-clicks on one of the items, it then appears in detail in a document window of its own. We used to have to load a conventional listbox; now, with Browser and VB 3.0, we can write the entire application in VB in a fraction of the time it used to take.

However, there is one improvement that would be really nice. Remember, Browser is an attempt to mimic the Browse mode of dBASE. However, in dBASE, you can *edit* fields as well as view them in Browse mode. Implementing this would be quite a challenge. Any takers?

# 9

# The Text File Viewer Control

In this chapter we'll build a flexible Text File Viewer control that will allow you to view text files. Although simple text-viewing windows have been built many times in other Windows programming books, our text viewer will be unique in that we'll be able to construct a full-fledged text editor from it in Chapter 10. Moreover, you'll be able to use this basic framework to create even more sophisticated editing controls—for example, text boxes that support full formatting.

his chapter will present the basic techniques for creating the Text File Viewer control. As we go along, we'll point out some of the important design decisions that were made so that we'll be able to easily extend the control in the next chapter.

# Designing a Text File Viewer Control

The Text File Viewer control (TextFileView) provides instant access to any text file. Where Windows' standard edit control must be "loaded" and is limited to 32K of data, the TextFileView control is available as soon as it is given a filename, and it supports as many as 32K *lines* of text.

If, in reading this description, you see parallels to the Virtual Listbox control presented in Chapter 6, don't be surprised. No sooner did Microsoft give us a fantastic control with generous limits, than we programmers found those limits too restraining.

Our TextFileView control won't be as easy to create as a Virtual Listbox control because we'll need to create it from scratch. (Recall that we used an Ownerdraw control as the foundation for the Virtual Listbox. Unfortunately, Windows does not provide an "Ownerdraw edit control" that we can use to build the Text File Viewer.)

Here are the major requirements of the TextFileView control:

• Its window must "own" up to 32K lines of text; that is, it must be able to pull text lines from disk and display them immediately.

• It must display a scroll bar if the number of lines in a file exceed the number that can be displayed at once. (This is the source of the 32K line limit, of course.)

• It must paint lines of text, placing the line indicated by the current scroll bar position at the top of the control's client area.

The viewer could be implemented as a trivial control. In fact, many Windows programming books present similar projects (although not in the form of a custom control). However, in the next chapter we'll add editing capability, and we intend to leave hooks enough to support full text formatting functions. That means we'll have to design this control carefully if we want to later build on our work.

When techniques for displaying lots of text are presented, they are usually handled in a manner which sacrifices good programming practice. Here, we'll not make such a compromise.

○　○　○

*To both make our job easier and to facilitate expanding this control in the next chapter, we'll also make use of some object-oriented techniques, even though we are writing in C.*

○　○　○

# Using Object-Oriented Techniques in a Non-OOP Language

Don't worry about our references to objects as we create TextFileView. We're not suddenly throwing C++ at you. We simply intend to use some object-oriented techniques to build the new control. The main one we'll use is called *encapsulation*. This involves taking all the code and data associated with a particular object and hiding them from the rest of the program. That is, the rest of the program can "see" a data structure (such as a Line descriptor), but it should never act on the data structure directly. Instead, a module containing all related functions acts as the interface.

A data structure implemented this way is often called a *control block*. You are probably already familiar with file control blocks. After all, the standard C library provides a whole set of functions that open, manipulate, and close files through control blocks that you never worry about. You just call the appropriate functions. This is a good example of encapsulation at work.

## Breaking a Project into Objects

One of the first steps in object-oriented design is to figure out how to break up a project into different objects. If you see your program as one, *giant* object, you are painting with strokes too broad. On the other hand, if you divide a project into too many objects, you'll end up with a program that's hard to manage.

In the case of TextFileView, we know that we have at least two overlapping components: the collection of *Lines* of text from the source file and the *View* of at least some of those lines. In some cases, a file will be small enough so that all its lines of text can be seen at once. In most cases it will not, and the user will need to scroll up and down to see the entire contents of the file. See Figure 9.1 for a pictorial representation.

The key aspect of encapsulation is that each of the three object types— *View, Line,* and *Lines*—must perform its unique job without interfering with

---

**Figure 9.1  The *View* object displays but does not store *Line* objects. The *Lines* collection stores *Line* objects but does not display them.**

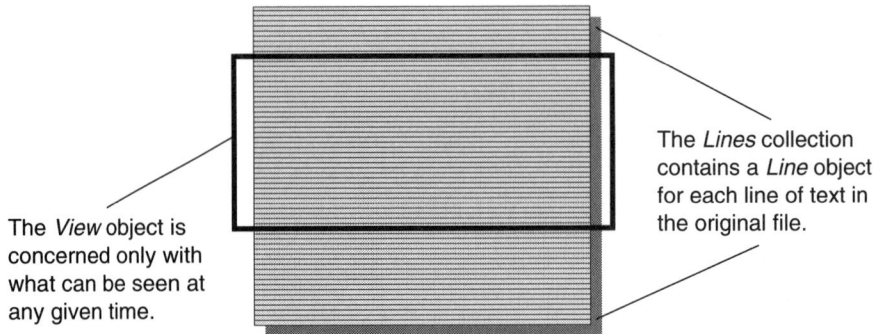

The *Lines* collection contains a *Line* object for each line of text in the original file.

The *View* object is concerned only with what can be seen at any given time.

---

how the *other* objects perform *their* jobs. You'll be amazed at how easy this approach makes putting together a complex piece of software.

○   ○   ○

*In object-oriented programming, a collection is just an object that contains other objects.*

○   ○   ○

## Managing 32,676 Lines of Text

Probably the most crucial component of the TextFileView control is the *Lines* collection of *Line* objects. This is implemented as a linked list that will allow us to manage the 32K lines of text. The TextFileView control only needs to append items until all lines of text have been read from disk, but the planned expansions must support the following tasks:

• Append characters to a line of text.
• Insert characters into a line of text.
• Delete characters from a line of text.
• Append a line of text to a file.
• Insert a line of text into a file.
• Delete a line of text from a file.

- Display a line of text in a client area.
- Write text to a disk.

In some collections, the collection object supplies most of the cohesion for the collected elements. However, since each *Line* object is a component of a linked list, the *Lines* collection is simply a focal point for the list of *Line* objects as a whole.

## Storing 32,676 Individual Strings

Storing individual strings is quite a challenge. Although any given string is not likely to be extremely large, it's just as likely there will be many of them. The standard Windows Edit control is limited to 32K data because it stores all of its strings in its local heap. To exceed that limit, we'll have to place the strings in the *global* heap. But if we allocate the memory for each string using *_fmalloc()*, we'll soon run out of global selectors (see the sidebar *Understanding Global Selectors*). Therefore, we need another memory allocation scheme, one that will allocate as few global segments as possible, then sub-allocate those segments as needed. We'll call the segments blocks, and the sub-allocations *parcels*, and implement the scheme in a module named BLOCK.C.

The Block Memory Manager's job is simple: It maintains a list of both the blocks that it has allocated and the parcels that it has defined within those allocated segments. Some of the parcels will be in use; some will be free. When a request is made for a parcel of a specified size, the Block Memory Manager will first try to find a free chunk of exactly the requested size. If this operation fails, it will try to find a larger chunk. If it finds one, it will create *two* parcels where there was one. Of the two, one will be the requested size (plus overhead); the other will be the remainder.

● ● ●

*The Block Memory Manager will allocate a new segment and supply the parcel from the segment only if it cannot find a free block of the desired size or larger.*

● ● ●

When a parcel is freed, the Block Memory Manager will try to consolidate the parcel with adjacent freed parcels. But the Block Memory Manager never shuffles parcels in memory to maximize space; that would invalidate the pointers to the parcels that are in use.

Since the Block Memory Manager was written with the object-oriented technique of encapsulation in mind, BLOCK.C isn't designed *just* for the

TextFileView control—you can plug it into any project where you need this type of memory management. To facilitate this, the Block Memory Manager even has its own header file.

## Understanding Global Selectors

In real mode and protected mode, pointers are composed of two components: the offset and segment. The least significant component, which is 16 bits wide, is the *offset*. It specifies the number of bytes that an address is *offset* from the place indicated by the most significant component. Here's an example:

| Real mode: Segment<br>Protected mode: Selector | Offset |
|---|---|

In real mode, the segment is just a paragraph address in which a value of one equals address location 16. In protected mode, this part of the address is called a *selector* because it selects a 48-bit address *descriptor* from an array of descriptors.

When an 80286 or better CPU is first powered up, it does so in real mode. This is necessary because in order for protected mode to work, several tables must be present—so the CPU uses its time in real mode to prepare those tables. One is the Global Descriptor Table (GDT). The hardware limits it to a single 64K segment; since each descriptor is 48 bits long, there can therefore be no more than 8,296 descriptors—making a larger number of selectors pointless.

Windows uses a hundred or so of these selectors for its own purposes. When you view Program Manager's About box, the "System Resources" figure is the result of a calculation involving both the amount of available memory *and* the number of available descriptors.

The selector is not called an index because it is not a simple, scalar value. The three least significant bits of a selector are used for another purpose entirely and don't affect which descriptor the selector accesses. Therefore, in a set of possible selectors, these four selectors all point to the *same* descriptor:

| |
|---|
| $1350 |
| $1351 |
| $1352 |
| $1353 |

This would be a tricky obstacle to overcome, but the newer C compilers have given us a workaround: the **huge** keyword. When you declare a variable to be **huge**, you tell the compiler to generate code that checks a pointer each time it is incremented or indexed, and to add 8—not 1—to the selector when the offset part of the address exceeds 0xFFFF.

## Reading a Text File

A standard edit control's contents are its "caption." The text in such an edit control is set via a *WM_SETTEXT* message and retrieved via a *WM_GETTEXT* message. Because the initial caption can be specified at creation time, an edit control can be initialized with small amounts of text as part of its description in the resource script (.RC) file.

We will not want to follow this pattern in the TextFileView control, whose *primary* text property (or "caption") will be the name of the file whose contents it displays.

Reading the file managed by the TextFileView control is not, in itself, a difficult task. We can use the *OpenFile(), _lread(),* and *_lwrite()* functions supplied with the Windows API.

## Displaying the Scroll Bar

A multi-line edit control displays a vertical scroll bar whenever it contains more lines than can be displayed at one time, given the size of the edit control window. We could create and destroy scroll bars as needed, but it's easier to give the window itself the *CS_VSCROLL* class style. As with any scroll bar, we'll have to send it a range of acceptable values, as well as the current value. If the range of values is empty—that is, the maximum and minimum values are the same—the scroll bar will disappear by itself.

## Painting the Text

Each of the controls we've presented in this book has had a module called PAINT.C but TextFileView will be an exception—sort of. In keeping with the object-oriented philosophy, the painting of this window will be managed by a *View* object. Of course, we could put the code for the *View* object in PAINT.C; but it will be more consistent with object-oriented programming methodologies to call the module VIEW.C, and that's what we'll do.

This is especially appropriate because the actual painting isn't *really* done by the *View* object itself. *View* manages the job, but we'll keep with the object-oriented philosophy that you don't do things "to" an object; you ask the object to do things—like painting—to "itself." The *View* object will be responsible for figuring out *what* to paint and *where*. But, given that information, the *Line* objects will have to paint themselves.

○   ○   ○

*You may have noticed that, in Visual Basic, filename properties use the File Open Common Dialog as an alternative to obtaining the name of the file for the property from the user. We will do the same, and because this is an operation we may need again, we'll put the code for this in a module of its own: FILEPROP.C.*

○   ○   ○

# Creating the TextFileView Control

The TextFileView control is implemented with the following modules:

```
TEXTVIEW.H
BLOCK.H
BLOCK.C
LINES.H
LINES.C
LINE.H
LINE.C
VIEW.H
VIEW.C
INTERNAL.H
MAIN.C
DIALOG.C
VISUAL.C
HELP.C
FILEPROP.C
TEXTVIEW.RC
TEXTVIEW.DEF
```

Notice that this control requires more header and source files than the other controls we have created. The additional files are needed to support the Block Memory Manager (BLOCK.H and BLOCK.C), object-oriented doubly-linked list (LINE.H and LINE.C), the Lines collection object (LINES.H and LINES.C), and the Visual Basic filename selector (FILEPROP.C).

In addition to these files, you'll need to include VBAPI.LIB in the list of libraries to be linked into the end-product DLL. This is required because TextFileView is implemented as both a standard and a visual custom control.

## TEXTVIEW.H

This **#include** file would be the only one which must be referenced by a programmer using TextFileView in a standard (non-Visual) Windows application. However, this header file is empty since there are no unique styles, messages, or notifications used by the TextFileView control. We'll keep it around to make it easier to expand TextFileView in the next chapter.

## BLOCK.H

Since the Block Memory Manager is not tied in any way to TextFileView or any other control, we have packaged it with its own header file. This way you can easily use it in any other project where it seems appropriate. Here's the contents of this header file:

```
#ifndef _BLOCK_H_
#define _BLOCK_H_
#include <windows.h>
#include <stdlib.h>
#include <string.h>

#define BLOCKERR_UnableToAllocateBlock 1
#define BLOCKERR_BlockCorrupted 2
#define BLOCKERR_RequestedSizeOutOfRange 3
#define BLOCKERR_UnableToAllocateLocalBlock 4

BOOL far pascal InitMem (void);
LPVOID far pascal GetMem (WORD Size);
LPVOID far pascal ReleaseMem (LPVOID Data);
void far pascal ReclaimMem (LPVOID Data);
LPVOID far pascal FreeMem (LPVOID Data);
void far pascal TermMem (void);

LPSTR far pascal StrNew (LPSTR Buffer);

#endif
```

As you can see, a few error numbers are defined to enhance the module's usefulness. We'll explain how the Block Memory Manager works next.

## BLOCK.C

The Block Memory Manager itself is composed of a series of functions that obtain and release blocks of memory. The idea here is to provide many small chunks of memory without using up any more global selectors than necessary.

One danger in using memory management routines is that, if the client application misuses the routines, the underlying control blocks can become confused, destroying data or even crashing the app. A way to avoid this is to mark each block with a *signature*. The signature provides a way of determining if the block is being used, or, at least, is valid. These techniques can range from elaborate checksumming schemes that provide absolute assurance at the expense of response time, to minimal routines that are likely to catch errors during development (when most occur) but won't slow the memory accesses by much. BLOCK.C is written using the latter approach. The signature, then, is a simple **long** value that can be checked with just a few machine instructions. It is defined at the top of the module:

```
#include "block.h"
#include <stdio.h>

#define SIGNATURE 0x424C4F4BL
#define BLOCKSIZE 65536L
```

We need terminology to distinguish between a block of memory, such as might be requested by a client application, and the global segments that are returned by the operating system. We'll name the latter *Blocks* and the former *Parcels*. Here are the structures that define them:

```
typedef struct tag_Block
    {
    long Signature;
    struct tag_Block far * NextBlock;
    long LargestFreeSpace;
    struct tag_Parcel far * FirstParcel;
    } BLOCK, far * LPBLOCK;

typedef struct tag_Parcel
    {
    long Signature;
    long Size;
    BOOL Free;
    struct tag_Block far * Block;
    struct tag_Parcel far * NextParcel;
    char Data[1];
    } PARCEL, far * LPPARCEL;
```

You will actually see how these structures work when we get to the code that manipulates them. For now, note that each contains a link to the *next* block or parcel—but not to the previous one. We were able to make this scheme much more efficient through the use of singly-linked lists, rather than the doubly-linked lists you may be more familiar with. (The LINE.C module, which we'll see later in this chapter, uses doubly-linked lists.) The idea of a singly-linked list, of course, is that you can traverse the list in a single direction only.

● ● ●

*Since our main goal in traversing a list of parcels or blocks is to find a free parcel or block of adequate size, making the trip in one direction is quite adequate.*

● ● ●

The next few lines supply a couple of **#define** statements and even a few static variables:

```
#define PARCELMAX (BLOCKSIZE - (long) sizeof (BLOCK) - (long) sizeof (PARCEL))
#define _offsetin(struc, fld) ((WORD)&(((struc *)0)->fld))

static LPBLOCK FirstBlock = NULL;
static WORD AccessCount = 0;
WORD Block_LastError = 0;
```

You don't often see static variables in our code, but it is essential to the workings of the Block Memory Manager that only one instance of it run per application. That means that *FirstBlock* can be set by the initialization function (which we'll see shortly) and referenced by all the other functions as needed. The *AccessCount* variable will allow nested initializations and terminations. *Block_LastError* borrows a trick from the standard C library; it is available to any other module that declares it as an **extern** variable, and it makes the most recent error (if there was one) available for inspection.

## Allocating Memory Blocks

The first function presented for our inspection is *AllocBlock()*. You can tell by the **static** keyword used to define *AllocBlock()* that this function is intended for internal use only:

```
static LPBLOCK near pascal AllocBlock (void)
  {
  HANDLE h = GlobalAlloc (GMEM_MOVEABLE, BLOCKSIZE);
  LPBLOCK Block;
  if (! h)
    {
    Block_LastError = BLOCKERR_UnableToAllocateBlock;
    return NULL;
```

```
    }
Block = (LPBLOCK) GlobalLock (h);
Block->Signature = SIGNATURE;
Block->LargestFreeSpace = PARCELMAX;
Block->NextBlock = NULL;
Block->FirstParcel = (LPPARCEL) &Block[1];
Block->FirstParcel->Signature = SIGNATURE;
Block->FirstParcel->Size = PARCELMAX;
Block->FirstParcel->Free = TRUE;
Block->FirstParcel->Block = Block;
Block->FirstParcel->NextParcel = NULL;
return Block;
}
```

As you can see, *AllocBlock()* uses the traditional call to *GlobalAlloc()* to actually obtain the desired memory block. This call could fail; if it does, the function sets *Block_LastError* and returns *NULL*. Otherwise, the various members of the structure are initialized and a pointer to the block is returned.

You may have noticed that we threw out the handle from *GlobalAlloc()*. In the old days when Windows could support real mode, you could not keep the pointer from *GlobalLock()* for any amount of time. Instead, whenever you needed a pointer, you had to re-lock the handle to get it. But nowadays all that is unnecessary. When it comes time to free the block, we can look up the handle required by *GlobalFree()* using the pointer we've saved.

The first public function in BLOCK.C is also the first one a client application will call:

```
BOOL far pascal InitMem (void)
  {
  if (! AccessCount++)
    {
    if (! (FirstBlock = AllocBlock()))
      return FALSE;
    Block_LastError = 0;
    }
  return TRUE;
  }
```

*InitMem()* is designed so that it can be called more than once. This allows the Block Memory Manager to be used in a subsystem that is then included in a larger subsystem or application that also wants to use it. *InitMem()* can be called as many times as needed, as long as *TermMem()* is called the same number of times. And only on its first call does *InitMem()* do its real job: allocate the first global block of memory by calling *AllocBlock()*.

The next function we'll look at, and the one most often used by a client application, is *GetMem()*. This function will be called whenever the client app needs a "parcel" of memory.

We have previously stated our preference for smaller functions, but unfortunately, *GetMem()* didn't lend itself to this approach. Therefore, we've marked out the various code components with actual *comments*:

```
LPVOID far pascal GetMem (WORD Size)
  {
  LPBLOCK Block = FirstBlock;
  LPPARCEL Parcel;

// Make sure requested size isn't larger than allowed
  if ((long) Size > PARCELMAX)
    {
    Block_LastError = BLOCKERR_RequestedSizeOutOfRange;
    return NULL;
    }

// Skip through list of blocks until one is found with a parcel
// of adequate size
  while (Block->LargestFreeSpace < (long) Size)
    {
    if (! Block->NextBlock)
      {
      if (! (Block->NextBlock = AllocBlock()))
        return NULL;
      }
    Block = Block->NextBlock;
    }

// Skip through that block's parcels until one is found
// of adequate size
  Parcel = Block->FirstParcel;
  while ((! Parcel->Free) || (Parcel->Size < Size))
    {
    Parcel = Parcel->NextParcel;
    if (Parcel->Signature != SIGNATURE)
      {
      Block_LastError = BLOCKERR_BlockCorrupted;
      return NULL;
      }
    }

// If parcel is bigger than needed, split off excess part
  if ((Parcel->Size - (long) sizeof (PARCEL) - (long) Size) > 16)
    {
    LPPARCEL NextParcel = (LPPARCEL) &Parcel->Data[Size];
```

```
      NextParcel->Signature = SIGNATURE;
      NextParcel->Size = Parcel->Size - (long) sizeof (PARCEL) - (long) Size;
      NextParcel->Free = TRUE;
      NextParcel->NextParcel = Parcel->NextParcel;
      Parcel->NextParcel = NextParcel;
      Parcel->Size = Size;
      }
   Parcel->Free = FALSE;
   Parcel->Block = Block;

// Recalculate max free block size
   Block->LargestFreeSpace = 0;
   {
   register LPPARCEL TestParcel = Block->FirstParcel;
   while (TestParcel)
      {
      if (TestParcel->Free)
        if (Block->LargestFreeSpace < TestParcel->Size)
          Block->LargestFreeSpace = TestParcel->Size;
      TestParcel = TestParcel->NextParcel;
      }
   }

   memset (Parcel->Data, 0, Size);
   Block_LastError = 0;
   return (LPSTR) &Parcel->Data;
   }
```

Because each block maintains an indicator of its largest free parcel, *GetMem()* doesn't have to waste time inspecting blocks whose free space is too small for the parcel being requested. If none of the previously allocated blocks has enough spare room, a new one is simply allocated and appended to the list. The new block is *sure* to have a large enough free parcel because we've already checked that the parcel being requested wasn't illegally large.

○   ○   ○

*A parcel is too large if it can't fit in a 64K block after subtracting the overhead for the block housekeeping, and that of the parcel itself.*

○   ○   ○

If an appropriate parcel is found, it is used—and split into two parcels if it is way larger than the size requested. The second parcel is marked as free. Finally, that block's free space is recalculated and the requested parcel is returned, after being initialized to zero bytes.

## Releasing Parcels

We said that *GetMem()* would be called by a client application more often than any other of these routines, but of course you thought we were mistaken. Surely it would be a tie between *GetMem()* and *FreeMem()*! But that's not quite right because parcels can be released in either of two ways.

The first function used to release parcels is *ReleaseMem()*:

```
LPVOID far pascal ReleaseMem (LPVOID Data)
  {
  LPPARCEL Parcel = (LPPARCEL) ((LPSTR) Data - _offsetin (PARCEL, Data));
  if (Parcel->Signature != SIGNATURE)
    Block_LastError = BLOCKERR_BlockCorrupted;
  else
    {
    Parcel->Free = TRUE;
    Block_LastError = 0;
    }
  return NULL;
  }
```

This function simply marks a parcel as being free—that is, no longer in use. It does not consolidate adjacent free parcels, and it does not deallocate a block whose parcels are all unused. *ReleaseMem()* is intended for those times in your application when you realize that you will be releasing many parcels at once. Why not call *ReleaseMem()*, with its minimal overhead, then call a function *ReclaimMem()* just once to do the cleanup?

Before we can look at *ReclaimMem()*, however, we must examine the **static** function *ReclaimMem_()* (note the trailing underscore) that makes *ReclaimMem()* work:

```
static void near pascal ReclaimMem_ (LPBLOCK Block)
  {
  register LPPARCEL Parcel = Block->FirstParcel;
  register LPPARCEL PrevParcel;
// Join any two contiguous free blocks
  Parcel = Block->FirstParcel;
  PrevParcel = NULL;
  while (Parcel)
    {
    if (PrevParcel && PrevParcel->Free && Parcel->Free)
      {
      PrevParcel->Size += (Parcel->Size + sizeof (PARCEL));
      PrevParcel->NextParcel = Parcel->NextParcel;
```

```
      }
    else
       PrevParcel = Parcel;
    Parcel = PrevParcel->NextParcel;
      }
// Recalculate max free block size
  Block->LargestFreeSpace = 0;
  Parcel = Block->FirstParcel;
  while (Parcel)
    {
    if (Parcel->Free)
      if (Block->LargestFreeSpace < Parcel->Size)
        Block->LargestFreeSpace = Parcel->Size;
    Parcel = Parcel->NextParcel;
    }
  }
```

This function performs two related tasks. First, it looks for adjacent, free parcels. If it finds any, it joins them into a single contiguous free parcel. Then, it recalculates the block's available free space, since there is less overhead taken by one free parcel than two.

This helper function is invoked by the routine the client application would call:

```
void far pascal ReclaimMem (LPVOID Data)
  {
  if (Data)
    {
    LPPARCEL Parcel = (LPPARCEL) ((LPSTR) Data - _offsetin (PARCEL, Data));
    ReclaimMem_ (Parcel->Block);
    }
  else
    {
    register LPBLOCK Block = FirstBlock;
    while (Block)
      {
      ReclaimMem_ (Block);
      Block = Block->NextBlock;
      }
    }
  }
```

*ReclaimMem()* invokes the internal *ReclaimMem_()* once for *each* block that has been allocated. Note that unused blocks are *not* released, although they will be reused.

❍ ❍ ❍

*You can implement the releasing of unused blocks if you change the singly-linked list to a doubly-linked list. We decided the performance penalty wasn't worth it.*

❍ ❍ ❍

Now how about those times when you *don't* intend to release a passel of parcels at once? Then you simply invoke *FreeMem()*:

```
LPVOID far pascal FreeMem (LPVOID Data)
  {
  if (Data)
    {
    ReleaseMem (Data);
    ReclaimMem (Data);
    }
  Block_LastError = 0;
  return NULL;
  }
```

Of course, *FreeMem()* invokes *ReleaseMem()* and *ReclaimMem()*, just as you'd expect. Note that we've included a safety check for a *NULL* pointer. Also, note that *FreeMem()* returns a *NULL* pointer, making it easy to assign it back to the original parcel pointer and thus clear it of a no-longer-valid address. (*ReleaseMem()* does the same.)

## Performing Cleanup Operations

Finally, when an application is ready to terminate, it should invoke *TermMem()*:

```
void far pascal TermMem (void)
  {
  register LPBLOCK Block = FirstBlock;
  if (! --AccessCount)
    {
    while (Block)
      {
      HANDLE h = LOWORD (GlobalHandle (HIWORD (Block)));
      Block = Block->NextBlock;
      GlobalUnlock (h);
      GlobalFree (h);
      }
    FirstBlock = NULL;
    }
  }
```

*TermMem()* decrements the *AccessCount* variable that *InitMem()* incremented; when the number of *TermMem()* calls is the same as the number of *InitMem()* calls, the memory blocks are released.

A side effect of this is that your application does not actually have to call *FreeMem()* (or (*ReleaseMem()*) for each allocated parcel during program shutdown. These calls could take time; but the call to *TermMem()* will release the blocks the parcels are in, and the blocks are all that Windows cares about.

## A Bonus Function

As a bonus, we've included one other function in BLOCK.C, even though it isn't used in this project. It's called *StrNew()*:

```
LPSTR far pascal StrNew (LPSTR Buffer)
   {
   LPSTR Str = GetMem (strlen (Buffer) + 1);
   strcpy (Str, Buffer);
   return Str;
   }
```

This function simply copies an existing string into a parcel newly allocated from the Block Memory Management system. *StrNew()* provides a shortcut for the common operation of measuring an existing string, allocating the space in which to store a copy, and then copying the original into the newly allocated space.

## LINE.H

Just as the Block Memory Management system is intended to be a "plug-in" component to any piece of code that needs it, so have we designed the *Line* object. Of course, the *Line* object is not as generally useful as BLOCK.C—but we will be borrowing it in the next chapter. Thus, we've constructed it in a more standalone manner, complete with its own header file:

```
#ifndef _LINE_H_
#define _LINE_H_

#include <windows.h>
#include "block.h"

typedef struct tagLine
   {
```

```
      struct tagLine far * Prev;
      struct tagLine far * Next;
      int Index;
      int CharCount;
      int Height;
      char Text[132];
      } LINE, far * LPLINE;

LPLINE far pascal LINE_Alloc (LPSTR Buffer, HDC dc);
void far pascal LINE_InsertBefore (LPLINE This, LPLINE Next);
void far pascal LINE_InsertAfter (LPLINE This, LPLINE Prev);
void far pascal LINE_Append (LPLINE This, LPLINE Root);
LPLINE far pascal LINE_GetFirst (LPLINE This);
LPLINE far pascal LINE_GetLast (LPLINE This);
LPLINE far pascal LINE_GetIndexed (LPLINE This, int Index);
LPLINE far pascal LINE_GetNext (LPLINE This);
LPLINE far pascal LINE_GetPrev (LPLINE This);
int far pascal LINE_GetHeight (LPLINE Line);
int far pascal LINE_GetIndex (LPLINE This);
void far pascal LINE_Remove (LPLINE This);
LPLINE far pascal LINE_Free (LPLINE This);
void far pascal LINE_Display (LPLINE This, HDC dc, LPPOINT Start);

#endif
```

As we mentioned in the design section of this chapter, a *Line* is basically an element of a doubly-linked list. Given any particular *Line*, you can access the previous or next *Line* through the *Prev* and *Next* pointers in the structure.

What makes a *Line* an "object?" Simply this: We will never access elements in the *LINE* structure outside of the LINE.C module, although the C compiler doesn't enforce this. We will restrict ourselves to the functions declared here to manipulate the structure—an example of encapsulation. We know that this seems like useless overhead to a traditional C programmer. But experience has shown that this technique really does produce more easily written and robust applications. (That's one reason the C++ language was written: to enforce the rules we will simply follow out of self-discipline.)

## LINE.C

LINE.C contains the actual functions that manipulate the *Line* objects. The first one we'll inspect is *LINE_Alloc()*:

```
#include "line.h"
#define _offsetin(struc, fld) ((WORD)&(((struc *)0)->fld))
```

```
LPLINE far pascal LINE_Alloc (LPSTR Buffer, HDC dc)
  {
  register Count = lstrlen (Buffer);
  LPLINE Line = GetMem (_offsetin (LINE, Text) + Count + 1);
  TEXTMETRIC tm;
  Line->Prev = NULL;
  Line->Next = NULL;
  Line->Index = 0;
  Line->CharCount = Count;
  lstrcpy (Line->Text, Buffer);
  GetTextMetrics (dc, &tm);
  Line->Height = HIWORD (GetTextExtent (dc,
    Count ? Buffer : " ",
    Count ? Count : 1));
  Line->Height += tm.tmExternalLeading;
  return Line;
  }
```

We've given all these functions—which in object-oriented terminology would be called "methods"—names that begin with the object type in capital letters. *LINE_Alloc()* simply allocates and initializes one object of the *Line* type. Although the structure's *Text* member is an array of 132 characters, *GetMem()* is only requested to provide as much space as the string actually requires (in addition to the structure overhead, of course). Also note that we store the string's character count. This will save us from having to tolerate the foolishness of the C standard library's compulsion to count every character in a string, every time the string is used.

One of the more interesting jobs *LINE_Alloc()* performs is to calculate the height of a text line, given the current font. (The device context *dc* that is passed to the routine should have had the current font, mapping mode, and so on already selected into it.) The usual algorithm for displaying text in Windows simply calculates the height of one line and leaves it at that. Although that technique would have sufficed for this control, remember that we want to provide for future enhancements. It makes sense, then, to leave this hook here.

Once a *Line* is allocated, it exists in a vacuum: Although potentially part of a linked list, it has no siblings to keep it company. To be useful, it must be inserted or appended to such a list. (Only the first *Line* will have no antecedents.)

Because of the use to which we intend to apply these *Lines*, one of their properties (excuse us, "member data items") is an index. Whenever a *Line* is inserted into the list, subsequent lines must be reindexed. That task is accomplished by this **static** function:

```
static void near pascal ReindexFrom (LPLINE This)
  {
  LPLINE Prev = This->Prev;
  register i = Prev ? Prev->Index : 0;
  while (This)
    {
    This->Index = ++i;
    This = This->Next;
    }
  }
```

The function is simply passed the newly inserted item—called *This*. The linked list is then traversed, setting the *Index* property for each member.

The only time the task of traversing the list is anything but straightforward is when the item *This* happens to be the very first *Line* in the chain. (We know that *This* is the first line when the pointer *This->Prev* is set to *NULL*.) In such a case, the *i* variable is initialized to zero. All other times *i* is simply set to the index of the previous item. This saves us from having to traverse the *entire* linked list every time an item is inserted. (Also note that, in this scheme, the index of the first item is one, not zero. This approach runs contrary to the C tradition where the first index is treated as zero.)

Because the *LINE_InsertBefore()* and *LINE_InsertAfter()* functions are nearly identical, let's look at them together:

```
void far pascal LINE_InsertBefore (LPLINE This, LPLINE Next)
  {
  LPLINE Prev = Next ? Next->Prev : NULL;
  if (Prev)
    Prev->Next = This;
  This->Prev = Prev;
  This->Next = Next;
  if (Next)
    Next->Prev = This;
  ReindexFrom (This);
  }


void far pascal LINE_InsertAfter (LPLINE This, LPLINE Prev)
  {
  LPLINE Next = Prev ? Prev->Next : NULL;
  if (Prev)
    Prev->Next = This;
  This->Prev = Prev;
  This->Next = Next;
  if (Next)
    Next->Prev = This;
  ReindexFrom (This);
  }
```

These functions are straight from the *Textbook of Linked Lists*, so there's little we can add. Note, however, that after the new *Line* has been inserted into the list, *ReindexFrom()* is invoked to make sure each *Line's Index* property remains consistent.

Now, to be honest, the functions that we just presented are included just to make this module complete. After all, the TextFileView control will never insert lines from a file, just append them. (The extra functions will be used in the next chapter, however.) Likewise, here's the *LINE_Append()* function:

```
void far pascal LINE_Append (LPLINE This, LPLINE Prev)
  {
  if (Prev)
    {
    Prev->Next = This;
    This->Index = Prev->Index + 1;
    }
  else
    This->Index = 1;
  This->Prev = Prev;
  This->Next = NULL;
  }
```

We do not have to invoke *ReindexFrom()* here because we know that the new *Line* is the last one in the list. The new index can easily be deduced.

## Navigating a List

The next several functions are used for list navigation operations. For example, given any particular member, you might need to go to the first or last item:

```
LPLINE far pascal LINE_GetFirst (LPLINE This)
  {
  register LPLINE This_ = This;
  while (This_ && This_->Prev)
    This_ = This_->Prev;
  return This_;
  }

LPLINE far pascal LINE_GetLast (LPLINE This)
  {
  register LPLINE This_ = This;
  while (This_ && This_->Next)
    This_ = This_->Next;
  return This_;
  }
```

We've used a trick here to speed up access. We copy the *This* pointer into a register—a stunt that will make traversing the list much faster. You'd think any optimizing compiler would do this for you, and perhaps some do—but by coding it this way, you can guarantee the fastest execution.

Likewise, it will sometimes be necessary to locate a particular *Line* from its *Index*:

```
LPLINE far pascal LINE_GetIndexed (LPLINE This, int Index)
  {
  register LPLINE This_ = This;
  while (This_ && (This_->Index > Index))
    This_ = This_->Prev;
  while (This_ && (This_->Index < Index))
    This_ = This_->Next;
  return This_;
  }
```

The next four functions simply return values stored in the *Line*'s structure. This is in keeping with our object-oriented programming approach (encapsulation). To obtain information, you call a function, rather than worrying about how the information is stored internally:

```
LPLINE far pascal LINE_GetNext (LPLINE This)
  {
  return This ? This->Next : NULL;
  }

LPLINE far pascal LINE_GetPrev (LPLINE This)
  {
  return This ? This->Prev : NULL;
  }

int far pascal LINE_GetHeight (LPLINE This)
  {
  return This->Height;
  }

int far pascal LINE_GetIndex (LPLINE This)
  {
  return This->Index;
  }
```

Just as a *Line* must be inserted into the linked list, it may on occasion need to be removed:

```
void far pascal LINE_Remove (LPLINE This)
  {
  LPLINE Prev = This->Prev;
  LPLINE Next = This->Next;
  if (Prev)
    Prev->Next = Next;
  if (Next)
    Next->Prev = Prev;
  This->Prev = NULL;
  This->Next = NULL;
  ReindexFrom (Next);
  }
```

*LINE_Remove()* simply "stitches" the former previous and next links together, and then it sets *This' Prev* and *Next* pointers to *NULL*. The line could then be reinserted at another location.

If, instead, you want to deallocate the *Line*, call *LINE_Free()*:

```
LPLINE far pascal LINE_Free (LPLINE This)
  {
  LINE_Remove (This);
  FreeMem ((LPSTR) This);
  return NULL;
  }
```

Since *LINE_Free()* invokes *LINE_Remove()*, you don't need to call *LINE_Remove()* yourself. On the other hand, there's no harm if you do—calling *LINE_Remove()* twice in a row causes no ill effects.

## Drawing Text Lines

We're now ready for the *piece de resistance*—the reason for all this code in the first place. We told you that a *Line* should be able to "draw" itself on screen. To accomplish this, we need the *LINE_Display()* function:

```
void far pascal LINE_Display (LPLINE This, HDC dc, LPPOINT Start)
  {
  TabbedTextOut (dc,
    Start->x, Start->y,
    This->Text,
    This->CharCount,
    0, NULL,
    Start->x);
  Start->y += This->Height;
  }
```

In addition to the pointer to the *Line* object (*This*), the function expects a device context *dc* and a pointer to a *POINT* structure. The structure is updated so that, in subsequent calls, each line can be drawn below the previous one.

## LINES.H

Just as we isolated the *Line* object components, we'll isolate the *Lines* collection object. Here is the header file:

```
#ifndef _LINES_H_
#define _LINES_H_

#include <stdio.h>
#include "line.c"

typedef struct
    {
    HWND Window;
    LPLINE TopLine;
    int  LinesCount;
    } LINES, far * LPLINES;

void far pascal LINES_Init (LPLINES This, HWND Window);
BOOL far pascal LINES_Load (LPLINES This, LPSTR Pathname, HDC dc);
void far pascal LINES_DeleteAll (LPLINES This);
LPLINE far pascal LINES_GetTopLine (LPLINES This);

#endif
```

The main purpose of the *Lines* collection object is to provide a focal point for the linked list of *Lines*. It will also provide methods—that is, functions—for operations that affect the list of *Lines* as a whole, such as reading them in from the source text file.

## LINES.C

As with most objects, a *Lines* collection must be initialized. The *LINES_Init()* function performs the initialization tasks:

```
#include "lines.h"

void far pascal LINES_Init (LPLINES This, HWND Window)
```

```
       {
       This->Window = Window;
       This->TopLine = NULL;
       This->LinesCount = 0;
       }
```

In this case, the initialization amounts to setting all the fields to *NULL*, except for the *Window* property, which is copied from the passed parameter. The *Lines* collection doesn't become interesting until it has been filled by the text of a disk file. A **static** helper function does most of the work:

```
static void near pascal LoadLines (LPLINES This, HDC dc, FILE * Stream)
   {
   char Buffer[256];
   LPLINE Line = NULL, Prev = NULL;
   while (Stream &&
         (! feof (Stream)) &&
         fgets (Buffer, sizeof Buffer, Stream))
     {
     register e = strlen (Buffer);
     if (e > 0)
       if (Buffer[--e] == '\n')
          Buffer[e] = 0;
     This->LinesCount++;
     Line = LINE_Alloc (Buffer, dc);
     LINE_Append (Line, Prev);
     if (! This->TopLine)
        This->TopLine = Line;
     Prev = Line;
     }
   InvalidateRect (This->Window, NULL, FALSE);
   }
```

At the time *LoadLines()* is invoked, the *Stream* property (a *FILE* pointer—one of the few "objects" in the standard C library) will already contain the information required to read a file. Therefore, the text will be read, line by line; each line will be used to create a *Line* object via *LINE_Alloc()*. Once allocated, each line will be appended to the previous ones via the call to *LINE_Append()*. The pointer to the first line, and the first line only, will also be assigned to the *Lines* collection's *TopLine* property. This data serves as the physical link between the *Lines* collection and the *Line* linked list. (Also notice that the link goes in one direction only. Given a *Line*, we don't need to get to the collection, since we can traverse the linked list itself.)

The *LoadLines()* helper function is called by *LINES_Load()*:

```
BOOL far pascal LINES_Load (LPLINES This, LPSTR Pathname, HDC dc)
  {
  FILE * Stream;
  BOOL Result = FALSE;
  if (This->TopLine)
     LINES_DeleteAll (This);
  Stream = fopen (Pathname, "rt");
  if (Stream)
     {
     LoadLines (This, dc);
     fclose (Stream);
     Result = TRUE;
     }
  SetScrollRange (This->Window, SB_VERT, 1, This->LinesCount, TRUE);
  return Result;
  }
```

The division of labor gives the outer function these tasks: clearing any previous contents, loading the new file (via *LoadLines()*), closing the file, and setting the scroll range with the appropriate number of lines. Notice that the lower range is set to one, which tallies nicely with the starting index of one we gave the first *Line* object.

You may have noticed that, if the *Lines* object was already in use, a function called *LINES_DeleteAll()* was invoked to clear it before the new file was loaded. Here is the function:

```
void far pascal LINES_DeleteAll (LPLINES This)
  {
  LPLINE Line = This->TopLine;
  while (Line)
     {
     register LPLINE Next = Line->Next;
     FreeMem (Line);
     Line = Next;
     }
  This->TopLine = NULL;
  }
```

It simply traverses the linked list, deallocating each *Line* object. It does *not* do so "properly," de-linking the objects as they are deallocated. That's because the entire list is being deleted; there's no point in housecleaning when the house is being destroyed.

The last function in the module returns the first *Line* in the collection:

```
LPLINE far pascal LINES_GetTopLine (LPLINES This)
  {
```

```
   return This->TopLine;
   }
```

Remember, once you have this *Line*, you can get to any line in the list.

# VIEW.H

The *View* object is roughly equivalent to the physical window in which the lines of text are to be displayed. Its header file is as follows:

```
#ifndef _VIEW_H_
#define _VIEW_H_

#include <windows.h>
#include "line.h"

typedef struct
   {
   HWND Window;
   int  Width, Height;
   int  LeftMargin;
   LPLINE TopVisibleLine;
   } VIEW, far * LPVIEW;

void far pascal VIEW_Init
       (
       LPVIEW View,
       HWND Window,
       int LeftMargin
       );
void far pascal VIEW_SetSize
       (
       LPVIEW View,
       int Width,
       int Height
       );
void far pascal VIEW_SetTopVisibleLine (LPVIEW View, LPLINE Line);
LPLINE far pascal VIEW_GetTopVisibleLine (LPVIEW View);
void far pascal VIEW_Display (LPVIEW View, HDC dc);
LPLINE far pascal VIEW_PageUp (LPVIEW View);
LPLINE far pascal VIEW_PageDown (LPVIEW View);

#endif
```

Of course, it's no surprise that the object structure tracks the height and width of the physical window. And, where the *Lines* collection notes the first line in the *Line* linked list, the *View* object is only interested in the top *visible* line of all those lines.

# VIEW.C

The VIEW.C module encapsulates the "methods" that manage the *View* object and, like the other "object" modules, it opens with an initialization function:

```
#include "view.h"

void far pascal VIEW_Init
    (
    LPVIEW View,
    HWND Window,
    int LeftMargin
    )
    {
    View->Window = Window;
    View->LeftMargin = LeftMargin;
    View->TopVisibleLine = NULL;
    }
```

The *VIEW_SetSize()* function will be invoked by the main window procedure whenever a *WM_SIZE* message is received:

```
void far pascal VIEW_SetSize
    (
    LPVIEW View,
    int Width,
    int Height
    )
    {
    View->Width = Width;
    View->Height = Height;
    }
```

The two functions which set and retrieve the top visible line are quite simple:

```
void far pascal VIEW_SetTopVisibleLine (LPVIEW View, LPLINE Line)
    {
    View->TopVisibleLine = Line;
    }
```

```
LPLINE far pascal VIEW_GetTopVisibleLine (LPVIEW View)
  {
  return View->TopVisibleLine;
  }
```

Where one of our previous controls would have called a *PaintMe()* function, the TextFileView control will call the *VIEW_Display()* function:

```
void far pascal VIEW_Display (LPVIEW View, HDC dc)
  {
  LPLINE Line = View->TopVisibleLine;
  POINT Start;
  Start.y = 0;
  Start.x = View->LeftMargin;
  while (Line && (Start.y <= View->Height))
    {
    LINE_Display (Line, dc, &Start);
    Line = Line->Next;
    }
  }
```

Notice that the function itself is quite simple. The object-oriented programming approach that we are using helps to keep individual functions small and simple. The tasks being accomplished are spread more evenly through the many functions. In this case, we start with the *Line* object that we know is the first one visible in the control window, and call that *Line*'s *LINE_Display()* function. We can then move to the next line, and the next, until we run out of lines or space in which to display them.

The next two functions are nearly identical, so we'll present them together. They are invoked when the user hits the Page Up or Page Down keys (or the scroll bar equivalents):

```
LPLINE far pascal VIEW_PageUp (LPVIEW View)
  {
  LPLINE Line = View->TopVisibleLine;
  register y = 0;
  while (Line)
    {
    y += LINE_GetHeight (Line);
    if (y > View->Height)
      break;
    Line = Line->Prev;
    }
  if (Line && Line->Next)
    Line = Line->Next;
  if (! Line)
```

```
      Line = LINE_GetFirst (View->TopVisibleLine);
   return Line;
   }

LPLINE far pascal VIEW_PageDown (LPVIEW View)
   {
   LPLINE Line = View->TopVisibleLine;
   register y = 0;
   while (Line)
      {
      y += LINE_GetHeight (Line);
      if (y > View->Height)
         break;
      Line = Line->Next;
      }
   if (Line && Line->Prev)
      Line = Line->Prev;
   if (! Line)
      Line = LINE_GetLast (View->TopVisibleLine);
   return Line;
   }
```

These functions are similar to *VIEW_Display()* except that they don't exactly display anything. Still, they start with the same top visible line and traverse the linked list until the cumulative *LINE_GetHeight()* values indicate that a "page" full of lines has been counted.

This may seem like a roundabout way to accomplish this task if all the lines are the same height. But if you want to enhance the control to process lines of different heights, you won't have to change this code.

## INTERNAL.H

We're now ready to examine the header file that is used by all the "regular" (non-utility, non-object) code modules in the project. Here is the entire file:

```
#include <windows.h>
#include "TEXTVIEW.H"
#include <vbapi.h>
#include <custcntl.h>
#include <string.h>
#include <direct.h>
#include <stdlib.h>
#include "block.h"
#include "line.h"
#include "lines.h"
#include "view.h"
```

```
#ifdef MAIN
HINSTANCE LibInstance = 0;
char far * ClassName = "TextFileView";
#else
extern HINSTANCE LibInstance;
extern char far * ClassName;
#endif

typedef struct
   {
   struct
      {
      UNIT :16;
      } CustomStyles;
   struct
      {
      UINT TabStop: 1;
      UINT Group: 1;
      UINT Thickframe: 1;
      UINT SysMenu: 1;
      UINT HScroll: 1;
      UINT VScroll: 1;
      UINT DlgFrame: 1;
      UINT Border: 1;
      UINT Maximize: 1;
      UINT ChipChildren: 1;
      UINT ClipSiblings: 1;
      UINT Disabled: 1;
      UINT Visible: 1;
      UINT Minimize: 1;
      UINT Child: 1;
      UINT Popup: 1;
      } StdStyles;
   } STYLEBITS, FAR * LPSTYLEBITS;

typedef struct
   {
   HFONT   Font;
   LINES   Lines;
   VIEW View;
   } MYDATA, far * LPMYDATA;

#define IDC_STATIC 0
#define IDC_GROUPBOX1 110
#define IDC_CAPTION 101
#define IDC_ID 102
#define IDC_BORDER 103
#define IDC_DISABLED 104
```

```
#define IDC_GROUP 105
#define IDC_TABSTOP 106
#define IDC_HSCROLL 107
#define IDC_VSCROLL 108
#define IDC_VISIBLE 109

HSZ far pascal GetAboutPropertyString (HCTL Control);
HWND far pascal PopupAbout (void);
void far pascal RegisterVbPopups (void);
void far pascal UnregisterVbPopups (void);
LPSTR far pascal HelpFileName (void);
BOOL far pascal vbm_Help
    (
    HWND Window,
    BYTE HelpType,
    BYTE i,
    PPROPINFO Properties[],
    PEVENTINFO Events[]
    );

void far pascal RegisterFileDlgPopup (void);
void far pascal UnregisterFileDlgPopup (void);
HWND far pascal PopupFileDlg
    (
    .HCTL Control_,
    HWND Window,
    LPSTR Title,
    int PropertyIndex_,
    LPSTR Filters,
    int FilterIndex,
    LPSTR DefaultExt,
    DWORD Flags
    );
```

You'll notice that there are a few new features. First, the list of **#include** files includes the header files for the new "objects": *View, Line,* and *Lines.* Second, there are a few additional function prototypes for the functions in FILEPROP.C, which we'll look at shortly.

Finally, the *MYDATA* structure contains a *Lines* and a *View* object.

## MAIN.C

Now we get to the module that contains the base code for the TextFileView control. It is based on the MAIN.C Skeleton module described in Chapter 3. As usual, it begins by allocating space for the *MyData* structure:

```
#define MAIN
#include "Internal.H"

#define GWL_MYDATA 0
#define GWW_EXTRA 4

#pragma argsused
static BOOL near pascal wm_NcCreate (HWND Window, LPCREATESTRUCT Create)
  {
  LPMYDATA MyData = (LPMYDATA) calloc (1, sizeof (MYDATA));
  if ((! MyData) || (! InitMem()))
    return FALSE;
  SetWindowLong (Window, GWL_MYDATA, (long) MyData);
  return TRUE;
  }
```

Note that part of TextFileView's initialization involves calling *InitMem()* from the BLOCK.C module. This call activates the Block Memory Manager. While we *allocate* space in the *wm_NcCreate()* function, we usually initialize the space in the *wm_Create()* function:

```
static long near pascal wm_SetText (HWND Window, LPSTR Buffer);

static void near pascal wm_Create (HWND Window, LPCREATESTRUCT Create)
  {
  LPMYDATA MyData = (LPMYDATA) GetWindowLong (Window, GWL_MYDATA);
  if (Create->lpszName && Create->lpszName[0])
    wm_SetText (Window, (LPSTR) Create->lpszName);
  LINES_Init (&MyData->Lines, Window);
  VIEW_Init (&MyData->View, Window,
    GetSystemMetrics (SM_CXVSCROLL) / 3);
  }
```

It is possible for the TextFileView control's caption, like any control's, to be preset. If this happens, the "caption" will arrive in the *Create* parameter's *lpszName* member. Remember, for the TextFileView control, this "caption" is actually the name of the file to be viewed. The easiest way to make this work, then, is to call the *wm_SetText()* function if a caption has been supplied. Because we didn't want to move this helper function from its usual location, we simply provided a prototype so the compiler would construct the correct set of parameters.

After (possibly) calling *wm_SetText()*, *wm_Create()*'s remaining job is to initialize the two *MyData* objects: *Lines* and *View*. The second parameter to *VIEW_Init()* is the desired left margin; we are supplying a value equal to one-third the system width of the vertical scroll bar.

## Handling Messages

The next two functions in MAIN.C handle the *WM_DESTROY* and *WM_NC-DESTROY* messages:

```
static void near pascal wm_Destroy (HWND Window)
   {
   LPMYDATA MyData = (LPMYDATA) GetWindowLong (Window, GWL_MYDATA);
   }

static void near pascal wm_NcDestroy (HWND Window)
   {
   LPMYDATA MyData = (LPMYDATA) GetWindowLong (Window, GWL_MYDATA);
   free (MyData);
   TermMem();
   }
```

As is often the case, we have nothing to destroy in the *wm_Destroy()* function. But don't miss the call to *TermMem()* in *wm_NcDestroy()*: This is the mate to the call to *InitMem()* in *wm_NcCreate()*.

The handler for the *WM_SIZE* message simply invokes the *VIEW_SetSize()* method for the *View* object:

```
static void near pascal wm_Size (HWND Window, int Width, int Height)
   {
   LPMYDATA MyData = (LPMYDATA) GetWindowLong (Window, GWL_MYDATA);
   VIEW_SetSize (&MyData->View, Width, Height);
   }
```

The next three functions are the standard ones used in the Skeleton control:

```
static long near pascal wm_GetDlgCode (HWND Window)
   {
   LPMYDATA MyData = (LPMYDATA) GetWindowLong (Window, GWL_MYDATA);
   return DLGC_STATIC;
   }

static void near pascal wm_SetFont (HWND Window, HFONT NewFont, BOOL Repaint)
   {
   LPMYDATA MyData = (LPMYDATA) GetWindowLong (Window, GWL_MYDATA);
   if (NewFont != MyData->Font)
      {
      MyData->Font = NewFont;
      if (Repaint)
         {
```

```
      InvalidateRect (Window, NULL, TRUE);
      UpdateWindow (Window);
      }
    }
  }

static HFONT near pascal wm_GetFont (HWND Window)
  {
  LPMYDATA MyData = (LPMYDATA) GetWindowLong (Window, GWL_MYDATA);
  HFONT Result = MyData->Font;
  if (! Result)
    Result = GetStockObject (SYSTEM_FONT);
  return Result;
  }
```

The *wm_Paint()* function is *almost* identical to the one in Skeleton except that, instead of calling *PaintMe()*, this new version invokes *VIEW_Display()*:

```
static void near pascal wm_Paint (HWND Window)
  {
  LPMYDATA MyData = (LPMYDATA) GetWindowLong (Window, GWL_MYDATA);
  PAINTSTRUCT ps;
  HDC dc = BeginPaint (Window, &ps);
  HBRUSH NewBrush = (HBRUSH) SendMessage (GetParent (Window),
    WM_CTLCOLOR,
    dc,
    MAKELONG (Window, CTLCOLOR_BTN));
  HBRUSH OldBrush;
  HFONT OldFont;
  HFONT NewFont = MyData->Font;
  if (NewBrush)
    OldBrush = SelectObject (dc, NewBrush);
  if (NewFont)
    OldFont = SelectObject (dc, NewFont);
  VIEW_Display (&MyData->View, dc);
  if (NewBrush)
    SelectObject (dc, OldBrush);
  if (NewFont)
    SelectObject (dc, OldFont);
  EndPaint (Window, &ps);
  }
```

The *wm_SetText()* function triggers the loading of the file into the *Lines* object. Of course, we wouldn't want to confuse the issue by allowing the "caption" to be set to an invalid filename or the name of a non-existent file, so we first verify the passed filename with a little *FileExists()* function derived from the *OpenFile()* Windows API call:

```
static BOOL near pascal FileExists (LPSTR Pathname)
  {
  OFSTRUCT of;
  return (OpenFile (Pathname, &of, OF_EXIST) != HFILE_ERROR);
  }

static long near pascal wm_SetText (HWND Window, LPSTR Buffer)
  {
  LPMYDATA MyData = (LPMYDATA) GetWindowLong (Window, GWL_MYDATA);
  if (FileExists (Buffer))
    {
    HDC dc = GetDC (Window);
    HFONT OldFont = NULL;
    if (MyData->Font)
      OldFont = SelectObject (dc, MyData->Font);
    LINES_Load (&MyData->Lines, Buffer, dc);
    if (OldFont)
      SelectObject (dc, OldFont);
    ReleaseDC (Window, dc);
    VIEW_SetTopVisibleLine (&MyData->View,
      LINES_GetTopLine (&MyData->Lines));
    InvalidateRect (Window, NULL, TRUE);
    return DefWindowProc (Window, WM_SETTEXT, 0, (long) Buffer);
    }
  else
    {
    LINES_DeleteAll (&MyData->Lines);
    InvalidateRect (Window, NULL, TRUE);
    return DefWindowProc (Window, WM_SETTEXT, 0, (long) "");
    }
  }
```

Note that a device context is obtained and the control's default font is selected into it. This is because *LINES_Load()* requires it; as each line is loaded and allocated, it uses the device context to calculate the height that the line will require to be displayed.

In previous controls that responded to the *WM_VSCROLL* message, we used the "traditional" method of handling it. However, with the *View* object in charge of which line is the top visible line, the technique of processing this message has changed as well:

```
static void near pascal wm_VScroll (HWND Window, WORD Code, int Position)
  {
```

```
LPMYDATA MyData = (LPMYDATA) GetWindowLong (Window, GWL_MYDATA);
LPLINE Line = VIEW_GetTopVisibleLine (&MyData->View);
switch (Code)
   {
   case SB_TOP:
      if (Line = LINES_GetTopLine (&MyData->Lines))
         VIEW_SetTopVisibleLine (&MyData->View, Line);
      break;
   case SB_BOTTOM:
      if (Line = LINE_GetLast (Line))
         VIEW_SetTopVisibleLine (&MyData->View, Line);
      break;
   case SB_LINEUP:
      if (Line = LINE_GetPrev (Line))
         VIEW_SetTopVisibleLine (&MyData->View, Line);
      break;
   case SB_LINEDOWN:
      if (Line = LINE_GetNext (Line))
         VIEW_SetTopVisibleLine (&MyData->View, Line);
      break;
   case SB_PAGEUP:
      if (Line = VIEW_PageUp (&MyData->View))
         VIEW_SetTopVisibleLine (&MyData->View, Line);
      break;
   case SB_PAGEDOWN:
      if (Line = VIEW_PageDown (&MyData->View))
         VIEW_SetTopVisibleLine (&MyData->View, Line);
      break;
   case SB_THUMBTRACK:
      if (Line = LINE_GetIndexed (Line, Position))
         VIEW_SetTopVisibleLine (&MyData->View, Line);
      break;
   }
if (Line)
   {
   register OldTopLine = GetScrollPos (Window, SB_VERT);
   register NewTopLine = LINE_GetIndex (Line);
   if (OldTopLine != NewTopLine)
      {
      SetScrollPos (Window, SB_VERT, NewTopLine, TRUE);
      InvalidateRect (Window, NULL, TRUE);
      UpdateWindow (Window);
      }
   }
}
```

Likewise, we've also simplified the keyboard interface to simply invoke the *wm_VScroll()* function appropriately. After all, why duplicate the code?

```
static void near pascal wm_KeyDown (HWND Window, WORD Key)
  {
  switch (Key)
    {
    case VK_HOME:
      wm_VScroll (Window, SB_TOP, 0);
      break;
    case VK_END:
      wm_VScroll (Window, SB_BOTTOM, 0);
      break;
    case VK_UP:
      wm_VScroll (Window, SB_LINEUP, 0);
      break;
    case VK_DOWN:
      wm_VScroll (Window, SB_LINEDOWN, 0);
      break;
    case VK_PRIOR:
      wm_VScroll (Window, SB_PAGEUP, 0);
      break;
    case VK_NEXT:
      wm_VScroll (Window, SB_PAGEDOWN, 0);
      break;
    }
  }
```

The main window procedure is the usual, simple message switch:

```
LRESULT far pascal _export FAR PASCAL WndProc
    (
    HWND Window,
    UINT Msg,
    WPARAM wParam,
    LPARAM lParam
    )
  {
  LRESULT Result = 0;
  switch (Msg)
    {
    case WM_NCCREATE:
      Result = wm_NcCreate (Window, (LPCREATESTRUCT) lParam);
      break;
    case WM_CREATE:
      wm_Create (Window, (LPCREATESTRUCT) lParam);
      break;
    case WM_DESTROY:
      wm_Destroy (Window);
      break;
    case WM_NCDESTROY:
```

```
        wm_NcDestroy (Window);
        break;
    case WM_SIZE:
        wm_Size (Window, LOWORD (lParam), HIWORD (lParam));
        break;
    case WM_GETDLGCODE:
        Result = wm_GetDlgCode (Window);
        break;
    case WM_GETFONT:
        Result = wm_GetFont (Window);
        break;
    case WM_SETFONT:
        wm_SetFont (Window, wParam, LOWORD (lParam));
        break;
    case WM_PAINT:
        wm_Paint (Window);
        break;
    case WM_SETTEXT:
        wm_SetText (Window, (LPSTR) lParam);
        break;
    case WM_VSCROLL:
        wm_VScroll (Window, wParam, LOWORD (lParam));
        break;
    case WM_KEYDOWN:
        wm_KeyDown (Window, wParam);
        break;
    default:
        Result = DefWindowProc (Window, Msg, wParam, lParam);
    }
    return Result;
    }
```

And the MAIN.C module closes in the usual way:

```
static WNDCLASS Class =
    {
    CS_HREDRAW | CS_VREDRAW | CS_DBLCLKS | CS_GLOBALCLASS,
    WndProc,
    0,
    GWW_EXTRA,
    0,
    NULL,
    NULL,
    COLOR_WINDOW + 1,
    NULL,
    NULL
    };
```

```
#pragma argsused
int far pascal LibMain
    (
    HINSTANCE hInstance,
    WORD DataSeg,
    WORD HeapSize,
    LPSTR CommandLine
    )
  {
  if (HeapSize > 0)
    UnlockData (0);
  LibInstance = hInstance;
  Class.hInstance = hInstance;
  Class.hCursor = LoadCursor (NULL, IDC_ARROW);
  Class.lpszClassName = ClassName;
  return RegisterClass (&Class) ? TRUE : FALSE;
  }
```

## DIALOG.C

The DIALOG.C module provides the hooks needed by the standard resource editors, such as Borland Resource Workshop and Microsoft's Dialog
Editor. This module has no special considerations compared to the version
that has appeared in the previous controls:

```
#include "Internal.h"

#pragma argsused
HGLOBAL far pascal _export Info (void)
  {
  typedef struct
    {
    UINT TypeStyle;
    UINT SuggestedWidth: 15;
    UINT WidthPixels: 1;
    UINT SuggestedHeight: 15;
    UINT HeightPixels: 1;
    DWORD DefaultStyle;
    char Description[22];
    HBITMAP ToolboxBitmap;
    HCURSOR DropCursor;
    } TYPEINFO;

  typedef struct
    {
    UINT Version;
```

```
        UINT TypeCount;
        char ClassName[CTLCLASS];
        char Title[94];
        char Reserved[10];
        TYPEINFO Type[1];
        } CONTROLINFO, FAR * LPCONTROLINFO;

    HGLOBAL hCtlInfo;
    LPCONTROLINFO CtlInfo;

    hCtlInfo = GlobalAlloc (GHND, sizeof (CONTROLINFO));
    if (hCtlInfo)
        {
        CtlInfo = (LPCONTROLINFO) GlobalLock (hCtlInfo);
        CtlInfo->Version = 100;
        CtlInfo->TypeCount = 1;
        lstrcpy (CtlInfo->ClassName, ClassName);
        lstrcpy (CtlInfo->Title, ClassName);
        CtlInfo->Type[0].SuggestedWidth = 50;
        CtlInfo->Type[0].SuggestedHeight = 40;
        CtlInfo->Type[0].DefaultStyle =
            WS_BORDER | WS_CHILD | WS_VISIBLE | WS_VSCROLL;
        lstrcpy (CtlInfo->Type[0].Description, ClassName);
        CtlInfo->Type[0].ToolboxBitmap =
            LoadBitmap (LibInstance, MAKEINTRESOURCE (100));
        CtlInfo->Type[0].DropCursor =
            LoadCursor (LibInstance, MAKEINTRESOURCE (100));
        GlobalUnlock (hCtlInfo);
        }
    return hCtlInfo;
    }


typedef struct
    {
    LPCTLSTYLE Style;
    LPFNSTRTOID String2ID;
    LPFNIDTOSTR ID2String;
    } STYLEDATA, FAR * LPSTYLEDATA;

static void near pascal wm_InitDialog
        (HWND Dialog, LPSTYLEDATA StyleData)
    {
    LPSTYLEBITS Styles =
        (LPSTYLEBITS) &StyleData->Style->dwStyle;
    char Buffer[64];
    if (Styles->StdStyles.TabStop)
        CheckDlgButton (Dialog, IDC_TABSTOP, 1);
    if (Styles->StdStyles.Group)
        CheckDlgButton (Dialog, IDC_GROUP, 1);
```

```
   if (Styles->StdStyles.HScroll)
     CheckDlgButton (Dialog, IDC_HSCROLL, 1);
   if (Styles->StdStyles.VScroll)
     CheckDlgButton (Dialog, IDC_VSCROLL, 1);
   if (Styles->StdStyles.Border)
     CheckDlgButton (Dialog, IDC_BORDER, 1);
   if (Styles->StdStyles.Disabled)
     CheckDlgButton (Dialog, IDC_DISABLED, 1);
   if (Styles->StdStyles.Visible)
     CheckDlgButton (Dialog, IDC_VISIBLE, 1);
   StyleData->ID2String (StyleData->Style->wId,
     Buffer, sizeof Buffer);
   SetDlgItemText (Dialog, IDC_ID, Buffer);
   SetDlgItemText (Dialog, IDC_CAPTION,
     StyleData->Style->szTitle);
   }


static void near pascal wm_Command_OK
     (HWND Dialog, LPSTYLEDATA StyleData)
   {
   LPSTYLEBITS Styles =
     (LPSTYLEBITS) &StyleData->Style->dwStyle;
   char Buffer[64];
   Styles->StdStyles.TabStop =
     IsDlgButtonChecked (Dialog, IDC_TABSTOP);
   Styles->StdStyles.Group =
     IsDlgButtonChecked (Dialog, IDC_GROUP);
   Styles->StdStyles.HScroll =
     IsDlgButtonChecked (Dialog, IDC_HSCROLL);
   Styles->StdStyles.VScroll =
     IsDlgButtonChecked (Dialog, IDC_VSCROLL);
   Styles->StdStyles.Border =
     IsDlgButtonChecked (Dialog, IDC_BORDER);
   Styles->StdStyles.Disabled =
     IsDlgButtonChecked (Dialog, IDC_DISABLED);
   Styles->StdStyles.Visible =
     IsDlgButtonChecked (Dialog, IDC_VISIBLE);
   GetDlgItemText (Dialog, IDC_ID,
     Buffer, sizeof Buffer);
   StyleData->Style->wId = StyleData->String2ID (Buffer);
   GetDlgItemText (Dialog, IDC_CAPTION,
     StyleData->Style->szTitle,
     sizeof StyleData->Style->szTitle);
   }


#pragma argsused
BOOL far pascal _export StyleProc
     (
     HWND Dialog,
```

```
      UINT Msg,
      WPARAM wParam,
      LPARAM lParam
      )
   {
   static LPSTYLEDATA StyleData;
   switch (Msg)
      {
      case WM_INITDIALOG:
         StyleData = (LPSTYLEDATA) lParam;
         wm_InitDialog (Dialog, StyleData);
         return TRUE;
      case WM_COMMAND:
         switch (wParam)
            {
            case IDOK:
               wm_Command_OK (Dialog, StyleData);
               EndDialog (Dialog, TRUE);
               break;
            case IDCANCEL:
               EndDialog (Dialog, FALSE);
               break;
            default:
               return FALSE;
            }
         break;
      default:
         return FALSE;
      }
   return TRUE;
   }

BOOL far pascal _export Style
      (
      HWND Window,
      HGLOBAL hCtlStyle,
      LPFNSTRTOID aString2ID,
      LPFNIDTOSTR aID2String
      )
   {
   BOOL Result;
   STYLEDATA StyleData;
   StyleData.Style = (LPCTLSTYLE) GlobalLock (hCtlStyle);
   StyleData.String2ID = aString2ID;
   StyleData.ID2String = aID2String;
   Result = DialogBoxParam (LibInstance,
      "Styles", Window, (FARPROC) StyleProc,
      (long) (LPSTYLEDATA) &StyleData);
   GlobalUnlock (hCtlStyle);
```

```
      return (Result == IDOK);
      }

#pragma argsused
UINT far pascal _export Flags
      (
      DWORD Flags,
      LPSTR Buffer,
      UINT BufferSize
      )
   {
   LPSTYLEBITS Styles = (LPSTYLEBITS) &Flags;
   Buffer[0] = 0;
   return lstrlen (Buffer);
   }

typedef HGLOBAL (CALLBACK *LPFNINFO)( void );
typedef BOOL (CALLBACK *LPFNSTYLE)
   (
   HWND hWnd,
   HGLOBAL hCntlStyle,
   LPFNSTRTOID lpfnSID,
   LPFNIDTOSTR lpfnIDS
   );
typedef UINT (CALLBACK *LPFNFLAGS)
   (
   DWORD  dwStyle,
   LPSTR  lpBuff,
   UINT wBuffLength
   );

typedef HGLOBAL (CALLBACK *LPFNLOADRES) (LPSTR szType, LPSTR szId);
typedef BOOL (CALLBACK *LPFNEDITRES) (LPSTR szType, LPSTR szId);

#pragma argsused
HGLOBAL far pascal _export ListClasses
      (
      LPSTR CallingClass,
      UINT Version,
      LPFNLOADRES Load,
      LPFNEDITRES Edit
      )
   {
   typedef struct
      {
      LPFNINFO  fnRWInfo;
      LPFNSTYLE fnRWStyle;
      LPFNFLAGS fnFlags;
      char ClassName[20];
      } RWCTLCLASS, FAR *LPRWCTLCLASS;
```

```
typedef struct {
  short  ClassCount;
  RWCTLCLASS Class[1];
  } CTLCLASSLIST, FAR *LPCTLCLASSLIST;

HGLOBAL hClassList = GlobalAlloc (GHND, sizeof (CTLCLASSLIST));
LPCTLCLASSLIST ClassList = (LPCTLCLASSLIST) GlobalLock (hClassList);

ClassList->ClassCount = 1;
ClassList->Class[0].fnRWInfo = Info;
ClassList->Class[0].fnRWStyle = Style;
ClassList->Class[0].fnFlags = Flags;
_fstrcpy (ClassList->Class[0].ClassName, ClassName);

GlobalUnlock (hClassList);
return hClassList;
}
```

# VISUAL.C

As in the Skeleton, the VISUAL.C module provides all the hooks needed to make the TextFileView accessible to a visual programming environment, such as Visual Basic. The properties are defined at the beginning of the module:

```
#include "internal.h"

#define _segment(p) ((unsigned intX((unsigned long) (void far *) (p)) >> 16L))
#define _offsetin(struc, fld) ((USHORT)&(((struc *)0)->fld))
#define VBERR_BADINDEX 381

static long Boolean[2] = { 0, -1 };

typedef struct
  {
  UINT : 16;
  } VBDATA;
typedef VBDATA far * LPVBDATA;

PROPINFO Property_About =
  {
  "(About)",
  DT_HSZ | PF_fNoRuntimeW | PF_fGetHszMsg,
  0, 0, 0, NULL, 0
  };

PROPINFO Property_Filename =
```

```
   {
   "Filename",
   DT_HSZ | PF_fGetMsg | PF_fSetMsg | PF_fSaveMsg,
   0, 0, 0, NULL, 0
   };

PPROPINFO Properties[] =
   {
   PPROPINFO_STD_NAME,
   PPROPINFO_STD_INDEX,
   PPROPINFO_STD_BACKCOLOR,
   PPROPINFO_STD_FORECOLOR,
   PPROPINFO_STD_LEFT,
   PPROPINFO_STD_TOP,
   PPROPINFO_STD_WIDTH,
   PPROPINFO_STD_HEIGHT,
   PPROPINFO_STD_FONTNAME,
   PPROPINFO_STD_FONTSIZE,
   PPROPINFO_STD_FONTBOLD,
   PPROPINFO_STD_FONTITALIC,
   PPROPINFO_STD_TABINDEX,
   PPROPINFO_STD_TABSTOP,
   PPROPINFO_STD_BORDERSTYLEON,
   PPROPINFO_STD_ENABLED,
   PPROPINFO_STD_PARENT,
   PPROPINFO_STD_TAG,
   PPROPINFO_STD_VISIBLE,
   PPROPINFO_STD_HELPCONTEXTID,
   PPROPINFO_STD_LAST,
   &Property_About,
   &Property_Filename,
   NULL
   };

typedef enum
   {
   IPROPINFO_STD_NAME,
   IPROPINFO_STD_INDEX,
   IPROPINFO_STD_BACKCOLOR,
   IPROPINFO_STD_FORECOLOR,
   IPROPINFO_STD_LEFT,
   IPROPINFO_STD_TOP,
   IPROPINFO_STD_WIDTH,
   IPROPINFO_STD_HEIGHT,
   IPROPINFO_STD_FONTNAME,
   IPROPINFO_STD_FONTSIZE,
   IPROPINFO_STD_FONTBOLD,
   IPROPINFO_STD_FONTITALIC,
   IPROPINFO_STD_TABINDEX,
```

```
IPROPINFO_STD_TABSTOP,
IPROPINFO_STD_BORDERSTYLEON,
IPROPINFO_STD_ENABLED,
IPROPINFO_STD_PARENT,
IPROPINFO_STD_TAG,
IPROPINFO_STD_VISIBLE,
IPROPINFO_STD_HELPCONTEXTID,
IPROPINFO_STD_LAST,
IPROPINFO_About,
IPROPINFO_Filename,
IPROPINFO_End
} PROPSIX;
```

The one new addition is the *FileName* property. Obviously, this property will provide the means by which the control will know what file's contents it is to display.

There are no non-standard events supported:

```
PEVENTINFO Events[] =
    {
    PEVENTINFO_STD_CLICK,
    PEVENTINFO_STD_DBLCLICK,
    PEVENTINFO_STD_DRAGDROP,
    PEVENTINFO_STD_DRAGOVER,
    PEVENTINFO_STD_GOTFOCUS,
    PEVENTINFO_STD_LOSTFOCUS,
    PEVENTINFO_STD_MOUSEDOWN,
    PEVENTINFO_STD_MOUSEMOVE,
    PEVENTINFO_STD_MOUSEUP,
    PEVENTINFO_STD_LAST,
    NULL
    };

typedef enum
    {
    IPEVENTINFO_STD_CLICK,
    IPEVENTINFO_STD_DBLCLK,
    IPEVENTINFO_STD_DRAGDROP,
    IPEVENTINFO_STD_DRAGOVER,
    IPEVENTINFO_STD_GOTFOCUS,
    IPEVENTINFO_STD_LOSTFOCUS,
    IPEVENTINFO_STD_MOUSEDOWN,
    IPEVENTINFO_STD_MOUSEMOVE,
    IPEVENTINFO_STD_MOUSEUP,
    IPEVENTINFO_STD_LAST,
    IPEVENTINFO_End
    } EVENTSIX;
```

We've removed the handlers for *vbm_NcCreate* and *vbm_NcDestroy*, since there are no special memory requirements at the visual layer. Likewise, we've removed the support for the *AddItem()* and *RemoveItem()* methods, which have no meaning for this control.

The *vbm_SetProperty()* and *vbm_GetProperty()* functions support the *FileName* property. Although at the visual level the file is set via this property, we know that at the standard level the filename is stored as the control's caption. Therefore, the property is set and read via the *SetWindowText()* and *GetWindowText()* functions from the Windows API:

```c
#pragma argsused
static BOOL near pascal vbm_SetProperty
    (
    HCTL Control,
    HWND Window,
    USHORT Property,
    long Value,
    long far * Error
    )
{
LPVBDATA VbData = (LPVBDATA) VBDerefControl (Control);
switch (Property)
    {
    case IPROPINFO_Filename:
      SetWindowText (Window, (LPSTR) Value);
      return TRUE;
    default:
      return FALSE;
    }
}


#pragma argsused
static BOOL near pascal vbm_GetProperty
    (
    HCTL Control,
    HWND Window,
    USHORT Property,
    LPVOID Value,
    long far * Error
    )
{
LPVBDATA VbData = (LPVBDATA) VBDerefControl (Control);
switch (Property)
    {
    case IPROPINFO_Filename:
      {
```

```
          char Buffer[128];
          GetWindowText (Window, Buffer, sizeof Buffer);
          *(HSZ far *)Value = VBCreateHsz (_segment (Control), Buffer);
          }
        return TRUE;
      default:               ,
        return FALSE;
      }
    }
```

We also support storing and loading this property to disk:

```
#pragma argsused
static BOOL near pascal vbm_LoadProperty
    (
    HCTL Control,
    HWND Window,
    USHORT Property,
    HFORMFILE FormFile,
    long far * Error
    )
  {
  LPVBDATA VbData = (LPVBDATA) VBDerefControl (Control);
  switch (Property)
    {
    case IPROPINFO_Filename:
      {
      BYTE Length;
      char Buffer[128];
      VBReadFormFile (FormFile, &Length, sizeof Length);
      VBReadFormFile (FormFile, Buffer, Length);
      Buffer[Length] = 0;
      SetWindowText (Window, Buffer);
      }
      return TRUE;
    default:
      return FALSE;
    }
  }

#pragma argsused
static BOOL near pascal vbm_SaveProperty
    (
    HCTL Control,
    HWND Window,
    USHORT Property,
    HFORMFILE FormFile,
    long far * Error
```

```
      )
   {
   LPVBDATA VbData = (LPVBDATA) VBDerefControl (Control);
   switch (Property)
      {
      case IPROPINFO_Filename:
         {
         BYTE Length;
         char Buffer[128];
         Length = GetWindowText (Window, Buffer, sizeof Buffer);
         VBWriteFormFile (FormFile, &Length, sizeof Length);
         VBWriteFormFile (FormFile, Buffer, Length);
         }
         return TRUE;
      default:
         return FALSE;
      }
   }
```

The control procedure adds just one new wrinkle: The *VBM_INIT-PROPPOPUP* message adds support for a Select File dialog for the new control:

```
long far pascal _export CtlProc
      (
      HCTL Control,
      HWND Window,
      USHORT Msg,
      USHORT wParam,
      long lParam
      )
   {
   long Error = 0;
   switch (Msg)
      {
      case WM_NCCREATE:
         wm_NcCreate (Control, (LPCREATESTRUCT) lParam);
         break;
      case VBM_METHOD:
         return vbm_Method (Control, Window, wParam, (void far *) lParam);
      case VBN_COMMAND:
         switch (HIWORD (lParam))
            {
            default:
               break;
            }
         break;
      case VBM_SETPROPERTY:
         if (vbm_SetProperty (Control, Window, wParam, lParam, &Error))
```

```
          return Error;
        break;
    case VBM_GETPROPERTY:
        if (vbm_GetProperty (Control, Window, wParam, (LPVOID) lParam, &Error))
          return Error;
        break;
    case VBM_LOADPROPERTY:
        if (vbm_LoadProperty (Control, Window, wParam, (HFORMFILE) lParam,
            &Error))
          return Error;
        break;
    case VBM_SAVEPROPERTY:
        if (vbm_SaveProperty (Control, Window, wParam, (HFORMFILE) lParam,
            &Error))
          return Error;
        break;
    case VBM_GETPROPERTYHSZ:
        switch (wParam)
          {
          case IPROPINFO_About:
            *((HSZ far *) lParam) = GetAboutPropertyString (Control);
            break;
          }
        return 0;
    case VBM_INITPROPPOPUP:
        switch (wParam)
          {
          case IPROPINFO_About:
            return PopupAbout ();
          case IPROPINFO_Filename:
            return PopupFileDlg (Control,
              Window,
              "Select Filename",
              IPROPINFO_Filename,
              "Text files\0*.txt\0All files\0*.*\0",
              1, "txt", 0);
          }
        break;
    case VBM_HELP:
        if (vbm_Help (Window,
            LOBYTE (wParam),
            HIBYTE (wParam),
            Properties, Events))
          return 0;
        break;
    case WM_DESTROY:
        WinHelp (Window, HelpFileName (), HELP_QUIT, 0);
        break;
```

```
      case WM_NCDESTROY:
        wm_NcDestroy (Control);
        break;
      }
    return VBDefControlProc (Control, Window, Msg, wParam, lParam);
    }
```

We'll see how the Select File dialog is managed when we review the
FILEPROP.C module shortly.

Finally, the last few lines of the VISUAL.C module are unchanged from
the Skeleton, except for the registering and unregistering of the FileName
dialog property:

```
MODEL Model =
    {
    VB_VERSION,
    MODEL_fFocusOk | MODEL_fArrows,
    (PCTLPROC) CtlProc,
    CS_VREDRAW | CS_HREDRAW,
    WS_BORDER,
    sizeof (VBDATA),
    8000,
    NULL,
    NULL,
    NULL,
    Properties,
    Events,
    IPROPINFO_STD_NAME,
    IPEVENTINFO_STD_CLICK,
    -1
    };

#pragma argsused
BOOL far pascal _export VBINITCC
    (
    USHORT Version,
    BOOL Runtime
    )
    {
    if (! Runtime)
        {
        RegisterVbPopups ();
        RegisterFileDlgPopup ();
        }
    Model.npszDefCtlName =
    Model.npszClassName =
    Model.npszParentClassName = (PSTR) ClassName;
```

```
    return VBRegisterModel (LibInstance, &Model);
    }

VOID FAR PASCAL _export VBTERMCC (void)
    {
    UnregisterVbPopups ();
    UnregisterFileDlgPopup ();
    }
```

# HELP.C

This module is unchanged from the Skeleton control; simply copy it to this project.

# FILEPROP.C

This module contains several functions that are similar to the About box support in HELP.C. That's because putting up a Select File dialog shares many of the same requirements.

You can include this module in any control in which one of the visual layer properties contains a filename. The module uses the Common Dialog *GetOpenFileName()* function to present the user with the dialog by which to make the choice. It starts with the **#include** directive for COMMDLG.H. Then, it allocates an initialized *OPENFILESTRUCT*:

```
#include "internal.h"
#pragma hdrstop
#include <commdlg.h>

#define _segment(p) ((unsigned int) (((unsigned long) (void far *) (p))
                    >> 16L))

static char Pathname[MAXPATH];
static HCTL Control;
static int PropertyIndex;

static OPENFILENAME DlgInit =
    {
    sizeof (OPENFILENAME),// lStructSize
    NULL,               // hwndOwner
    NULL,               // hInstance of Dlg Template
    NULL,               // lpstrFilter
    NULL,               // lpstrCustomFilter
```

```
0,                    // nMaxCustomFilter
0,                    // nFilterIndex
Pathname,             // lpstrFile
MAXPATH,              // nMaxFile
NULL,                 // lpstrFileTitle
MAXFILE + MAXEXT,     // nMaxFileTitle
NULL,                 // lpstrInitialDir
NULL,                 // lpstrTitle
0,                    // Flags
0,                    // nFileOffset
0,                    // nFileExtension
"txt",                // lpstrDefExt
0,                    // lCustData
NULL,                 // lpfnHook
NULL                  // lpTemplateName
};
```

Just as HELP.C's *AboutPopupWndProc* must respond to the *WM_SHOW-WINDOW* message by posting the popup with a *WM_USER* message to display the actual dialog, so must *FileDlgPopupWndProc* do the same to call *GetOpenFileDlg()*:

```
LONG _export FAR PASCAL FileDlgPopupWndProc
    (
    HWND Window,
    USHORT Message,
    USHORT wParam,
    LONG lParam
    )
{
switch (Message)
    {
    case WM_SHOWWINDOW:
        if (wParam)
            {
            ShowWindow (Window, SW_HIDE);
            PostMessage (Window, WM_USER, 0, 0);
            return 0;
            }
        break;
    case WM_USER:
        if (GetOpenFileName (&DlgInit))
            VBSetControlProperty (Control,
                PropertyIndex,
                (long)(LPSTR) Pathname);
        return 0;
    }
```

```
    return DefWindowProc (Window, Message, wParam, lParam);
    }

static char FileDlgPopupClass[] = "FileDlgPopup";
```

*GetOpenFileName()* returns *TRUE* or *FALSE* depending on whether the user hit the OK button on the dialog. So, if the function returns *TRUE*, we call the *VBSetControlProperty()* function to set the property to whatever filename the user chose.

When the dialog first appears, of course, we'd like to initialize it with the previous value of the property. We can get that property and put it in a place the dialog expects to find it with this function:

```
static void near pascal GetCurrentFilename
    (
    HCTL Control,
    int PropertyIndex
    )
{
HSZ Pathname_;
VBGetControlProperty (Control, PropertyIndex, &Pathname_);
lstrcpy (Pathname, VBDerefHsz (Pathname_));
VBDestroyHsz (Pathname_);
}
```

The following function, *PopupFileDlg()*, is analogous to *PopupAboutDlg()* and is called by the control procedure in response to the *VBM_INITPROPPOPUP* message:

```
HWND far pascal PopupFileDlg
    (
    HCTL Control_,
    HWND Window,
    LPSTR Title,
    int PropertyIndex_,
    LPSTR Filters,
    int FilterIndex,
    LPSTR DefaultExt,
    DWORD Flags
    )
{
Control = Control_;
PropertyIndex = PropertyIndex_;
DlgInit.hwndOwner = Window;
DlgInit.lpstrTitle = Title;
```

```
GetCurrentFilename (Control, PropertyIndex);
DlgInit.lpstrFilter = Filters;
DlgInit.nFilterIndex = FilterIndex;
DlgInit.lpstrDefExt = DefaultExt;
DlgInit.Flags = Flags;
return CreateWindow
   (
   FileDlgPopupClass,
   NULL,
   WS_POPUP,
   0, 0, 0, 0,
   NULL,
   NULL,
   LibInstance,
   NULL
   );
}
```

The remainder of the file contains the same support for the file popup as is found for the About popup in HELP.C:

```
static HANDLE IdeTask = FALSE;

static WNDCLASS Class =
   {
   0,
   (WNDPROC) FileDlgPopupWndProc,
   0,
   0,
   0,
   NULL,
   NULL,
   NULL,
   NULL,
   NULL
   };

void far pascal RegisterFileDlgPopup (void)
   {
   Class.hInstance = LibInstance;
   Class.lpszClassName = FileDlgPopupClass;
   RegisterClass (&Class);
   }

void far pascal UnregisterFileDlgPopup (void)
   {
   if (IdeTask == GetCurrentTask())
```

```
    {
    UnregisterClass (FileDlgPopupClass, LibInstance);
    IdeTask = NULL;
    }
}
```

# TEXTVIEW.DEF

The TextFileView's module definition file comes directly from Skeleton, with (of course) the module name changed:

```
LIBRARY TextView
EXETYPE   WINDOWS
CODE    PRELOAD MOVEABLE DISCARDABLE
DATA    PRELOAD MOVEABLE SINGLE
HEAPSIZE 0
EXPORTS
        WEP         RESIDENTNAME
        Info      @2
        Style      @3
        Flags      @4
        WndProc    @5
        StyleProc  @6
        ListClasses
```

Remember that *WEP* should be marked *PRIVATE* instead of *RESIDENTNAME* if you are using the newer Microsoft linker.

# TEXTVIEW.RC

The TextFileView resources are derived from the Skeleton resources, as usual. To support the Dialog Editor, we supply a Styles dialog (shown in Figure 9.2). Here is the complete listing of TEXTVIEW.RC:

**Figure 9.2  The TextFileView Styles dialog box for Dialog Editor.**

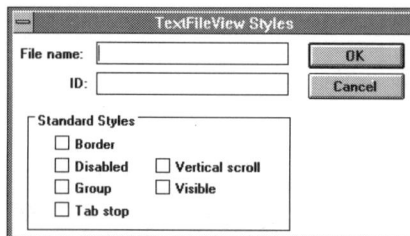

```
#include "internal.h"

// For Dialog Editor
Styles DIALOG 0, 0, 210, 147
STYLE DS_MODALFRAME | WS_POPUP | WS_VISIBLE | WS_CAPTION | WS_SYSMENU
CAPTION "TextFileView Styles"
FONT 8, "MS Sans Serif"
{
  CONTROL "File name:", IDC_STATIC, "STATIC", SS_RIGHT | WS_CHILD |
          WS_VISIBLE | WS_GROUP, 3, 7, 35, 7
  CONTROL "", IDC_CAPTION, "EDIT", ES_LEFT | ES_AUTOHSCROLL | WS_CHILD |
          WS_VISIBLE | WS_BORDER | WS_TABSTOP, 44, 4, 100, 12
  CONTROL "ID:", IDC_STATIC, "STATIC", SS_RIGHT | WS_CHILD | WS_VISIBLE |
          WS_GROUP, 5, 23, 35, 7
  CONTROL "", IDC_ID, "EDIT", ES_LEFT | ES_AUTOHSCROLL | WS_CHILD |
          WS_VISIBLE | WS_BORDER | WS_TABSTOP, 44, 21, 100, 12
  CONTROL "Standard Styles", IDC_STATIC, "BUTTON", BS_GROUPBOX | WS_CHILD |
          WS_VISIBLE | WS_TABSTOP, 8,41,137,66
  CONTROL "Border", IDC_BORDER, "Button", BS_AUTOCHECKBOX | WS_CHILD |
          WS_VISIBLE | WS_TABSTOP, 22, 55, 48, 10
  CONTROL "Disabled", IDC_DISABLED, "Button", BS_AUTOCHECKBOX | WS_CHILD |
          WS_VISIBLE | WS_TABSTOP, 22,67,44,10
  CONTROL "Group", IDC_GROUP, "Button", BS_AUTOCHECKBOX | WS_CHILD |
          WS_VISIBLE | WS_TABSTOP, 22,79,34,10
  CONTROL "Tab stop", IDC_TABSTOP, "Button", BS_AUTOCHECKBOX | WS_CHILD |
          WS_VISIBLE | WS_TABSTOP, 22,91,46,10
  CONTROL "Horizontal scroll", IDC_HSCROLL, "Button", BS_AUTOCHECKBOX |
          WS_CHILD | WS_VISIBLE | WS_TABSTOP, 75,55,66,10
  CONTROL "Vertical scroll", IDC_VSCROLL, "Button", BS_AUTOCHECKBOX |
          WS_CHILD | WS_VISIBLE | WS_TABSTOP, 75,67,61,10
  CONTROL "OK", IDOK, "BUTTON", BS_DEFPUSHBUTTON | WS_CHILD | WS_VISIBLE |
          WS_TABSTOP, 154, 4, 50, 14
  CONTROL "Cancel", IDCANCEL, "BUTTON", BS_PUSHBUTTON | WS_CHILD |
          WS_VISIBLE | WS_TABSTOP, 154, 21, 50, 14
  CONTROL "Visible", IDC_VISIBLE, "Button", BS_AUTOCHECKBOX | WS_CHILD |
          WS_VISIBLE | WS_TABSTOP, 75, 79, 61, 10
}

// For Resource Workshop
100 BITMAP "tbx.bmp"
100 CURSOR "tbx.cur"

// For Visual Basic
8000 BITMAP "8000.bmp"
8001 BITMAP "8001.bmp"
8003 BITMAP "8003.bmp"
8006 BITMAP "8006.bmp"

ABOUT DIALOG 41, 45, 192, 125
STYLE DS_MODALFRAME | WS_POPUP | WS_CAPTION
```

```
CAPTION "About Text File Viewer Control"
FONT 8, "MS Sans Serif"
BEGIN
    CONTROL "Text File Viewer Control", 0, "STATIC", SS_CENTER | WS_CHILD |
            WS_VISIBLE, 0, 8, 190, 8
    CONTROL "by Paul S. Cilwa", 0, "STATIC", SS_CENTER | WS_CHILD |
            WS_VISIBLE, 0, 16, 190, 8
    CONTROL "MAIN", 0, "STATIC", SS_ICON | WS_CHILD | WS_VISIBLE, 87, 29,
            18, 20
    CONTROL "Version 1.0", 0, "STATIC", SS_CENTER | WS_CHILD | WS_VISIBLE,
            0, 59, 190, 8
    CONTROL "\2511993 by Paul S. Cilwa", 0, "STATIC", SS_CENTER | WS_CHILD
            | WS_VISIBLE, 0, 79, 190, 8
    CONTROL "All Rights Reserved", 0, "STATIC", SS_CENTER | WS_CHILD |
            WS_VISIBLE, 0, 88, 190, 8
    CONTROL "OK", IDOK, "BUTTON", BS_PUSHBUTTON | WS_CHILD | WS_VISIBLE |
            WS_TABSTOP, 74, 102, 45, 15
END


MAIN ICON "TextView.ico"


1 VERSIONINFO LOADONCALL MOVEABLE DISCARDABLE
FILEVERSION 1, 0, 0, 0
PRODUCTVERSION 1, 0, 0, 0
FILEOS VOS__WINDOWS16
FILETYPE VFT_DLL
BEGIN
    BLOCK "StringFileInfo"
    BEGIN
        BLOCK "040904E4"
        BEGIN
            VALUE "CompanyName", "Coriolis Group\000"
            VALUE "FileDescription", "TextFileViewer Control for Visual Basic
                and Windows\000"
            VALUE "FileVersion", "1.0.0.0\000"
            VALUE "InternalName", "TEXTVIEW\000"
            VALUE "LegalCopyright", "Copyright © Paul S. Cilwa 1993\000"
            VALUE "OriginalFilename", "textview.vbx\000"
            VALUE "ProductName", "Windows Programming Power\000"
            VALUE "ProductVersion", "1.0.0.0\000"
            VALUE "Comments", "\000"
        END
    END
END
```

To support Borland's Resource Workshop, we need to add a toolbox bitmap and a cursor. The bitmap and cursor are shown in Figure 9.3. The statements that include them in the application's resource pool are as follows:

```
// For Resource Workshop
100 BITMAP "tbx.bmp"
100 CURSOR "tbx.cur"
```

Visual Basic requires the set of toolbox bitmaps shown in Figure 9.4. An About box and program icon are also needed. These are shown in Figures 9.5 and 9.6, respectively.

# Enhancing the Text File Viewer

Static controls don't usually support the Clipboard, but you could make a case for adding the ability to mark text and copy it, as well as to pull from the control text on a line-by-line basis. However, we didn't do any of those things in this chapter, because the *next* chapter features the TextFileEdit control which will include those features and more.

---

**Figure 9.3   The TextFileView bitmap and cursor for Resource Workshop.**

---

**Figure 9.4   The TextFileView toolbar bitmaps for Visual Basic.**

---

**Figure 9.5   The TextFileView About box for Visual Basic.**

**Figure 9.6  The TextFileView icon for Visual Basic.**

# 10

# The Text File
# Editor Control

In the previous chapter we built the
TextFileView control to display the contents of a text file. We are now going to
build on this control and create a basic text
editor control called TextFileEdit that supports up
to 32K lines (not characters) of text. With this control
you'll be able to read in text files and perform editing
operations such as selecting text, copying selected text
into the Clipboard, deleting selected text, and inserting
new text. You'll also be able to save your changes back
into the original text file.

ecause we did such a good job of designing the TextFileView control, you'll find that editing features can be added without too much fuss. We'll start by showing you which enhancements need to be made; then, we'll get to the actual work of writing the code.

# Designing the TextFileEdit Control

Ideally, the TextFileEdit control should behave *exactly* like a standard edit control (or, as it's called in Visual Basic, a "Text Box"), with the added feature of automatically loading and saving to disk. Unfortunately, the basic Edit control is *so* feature-filled we could dedicate an entire book to the code duplicating all those features. Therefore, we'll just build a basic TextFileEdit control that performs the basic editing features of adding and deleting text, and copying and pasting text from the Clipboard.

Because we are starting with the TextFileView control from the previous chapter, we'll only need to enhance a few areas in order to support text editing. Here are the changes we'll need to make:

- Change the default cursor from the arrow to the "I-beam" (this is a trivial step).
- Add an "insertion caret," the little blinking line that tells the user where the next typed character will be inserted.
- Alter the keyboard interface to the Scrollbar so that it controls the insertion caret instead.
- Recognize mouse drags and certain key combinations to allow the user to select blocks of text for copying and cutting text.
- Intercept *WM_CHAR* messages and use them to insert characters at the insertion point.
- Implement a new message to allow selected text to be placed or retrieved programmatically (specifically, by the visual layer).

Wow! Sounds like quite an ambitious project, doesn't it? Fortunately, we laid a firm foundation in the previous chapter by using object-oriented programming techniques to build TextFileView. It turns out that most of the enhancements in our list can be implemented by just making the TextFileView objects (such as *Lines* and *Line* objects) a little smarter—that is, by adding a few properties and methods to each object.

## Manipulating the Insertion Caret

The first item on our list involves changing the normal arrow mouse cursor to an "I-Beam." This is an easy task and you'll see how to do it when we get to the code section. Manipulating the insertion caret, on the other hand, requires more planning, so let's consider it here.

### Creating an Insertion Caret

The *insertion caret*—usually just called the *caret*—is generally a blinking, vertical line that users have come to associate with an edit control. By letting you know where the next character you type will be inserted, it serves the same purpose as the little hammer guides on old-fashioned typewriters.

A less commonly known fact is that the insertion caret doesn't *have* to be a vertical line. When you create the thing, *you* specify its height *and* width. Thus, you can make a large block or a horizontal line caret as easily as the standard vertical one.

Still, users appreciate not being surprised by unconventional behavior in their Windows applications. So, for an editing control that is supposed to *look* like an editing control, the vertical line is our best bet.

○   ○   ○

*Remember the possibilities available for creating carets if you ever find yourself creating something other than a text editor.*

○   ○   ○

The caret is a "system resource," which means that there is only one, and it must be shared among all active applications. You may have noticed that only one edit control in a dialog ever has a caret at one time. In fact, that's how you identify *which* edit control has the focus. This suggests that your control must get the caret (if it wants it) when the *WM_GETFOCUS* message arrives. Likewise, if your control uses the caret, it must explicitly relinquish the caret when it receives a *WM_KILLFOCUS* message.

The function you call to obtain the caret is named *CreateCaret()*, although the caret already exists. Likewise, to "relinquish" the caret, you invoke *DestroyCaret()*.

The caret's height and width is specified in the call to *CreateCaret()*. You cannot specify a color, however. Although you may think the caret is black, look more closely; Windows actually performs an *inversion* of the underlying pixels when the caret is displayed. For example, if the background is blue, the caret will be yellow.

After the caret has been created, it must be positioned. This is done by calling *SetCaretPos()*. You might think you could call *SetCaretPos()* safely any time the insertion point changes—but wait a moment. What if the insertion point changes because of a *programmatic* manipulation while the control doesn't have the focus? You shouldn't try to position a caret you don't own. That's why we're going to design a *Caret* object instead of presenting the caret-management code in-line in the Window procedure, as most Windows programming books do. Our *Caret* object can obtain the insertion point from the *Lines* object and reposition itself when needed. It can also create and destroy the physical caret when *WM_GETFOCUS* and *WM_KILLFOCUS* messages are received.

◦  ◦  ◦

*In effect, we'll create our own caret and we won't have to think of it as being a shared object because the underlying mechanism of the physical caret will be self-contained in the* Caret *object. That's what encapsulation is all about.*

◦  ◦  ◦

## Positioning the Caret

We implied earlier that the *Lines* and *Line* objects will "know" where the current insertion point is...somehow. They need to know this so that the *Caret* object can figure out where to position itself. To implement this feature, we'll need to enhance several objects in the TextFileView control.

The first object we'll enhance is the *Lines* collection. Because it already has a *TopLine* property, it can find the beginning of the linked list of *Line* objects. However, it will need a new property to point to the *Line* that has the insertion point. In the TextFileView control, an empty file could generate no lines at all. We'll have to make sure that the *Lines* collection always has at least one *Line*—even if the line is blank—to guarantee an insertion point.

We also must enhance the *Line* object so that it knows the actual character position of the insertion point. We can borrow a technique from the Listbox control and use a value of -1 to indicate that the insertion point isn't on the *Line* at all. Any other value will be the index into the *Text* array to indicate where new characters will be inserted.

When the *Caret* property is activated (during processing of a *WM_GETFOCUS* message), it will need to query the *Lines* object for its display position. The *Lines* object, knowing which *Line* has the insertion point, can pass the query on to the *Line*. By tossing in a pointer to the *View* object, which knows which line is at the top of the control's display, the

*Line* object will be able to return the x and y coordinates of the insertion point to the *Lines* object. The object will then pass the coordinates on to the *Caret* object which can use them to position itself. Don't panic! It sounds complicated, but object-oriented programming usually involves many pieces doing small amounts of coordinated work. See Figure 10.1 for a visual aid of this process.

The question that may be troubling you is: How can a *Line* object convert a text array index into a display coordinate? After all, the DOS days of 80 x 25 character display grids are long gone. (Thank goodness!) Windows text might be any size and is usually proportionally spaced, to boot.

Well, the solution is simple. All we have to do is call *GetTextExtent()*, passing it the *Line*'s text but giving it the insertion point index instead of the line length. *GetTextExtent()* will then tell us exactly where the next character—and, therefore, the insertion point—should go.

## Locating Mouse Clicks

In a way, the processing of mouse clicks gives us the opposite problem encountered with carets. Given the pair of screen coordinates that arrive with a *WM_LBUTTONDOWN* message, how can we determine what the new insertion point should become?

And yet, using *Lines*, *Line*, and *View* objects, the flow is quite similar. Since a mouse click can only occur in the visible window (the area managed by *View)*, the click point can be sent to *View*, which can query each

**Figure 10.1   How the *Caret* positions itself.**

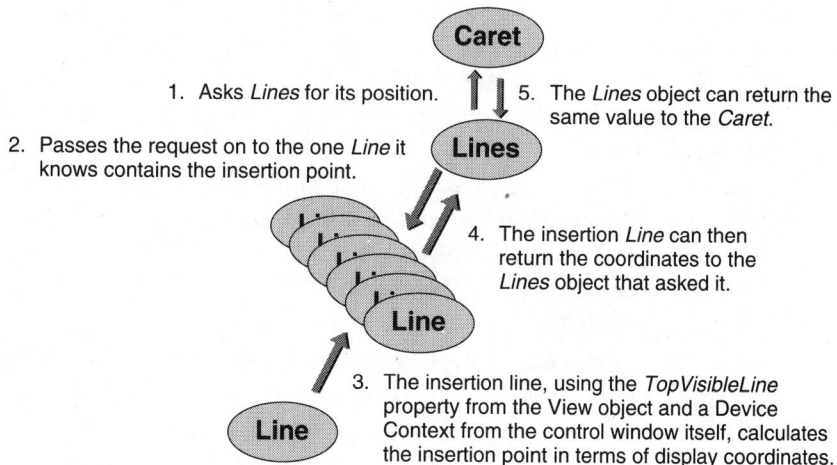

1. Asks *Lines* for its position.

5. The *Lines* object can return the same value to the *Caret*.

2. Passes the request on to the one *Line* it knows contains the insertion point.

4. The insertion *Line* can then return the coordinates to the *Lines* object that asked it.

3. The insertion line, using the *TopVisibleLine* property from the View object and a Device Context from the control window itself, calculates the insertion point in terms of display coordinates.

*Line* starting with *TopVisibleLine* to see if it is the *Line* that contains the point in question. If it is, *View* can ask the *Lines* collection to reset the insertion point to that *Line*. (*Lines* must be in charge because the *Line* which previously held the insertion point must be informed that it can't keep the insertion point any longer.) The new insertion *Line* will further refine the point to the correct character location. Finally, the *Caret* object can be notified that the insertion point has changed; it can then reposition itself using the algorithm previously described.

If proportionally spaced fonts are used, how can we determine *which* characters the insertion point now lies between? We'll tell you, but we know you'll cringe. We must call *GetTextExtent()* repeatedly, starting with a buffer of zero characters and working our way up until the length returned by *GetTextExtent()* has exceeded the point we're looking for. Does this sound terribly inefficient? You bet! We can only assure you that it doesn't seem to take any time at all. The visual response seems to be instantaneous, and that's what counts, after all.

○    ○    ○

*Notice that only a small amount of our code directly interacts with the Windows API. Our job, as Windows programmers, should not be to overwhelm ourselves with API calls but rather to concentrate on getting the elements of our application—Windows and otherwise—to work together.*

○    ○    ○

## Tracking the Selection Rectangle

As a user of Windows applications, you might think that the insertion point isn't always just one point—sometimes it's a whole slew of characters, which may have been selected by dragging the mouse or using the keyboard. When the next character arrives, the selected group will be replaced by the new character.

Well, certainly there is a selection block. However, we see it as being distinct from the insertion point, even though one end of the selection block always *coincides* with the insertion point, and an insertion operation first deletes the characters in the selection block (if there are any).

Another distinction is that the selection block is not painted the same colors as regular text. In fact, a set of colors is defined in the standard Windows palette (which users can change using the Control Panel) for highlighted (selected) text. To identify which portions of text are to be painted in what colors, the *Line* objects in the middle of a selection block will each have a *StartSelection* set to the beginning of the *Line*, and an *EndSelection* set to the end of it.

When a user presses the left mouse button over the TextFileEdit window, an "anchor" point is set. Dragging the mouse from that point changes the "selection" point. In a simple click, the anchor and selection points are the same.

Creating the selection rectangle is just an extension of what we already planned with the insertion point. We know that the *Lines* collection will have been notified of the receipt of a *WM_LBUTTONDOWN* message. It will have to set an internal flag noting this. If the next message is a *WM_LBUTTONUP* message, then an insertion point has been set and that's all; the flag can be reset. If, on the other hand, *WM_MOUSEMOVE* messages intervene, a selection block is being marked. The *Lines* object, through manipulating its individual *Line* objects, will have to mark and repaint the text until that *WM_LBUTTONUP* message finally arrives.

## Inserting Additional Text

Once the problem of determining *where* a text insertion will take place has been solved, we get to the fun part of actually *inserting* the text! Text usually arrives in the form of characters, one at a time, conveyed in *WM_CHAR* messages. However, the *WM_PASTE* message is a signal to copy the contents of the Clipboard into the current insertion point, and that usually involves more than one character. In fact, it may involve many *lines* of text. Also, we'll want to provide a programmatic method of inserting text, as standard edit controls do.

To accommodate these needs, we're going to give the *Lines* object a *LINES_Insert()* method. This method will place text, whether one character or many, starting at the insertion point (and moving the insertion point beyond each character that is added). Of course, *Lines* will accomplish this by deleting the selected text, if any, before sending the insertion text to the *Line* that has the insertion point. That *Line* will allocate additional space as needed, and even insert new *Lines* after itself if the text being inserted includes new line characters.

## Keeping the Device in Context

While a simple app can succeed with the basic device context management approach we've been using all along, TextFileEdit will need much more frequent access to a device context for us to get away with such a simple system. For example, each line of text needs to have its height specially measured (you may want to add multiple font capability to this control someday). Also, a device context is required for all those calls to *GetTextExtent()* used to place the caret. We could ask for a *DC* whenever one is required, but we'd have to select the current font into it every time (otherwise the measurements calculated would not be accurate). Overall, it will be much more efficient to create a *device context* object to both work with the *DC* supplied by the *WM_PAINT* message and to create a *DC* whenever one is needed for measuring.

## Memory Management

If a *Line* allocated additional space each time a character was added, adding text to a TextFileEdit control would be accomplished about as fast as health care reform. Each *Line*, you'll recall, is initially given exactly the space it needs to store its text. However, most people don't usually add a character to *every* line in a file; they tend to concentrate on a few lines. Therefore, we can safely add, say, 50 bytes to each *Line* as it is needed, thus reducing the re-allocations to a manageable number. To implement this technique, we'll need to add an *AllocatedLength* property to the *Line* objects so they can tell when they're running out of space.

# Extracting Text

We'll need to programmatically pull text out of the TextFileEdit control in response to *WM_COPY* messages. (These messages are sent to instruct the control to copy the current selection to the Clipboard.) We'll also need to pull out text in response to other messages we define for this purpose so that the parent window can manipulate the text. We will not, however, provide a "get all text" message. The parent window can always select the entire contents of a file if it really wants it. Since a file can contain many characters, the parent will need to pass a **huge** pointer for such a transfer. For TextFileEdit's part, a **huge** pointer will always be assumed.

◦　◦　◦

*If the parent window doesn't pass a **huge** pointer, there won't be a problem as long as the actual text being transferred does not exceed the target buffer's 64K boundary.*

◦　◦　◦

# Creating the TextFileEdit Control

The TextFileEdit is implemented in C with the following modules:

```
TEXTEDIT.H
INTERNAL.H
BLOCK.H / BLOCK.C
DC.H / DC.C
CARET.H / CARET.C
LINES.H / LINES.C
LINE.H / LINE.C
VIEW.C
MAIN.C
DIALOG.C
VISUAL.C
HELP.C
FILEPROP.C
TEXTEDIT.RC
TEXTEDIT.DEF
TEXTEDIT.BAS
```

Because the TextFileEdit control is implemented as both a standard and a visual custom control, you'll need to include VBAPI.LIB in the list of libraries to be linked into the end-product DLL.

## TEXTEDIT.H

This **#include** file is the only one which must be referenced by a programmer using the TextFileEdit control in a standard (non-Visual) Windows app. It provides the **#define** directives for the messages and notifications:

```
#ifndef _TEXTFILE_H_
#define _TEXTFILE_H_

#define TEM_GETSEL (WM_USER+200)
#define TEM_SETSEL (WM_USER+201)
#define TEM_INSERTTEXT (WM_USER+202)
#define TEM_STOREDATA (WM_USER+203)
#define TEM_GETMODIFIED (WM_USER+204)
#define TEM_SETMODIFIED (WM_USER+205)
#define TEM_GETSELTEXT (WM_USER+206)
#define TEM_GETTEXT (WM_USER+207)

#define TEN_CHANGE 1
```

```
#define TEN_KILLFOCUS 2
#define TEN_SETFOCUS 3

#endif
```

## BLOCK.H and BLOCK.C

These files comprise the same memory management scheme used in Chapter 9, and are unchanged. Thus, you can simply copy them into the subdirectory for this chapter's project.

## DC.H

Both DC.H and DC.C implement the Device Context object. The header file, DC.H, describes the object's structure and callable routines. Notice that this object is packaged so that you can use it in other projects as well. Here is the complete DC.H file:

```
#ifndef _DC_H_
#define _DC_H_

#include <windows.h>

typedef struct
   {
   HWND Window;
   HDC Value;
   BOOL Owned;
   HFONT Font, OldFont;
   HBRUSH Brush, OldBrush;
   HPEN Pen, OldPen;
   COLORREF TextColor;
   COLORREF BkColor;
   } DC, far * LPDC;

void far pascal DC_Init (LPDC dc, HWND Window);
void far pascal DC_SetFont (LPDC dc, HFONT Font);
HFONT far pascal DC_GetFont (LPDC dc);
void far pascal DC_SetBrush (LPDC dc, HBRUSH Brush);
HBRUSH far pascal DC_GetBrush (LPDC dc);
void far pascal DC_SetPen (LPDC dc, HPEN Pen);
HPEN far pascal DC_GetPen (LPDC dc);
void far pascal DC_SetTextColor (LPDC dc, COLORREF Color);
void far pascal DC_SetBkColor (LPDC dc, COLORREF Color);
```

```
static void near Adjust (LPDC dc);
HDC far pascal DC_Get (LPDC dc);
void far pascal DC_Release (LPDC dc);
HDC far pascal DC_Use (LPDC dc, HDC hDC);

#endif
```

A glance at the *DC* structure explains what we're trying to do here. Recall from Chapter 3 that whenever a font, pen, or brush is selected into a device context, the original font, pen, or brush must be returned before you release the DC. Our *DC* structure supports this requirement by providing not only "pockets" for the replacement GDI objects, but places for the original values as well.

○   ○   ○

*Although it is possible for an app to "own" a permanent DC, which the app typically customizes at initialization and finally releases when it terminates, most apps just "borrow" one from the system and return it when through.*

○   ○   ○

Because there are only five "free-lance" DCs available at any given time, it is imperative that no one application grab a DC and hog it. Thus, we've designed the Device Context object so that it can store our font, pen, and brush preferences, but not actually keep a DC hanging around until we need it.

To see how the *DC* structure is managed in general, just look at the assortment of functions provided to manage this object: Any GDI object can be added to the structure at any time, whether the DC is "active" or not. That way you can call the *DC_Get()* function as often as you need to, confident that the DC you receive will always come pre-loaded with your required set of GDI objects. You'll also know that the proper housekeeping tasks will take place when you are done with the DC.

## DC.C

To see how the Device Context object is managed in detail, it is necessary to study the source code, contained in DC.C.

First off, you must initialize the Device Context object before using it by calling the *DC_Init()* function:

```
#include "dc.h"
```

```
void far pascal DC_Init (LPDC dc, HWND Window)
  {
  dc->Window = Window;
  dc->Value =
  dc->Font = dc->OldFont =
  dc->Brush = dc->OldBrush =
  dc->Pen = dc->OldPen = 0;
  dc->TextColor = GetSysColor (COLOR_WINDOWTEXT);
  dc->BkColor = GetSysColor (COLOR_WINDOW);
  }
```

Most of the fields are simply preset to zero. However, two of the fields, *TextColor* and *BkColor*, are set to the appropriate system values. These are the colors the user has chosen for his or her system.

Our primary motivation in creating this object was to provide an easy way to get a DC whenever we need one, pre-loaded with the correct font. (Recall that our most frequent reason for needing a DC is to measure text with it.) The following two functions load a font, and make it available:

```
void far pascal DC_SetFont (LPDC dc, HFONT Font)
  {
  dc->Font = Font;
  if (dc->Value)
    if (! dc->OldFont)
      dc->OldFont = SelectObject (dc->Value, dc->Font);
    else
      SelectObject (dc->Value, dc->Font);
  }

HFONT far pascal DC_GetFont (LPDC dc)
  {
  return dc->Font ? dc->Font : GetStockObject (SYSTEM_FONT);
  }
```

Note that the *DC_SetFont()* function is written to accommodate changing the font, whether the DC is currently in use or not. Likewise, if the DC is active and the new font is replacing a previous custom font, the original font is undisturbed. (It will have to be re-selected into the DC just before releasing it.)

The jobs of loading pens and brushes is virtually identical to that of loading fonts. Here are the pen and brush functions:

```
void far pascal DC_SetBrush (LPDC dc, HBRUSH Brush)
  {
```

```
    dc->Brush = Brush;
    if (dc->Value)
      if (! dc->OldBrush)
        dc->OldBrush = SelectObject (dc->Value, dc->Brush);
      else
        SelectObject (dc->Value, dc->Brush);
    }

HBRUSH far pascal DC_GetBrush (LPDC dc)
    {
    return dc->Brush ? dc->Brush : GetStockObject (WHITE_BRUSH);
    }

void far pascal DC_SetPen (LPDC dc, HPEN Pen)
    {
    dc->Pen = Pen;
    if (dc->Value)
      if (! dc->OldPen)
        dc->OldPen = SelectObject (dc->Value, dc->Pen);
      else
        SelectObject (dc->Value, dc->Pen);
    }

HPEN far pascal DC_GetPen (LPDC dc)
    {
    return dc->Pen ? dc->Pen : GetStockObject (BLACK_PEN);
    }
```

Although most applications shouldn't change the color of the text and background from the user's Control Panel-set preferences, sometimes there are good reasons to. In such a case, your application could call the following two functions:

```
void far pascal DC_SetTextColor (LPDC dc, COLORREF Color)
    {
    dc->TextColor = Color;
    if (dc->Value)
      SetTextColor (dc->Value, dc->TextColor);
    }

void far pascal DC_SetBkColor (LPDC dc, COLORREF Color)
    {
    dc->BkColor = Color;
    if (dc->Value)
      SetBkColor (dc->Value, dc->BkColor);
    }
```

Although *SetTextColor()* and *SetBkColor()* each returns the previous color (just as *SelectObject()* returns the previous font, pen, or brush), we don't bother saving them. Not returning a GDI object such as a pen can result in your app's having a memory leak; but there's no harm in leaving the text color changed as long as you've created the DC yourself (or have received it via a *WM_PAINT* message).

Our Device Context object needs to apply our customizations as well as to restore the original values. That's what these two local functions are for:

```
static void near Adjust (LPDC dc)
   {
   if (dc->Font)
     dc->OldFont = SelectObject (dc->Value, dc->Font);
   if (dc->Brush)
     dc->OldBrush = SelectObject (dc->Value, dc->Brush);
   if (dc->Pen)
     dc->OldPen = SelectObject (dc->Value, dc->Pen);
   SetTextColor (dc->Value, dc->TextColor);
   SetBkColor (dc->Value, dc->BkColor);
   }

static void near pascal Restore (LPDC dc)
   {
   if (dc->OldFont)
     {
     SelectObject (dc->Value, dc->OldFont);
     dc->OldFont = 0;
     }
   if (dc->OldBrush)
     {
     SelectObject (dc->Value, dc->OldBrush);
     dc->OldBrush = 0;
     }
   if (dc->OldPen)
     {
     SelectObject (dc->Value, dc->OldPen);
     dc->OldPen = 0;
     }
   }
```

A DC can come from two places: the *WM_PAINT* message (actually, the *PAINTSTRUCT* that the message provides) and a specific request by your application. The *DC_Get()* function accommodates the latter:

```
HDC far pascal DC_Get (LPDC dc)
   {
```

```
if (! dc->Value)
   {
   dc->Value = GetDC (dc->Window);
   dc->Owned = TRUE;
   Adjust (dc);
   }
return dc->Value;
}
```

Notice the *Owned* flag: This tells the object that the DC in the *Value* field was actually obtained by *DC_Get()* and will have to be released later. Also, notice that the function is designed to be called as often as desired without calling *DC_Release()* in between. After the first call, it simply returns the DC that it's already obtained. This can be handy if you need to call *DC_Get()* a couple of times in succession but don't want to clutter your code with another variable to hold the DC that *DC_Get()* returns.

If you are processing a *WM_PAINT* message, you'll still want the Device Context object to customize a DC—but it'll be the one that comes with the message. The *DC_Use()* function is designed especially for that:

```
HDC far pascal DC_Use (LPDC dc, HDC hDC)
   {
   dc->Value = hDC;
   dc->Owned = FALSE;
   Adjust (dc);
   return dc->Value;
   }
```

Notice that in this routine, the *Owned* flag is set to *FALSE*. The *DC_Release()* function will call the Windows *ReleaseDC()* function only if the *Owned* flag is true:

```
void far pascal DC_Release (LPDC dc)
   {
   Restore (dc);
   if (dc->Owned)
      ReleaseDC (dc->Window, dc->Value);
   dc->Value = 0;
   }
```

Obviously, putting this functionality in a Device Context object means we won't need the *wm_Paint()* function in the MAIN.C module to do as much as it usually does. We'll see how simple managing the Device Context becomes in just a few pages.

## CARET.H

The *Caret* object encapsulates the management of the system resource that visually cues the user where the next typed letters are to go. Here is the header file for this object, which you can reuse in other projects if you like:

```c
#ifndef _CARET_H_
#define _CARET_H_

#include <windows.h>

typedef struct
  {
  HWND Window;
  int Height;
  int Width;
  BOOL Created: 1;
  BOOL Visible: 1;
  POINT Location;
  int LeftMargin;
  } CARET, far * LPCARET;

void far pascal CARET_Init (LPCARET Caret, HWND Window);
void far pascal CARET_GetFocus (LPCARET Caret);
void far pascal CARET_LoseFocus (LPCARET Caret);
void far pascal CARET_Show (LPCARET Caret);
void far pascal CARET_Hide (LPCARET Caret);
void far pascal CARET_SetLeftMargin (LPCARET Caret, int LeftMargin);
void far pascal CARET_SetPosition (LPCARET Caret, POINT Point);
void far pascal CARET_SetWidth (LPCARET Caret, int Width);
void far pascal CARET_SetHeight (LPCARET Caret, int Height);

#endif
```

## CARET.C

The functions declared in CARET.H are defined in CARET.C, the *Caret* object's implementation file. The caret itself is simple, both in management and in design. We explained how the Windows caret is used earlier in this chapter. Now, we'll look closely at the supporting code.

To use our *Caret* object, we must first call *CARET_Init()* to initialize the object:

```c
#include "caret.h"
```

```
void far pascal CARET_Init (LPCARET Caret, HWND Window)
  {
  Caret->Window = Window;
  Caret->Height = GetSystemMetrics (SM_CYHSCROLL);
  Caret->Width = GetSystemMetrics (SM_CXBORDER) * 2;
  Caret->Created = FALSE;
  Caret->Visible = FALSE;
  Caret->Location.x =
  Caret->Location.y = 0;
  Caret->LeftMargin = 0;
  }
```

The only metrics we are interested in are the caret's height and width. By default, the caret is one pixel wide; this makes it visible, but just barely. We'll make it twice the width of a system border, or two pixels wide on most monitors. The default height, on the other hand, is just a dot—*very* hard to see. Windows users typically see carets displayed as the height of an average character in the current font. Since we won't know which font will be used at initialization time, we'll guess at a usable value. We'll also supply a means for an application to change the caret height later.

If a window is to have a caret, the caret must be enabled during processing of the *WM_GETFOCUS* message:

```
void far pascal CARET_GetFocus (LPCARET Caret)
  {
  CreateCaret (Caret->Window,
    NULL, Caret->Width, Caret->Height);
  Caret->Created = TRUE;
  SetCaretPos (Caret->Location.x + Caret->LeftMargin,
    Caret->Location.y);
  CARET_Show (Caret);
  }
```

Likewise, the caret must be relinquished when the *WM_KILLFOCUS* message is handled:

```
void far pascal CARET_LoseFocus (LPCARET Caret)
  {
  CARET_Hide (Caret);
  DestroyCaret ();
  Caret->Created = FALSE;
  }
```

If your application needs to paint the screen at a time when *WM_PAINT* is *not* being processed, you must hide the caret while you do your illustrating. The following two functions simplify this chore:

```
void far pascal CARET_Show (LPCARET Caret)
  {
  if (! Caret->Visible)
    {
    ShowCaret (Caret->Window);
    Caret->Visible = TRUE;
    }
  }

void far pascal CARET_Hide (LPCARET Caret)
  {
  if (Caret->Visible)
    {
    HideCaret (Caret->Window);
    Caret->Visible = FALSE;
    }
  }
```

Since the height and width of a caret must be specified *before* the caret is displayed, the functions that set these dimensions are extremely simple:

```
void far pascal CARET_SetWidth (LPCARET Caret, int Width)
  {
  Caret->Width = Width;
  }

void far pascal CARET_SetHeight (LPCARET Caret, int Height)
  {
  Caret->Height = Height;
  }
```

If you are wondering why we need functions to perform operations you could accomplish slightly faster without calling a function, we can only say that this is in keeping with our object-oriented programming style. One benefit is that it allows you to modify your object's storage implementation, without requiring that other modules that call on your object be recompiled.

## LINES.H

As in the TextFileView control, the *Lines* object manages the lines of text from a file. The version used with TextFileEdit is quite similar although features have been added for tracking the anchor and selection points, and for writing the changed contents of the control back out to disk. Here is the entire header file, LINES.H:

```c
#ifndef _LINES_H_
#define _LINES_H_

#include <stdio.h>
#include "line.h"
#include "dc.h"
#include "caret.h"

typedef struct
    {
    HWND Window;
    LPLINE  TopLine;
    int LinesCount;
    LPLINE Anchor,
        Selection;
    LPCARET Caret;
    BOOL Modified;
    } LINES, far * LPLINES;

void far pascal LINES_Init
    (
    LPLINES This,
    HWND Window,
    LPCARET Caret
    );
BOOL far pascal LINES_Load (LPLINES This, LPSTR Pathname, HDC dc);
void far pascal LINES_DeleteAll (LPLINES This);
LPLINE far pascal LINES_GetTopLine (LPLINES This);
void far pascal LINES_DropAnchor
    (
    LPLINES This,
    LPLINE Line,
    HDC dc,
    int x
    );
LPLINE far pascal LINES_GetSelection (LPLINES This);
void far pascal LINES_ExtendSelection
    (
    LPLINES This,
    LPLINE Line,
    HDC dc,
    int x
    );
void far pascal LINES_GoHome (LPLINES This, BOOL Extend, HDC dc);
void far pascal LINES_GoEnd (LPLINES This, BOOL Extend, HDC dc);
void far pascal LINES_GoUp (LPLINES This, BOOL Extend, HDC dc);
void far pascal LINES_GoDown (LPLINES This, BOOL Extend, HDC dc);
void far pascal LINES_GoLeft (LPLINES This, BOOL Extend);
void far pascal LINES_GoRight (LPLINES This, BOOL Extend);
```

```
void far pascal LINES_DeleteSelection (LPLINES This, HDC dc);
void far pascal LINES_InsertText (LPLINES This, LPSTR Buffer, HDC dc);
void far pascal LINES_SetModified (LPLINES This, BOOL Modified);
BOOL far pascal LINES_GetModified (LPLINES This);
void far pascal LINES_GetSelectionRect (LPLINES This, LPRECT Rect);
void far pascal LINES_SetSelectionRect (LPLINES This, LPRECT Rect);
void far pascal LINES_GetSelectedText (LPLINES This, LPSTR Buffer);
void far pascal LINES_GetText (LPLINES This, LPSTR Buffer);
BOOL far pascal LINES_Store (LPLINES This, LPSTR Pathname);
#endif
```

# LINES.C

The first function in LINES.C, the implementation file for the *Lines* object, is
still *LINES_Init()*. We've added initialization code for the new data members:

```
#include "lines.h"

void far pascal LINES_Init
    (
    LPLINES This,
    HWND Window,
    LPCARET Caret
    )
{
This->Window = Window;
This->TopLine = NULL;
This->LinesCount = 0;
This->Anchor =
This->Selection = NULL;
This->Caret = Caret;
This->Modified = FALSE;
}
```

The *LoadLines()* function called by *LINES_Loud()* hasn't changed:

```
static void near pascal LoadLines (LPLINES This, HDC dc, FILE * Stream)
{
char Buffer[256];
LPLINE Line = NULL, Prev = NULL;
while (Stream &&
    (! feof (Stream)) &&
    fgets (Buffer, sizeof Buffer, Stream))
    {
    register e = strlen (Buffer);
    if (e > 0)
        if (Buffer[-e] == '\n')
```

```
        Buffer[e] = 0;
    This->LinesCount++;
    Line = LINE_Alloc (Buffer, dc);
    LINE_Append (Line, Prev);
    if (! This->TopLine)
      This->TopLine = Line;
    Prev = Line;
    }
  InvalidateRect (This->Window, NULL, FALSE);
  }
```

However, the *LINES_Load()* function now calls an additional helper
function if it cannot open the requested file. The helper function's name is
*CreateBlankLine()*. Since the control is designed to allow editing, it requires
at least one blank line to provide a starting point for any editing:

```
static void near pascal CreateBlankLine (LPLINES This, HDC dc)
  {
  LPLINE Line = LINE_Alloc ("", dc);
  This->LinesCount = 1;
  This->TopLine = Line;
  }
```

Other than that, the biggest change in *LINES_Load()* is that
*LINES_DropAnchor()* is now called to place the insertion point firmly in the
window, before the first character of the first line:

```
BOOL far pascal LINES_Load (LPLINES This, LPSTR Pathname, HDC dc)
  {
  FILE * Stream;
  BOOL Result = FALSE;
  if (This->TopLine)
    LINES_DeleteAll (This);
  Stream = fopen (Pathname, "rt");
  if (Stream)
    {
    LoadLines (This, dc, Stream);
    fclose (Stream);
    Result = TRUE;
    This->Modified = TRUE;
    }
  else
    CreateBlankLine (This, dc);
  LINES_DropAnchor (This, This->TopLine, dc, 0);
  SetScrollRange (This->Window, SB_VERT,
    1, This->LinesCount, TRUE);
  return Result;
  }
```

*LINES_DeleteAll()* and *LINES_GetTopLine()* have not changed since the previous chapter:

```
void far pascal LINES_DeleteAll (LPLINES This)
  {
  LPLINE Line = This->TopLine;
  while (Line)
    {
    register LPLINE Next = Line->Next;
    FreeMem (Line);
    Line = Next;
    }
  This->TopLine = NULL;
  }

LPLINE far pascal LINES_GetTopLine (LPLINES This)
  {
  return This->TopLine;
  }
```

## Selecting Text

The remaining functions in this module, except one, implement the editing side of the TextFileEdit control. First up is a function that clears any selection that may have been in effect when the user clicked on some location with the mouse. Such an action marks a new selection, so the old one must be cleared:

```
static void near pascal ResetSelection (LPLINES This)
  {
  BOOL Forward = (LINE_GetIndex (This->Anchor) <=
    LINE_GetIndex (This->Selection));
  while (This->Anchor != This->Selection)
    {
    LINE_ResetSelection (This->Selection);
    if (Forward)
      This->Selection = LINE_GetPrev (This->Selection);
    else
      This->Selection = LINE_GetNext (This->Selection);
    }
  if (This->Anchor)
    LINE_ResetSelection (This->Anchor);
  }
```

Note that the function was written to be "NULL-pointer" safe. You'll see why in a moment when you look at the *LINES_DropAnchor()* function:

```
void far pascal LINES_DropAnchor
    (
    LPLINES This,
    LPLINE Line,
    HDC dc,
    int x
    )
{
ResetSelection (This);
This->Anchor =
This->Selection = Line;
LINE_DropAnchor (Line, dc, x);
InvalidateRect (This->Window, NULL, FALSE);
}
```

This routine is called to start a selection. However, it is called at least once, not by a user, but by the *Lines* object itself during initialization. At this time, no selection could be made. Knowing that it could be called with *NULL* pointers, *ResetSelection()* was written to handle that situation gracefully.

Once the anchor has been dropped, we have a legal "selection" of zero characters at a specific location. This selection implies an insertion point. Occasionally, we'll need to access the line using the insertion point. The following *LINES_GetSelection()* function is needed for this purpose:

```
LPLINE far pascal LINES_GetSelection (LPLINES This)
    {
    return This->Selection;
    }
```

Once the anchor point has been dropped, the user can go up, down, left, or right with the cursor. The selection scheme must be able to handle all these cases:

```
void far pascal LINES_ExtendSelection
    (
    LPLINES This,
    LPLINE Line,
    HDC dc,
    int x
    )
{
ResetSelection (This);
if (LINE_GetIndex (This->Anchor) == LINE_GetIndex (Line))
    LINE_ExtendRight (This->Anchor, dc, x);
else if (LINE_GetIndex (Line) > LINE_GetIndex (This->Anchor))
```

```
        {
      while (This->Selection != Line)
        {
        LINE_ExtendRight (This->Selection, dc, 0x7FFF);
        This->Selection = LINE_GetNext (This->Selection);
        }
      LINE_ExtendRight (This->Selection, dc, x);
      }
    else
      {
      LINE_ExtendRight (This->Selection, dc, x);
      while (This->Selection != Line)
        {
        LINE_ExtendRight (This->Selection, dc, 0x7FFF);
        This->Selection = LINE_GetPrev (This->Selection);
        }
      LINE_ExtendLeft (This->Selection, dc, x);
      }
    InvalidateRect (This->Window, NULL, FALSE);
    }
```

This function determines whether the mouse is moving up or down and behaves accordingly. Notice that we are using the hexadecimal number 0x7FFF as the farthest possible point on a line. (The *Line* object functions will not allow a selection point to go past the end of a line.)

As useful as the mouse is for navigating around the screen, many people prefer the keyboard. Some of the keystrokes that controlled the scroll bar in TextFileView have been commandeered by TextFileEdit to serve more appropriate roles in a text editor. For example, the Home, End, Right, and Left arrows now have navigational functions:

```
void far pascal LINES_GoHome (LPLINES This, BOOL Extend, HDC dc)
  {
  if (! Extend)
    LINES_DropAnchor (This, This->Selection, dc, 0);
  else
    LINES_ExtendSelection (This, This->Selection, dc, 0);
  }

void far pascal LINES_GoEnd (LPLINES This, BOOL Extend, HDC dc)
  {
  if (! Extend)
    LINES_DropAnchor (This, This->Selection, dc, 0x7FFF);
  else
    LINES_ExtendSelection (This, This->Selection, dc, 0x7FFF);
  }
```

```
void far pascal LINES_GoUp (LPLINES This, BOOL Extend, HDC dc)
  {
  LPLINE NewLine = LINE_GetPrev (This->Selection);
  if (NewLine)
    {
    int x = LINE_GetCaretPoint (This->Selection, dc);
    if (! Extend)
      LINES_DropAnchor (This, NewLine, dc, x);
    else
      LINES_ExtendSelection (This, NewLine, dc, x);
    }
  }

void far pascal LINES_GoDown (LPLINES This, BOOL Extend, HDC dc)
  {
  LPLINE NewLine = LINE_GetNext (This->Selection);
  if (NewLine)
    {
    int x = LINE_GetCaretPoint (This->Selection, dc);
    if (! Extend)
      LINES_DropAnchor (This, NewLine, dc, x);
    else
      LINES_ExtendSelection (This, NewLine, dc, x);
    }
  }
```

The *Extend* parameter is used to support the Shift key to extend a selection beyond the anchor point.

Moving left or right on the line is an action best deferred to the *Line* with the insertion point:

```
void far pascal LINES_GoLeft (LPLINES This, BOOL Extend)
  {
  LINE_GoLeft (This->Selection, Extend, 1);
  }

void far pascal LINES_GoRight (LPLINES This, BOOL Extend)
  {
  LINE_GoRight (This->Selection, Extend, 1);
  }
```

## Deleting and Inserting Text

The next function is invoked when text that has been selected is deleted:

```
void far pascal LINES_DeleteSelection (LPLINES This, HDC dc)
  {
```

```
if (LINE_GetIndex (This->Anchor) <= LINE_GetIndex (This->Selection))
  This->Anchor = LINE_DeleteSelection (This->Anchor, dc);
 else
  This->Anchor = LINE_DeleteSelection (This->Selection, dc);
This->Selection = This->Anchor;
This->Modified = TRUE;
InvalidateRect (This->Window, NULL, TRUE);
}
```

Again, the actual text deletion takes place in the *Line* object. (We'll show you how this works when we look at the LINE.C module.) From the *Lines'* point of view, the deletions either start from the anchor or the end of the selection, whichever happens to come first. (Remember, the user may have dragged the selection upwards rather than downwards.)

Inserting text is a similar operation:

```
void far pascal LINES_InsertText (LPLINES This, LPSTR Buffer, HDC dc)
  {
  LINES_DeleteSelection (This, dc);
  This->Anchor = LINE_InsertText (This->Selection, Buffer, dc);
  This->Selection = This->Anchor;
  This->Modified = TRUE;
  }
```

Note that *LINES_InsertText()* automatically calls *LINES_DeleteSelection()* when it starts. All inserts to the insertion point first delete the selection.

We've been maintaining the modification flag, *Modified*, by setting it to *FALSE* when loading a file and to *TRUE* when text is inserted or deleted. We also want to provide programmatic control of this flag with the next two functions:

```
void far pascal LINES_SetModified (LPLINES This, BOOL Modified)
  {
  This->Modified = Modified;
  }

BOOL far pascal LINES_GetModified (LPLINES This)
  {
  return This->Modified;
  }
```

We'll want to provide a means for programmatic determination of the selection rectangle, in terms of line numbers and character positions:

```
void far pascal LINES_GetSelectionRect (LPLINES This, LPRECT Rect)
   {
   RECT Anchor, Selection;
   LINE_GetSelectionRect (This->Anchor, &Anchor);
   LINE_GetSelectionRect (This->Selection, &Selection);
   Rect->top = Anchor.top;
   Rect->left = Anchor.left;
   Rect->bottom = Selection.bottom;
   Rect->right = Selection.right;
   }
```

Likewise, we'll want to allow programmatic setting of the selection:

```
void far pascal LINES_SetSelectionRect (LPLINES This, LPRECT Rect)
   {
   RECT Anchor, Selection;
   This->Anchor = LINE_GetIndexed (This->Anchor, Rect->top);
   This->Selection = LINE_GetIndexed (This->Anchor, Rect->bottom);
   if (Rect->top == Rect->bottom)
      {
      Anchor = *Rect;
      Selection = *Rect;
      }
   else
      {
      Anchor.left = 0;
      Anchor.right = Rect->left;
      Selection.left = Rect->right;
      Selection.right = 0;
      }
   LINE_SetSelectionRect (This->Anchor, &Anchor);
   LINE_SetSelectionRect (This->Selection, &Selection);
   }
```

The input rectangle may describe a selection of one line, or of more than one line. If a single line is involved, the *left* and *right* fields of the input rectangle refer to that one line. On the other hand, if a range of lines is indicated, the input rectangle's *left* field points to the selection start on the top line of the selection, and the *right* field points to the selection's end on the last line.

Given that there's a selection, the user may want to copy that selection into the Clipboard. We may also want to provide programmatic access to it. The following function places the selected text into a buffer:

```
void far pascal LINES_GetSelectedText (LPLINES This, LPSTR Buffer)
  {
  LPLINE Line;
  char Temp[132];
  Line =
    (LINE_GetIndex (This->Anchor) <= LINE_GetIndex (This->Selection)) ?
    This->Anchor : This->Selection;
  Buffer[0] = 0;
  while (Line && LINE_GetSelectedText (Line, Temp))
    {
    lstrcat (Buffer, Temp);
    Line = LINE_GetNext (Line);
    }
  }
```

Of course, the work is mostly delegated to each of the *Line* objects in the selection, just as it is in the next function, which retrieves *all* the text:

```
void far pascal LINES_GetText (LPLINES This, LPSTR Buffer)
  {
  LPLINE Line = This->TopLine;
  LPSTR Ptr = Buffer;
  while (Line)
    {
    Ptr = &Ptr[LINE_GetText (Line, Ptr)];
    Line = LINE_GetNext (Line);
    }
  }
```

The last components of this module are the ones that, upon command, write the contents of the control *back out* to the file from which they came:

```
static void near pascal StoreLines (LPLINES This, FILE * Stream)
  {
  LPLINE register Line = This->TopLine;
  while (Line)
    {
    LINE_Store (Line, Stream);
    Line = LINE_GetNext (Line);
      }
    }

BOOL far pascal LINES_Store (LPLINES This, LPSTR Pathname)
  {
  FILE * Stream;
  BOOL Result = FALSE;
```

```
Stream = fopen (Pathname, "wt");
if (Stream)
   {
   StoreLines (This, Stream);
   fclose (Stream);
   Result = TRUE;
   This->Modified = FALSE;
   }
return Result;
}
```

Unlike *LINES_Load()*, *LINES_Unload()* doesn't do the work itself. That's because when the text was being read from the file, the *Line* objects didn't exist yet. Now they do, however, and each one can "write itself" to the output file. The *Lines* collection handles the housekeeping—opening and closing the file—and making sure the *Line* objects write themselves in the correct order.

## LINE.H

As the *Lines* object has been enhanced for editing, so has the *Line* object. Here is the entire header file:

```
#ifndef _LINE_H_
#define _LINE_H_

#include <windows.h>
#include <stdio.h>
#include "block.h"

typedef struct tagLine
   {
   struct tagLine far * Prev;
   struct tagLine far * Next;
   int Index;
   int CharCount;
   int Height;
   int Anchor,
     Selection;
   BOOL Left;
   char Text[132];
   } LINE, far * LPLINE;

LPLINE far pascal LINE_Alloc (LPSTR Buffer, HDC dc);
void far pascal LINE_InsertBefore (LPLINE This, LPLINE Next);
void far pascal LINE_InsertAfter (LPLINE This, LPLINE Prev);
```

```
void far pascal LINE_Append (LPLINE This, LPLINE Root);
LPLINE far pascal LINE_GetFirst (LPLINE This);
LPLINE far pascal LINE_GetLast (LPLINE This);
LPLINE far pascal LINE_GetIndexed (LPLINE This, int Index);
LPLINE far pascal LINE_GetNext (LPLINE This);
LPLINE far pascal LINE_GetPrev (LPLINE This);
int far pascal LINE_GetHeight (LPLINE Line);
int far pascal LINE_GetIndex (LPLINE This);
void far pascal LINE_Remove (LPLINE This);
LPLINE far pascal LINE_Free (LPLINE This);
void far pascal LINE_Display (LPLINE This, HDC dc, LPPOINT Start);
void far pascal LINE_ResetSelection (LPLINE This);
void far pascal LINE_DropAnchor
    (
    LPLINE This,
    HDC dc,
    int x
    );
int far pascal LINE_GetCaretPoint (LPLINE This, HDC dc);
void far pascal LINE_ExtendRight
    (
    LPLINE This,
    HDC dc,
    int x
    );
void far pascal LINE_ExtendLeft
    (
    LPLINE This,
    HDC dc,
    int x
    );
void far pascal LINE_GoLeft (LPLINE This, BOOL Extend, int Count);
void far pascal LINE_GoRight (LPLINE This, BOOL Extend, int Count);
LPLINE far pascal LINE_DeleteSelection (LPLINE This, HDC dc);
LPLINE far pascal LINE_InsertText (LPLINE This, LPSTR Text, HDC dc);
void far pascal LINE_GetSelectionRect (LPLINE This, LPRECT Rect);
void far pascal LINE_SetSelectionRect (LPLINE This, LPRECT Rect);
BOOL far pascal LINE_GetSelectedText (LPLINE This, LPSTR Buffer);
int far pascal LINE_GetText (LPLINE This, LPSTR Buffer);
void far pascal LINE_Store (LPLINE This, FILE * Stream);
```

```
#endif
```

As we planned, *Anchor* and *Selection* fields are provided to help us track selected text. In addition, new functions have been added to support editing features, as we'll see next.

## LINE.C

The first function that appears in LINE.C is *LINE_Alloc()*. Its job is to initialize the additional fields, as well as the original ones:

```c
#include "line.h"
#define _offsetin(struc, fld) ((WORD)&(((struc *)0)->fld))

LPLINE far pascal LINE_Alloc (LPSTR Buffer, HDC dc)
   {
   register Count = lstrlen (Buffer);
   LPLINE Line = GetMem (_offsetin (LINE, Text) + Count + 1);
   TEXTMETRIC tm;
   Line->Prev = NULL;
   Line->Next = NULL;
   Line->Index = 0;
   Line->CharCount = Count;
   Line->Anchor =
   Line->Selection = 0;
   Line->Left = FALSE;
   lstrcpy (Line->Text, Buffer);
   GetTextMetrics (dc, &tm);
   Line->Height = HIWORD (GetTextExtent (dc,
     Count ? Buffer : " ",
     Count ? Count : 1));
   Line->Height += tm.tmExternalLeading;
   return Line;
   }
```

The next several functions are copied directly from the previous chapter, and are reproduced here solely for completeness' sake:

```c
static void near pascal ReindexFrom (LPLINE This)
   {
   LPLINE register This_ = This;
   LPLINE Prev = This_->Prev;
   register i = Prev ? Prev->Index : 0;
   while (This_)
      {
      This_->Index = ++i;
      This_ = This_->Next;
      }
   }


void far pascal LINE_InsertBefore (LPLINE This, LPLINE Next)
   {
```

```
    LPLINE Prev = Next ? Next->Prev : NULL;
    if (Prev)
       Prev->Next = This;
    This->Prev = Prev;
    This->Next = Next;
    if (Next)
       Next->Prev = This;
    ReindexFrom (This);
    }

void far pascal LINE_InsertAfter (LPLINE This, LPLINE Prev)
    {
    LPLINE Next = Prev ? Prev->Next : NULL;
    if (Prev)
       Prev->Next = This;
    This->Prev = Prev;
    This->Next = Next;
    if (Next)
       Next->Prev = This;
    ReindexFrom (This);
    }

void far pascal LINE_Append (LPLINE This, LPLINE Prev)
    {
    if (Prev)
       {
       Prev->Next = This;
       This->Index = Prev->Index + 1;
       }
    else
       This->Index = 1;
    This->Prev = Prev;
    This->Next = NULL;
    }

LPLINE far pascal LINE_GetFirst (LPLINE This)
    {
    register LPLINE This_ = This;
    while (This_ && This_->Prev)
       This_ = This_->Prev;
    return This_;
    }

LPLINE far pascal LINE_GetLast (LPLINE This)
    {
    register LPLINE This_ = This;
    while (This_ && This_->Next)
       This_ = This_->Next;
    return This_;
    }
```

```
LPLINE far pascal LINE_GetIndexed (LPLINE This, int Index)
   {
   register LPLINE This_ = This;
   while (This_ && (This_->Index > Index))
     This_ = This_->Prev;
   while (This_ && (This_->Index < Index))
     This_ = This_->Next;
   return This_;
   }

LPLINE far pascal LINE_GetNext (LPLINE This)
   {
   return This ? This->Next : NULL;
   }

LPLINE far pascal LINE_GetPrev (LPLINE This)
   {
   return This ? This->Prev : NULL;
   }

int far pascal LINE_GetHeight (LPLINE This)
   {
   return This->Height;
   }

int far pascal LINE_GetIndex (LPLINE This)
   {
   return This ? This->Index : -1;
   }

void far pascal LINE_Remove (LPLINE This)
   {
   LPLINE register Prev = This->Prev;
   LPLINE register Next = This->Next;
   This->Prev = NULL;
   This->Next = NULL;
   if (Prev)
     Prev->Next = Next;
   if (Next)
     {
     Next->Prev = Prev;
     ReindexFrom (Next);
     }
   }

LPLINE far pascal LINE_Free (LPLINE This)
   {
   LINE_Remove (This);
   FreeMem ((LPSTR) This);
   return NULL;
   }
```

However, *LINE_Display()* is now much more complex than it was. The reason is that a line is no longer displayed in just one color; if a portion of a line is selected, that portion must be displayed in the colors the user has chosen for selected text. The selection could occur at the beginning, middle, or end of a line; it can span lines as well. The following code produces the desired result:

```
void far pascal LINE_Display (LPLINE This, HDC dc, LPPOINT Start)
   {
   register x = Start->x;
   register SelStart, SelStop;

   if (This->Left)
      {
      SelStart = This->Selection;
      SelStop = This->CharCount;
      }
   else if (This->Anchor < This->Selection)
      {
      SelStart = This->Anchor;
      SelStop = This->Selection;
      }
   else
      {
      SelStart = This->Selection;
      SelStop = This->Anchor;
      }

   // Write any characters prior to a selection
   if (SelStart > 0)
      x += LOWORD (TabbedTextOut (dc,
         x, Start->y,
         &This->Text[0],
         SelStart,
         0, NULL,
         Start->x));

   // Write the selection if there is one
   if (SelStop > 0)
      {
      COLORREF OldTextColor, OldBkColor;
      OldTextColor = SetTextColor (dc, GetSysColor (COLOR_HIGHLIGHTTEXT));
      OldBkColor = SetBkColor (dc, GetSysColor (COLOR_HIGHLIGHT));
      x += LOWORD (TabbedTextOut (dc,
         x, Start->y,
         &This->Text[SelStart],
         SelStop - SelStart,
         0, NULL,
```

```
         Start->x));
     SetTextColor (dc, OldTextColor);
     SetBkColor (dc, OldBkColor);
     }

  // Write the remaining characters
  if (SelStop < This->CharCount)
    TabbedTextOut (dc,
        x, Start->y,
        &This->Text[SelStop],
        This->CharCount - SelStop,
        0, NULL,
        Start->x);

  Start->y += This->Height;
  }
```

The function begins by identifying the beginning and end of a selection, if there is one on this line. (According to our design, remember, a selection can span lines, but the portion of each line that is selected is marked at the *Line* level.) Conceptually, every line begins with an unselected portion—which may be of zero length—followed by a selected portion, which again may be of zero length. Any characters remaining on the line after the selection are then displayed using the colors for unselected text. This allows us to treat lines with a selection and without one, in the same way.

Resetting the selected area of a line means setting the *Selection* field to be the same as the *Anchor* field, and setting the *Left* direction flag to *FALSE:*

```
void far pascal LINE_ResetSelection (LPLINE This)
  {
  This->Selection = This->Anchor;
  This->Left = FALSE;
  }
```

The first step in marking a selection is to drop the selection anchor. To do this, we'll have to first convert from a point in the client area to the corresponding character within the line:

```
static int near pascal PointToIndex (LPLINE This, HDC dc, int x)
  {
  register i;
  for (i = 0; i < This->CharCount; i++)
    if (LOWORD (GetTabbedTextExtent
        (
        dc,
        This->Text,
```

```
            i,
            0,
            NULL
            )) >= x)
        break;
    return i;
    }

void far pascal LINE_DropAnchor
    (
    LPLINE This,
    HDC dc,
    int x
    )
    {
    This->Anchor =
    This->Selection = PointToIndex (This, dc, x);
    }
```

Of course, we'll also need to convert back to the screen coordinates to properly position the caret:

```
int far pascal LINE_GetCaretPoint (LPLINE This, HDC dc)
    {
    return LOWORD (GetTabbedTextExtent (dc,
      This->Text, This->Selection,
      0, NULL));
    }
```

Once the anchor is dropped, the user may drag in either direction—up or down. Depending on the direction in which the user drags, the *Left* direction flag will or will not be set:

```
void far pascal LINE_ExtendRight
    (
    LPLINE This,
    HDC dc,
    int x
    )
    {
    This->Left = FALSE;
    This->Selection = PointToIndex (This, dc, x);
    }

void far pascal LINE_ExtendLeft
    (
    LPLINE This,
```

```
    HDC dc,
    int x
    )
{
This->Left = TRUE;
This->Selection = PointToIndex (This, dc, x);
}
```

The selection may also be extended in either direction by using the arrow keys. In such a case, the extension is done by character count, rather than a physical location:

```
void far pascal LINE_GoLeft (LPLINE This, BOOL Extend, int Count)
  {
  This->Selection -= Count;
  if (This->Selection < 0)
    This->Selection = 0;
  if (! Extend)
    This->Anchor = This->Selection;
  }

void far pascal LINE_GoRight (LPLINE This, BOOL Extend, int Count)
  {
  This->Selection += Count;
  if (This->Selection > This->CharCount)
    This->Selection = This->CharCount;
  if (! Extend)
    This->Anchor = This->Selection;
  }
```

Deleting the selection means identifying its start and stop locations on the line:

```
LPLINE far pascal LINE_DeleteSelection (LPLINE This, HDC dc)
  {
  LPLINE register Prev;
  register SelStart, SelStop;
  char Buffer[132];
  while (This && (This->Anchor || This->Selection))
    {
    Prev = This;
    if (This->Left)
      {
      SelStart = This->Selection;
      SelStop = This->CharCount;
      }
    else if (This->Anchor < This->Selection)
```

```
         {
      SelStart = This->Anchor;
      SelStop = This->Selection;
      }
   else
      {
      SelStart = This->Selection;
      SelStop = This->Anchor;
      }
   This = This->Next;
   }
This = Prev;

if (SelStart == SelStop)
   if (SelStop < This->CharCount)
      SelStop++;

_fstrcpy (Buffer, &This->Text[0]);
Buffer[SelStart] = 0;
lstrcat (Buffer, &This->Text[SelStop]);

if ((lstrlen (Buffer) > 0) ||
    (This->Anchor && This->Selection))
   {
   LPLINE NewLine;
   NewLine = LINE_Alloc (Buffer, dc);
   NewLine->Anchor = This->Anchor;
   NewLine->Selection = NewLine->Anchor;
   LINE_InsertBefore (NewLine, This);
   LINE_Free (This);
   This = NewLine;
   }
else
   {
   LINE_Free (This);
   This = Prev;
   }

return This;
}
```

If a portion of the line was deleted, as opposed to the entire line, then the remainder is copied into a new *Line* object which then replaces the old one.

A new *Line* must also replace an old one if text is being added at the insertion point:

```
LPLINE far pascal LINE_InsertText (LPLINE This, LPSTR Text, HDC dc)
   {
```

```
   char Buffer[132];
   register SelStart, SelStop;
   LPLINE NewLine;

   if (This->Left)
      {
      SelStart = This->Selection;
      SelStop = This->CharCount;
      }
   else if (This->Anchor < This->Selection)
      {
      SelStart = This->Anchor;
      SelStop = This->Selection;
      }
   else
      {
      SelStart = This->Selection;
      SelStop = This->Anchor;
      }

   _fstrcpy (Buffer, &This->Text[0]);
   Buffer[SelStart] = 0;
   lstrcat (Buffer, Text);
   lstrcat (Buffer, &This->Text[SelStop]);

   NewLine = LINE_Alloc (Buffer, dc);
   NewLine->Anchor = This->Anchor + lstrlen (Buffer);
   NewLine->Selection = NewLine->Anchor;

   LINE_InsertBefore (NewLine, This);
   LINE_Free (This);

   return NewLine;
   }
```

We'll have to provide for programmatic reading of the selection points of a given line:

```
void far pascal LINE_GetSelection (LPLINE This, LPRECT Rect)
   {
   Rect->top =
   Rect->bottom = This->Index;
   if (This->Left)
      {
      Rect->left = This->Selection;
      Rect->right = This->Anchor;
      }
   else
```

```
      {
      Rect->left = This->Anchor;
      Rect->right = This->Selection;
      }
    }
```

And we'll have to allow programmatic setting of the selection, as well:

```
void far pascal LINE_SetSelection (LPLINE This, LPRECT Rect)
  {
  This->Left = FALSE;
  This->Anchor = Rect->left;
  This->Selection = Rect->right;
  }
```

To implement copying the selected text into the Clipboard, we'll need to be able to copy the selected text into a buffer:

```
BOOL far pascal LINE_GetSelectedText (LPLINE This, LPSTR Buffer)
  {
  BOOL Result = FALSE;
  if (This->Anchor || This->Selection)
    {
    register SelStart, SelStop;
    if (This->Left)
      {
      SelStart = This->Selection;
      SelStop = This->CharCount;
      }
    else if (This->Anchor < This->Selection)
      {
      SelStart = This->Anchor;
      SelStop = This->Selection;
      }
    else
      {
      SelStart = This->Selection;
      SelStop = This->Anchor;
      }
    lstrcpy (Buffer, This->Text);
    Buffer[SelStop] = 0;
    lstrcpy (Buffer, &Buffer[SelStart]);
    if (SelStop == This->CharCount)
      lstrcat (Buffer, "\n");
    Result = TRUE;
    }
  return Result;
  }
```

We also want to allow the entire text of a given line to be retrieved:

```
int far pascal LINE_GetText (LPLINE This, LPSTR Buffer)
  {
  lstrcpy (Buffer, This->Text);
  lstrcat (Buffer, "\n");
  return lstrlen (Buffer);
  }
```

The only thing left for a *Line* to do, then, is to store itself onto disk when the *Lines* collection requests it:

```
void far pascal LINE_Store (LPLINE This, FILE * Stream)
  {
  fwrite (This->Text, 1, This->CharCount, Stream);
  fwrite ("\n", 1, 1, Stream);
  }
```

## VIEW.H

As with *Lines* and *Line* objects, the *View* object starts off as it was in the TextFileViiew control, with new functions added to support the caret and text selection. Here is the entire header file, VIEW.H:

```
#ifndef _VIEW_H_
#define _VIEW_H_

#include <windows.h>
#include "line.h"

typedef struct
  {
  HWND Window;
  int Width, Height;
  int LeftMargin;
  LPLINE TopVisibleLine;
  } VIEW, far * LPVIEW;

void far pascal VIEW_Init
    (
    LPVIEW View,
    HWND Window,
    int LeftMargin
    );
void far pascal VIEW_SetSize
    (
    LPVIEW View,
```

```
    int Width,
    int Height
    );
void far pascal VIEW_SetTopVisibleLine (LPVIEW View, LPLINE Line);
LPLINE far pascal VIEW_GetTopVisibleLine (LPVIEW View);
void far pascal VIEW_Display (LPVIEW View, HDC dc);
LPLINE far pascal VIEW_PageUp (LPVIEW View);
LPLINE far pascal VIEW_PageDown (LPVIEW View);
LPLINE far pascal VIEW_FindLineFromPoint (LPVIEW View, LPPOINT Point);
int far pascal VIEW_GetLeftMargin (LPVIEW View);
void far pascal VIEW_SetLeftMargin (LPVIEW View, int LeftMargin);
POINT far pascal VIEW_GetCaretPoint
    (
    LPVIEW View,
    LPLINE Selection,
    HDC dc
    );
void far pascal VIEW_ScrollCaretIntoView
    (
    LPVIEW View,
    LPLINE Selection,
    HDC dc
    );

#endif
```

## VIEW.C

The source code in VIEW.C also begins identically to the source code in the TEXTFILEVIEW control:

```
#include "view.h"

void far pascal VIEW_Init
    (
    LPVIEW View,
    HWND Window,
    int LeftMargin
    )
  {
  View->Window = Window;
  VIEW_SetLeftMargin (View, LeftMargin);
  View->TopVisibleLine = NULL;
  }


void far pascal VIEW_SetSize
    (
```

```
    LPVIEW View,
    int Width,
    int Height
    )
  {
  View->Width = Width;
  View->Height = Height;
  }

void far pascal VIEW_SetTopVisibleLine (LPVIEW View, LPLINE Line)
  {
  View->TopVisibleLine = Line;
  }

LPLINE far pascal VIEW_GetTopVisibleLine (LPVIEW View)
  {
  return View->TopVisibleLine;
  }

void far pascal VIEW_Display (LPVIEW View, HDC dc)
  {
  LPLINE register Line = View->TopVisibleLine;
  POINT Start;
  Start.y = 0;
  Start.x = View->LeftMargin;
  while (Line && (Start.y <= View->Height))
    {
    LINE_Display (Line, dc, &Start);
    Line = Line->Next;
    }
  }

LPLINE far pascal VIEW_PageUp (LPVIEW View)
  {
  LPLINE Line = View->TopVisibleLine;
  register y = 0;
  while (Line)
    {
    y += LINE_GetHeight (Line);
    if (y > View->Height)
      break;
    Line = Line->Prev;
    }
  if (Line && Line->Next)
    Line = Line->Next;
  if (! Line)
    Line = LINE_GetFirst (View->TopVisibleLine);
  return Line;
  }
```

```
LPLINE far pascal VIEW_PageDown (LPVIEW View)
  {
  LPLINE Line = View->TopVisibleLine;
  register y = 0;
  while (Line)
    {
    y += LINE_GetHeight (Line);
    if (y > View->Height)
      break;
    Line = Line->Next;
    }
  if (Line && Line->Prev)
    Line = Line->Prev;
  if (! Line)
    Line = LINE_GetLast (View->TopVisibleLine);
  return Line;
  }
```

For editing, it will often be necessary to determine which *Line* lies at a given screen location:

```
LPLINE far pascal VIEW_FindLineFromPoint (LPVIEW View, LPPOINT Point)
  {
  LPLINE Line = View->TopVisibleLine;
  register h = 0;
  Point->x -= View->LeftMargin;
  if (Point->x < 0)
    Point->x = 0;
  while (Line)
    {
    h += LINE_GetHeight (Line);
    if (h >= Point->y)
      break;
    Line = LINE_GetNext (Line);
    }
  return Line;
  }
```

The left margin must also be available for programmatic query and change:

```
int far pascal VIEW_GetLeftMargin (LPVIEW View)
  {
  return View->LeftMargin;
  }
```

```
void far pascal VIEW_SetLeftMargin (LPVIEW View, int LeftMargin)
    {
    View->LeftMargin = LeftMargin;
    }
```

We'll also need to determine the current insertion point so we'll know
where to place the caret:

```
POINT far pascal VIEW_GetCaretPoint
     (
     LPVIEW View,
     LPLINE Selection,
     HDC dc
     )
    {
    register POINT Point;
    LPLINE Line = View->TopVisibleLine;
    if (LINE_GetIndex (Selection) < LINE_GetIndex (Line))
       Point.x = Point.y = -10000;
    else
       {
       Point.x = Point.y = 0;
       while (Line && (Line != Selection))
          {
          Point.y += LINE_GetHeight (Line);
          if (Point.y > View->Height)
             {
             Point.y = -10000;
              return Point;
             }
          Line = LINE_GetNext (Line);
          }
       Point.x = LINE_GetCaretPoint (Line, dc);
       }
    return Point;
    }
```

Notice that we don't bother to calculate the caret position if it won't be
in the visible part of the window.

Given that the caret is somewhere in the "virtual" view, perhaps lying
beyond the extent of the physical porthole, the *View* object may be requested to scroll the part of the text containing the caret into view:

```
void far pascal VIEW_ScrollCaretIntoView
     (
     LPVIEW View,
```

```
      LPLINE Selection,
      HDC dc
      )
  {
  POINT Point = VIEW_GetCaretPoint (View, Selection, dc);
  if (LINE_GetIndex (View->TopVisibleLine) < LINE_GetIndex (Selection))
     while (Point.y < 0)
        {
        View->TopVisibleLine = LINE_GetNext (View->TopVisibleLine);
        Point = VIEW_GetCaretPoint (View, Selection, dc);
        }
  else
     View->TopVisibleLine = Selection;
  }
```

As you look at these functions, it may occur to you that you don't know from where they are going to be called. As they move toward object-oriented programming, a lot of people become concerned, feeling that the "big picture" is slipping away from them. But this, too, is a feature of encapsulation. You aren't *supposed* to look at the "big picture," except as it is implemented in your "application object"—a level represented by the message switch in the MAIN.C module, which we haven't seen yet. When dealing with the *View* object, you don't need to concern yourself with what other object might want the *View* to scroll the line containing the caret into sight. You content yourself with giving the *View* object the ability to perform this task if asked. Later, when you *do* encounter a situation where this ability is needed, well—there it is, simply another tool in your toolbox.

## TEXTEDIT.BAS

The TEXTEDIT.BAS module has a very simple job: It saves the Visual Basic programmer from having to remember the one numeric value required by the *Action* property. Here is the entire content of the module:

```
Global Const Action_STOREDATA = 1
```

We'll grant you, creating a whole module to house a single constant seems a tad overblown. But sometimes principles are worth following even when, occasionally, they seem unnecessary. If you always include a .BAS module with any visual control that defines constants, your users (visual programmers) will always know where to find those constants. Sure, TextFileEdit only has one; but some other control—or even a future version of TextFileEdit that you, yourself, create—may have a dozen or more. By following this consistent naming convention, and making sure the module is always supplied, you'll never have to waste time trying to find one. (Of course, we aren't *totally* neurotic. In other controls where this module would have been empty, we did omit it.)

## INTERNAL.H

This header file is used internally to enforce consistent use of inter-segment functions, and to provide IDs for the controls in the dialog boxes referenced by the DIALOG.C module. Here is the entire file:

```c
#include <windows.h>
#include "TEXTEDIT.H"
#include <vbapi.h>
#include <custcntl.h>
#include <string.h>
#include <direct.h>
#include <stdlib.h>
#include "block.h"
#include "dc.h"
#include "line.h"
#include "lines.h"
#include "view.h"

#ifdef MAIN
HINSTANCE LibInstance = 0;
char far * ClassName = "TextFileEdit";
#else
extern HINSTANCE LibInstance;
extern char far * ClassName;
#endif

typedef struct
    {
    struct
        {
        UINT :16;
        } CustomStyles;
    struct
        {
        UINT TabStop: 1;
        UINT Group: 1;
        UINT Thickframe: 1;
        UINT SysMenu: 1;
        UINT HScroll: 1;
        UINT VScroll: 1;
        UINT DlgFrame: 1;
```

```
        UINT Border: 1;
        UINT Maximize: 1;
        UINT ChipChildren: 1;
        UINT ClipSiblings: 1;
        UINT Disabled: 1;
        UINT Visible: 1;
        UINT Minimize: 1;
        UINT Child: 1;
        UINT Popup: 1;
        } StdStyles;
    } STYLEBITS, FAR * LPSTYLEBITS;

typedef struct
    {
    DC   DeviceContext;
    CARET  Caret;
    LINES  Lines;
    VIEW View;
    BOOL Dragging;
    } MYDATA, far * LPMYDATA;

#define IDC_STATIC 0
#define IDC_GROUPBOX1 110
#define IDC_CAPTION 101
#define IDC_ID 102
#define IDC_BORDER 103
#define IDC_DISABLED 104
#define IDC_GROUP 105
#define IDC_TABSTOP 106
#define IDC_HSCROLL 107
#define IDC_VSCROLL 108
#define IDC_VISIBLE 109

HSZ far pascal GetAboutPropertyString (HCTL Control);
HWND far pascal PopupAbout (void);
void far pascal RegisterVbPopups (void);
void far pascal UnregisterVbPopups (void);
LPSTR far pascal HelpFileName (void);
BOOL far pascal vbm_Help
    (
    HWND Window,
    BYTE HelpType,
    BYTE i,
    PPROPINFO Properties[],
    PEVENTINFO Events[]
    );
```

```
void far pascal RegisterFileDlgPopup (void);
void far pascal UnregisterFileDlgPopup (void);
HWND far pascal PopupFileDlg
    (
    HCTL Control_,
    HWND Window,
    LPSTR Title,
    int PropertyIndex_,
    LPSTR Filters,
    int FilterIndex,
    LPSTR DefaultExt,
    DWORD Flags
    );
```

```
#define Action_STOREDATA 1
```

INTERNAL.H follows the pattern we've presented in the preceding chapters, particularly the TextFileView chapter. The *MyData* structure does have new members: *Device Context* and *Caret* objects, and a *Dragging* flag that will help implement text selection by mouse. Another addition to the file is the *Action_STOREDATA* define at the end. We'll see that used when we look at the VISUAL.C module, shortly.

## MAIN.C

This module contains the main code for the TextFileEdit control. It is based on the MAIN.C module described in Chapter 9. This time, a few extra objects in the *MyData* structure need to be initialized:

```
#define MAIN
#include "Internal.H"

#define GWL_MYDATA 0
#define GWW_EXTRA 4

static void near pascal NotifyParent
    (
    HWND  Window,
    WORD  Notification
    )
  {
  SendMessage (GetParent (Window),
    WM_COMMAND,
    GetWindowWord (Window, GWW_ID),
```

```
          MAKELONG (Window, Notification));
    }


#pragma argsused
static BOOL near pascal wm_NcCreate (HWND Window, LPCREATESTRUCT Create)
    {
    LPMYDATA MyData = (LPMYDATA) calloc (1, sizeof (MYDATA));
    if ((! MyData) || (! InitMem()))
       return FALSE;
    SetWindowLong (Window, GWL_MYDATA, (long) MyData);
    return TRUE;
    }


static long near pascal wm_SetText (HWND Window, LPSTR Buffer);


static void near pascal wm_Create (HWND Window, LPCREATESTRUCT Create)
    {
    LPMYDATA MyData = (LPMYDATA) GetWindowLong (Window, GWL_MYDATA);
    DC_Init (&MyData->DeviceContext, Window);
    CARET_Init (&MyData->Caret, Window);
    LINES_Init (&MyData->Lines, Window,
      &MyData->Caret);
    VIEW_Init (&MyData->View, Window,
      GetSystemMetrics (SM_CXVSCROLL) / 3);
    CARET_SetLeftMargin (&MyData->Caret,
      VIEW_GetLeftMargin (&MyData->View));
    MyData->Dragging = FALSE;
    if (Create->lpszName && Create->lpszName[0])
      wm_SetText (Window, (LPSTR) Create->lpszName);
    }
```

Application termination also proceeds along familiar lines:

```
static void near pascal wm_Destroy (HWND Window)
    {
    LPMYDATA MyData = (LPMYDATA) GetWindowLong (Window, GWL_MYDATA);
    }


static void near pascal wm_NcDestroy (HWND Window)
    {
    LPMYDATA MyData = (LPMYDATA) GetWindowLong (Window, GWL_MYDATA);
    free (MyData);
    TermMem();
    }
```

The next two functions are copied, unchanged:

```
static void near pascal wm_Size (HWND Window, int Width, int Height)
  {
  LPMYDATA MyData = (LPMYDATA) GetWindowLong (Window, GWL_MYDATA);
  VIEW_SetSize (&MyData->View, Width, Height);
  }

static long near pascal wm_GetDlgCode (HWND Window)
  {
  LPMYDATA MyData = (LPMYDATA) GetWindowLong (Window, GWL_MYDATA);
  return DLGC_STATIC;
  }
```

However, notice how the code for getting and setting the font have changed since we added a *DeviceContext* object to *MyData*:

```
static void near pascal wm_SetFont (HWND Window, HFONT NewFont, BOOL Repaint)
  {
  LPMYDATA MyData = (LPMYDATA) GetWindowLong (Window, GWL_MYDATA);
  if (NewFont != DC_GetFont (&MyData->DeviceContext))
    {
    DC_SetFont (&MyData->DeviceContext, NewFont);
    if (Repaint)
      {
      InvalidateRect (Window, NULL, TRUE);
      UpdateWindow (Window);
      }
    }
  }

static HFONT near pascal wm_GetFont (HWND Window)
  {
  LPMYDATA MyData = (LPMYDATA) GetWindowLong (Window, GWL_MYDATA);
  return DC_GetFont (&MyData->DeviceContext);
  }
```

Likewise, the *wm_Paint()* function is simplified since the code for modifying the passed device context no longer resides there:

```
static void near pascal wm_Paint (HWND Window)
  {
  LPMYDATA MyData = (LPMYDATA) GetWindowLong (Window, GWL_MYDATA);
  PAINTSTRUCT ps;
  HDC dc = BeginPaint (Window, &ps);
```

```
    HBRUSH NewBrush = (HBRUSH) SendMessage (GetParent (Window),
      WM_CTLCOLOR,
      dc,
      MAKELONG (Window, CTLCOLOR_BTN));
    if (NewBrush && (NewBrush != DC_GetBrush (&MyData->DeviceContext)))
      DC_SetBrush (&MyData->DeviceContext, NewBrush);
    VIEW_Display (&MyData->View, DC_Use (&MyData->DeviceContext, dc));
    DC_Release (&MyData->DeviceContext);
    EndPaint (Window, &ps);
    }
```

The work of verifying and opening the input file hasn't changed:

```
static BOOL near pascal FileExists (LPSTR Pathname)
    {
    OFSTRUCT of;
    return (OpenFile (Pathname, &of, OF_EXIST) != HFILE_ERROR);
    }


static long near pascal wm_SetText (HWND Window, LPSTR Buffer)
    {
    LPMYDATA MyData = (LPMYDATA) GetWindowLong (Window, GWL_MYDATA);
    if (FileExists (Buffer))
      {
      LINES_Load (&MyData->Lines, Buffer,
        DC_Get (&MyData->DeviceContext));
      VIEW_SetTopVisibleLine (&MyData->View,
        LINES_GetTopLine (&MyData->Lines));
      InvalidateRect (Window, NULL, TRUE);
      return DefWindowProc (Window, WM_SETTEXT, 0, (long) Buffer);
      }
    else
      {
      LINES_DeleteAll (&MyData->Lines);
      InvalidateRect (Window, NULL, TRUE);
      return DefWindowProc (Window, WM_SETTEXT, 0, (long) "");
      }
    }
```

## Supporting Scrolling

Scrolling text in the TextFileEdit control becomes a little more complex because the caret must be scrolled with the text. Therefore, we've added a little helper function, *UpdateCaret()*, to assist:

```
static void near pascal UpdateCaret (HWND Window)
  {
  LPMYDATA MyData = (LPMYDATA) GetWindowLong (Window, GWL_MYDATA);
  register HDC dc = DC_Get (&MyData->DeviceContext);
  CARET_SetPosition (&MyData->Caret,
    VIEW_GetCaretPoint (&MyData->View,
      LINES_GetSelection (&MyData->Lines),
      dc));
  DC_Release (&MyData->DeviceContext);
  }

static void near pascal wm_VScroll (HWND Window, WORD Code, int Position)
  {
  LPMYDATA MyData = (LPMYDATA) GetWindowLong (Window, GWL_MYDATA);
  LPLINE Line = VIEW_GetTopVisibleLine (&MyData->View);
  switch (Code)
    {
    case SB_TOP:
      if (Line = LINES_GetTopLine (&MyData->Lines))
        VIEW_SetTopVisibleLine (&MyData->View, Line);
      break;
    case SB_BOTTOM:
      if (Line = LINE_GetLast (Line))
        VIEW_SetTopVisibleLine (&MyData->View, Line);
      break;
    case SB_LINEUP:
      if (Line = LINE_GetPrev (Line))
        VIEW_SetTopVisibleLine (&MyData->View, Line);
      break;
    case SB_LINEDOWN:
      if (Line = LINE_GetNext (Line))
        VIEW_SetTopVisibleLine (&MyData->View, Line);
      break;
    case SB_PAGEUP:
      if (Line = VIEW_PageUp (&MyData->View))
        VIEW_SetTopVisibleLine (&MyData->View, Line);
      break;
    case SB_PAGEDOWN:
      if (Line = VIEW_PageDown (&MyData->View))
        VIEW_SetTopVisibleLine (&MyData->View, Line);
      break;
    case SB_THUMBTRACK:
      if (Line = LINE_GetIndexed (Line, Position))
        VIEW_SetTopVisibleLine (&MyData->View, Line);
      break;
    }
  if (Line)
    {
```

```
register OldTopLine = GetScrollPos (Window, SB_VERT);
register NewTopLine = LINE_GetIndex (Line);
if (OldTopLine != NewTopLine)
  {
  SetScrollPos (Window, SB_VERT, NewTopLine, TRUE);
  UpdateCaret (Window);
  InvalidateRect (Window, NULL, TRUE);
  UpdateWindow (Window);
  }
 }
}
```

Remember the *VIEW_ScrollCaretIntoView()* function? You may have been wondering where it might get used. We're a little closer to answering this question now:

```
static void near pascal ScrollCaretIntoView (HWND Window, LPMYDATA MyData)
  {
  register HDC dc = DC_Get (&MyData->DeviceContext);
  VIEW_ScrollCaretIntoView (&MyData->View,
    LINES_GetSelection (&MyData->Lines),
    dc);
  CARET_SetPosition (&MyData->Caret,
    VIEW_GetCaretPoint (&MyData->View,
      LINES_GetSelection (&MyData->Lines),
      dc));
  DC_Release ( &MyData->DeviceContext);
  InvalidateRect (Window, NULL, TRUE);
  }
```

But when exactly will this helper function be called? Well, special keys such as Home and End no longer affect text scrolling as they did with the TextFileView control. In TextFileEdit, these keys control the caret; when the caret is moved, it should be brought into view:

```
static void near pascal wm_KeyDown (HWND Window, WORD Key)
  {
  LPMYDATA MyData = (LPMYDATA) GetWindowLong (Window, GWL_MYDATA);
  BOOL Shifted = GetKeyState (VK_SHIFT) >> 15;
  switch (Key)
    {
    case VK_HOME:
      LINES_GoHome (&MyData->Lines, Shifted,
        DC_Get (&MyData->DeviceContext));
      DC_Release (&MyData->DeviceContext);
```

```
      ScrollCaretIntoView (Window, MyData);
      break;
    case VK_END:
      LINES_GoEnd (&MyData->Lines, Shifted,
        DC_Get (&MyData->DeviceContext));
      DC_Release (&MyData->DeviceContext);
      ScrollCaretIntoView (Window, MyData);
      break;
    case VK_UP:
      LINES_GoUp (&MyData->Lines, Shifted,
        DC_Get (&MyData->DeviceContext));
      DC_Release (&MyData->DeviceContext);
      ScrollCaretIntoView (Window, MyData);
      break;
    case VK_DOWN:
      LINES_GoDown (&MyData->Lines, Shifted,
        DC_Get (&MyData->DeviceContext));
      DC_Release (&MyData->DeviceContext);
      ScrollCaretIntoView (Window, MyData);
      break;
    case VK_LEFT:
      LINES_GoLeft (&MyData->Lines, Shifted);
      ScrollCaretIntoView (Window, MyData);
      break;
    case VK_RIGHT:
      LINES_GoRight (&MyData->Lines, Shifted);
      ScrollCaretIntoView (Window, MyData);
      break;
    case VK_PRIOR:
      wm_VScroll (Window, SB_PAGEUP, 0);
      break;
    case VK_NEXT:
      wm_VScroll (Window, SB_PAGEDOWN, 0);
      break;
    case VK_DELETE:
      LINES_DeleteSelection (&MyData->Lines,
        DC_Get (&MyData->DeviceContext));
      DC_Release (&MyData->DeviceContext);
      ScrollCaretIntoView (Window, MyData);
      break;
    }
  }
```

As noted earlier, the *Caret* object must be informed of when the window gets and loses the input focus. This is required because the physical caret must be "created" and "destroyed" when the window gets or loses the focus:

```
static void near pascal wm_SetFocus (HWND Window)
  {
  LPMYDATA MyData = (LPMYDATA) GetWindowLong (Window, GWL_MYDATA);
  CARET_GetFocus (&MyData->Caret);
  NotifyParent (Window, TEN_SETFOCUS);
  }

static void near pascal wm_KillFocus (HWND Window)
  {
  LPMYDATA MyData = (LPMYDATA) GetWindowLong (Window, GWL_MYDATA);
  CARET_LoseFocus (&MyData->Caret);
  NotifyParent (Window, TEN_KILLFOCUS);
  }
```

## Supporting Text Selection

Supporting text selection by mouse requires handling several different messages. First, when the left mouse button is pressed, the selection process begins:

```
static void near pascal wm_LButtonDown (HWND Window, POINT Point)
  {
  LPMYDATA MyData = (LPMYDATA) GetWindowLong (Window, GWL_MYDATA);
  LPLINE Line = VIEW_FindLineFromPoint (&MyData->View, &Point);
  register HDC dc = DC_Get (&MyData->DeviceContext);
  LINES_DropAnchor (&MyData->Lines, Line, dc, Point.x);
  CARET_SetPosition (&MyData->Caret,
    VIEW_GetCaretPoint (&MyData->View,
      LINES_GetSelection (&MyData->Lines),
      dc));
  DC_Release (&MyData->DeviceContext);
  MyData->Dragging = TRUE;
  }
```

Note that the *Dragging* flag from *MyData* is set by this message. That flag is used to determine whether *WM_MOUSEMOVE* messages should be ignored because they are significant only during a drag operation:

```
static void near pascal wm_MouseMove (HWND Window, POINT Point)
  {
  LPMYDATA MyData = (LPMYDATA) GetWindowLong (Window, GWL_MYDATA);
  if (MyData->Dragging)
    {
    LPLINE Line = VIEW_FindLineFromPoint (&MyData->View, &Point);
    register HDC dc = DC_Get (&MyData->DeviceContext);
```

```
        LINES_ExtendSelection (&MyData->Lines, Line, dc, Point.x);
        CARET_SetPosition (&MyData->Caret,
          VIEW_GetCaretPoint (&MyData->View,
            LINES_GetSelection (&MyData->Lines),
            dc));
        DC_Release (&MyData->DeviceContext);
        }
    }
```

Next, when the mouse button is released, the operation is completed:

```
static void near pascal wm_LButtonUp (HWND Window, POINT Point)
  {
  LPMYDATA MyData = (LPMYDATA) GetWindowLong (Window, GWL_MYDATA);
  LPLINE Line = VIEW_FindLineFromPoint (&MyData->View, &Point);
  register HDC dc = DC_Get (&MyData->DeviceContext);
  LINES_ExtendSelection (&MyData->Lines, Line, dc, Point.x);
  CARET_SetPosition (&MyData->Caret,
    VIEW_GetCaretPoint (&MyData->View,
      LINES_GetSelection (&MyData->Lines),
      dc));
  DC_Release (&MyData->DeviceContext);
  MyData->Dragging = FALSE;
  }
```

Note the similarity of how the *WM_MOUSEMOVE* and *WM_LBUTTONUP*
messages are handled. The only real difference is that the *Dragging* flag is
reset when the mouse button is released. Processing the *WM_MOUSEMOVE*
messages is only required to provide visual feedback during the dragging
operation by actually changing the selection parameters as the mouse is
positioned.

  *WM_CHAR* messages arrive when the user types some text into the
TextFileEdit control:

```
static void near pascal wm_Char (HWND Window, char Character)
  {
  LPMYDATA MyData = (LPMYDATA) GetWindowLong (Window, GWL_MYDATA);
  char Buffer[2];
  register HDC dc = DC_Get (&MyData->DeviceContext);
  Buffer[0] = Character;
  Buffer[1] = 0;
  LINES_InsertText (&MyData->Lines, Buffer, dc);
  DC_Release (&MyData->DeviceContext);
  ScrollCaretIntoView (Window, MyData);
  }
```

We simply turn the single character into a standard C-style string, and pass it to *LINES_InsertText()*. To mimic the standard edit control, we also call *ScrollCaretIntoView()* to make sure the insertion point, and therefore the new character, is visible.

## Managing Clipboard Messages

In the Skeleton control, we included references to the three Clipboard-related messages, but supplied no code to go with them. They were simply there to remind us to implement them when appropriate.

Now is the time. The three Clipboard-related messages are *WM_COPY*, *WM_CUT*, and *WM_PASTE*. Here's the function that handles the *WM_COPY* message:

```
static void near pascal wm_Copy (HWND Window)
  {
  LPMYDATA MyData = (LPMYDATA) GetWindowLong (Window, GWL_MYDATA);
  if (OpenClipboard (Window))
    {
    HANDLE h = GlobalAlloc (GMEM_DDESHARE, 0xFFFF);
    LPSTR Buffer = GlobalLock (h);
    LINES_GetSelectedText (&MyData->Lines, Buffer);
    GlobalUnlock (h);
    GlobalReAlloc (h, lstrlen (Buffer) + 1, GMEM_DDESHARE);
    EmptyClipboard();
    SetClipboardData (CF_TEXT, h);
    CloseClipboard();
    }
  }
```

This is not the place to describe the intricate details of Clipboard manipulation; but here's a brief description of the code. First, the Clipboard is "opened" by calling the *OpenClipboard()* function.

○   ○   ○

*Under Windows 3.1, the operation of opening the Clipboard cannot fail. But in Windows NT under a multi-processor system, it may be possible that another application has the Clipboard opened; so we check the return from* OpenClipboard() *just in case.*

○   ○   ○

With the Clipboard available, we allocate a full 64K block—with the *GMEM_DDESHARE* flag—and copy the currently selected text into it, afterwards reallocating the block so that it takes up no more space than it needs. We then empty the Clipboard of its previous contents, present it with the global handle to the copied text, and close it. That's all there is to it.

The *WM_CUT* operation is very simple because it builds on existing code:

```
static void near pascal wm_Cut (HWND Window)
  {
  wm_Copy (Window);
  wm_KeyDown (Window, VK_DELETE);
  }
```

A *cut* operation is just a *copy* followed by a *delete*, and we already have routines to perform those two operations. So, we just invoke them.

The *WM_PASTE* message is a little more intricate:

```
static void near pascal wm_Paste (HWND Window)
  {
  LPMYDATA MyData = (LPMYDATA) GetWindowLong (Window, GWL_MYDATA);
  if (IsClipboardFormatAvailable (CF_TEXT) && OpenClipboard (Window))
    {
    HANDLE h = GetClipboardData (CF_TEXT);
    LPSTR Buffer = GlobalLock (h);
    LINES_InsertText (&MyData->Lines, Buffer,
      DC_Get (&MyData->DeviceContext));
    DC_Release (&MyData->DeviceContext);
    GlobalUnlock (h);
    CloseClipboard ();
    NotifyParent (Window, TEN_CHANGE);
    }
  }
```

This time we get the global handle *from* the Clipboard, instead of *giving* it—that is, *if* the Clipboard has data in the *CF_TEXT* format. *GlobalLock()* gives us the pointer to the data, which we then pass on to *LINES_InsertText()*. Note that we unlock the global handle, but do not free it: It belongs to the Clipboard, not us.

## Implementing the Custom Messages

We then turn to implementing the custom messages for this control, starting with *TEM_GETSEL* and *TEM_SETSEL*, the messages that allow for programmatic manipulation of the selection rectangle:

```
static void near pascal tem_GetSel (HWND Window, LPRECT Rect)
  {
  LPMYDATA MyData = (LPMYDATA) GetWindowLong (Window, GWL_MYDATA);
  LINES_GetSelectionRect (&MyData->Lines, Rect);
  }

static void near pascal tem_SetSel (HWND Window, LPRECT Rect)
  {
  LPMYDATA MyData = (LPMYDATA) GetWindowLong (Window, GWL_MYDATA);
  LINES_SetSelectionRect (&MyData->Lines, Rect);
  }
```

The *TEM_INSERTTEXT* message replaces the current selection with text supplied by the message (pointed to by the *lParam* parameter):

```
static void near pascal tem_InsertText (HWND Window, LPSTR Buffer)
  {
  LPMYDATA MyData = (LPMYDATA) GetWindowLong (Window, GWL_MYDATA);
  LINES_InsertText (&MyData->Lines, Buffer);
  NotifyParent (Window, TEN_CHANGE);
  }
```

*TEM_GETSELTEXT* does the inverse; it retrieves the selected portion of the text:

```
static void near pascal tem_GetSelText (HWND Window, LPSTR Buffer)
  {
  LPMYDATA MyData = (LPMYDATA) GetWindowLong (Window, GWL_MYDATA);
  LINES_GetSelectedText (&MyData->Lines, Buffer);
  }
```

We also permit the entire text (up to 64K) to be programmatically referenced:

```
static void near pascal tem_GetText (HWND Window, LPSTR Buffer)
  {
  LPMYDATA MyData = (LPMYDATA) GetWindowLong (Window, GWL_MYDATA);
  LINES_GetText (&MyData->Lines, Buffer);
  }
```

*TEM_STOREDATA* triggers the saving of the text in the control, which presumably has been changed, back to disk:

```
static void near pascal tem_StoreData (HWND Window)
  {
```

```
LPMYDATA MyData = (LPMYDATA) GetWindowLong (Window, GWL_MYDATA);
char Buffer[128];
GetWindowText (Window, Buffer, sizeof Buffer);
LINES_Store (&MyData->Lines, Buffer);
}
```

Finally, we have the two messages which set and get the state of the *Modified* flag:

```
static BOOL near pascal tem_GetModified (HWND Window)
  {
  LPMYDATA MyData = (LPMYDATA) GetWindowLong (Window, GWL_MYDATA);
  return LINES_GetModified (&MyData->Lines);
  }

static void near pascal tem_SetModified (HWND Window, BOOL Modified)
  {
  LPMYDATA MyData = (LPMYDATA) GetWindowLong (Window, GWL_MYDATA);
  LINES_SetModified (&MyData->Lines, Modified);
  }
```

The window procedure, as always, is a simple (if lengthy) message switch:

```
LRESULT far pascal _export FAR PASCAL WndProc
    (
    HWND Window,
    UINT Msg,
    WPARAM wParam,
    LPARAM lParam
    )
  {
  LRESULT Result = 0;
  switch (Msg)
    {
    case WM_NCCREATE:
      Result = wm_NcCreate (Window, (LPCREATESTRUCT) lParam);
      break;
    case WM_CREATE:
      wm_Create (Window, (LPCREATESTRUCT) lParam);
      break;
    case WM_DESTROY:
      wm_Destroy (Window);
      break;
    case WM_NCDESTROY:
      wm_NcDestroy (Window);
      break;
```

```
      case WM_SIZE:
        wm_Size (Window, LOWORD (lParam), HIWORD (lParam));
        break;
      case WM_GETDLGCODE:
        Result = wm_GetDlgCode (Window);
        break;
      case WM_GETFONT:
        Result = wm_GetFont (Window);
        break;
      case WM_SETFONT:
        wm_SetFont (Window, wParam, LOWORD (lParam));
        break;
      case WM_PAINT:
        wm_Paint (Window);
        break;
      case WM_SETTEXT:
        wm_SetText (Window, (LPSTR) lParam);
        break;
      case WM_VSCROLL:
        wm_VScroll (Window, wParam, LOWORD (lParam));
        break;
      case WM_KEYDOWN:
        wm_KeyDown (Window, wParam);
        break;
      case WM_SETFOCUS:
        wm_SetFocus (Window);
        break;
      case WM_KILLFOCUS:
        wm_KillFocus (Window);
        break;
      case WM_LBUTTONDOWN:
        wm_LButtonDown (Window, MAKEPOINT (lParam));
        break;
      case WM_MOUSEMOVE:
        wm_MouseMove (Window, MAKEPOINT (lParam));
        break;
      case WM_LBUTTONUP:
        wm_LButtonUp (Window, MAKEPOINT (lParam));
        break;
      case WM_CHAR:
        wm_Char (Window, wParam);
        break;
      case TEM_GETSEL:
        tem_GetSel (Window, (LPRECT) lParam);
        break;
      case TEM_SETSEL:
        tem_SetSel (Window, (LPRECT) lParam);
        break;
```

```
    case TEM_INSERTTEXT:
      tem_InsertText (Window, (LPSTR) lParam);
      break;
    case TEM_GETSELTEXT:
      tem_GetSelText (Window, (LPSTR) lParam);
      break;
    case TEM_GETTEXT:
      tem_GetText (Window, (LPSTR) lParam);
      break;
    case TEM_STOREDATA:
      tem_StoreData (Window);
      break;
    case TEM_GETMODIFIED:
      Result = tem_GetModified (Window);
      break;
    case TEM_SETMODIFIED:
      tem_SetModified (Window, wParam);
      break;
    default:
      Result = DefWindowProc (Window, Msg, wParam, lParam);
    }
  return Result;
  }
```

## Wrapping Up MAIN.C

We close off the module with the *LibMain()* function which is called to register our new window class when the DLL is loaded:

```
static WNDCLASS Class =
  {
  CS_HREDRAW | CS_VREDRAW | CS_DBLCLKS | CS_GLOBALCLASS,
  WndProc,
  0,
  GWW_EXTRA,
  0,
  NULL,
  NULL,
  COLOR_WINDOW + 1,
  NULL,
  NULL
  };

#pragma argsused
int far pascal LibMain
    (
    HINSTANCE hInstance,
```

```
          WORD DataSeg,
          WORD HeapSize,
          LPSTR CommandLine
          )
       {
       if (HeapSize > 0)
          UnlockData (0);
       LibInstance = hInstance;
       Class.hInstance = hInstance;
       Class.hCursor = LoadCursor (NULL, IDC_IBEAM);
       Class.lpszClassName = ClassName;
       return RegisterClass (&Class) ? TRUE : FALSE;
       }
```

## DIALOG.C

The DIALOG.C module provides the hooks needed by the standard resource editors, such as Borland Resource Workshop and Microsoft's Dialog
Editor. This module is not really any different than the version that has
appeared in the other controls:

```
#pragma argsused
HGLOBAL far pascal _export Info (void)
   {
   typedef struct
      {
      UINT TypeStyle;
      UINT SuggestedWidth: 15;
      UINT WidthPixels: 1;
      UINT SuggestedHeight: 15;
      UINT HeightPixels: 1;
      DWORD DefaultStyle;
      char Description[22];
      HBITMAP ToolboxBitmap;
      HCURSOR DropCursor;
      } TYPEINFO;

   typedef struct
      {
      UINT Version;
      UINT TypeCount;
      char ClassName[CTLCLASS];
      char Title[94];
      char Reserved[10];
      TYPEINFO Type[1];
      } CONTROLINFO, FAR * LPCONTROLINFO;
```

```
    HGLOBAL hCtlInfo;
    LPCONTROLINFO CtlInfo;

    hCtlInfo = GlobalAlloc (GHND, sizeof (CONTROLINFO));
    if (hCtlInfo)
        {
        CtlInfo = (LPCONTROLINFO) GlobalLock (hCtlInfo);
        CtlInfo->Version = 100;
        CtlInfo->TypeCount = 1;
        lstrcpy (CtlInfo->ClassName, ClassName);
        lstrcpy (CtlInfo->Title, ClassName);
        CtlInfo->Type[0].SuggestedWidth = 50;
        CtlInfo->Type[0].SuggestedHeight = 40;
        CtlInfo->Type[0].DefaultStyle =
            WS_BORDER | WS_CHILD | WS_VISIBLE | WS_VSCROLL;
        lstrcpy (CtlInfo->Type[0].Description, ClassName);
        CtlInfo->Type[0].ToolboxBitmap =
            LoadBitmap (LibInstance, MAKEINTRESOURCE (100));
        CtlInfo->Type[0].DropCursor =
            LoadCursor (LibInstance, MAKEINTRESOURCE (100));
        GlobalUnlock (hCtlInfo);
        }
    return hCtlInfo;
    }


typedef struct
    {
    LPCTLSTYLE Style;
    LPFNSTRTOID String2ID;
    LPFNIDTOSTR ID2String;
    } STYLEDATA, FAR * LPSTYLEDATA;

static void near pascal wm_InitDialog
    (HWND Dialog, LPSTYLEDATA StyleData)
    {
    LPSTYLEBITS Styles =
        (LPSTYLEBITS) &StyleData->Style->dwStyle;
    char Buffer[64];
    if (Styles->StdStyles.TabStop)
        CheckDlgButton (Dialog, IDC_TABSTOP, 1);
    if (Styles->StdStyles.Group)
        CheckDlgButton (Dialog, IDC_GROUP, 1);
    if (Styles->StdStyles.HScroll)
        CheckDlgButton (Dialog, IDC_HSCROLL, 1);
    if (Styles->StdStyles.VScroll)
        CheckDlgButton (Dialog, IDC_VSCROLL, 1);
    if (Styles->StdStyles.Border)
        CheckDlgButton (Dialog, IDC_BORDER, 1);
```

```
      if (Styles->StdStyles.Disabled)
         CheckDlgButton (Dialog, IDC_DISABLED, 1);
      if (Styles->StdStyles.Visible)
         CheckDlgButton (Dialog, IDC_VISIBLE, 1);
      StyleData->ID2String (StyleData->Style->wId,
         Buffer, sizeof Buffer);
      SetDlgItemText (Dialog, IDC_ID, Buffer);
      SetDlgItemText (Dialog, IDC_CAPTION,
         StyleData->Style->szTitle);
      }

   static void near pascal wm_Command_OK
         (HWND Dialog, LPSTYLEDATA StyleData)
      {
      LPSTYLEBITS Styles =
         (LPSTYLEBITS) &StyleData->Style->dwStyle;
      char Buffer[64];
      Styles->StdStyles.TabStop =
         IsDlgButtonChecked (Dialog, IDC_TABSTOP);
      Styles->StdStyles.Group =
         IsDlgButtonChecked (Dialog, IDC_GROUP);
      Styles->StdStyles.HScroll =
         IsDlgButtonChecked (Dialog, IDC_HSCROLL);
      Styles->StdStyles.VScroll =
         IsDlgButtonChecked (Dialog, IDC_VSCROLL);
      Styles->StdStyles.Border =
         IsDlgButtonChecked (Dialog, IDC_BORDER);
      Styles->StdStyles.Disabled =
         IsDlgButtonChecked (Dialog, IDC_DISABLED);
      Styles->StdStyles.Visible =
         IsDlgButtonChecked (Dialog, IDC_VISIBLE);
      GetDlgItemText (Dialog, IDC_ID,
         Buffer, sizeof Buffer);
      StyleData->Style->wId = StyleData->String2ID (Buffer);
      GetDlgItemText (Dialog, IDC_CAPTION,
         StyleData->Style->szTitle,
         sizeof StyleData->Style->szTitle);
      }

   #pragma argsused
   BOOL far pascal _export StyleProc
         (
         HWND Dialog,
         UINT Msg,
         WPARAM wParam,
         LPARAM lParam
         )
      {
```

```
    static LPSTYLEDATA StyleData;
    switch (Msg)
      {
      case WM_INITDIALOG:
        StyleData = (LPSTYLEDATA) lParam;
        wm_InitDialog (Dialog, StyleData);
        return TRUE;
      case WM_COMMAND:
        switch (wParam)
          {
          case IDOK:
            wm_Command_OK (Dialog, StyleData);
            EndDialog (Dialog, TRUE);
            break;
          case IDCANCEL:
            EndDialog (Dialog, FALSE);
            break;
          default:
            return FALSE;
          }
        break;
      default:
        return FALSE;
      }
    return TRUE;
    }

BOOL far pascal _export Style
      (
      HWND Window,
      HGLOBAL hCtlStyle,
      LPFNSTRTOID aString2ID,
      LPFNIDTOSTR aID2String
      )
    {
    BOOL Result;
    STYLEDATA StyleData;
    StyleData.Style = (LPCTLSTYLE) GlobalLock (hCtlStyle);
    StyleData.String2ID = aString2ID;
    StyleData.ID2String = aID2String;
    Result = DialogBoxParam (LibInstance,
      "Styles", Window, (FARPROC) StyleProc,
      (long) (LPSTYLEDATA) &StyleData);
    GlobalUnlock (hCtlStyle);
    return (Result == IDOK);
    }

#pragma argsused
```

```
UINT far pascal _export Flags
    (
    DWORD Flags,
    LPSTR Buffer,
    UINT BufferSize
    )
    {
    LPSTYLEBITS Styles = (LPSTYLEBITS) &Flags;
    Buffer[0] = 0;
    return lstrlen (Buffer);
    }

typedef HGLOBAL (CALLBACK *LPFNINFO)( void );
typedef BOOL (CALLBACK *LPFNSTYLE)
    (
    HWND hWnd,
    HGLOBAL hCntlStyle,
    LPFNSTRTOID lpfnSID,
    LPFNIDTOSTR lpfnIDS
    );
typedef UINT (CALLBACK *LPFNFLAGS)
    (
    DWORD   dwStyle,
    LPSTR   lpBuff,
    UINT    wBuffLength
    );

typedef HGLOBAL (CALLBACK *LPFNLOADRES) (LPSTR szType, LPSTR szId);
typedef BOOL (CALLBACK *LPFNEDITRES) (LPSTR szType, LPSTR szId);

#pragma argsused
HGLOBAL far pascal _export ListClasses
    (
    LPSTR CallingClass,
    UINT Version,
    LPFNLOADRES Load,
    LPFNEDITRES Edit
    )
    {
    typedef struct
        {
        LPFNINFO   fnRWInfo;
        LPFNSTYLE  fnRWStyle;
        LPFNFLAGS  fnFlags;
        char   ClassName[20];
        } RWCTLCLASS, FAR *LPRWCTLCLASS;

    typedef struct {
```

```
    short   ClassCount;
    RWCTLCLASS Class[1];
    } CTLCLASSLIST, FAR *LPCTLCLASSLIST;

HGLOBAL hClassList = GlobalAlloc (GHND, sizeof (CTLCLASSLIST));
LPCTLCLASSLIST ClassList = (LPCTLCLASSLIST) GlobalLock (hClassList);

ClassList->ClassCount = 1;
ClassList->Class[0].fnRWInfo = Info;
ClassList->Class[0].fnRWStyle = Style;
ClassList->Class[0].fnFlags = Flags;
_fstrcpy (ClassList->Class[0].ClassName, ClassName);

GlobalUnlock (hClassList);
return hClassList;
}
```

# VISUAL.C

As in the Skeleton, the VISUAL.C module provides all the hooks needed to make the TextFileEdit control accessible to a visual programming environment, such as Visual Basic. At the beginning of the module, the properties are defined:

```
#include "internal.h"

#define _segment(p) ((unsigned int) (((unsigned long) (void far *) (p)) >>
16L))
#define _offsetin(struc, fld) ((USHORT)&(((struc *)0)->fld))
#define VBERR_BADINDEX 381

static long Boolean[2] = { 0, -1 };

typedef struct
  {
  UINT : 16;
  } VBDATA;
typedef VBDATA far * LPVBDATA;

PROPINFO Property_About =
  {
  "(About)",
  DT_HSZ | PF_fNoRuntimeW | PF_fGetHszMsg,
  0, 0, 0, NULL, 0
  };
```

```
PROPINFO Property_Filename =
  {
  "Filename",
  DT_HSZ | PF_fGetMsg | PF_fSetMsg | PF_fSaveMsg | PF_fEditable,
  0, 0, 0, NULL, 0
  };

PROPINFO Property_Modified =
  {
  "Modified",
  DT_BOOL | PF_fGetMsg | PF_fSetMsg | PF_fNoShow,
  0, 0, 0, NULL, 0
  };

PROPINFO Property_Action =
  {
  "Action",
  DT_SHORT | PF_fSetMsg | PF_fNoShow | PF_fNoRuntimeR,
  0, 0, 0, NULL, 0
  };

PROPINFO Property_SelStartPos =
  {
  "SelStartPos",
  DT_SHORT | PF_fSetMsg | PF_fGetMsg | PF_fNoShow,
  0, 0, 0, NULL, 0
  };

PROPINFO Property_SelStartLine =
  {
  "SelStartLine",
  DT_SHORT | PF_fSetMsg | PF_fGetMsg | PF_fNoShow,
  0, 0, 0, NULL, 0
  };

PROPINFO Property_SelStopPos =
  {
  "SelStopPos",
  DT_SHORT | PF_fSetMsg | PF_fGetMsg | PF_fNoShow,
  0, 0, 0, NULL, 0
  };

PROPINFO Property_SelStopLine =
  {
  "SelStopLine",
  DT_SHORT | PF_fSetMsg | PF_fGetMsg | PF_fNoShow,
  0, 0, 0, NULL, 0
  };
```

```
PROPINFO Property_SelText =
   {
   "SelText",
   DT_HSZ | PF_fSetMsg | PF_fGetMsg | PF_fNoShow,
   0, 0, 0, NULL, 0
   };

PROPINFO Property_Text =
   {
   "Text",
   DT_HSZ | PF_fSetMsg | PF_fGetMsg | PF_fNoShow | PF_fNoRuntimeW,
   0, 0, 0, NULL, 0
   };

PPROPINFO Properties[] =
   {
   PPROPINFO_STD_NAME,
   PPROPINFO_STD_INDEX,
   PPROPINFO_STD_BACKCOLOR,
   PPROPINFO_STD_FORECOLOR,
   PPROPINFO_STD_LEFT,
   PPROPINFO_STD_TOP,
   PPROPINFO_STD_WIDTH,
   PPROPINFO_STD_HEIGHT,
   PPROPINFO_STD_FONTNAME,
   PPROPINFO_STD_FONTSIZE,
   PPROPINFO_STD_FONTBOLD,
   PPROPINFO_STD_FONTITALIC,
   PPROPINFO_STD_TABINDEX,
   PPROPINFO_STD_TABSTOP,
   PPROPINFO_STD_BORDERSTYLEON,
   PPROPINFO_STD_ENABLED,
   PPROPINFO_STD_PARENT,
   PPROPINFO_STD_TAG,
   PPROPINFO_STD_VISIBLE,
   PPROPINFO_STD_HELPCONTEXTID,
   PPROPINFO_STD_LAST,
   &Property_About,
   &Property_Filename,
   &Property_Modified,
   &Property_Action,
   &Property_SelStartPos,
   &Property_SelStartLine,
   &Property_SelStopPos,
   &Property_SelStopLine,
   &Property_SelText,
   &Property_Text,
   NULL
```

```
    };

typedef enum
    {
    IPROPINFO_STD_NAME,
    IPROPINFO_STD_INDEX,
    IPROPINFO_STD_BACKCOLOR,
    IPROPINFO_STD_FORECOLOR,
    IPROPINFO_STD_LEFT,
    IPROPINFO_STD_TOP,
    IPROPINFO_STD_WIDTH,
    IPROPINFO_STD_HEIGHT,
    IPROPINFO_STD_FONTNAME,
    IPROPINFO_STD_FONTSIZE,
    IPROPINFO_STD_FONTBOLD,
    IPROPINFO_STD_FONTITALIC,
    IPROPINFO_STD_TABINDEX,
    IPROPINFO_STD_TABSTOP,
    IPROPINFO_STD_BORDERSTYLEON,
    IPROPINFO_STD_ENABLED,
    IPROPINFO_STD_PARENT,
    IPROPINFO_STD_TAG,
    IPROPINFO_STD_VISIBLE,
    IPROPINFO_STD_HELPCONTEXTID,
    IPROPINFO_STD_LAST,
    IPROPINFO_About,
    IPROPINFO_Filename,
    IPROPINFO_Modified,
    IPROPINFO_Action,
    IPROPINFO_SelStartPos,
    IPROPINFO_SelStartLine,
    IPROPINFO_SelStopPos,
    IPROPINFO_SelStopLine,
    IPROPINFO_SelText,
    IPROPINFO_Text,
    IPROPINFO_End
    } PROPSIX;
```

The events come next:

```
EVENTINFO Event_Change = { "Change", 0, 0, NULL, NULL };

PEVENTINFO Events[] =
    {
    PEVENTINFO_STD_CLICK,
    PEVENTINFO_STD_DBLCLICK,
    PEVENTINFO_STD_DRAGDROP,
    PEVENTINFO_STD_DRAGOVER,
```

```
        PEVENTINFO_STD_GOTFOCUS,
        PEVENTINFO_STD_LOSTFOCUS,
        PEVENTINFO_STD_MOUSEDOWN,
        PEVENTINFO_STD_MOUSEMOVE,
        PEVENTINFO_STD_MOUSEUP,
          PEVENTINFO_STD_LAST,
        &Event_Change,
        NULL
        };

typedef enum
        {
        IPEVENTINFO_STD_CLICK,
        IPEVENTINFO_STD_DBLCLK,
        IPEVENTINFO_STD_DRAGDROP,
        IPEVENTINFO_STD_DRAGOVER,
        IPEVENTINFO_STD_GOTFOCUS,
        IPEVENTINFO_STD_LOSTFOCUS,
        IPEVENTINFO_STD_MOUSEDOWN,
        IPEVENTINFO_STD_MOUSEMOVE,
        IPEVENTINFO_STD_MOUSEUP,
        IPEVENTINFO_STD_LAST,
        IPEVENTINFO_Change,
        IPEVENTINFO_End
        } EVENTSIX;
```

The next function sets property values:

```
#pragma argsused
static BOOL near pascal vbm_SetProperty
        (
        HCTL Control,
        HWND Window,
        USHORT Property,
        long Value,
        long far * Error
        )
        {
        LPVBDATA VbData = (LPVBDATA) VBDerefControl (Control);
        RECT Rect;
        switch (Property)
            {
            case IPROPINFO_Filename:
              SetWindowText (Window, (LPSTR) Value);
              return TRUE;
            case IPROPINFO_Modified:
              SendMessage (Window, TEM_SETMODIFIED, (WORD) Value, 0);
              return TRUE;
```

```
        case IPROPINFO_Action:
          switch ((int) Value)
            {
            case Action_STOREDATA:
              SendMessage (Window, TEM_STOREDATA, 0, 0);
              break;
              }
          return TRUE;
        case IPROPINFO_SelStartPos:
          SendMessage (Window, TEM_GETSEL, 0, (long) (LPRECT) &Rect);
          Rect.left = (int) Value;
          SendMessage (Window, TEM_SETSEL, 0, (long) (LPRECT) &Rect);
          return TRUE;
        case IPROPINFO_SelStartLine:
          SendMessage (Window, TEM_GETSEL, 0, (long) (LPRECT) &Rect);
          Rect.top = (int) Value;
          SendMessage (Window, TEM_SETSEL, 0, (long) (LPRECT) &Rect);
          return TRUE;
        case IPROPINFO_SelStopPos:
          SendMessage (Window, TEM_GETSEL, 0, (long) (LPRECT) &Rect);
          Rect.right = (int) Value;
          SendMessage (Window, TEM_SETSEL, 0, (long) (LPRECT) &Rect);
          return TRUE;
        case IPROPINFO_SelStopLine:
          SendMessage (Window, TEM_GETSEL, 0, (long) (LPRECT) &Rect);
          Rect.bottom = (int) Value;
          SendMessage (Window, TEM_SETSEL, 0, (long) (LPRECT) &Rect);
          return TRUE;
        case IPROPINFO_SelText:
          SendMessage (Window, TEM_INSERTTEXT, 0, (long) (LPSTR) Value);
          return TRUE;
        default:
          return FALSE;
        }
    }
```

This function, *Vbm_SetProperty()*, is interesting because of the *Action*
property. For some reason, Visual Basic's API allows you to create an
indefinite number of custom properties and events. But the list of methods
is finite and pre-defined. If you want your control to support a method
that's not on the list, you can't do it—except by using this kludge: Create an
"Action" property that produces different effects depending on the numeric
value it's assigned. This is the technique used by the Common Dialog
control. We'll also use it here. The missing method in this case is the one
that stores the control's text back to disk.

The four selection properties are each set by obtaining the selection rectangle, changing the one value of interest, then reassigning the (altered) rectangle.

The next function obtains property values. You'll note that *Action,* a write-only property, is not represented here:

```
static BOOL near pascal vbm_GetProperty
    (
    HCTL Control,
    HWND Window,
    USHORT Property,
    LPVOID Value,
    long far * Error
    )
{
LPVBDATA VbData = (LPVBDATA) VBDerefControl (Control);
RECT Rect;
switch (Property)
    {
    case IPROPINFO_Filename:
        {
        char Buffer[128];
        GetWindowText (Window, Buffer, sizeof Buffer);
        *(HSZ far *)Value = VBCreateHsz (_segment (Control), Buffer);
        }
        return TRUE;
    case IPROPINFO_Modified:
        *(long far *)Value = SendMessage (Window, TEM_GETMODIFIED, 0, 0);
        return TRUE;
    case IPROPINFO_SelStartPos:
        SendMessage (Window, TEM_GETSEL, 0, (long) (LPRECT) &Rect);
        *(long far *) Value = Rect.left;
        return TRUE;
    case IPROPINFO_SelStartLine:
        SendMessage (Window, TEM_GETSEL, 0, (long) (LPRECT) &Rect);
        *(long far *) Value = Rect.top;
        return TRUE;
    case IPROPINFO_SelStopPos:
        SendMessage (Window, TEM_GETSEL, 0, (long) (LPRECT) &Rect);
        *(long far *) Value = Rect.right;
        return TRUE;
    case IPROPINFO_SelStopLine:
        SendMessage (Window, TEM_GETSEL, 0, (long) (LPRECT) &Rect);
        *(long far *) Value = Rect.bottom;
        return TRUE;
    case IPROPINFO_SelText:
        {
```

```
        HANDLE h = GlobalAlloc (GMEM_MOVEABLE, 0xFFFF);
        LPSTR Buffer = GlobalLock (h);
        SendMessage (Window, TEM_GETSELTEXT, 0, (long) Buffer);
        *(HSZ far *)Value = VBCreateHsz (_segment (Control), Buffer);
        GlobalUnlock (h);
        GlobalFree (h);
        }
        return TRUE;
      case IPROPINFO_Text:
        {
        HANDLE h = GlobalAlloc (GMEM_MOVEABLE, 0xFFFF);
        LPSTR Buffer = GlobalLock (h);
        SendMessage (Window, TEM_GETTEXT, 0, (long) Buffer);
        *(HSZ far *)Value = VBCreateHsz (_segment (Control), Buffer);
        GlobalUnlock (h);
        GlobalFree (h);
        }
        return TRUE;
      default:
        return FALSE;
      }
    }
```

The functions that load and save properties at design time are short; only one custom property (*FileName*) is needed. This property can be set at design time:

```
#pragma argsused
static BOOL near pascal vbm_LoadProperty
    (
    HCTL Control,
    HWND Window,
    USHORT Property,
    HFORMFILE FormFile,
    long far * Error
    )
{
LPVBDATA VbData = (LPVBDATA) VBDerefControl (Control);
switch (Property)
    {
    case IPROPINFO_Filename:
        {
        BYTE Length;
        char Buffer[128];
        VBReadFormFile (FormFile, &Length, sizeof Length);
        VBReadFormFile (FormFile, Buffer, Length);
        Buffer[Length] = 0;
```

```
         SetWindowText (Window, Buffer);
         }
       return TRUE;
     default:
       return FALSE;
     }
   }


#pragma argsused
static BOOL near pascal vbm_SaveProperty
     (
     HCTL Control,
     HWND Window,
     USHORT Property,
     HFORMFILE FormFile,
     long far * Error
     )
   {
   LPVBDATA VbData = (LPVBDATA) VBDerefControl (Control);
   switch (Property)
     {
     case IPROPINFO_Filename:
       {
       BYTE Length;
       char Buffer[128];
       Length = GetWindowText (Window, Buffer, sizeof Buffer);
       VBWriteFormFile (FormFile, &Length, sizeof Length);
       VBWriteFormFile (FormFile, Buffer, Length);
       }
       return TRUE;
     default:
       return FALSE;
     }
   }
```

To finish up the module, we have the control procedure:

```
long far pascal _export CtlProc
     (
     HCTL Control,
     HWND Window,
     USHORT Msg,
     USHORT wParam,
     long lParam
     )
   {
   long Error = 0;
   switch (Msg)
```

```
     {
case VBN_COMMAND:
   switch (HIWORD (lParam))
      {
      case TEN_SETFOCUS:
         VBFireEvent (Control, IPEVENTINFO_STD_GOTFOCUS, NULL);
         break;
      case TEN_KILLFOCUS:
         VBFireEvent (Control, IPEVENTINFO_STD_LOSTFOCUS, NULL);
         break;
      case TEN_CHANGE:
         VBFireEvent (Control, IPEVENTINFO_Change, NULL);
         break;
      default:
         break;
      }
   break;
case VBM_SETPROPERTY:
   if (vbm_SetProperty (Control, Window, wParam, lParam, &Error))
      return Error;
   break;
case VBM_GETPROPERTY:
   if (vbm_GetProperty (Control, Window, wParam,
      (LPVOID) lParam, &Error))
      return Error;
   break;
case VBM_LOADPROPERTY:
   if (vbm_LoadProperty (Control, Window, wParam,
      (HFORMFILE) lParam, &Error))
      return Error;
   break;
case VBM_SAVEPROPERTY:
   if (vbm_SaveProperty (Control, Window, wParam,
      (HFORMFILE) lParam, &Error))
      return Error;
   break;
case VBM_GETPROPERTYHSZ:
   switch (wParam)
      {
      case IPROPINFO_About:
         *((HSZ far *) lParam) = GetAboutPropertyString (Control);
         break;
      }
   return 0;
case VBM_INITPROPPOPUP:
   switch (wParam)
      {
      case IPROPINFO_About:
```

```
                return PopupAbout ();
            case  IPROPINFO_Filename:
                return PopupFileDlg (Control,
                    Window,
                    "Select Filename",
                    IPROPINFO_Filename,
                    "Text files\0*.txt\0All files\0*.*\0",
                    1, "txt", 0);
            }
        break;
    case VBM_HELP:
        if (vbm_Help (Window,
                LOBYTE (wParam),
                HIBYTE (wParam),
                Properties, Events))
            return 0;
        break;
    case WM_DESTROY:
        WinHelp (Window, HelpFileName (), HELP_QUIT, 0);
        break;
    }
    return VBDefControlProc (Control, Window, Msg, wParam, lParam);
    }
```

And here are the hooks required to support the Visual Basic environment:

```
MODEL Model =
    {
    VB_VERSION,
    MODEL_fFocusOk | MODEL_fArrows,
    (PCTLPROC) CtlProc,
    CS_VREDRAW | CS_HREDRAW,
    WS_BORDER,
    sizeof (VBDATA),
    8000,
    NULL,
    NULL,
    NULL,
    Properties,
    Events,
    IPROPINFO_STD_NAME,
    IPEVENTINFO_Change,
    -1
    };

#pragma argsused
BOOL far pascal _export VBINITCC
    (
```

```
    USHORT Version,
    BOOL Runtime
    )
{
if (! Runtime)
    {
    RegisterVbPopups ();
    RegisterFileDlgPopup ();
    }
Model.npszDefCtlName =
Model.npszClassName =
Model.npszParentClassName = (PSTR) ClassName;
return VBRegisterModel (LibInstance, &Model);
}

VOID FAR PASCAL _export VBTERMCC (void)
    {
    UnregisterVbPopups ();
    UnregisterFileDlgPopup ();
    }
```

## HELP.C

This module is unchanged from the Skeleton control; simply copy it to this project.

## FILEPROP.C

This module is unchanged from the TextFileView control; simply copy it to this project.

## TEXTEDIT.DEF

The TextFileEdit's module definition file comes directly from Skeleton, with (of course) the module name changed:

```
LIBRARY TEXTEDIT
EXETYPE WINDOWS
CODE PRELOAD MOVEABLE DISCARDABLE
DATA PRELOAD MOVEABLE SINGLE
HEAPSIZE 0
EXPORTS
        WEP         RESIDENTNAME
        Info        @2
        Style       @3
```

```
Flags       @4
WndProc     @5
StyleProc   @6
ListClasses
```

Remember that *WEP* should be marked *PRIVATE* instead of *RESIDENTNAME* if you are using the newer Microsoft linker.

## TEXTEDIT.RC

The TextFileEdit resources are derived from the ones used with the TextFileView control. Here is the entire resource script:

```
#include "internal.h"

// For Dialog Editor
Styles DIALOG 0, 0, 210, 111
STYLE DS_MODALFRAME | WS_POPUP | WS_VISIBLE | WS_CAPTION | WS_SYSMENU
CAPTION "TextFileEdit Styles"
FONT 8, "MS Sans Serif"
BEGIN
    RTEXT "File name:", IDC_STATIC, 3, 7, 35, 7
    CONTROL "", IDC_CAPTION, "EDIT", ES_LEFT | ES_AUTOHSCROLL | WS_CHILD |
WS_VISIBLE | WS_BORDER | WS_TABSTOP, 44, 4, 100, 12
    RTEXT "ID:", IDC_STATIC, 5, 23, 35, 7
    CONTROL "", IDC_ID, "EDIT", ES_LEFT | ES_AUTOHSCROLL | WS_CHILD |
WS_VISIBLE | WS_BORDER | WS_TABSTOP, 44, 21, 100, 12
    GROUPBOX "Standard Styles", IDC_STATIC, 8,41,137,66
    CONTROL "Border", IDC_BORDER, "Button", BS_AUTOCHECKBOX | WS_CHILD |
WS_VISIBLE | WS_TABSTOP, 22, 55, 48, 10
    CONTROL "Disabled", IDC_DISABLED, "Button", BS_AUTOCHECKBOX | WS_CHILD
| WS_VISIBLE | WS_TABSTOP, 22,67,44,10
    CONTROL "Group", IDC_GROUP, "Button", BS_AUTOCHECKBOX | WS_CHILD |
WS_VISIBLE | WS_TABSTOP, 22,79,34,10
    CONTROL "Tab stop", IDC_TABSTOP, "Button", BS_AUTOCHECKBOX | WS_CHILD |
WS_VISIBLE | WS_TABSTOP, 22,91,46,10
    CONTROL "Vertical scroll", IDC_VSCROLL, "Button", BS_AUTOCHECKBOX |
WS_CHILD | WS_VISIBLE | WS_TABSTOP, 75,67,61,10
    DEFPUSHBUTTON "OK", IDOK, 154, 4, 50, 14
    PUSHBUTTON "Cancel", IDCANCEL, 154, 21, 50, 14
    CONTROL "Visible", IDC_VISIBLE, "Button", BS_AUTOCHECKBOX | WS_CHILD |
WS_VISIBLE | WS_TABSTOP, 75, 79, 61, 10
END

// For Resource Workshop
100 BITMAP "tbx.bmp"
100 CURSOR "tbx.cur"
```

```
// For Visual Basic
8000 BITMAP "8000.bmp"
8001 BITMAP "8001.bmp"
8003 BITMAP "8003.bmp"
8006 BITMAP "8006.bmp"


ABOUT DIALOG 41, 45, 192, 125
STYLE DS_MODALFRAME | WS_POPUP | WS_CAPTION
CAPTION "About Text File Editor Control"
FONT 8, "MS Sans Serif"
BEGIN
   CONTROL "Text File Editor Control", 0, "STATIC", SS_CENTER | WS_CHILD |
WS_VISIBLE, 0, 8, 190, 8
   CONTROL "by Paul S. Cilwa", 0, "STATIC", SS_CENTER | WS_CHILD |
WS_VISIBLE, 0, 16, 190, 8
   ICON "MAIN", 0, 87, 29, 18, 20
   CONTROL "Version 1.0", 0, "STATIC", SS_CENTER | WS_CHILD | WS_VISIBLE,
0, 59, 190, 8
   CONTROL "\2511993 by Paul S. Cilwa", 0, "STATIC", SS_CENTER | WS_CHILD
| WS_VISIBLE, 0, 79, 190, 8
   CONTROL "All Rights Reserved", 0, "STATIC", SS_CENTER | WS_CHILD |
WS_VISIBLE, 0, 88, 190, 8
   PUSHBUTTON "OK", IDOK, 74, 102, 45, 15
END


MAIN ICON "textedit.ico"

1 VERSIONINFO LOADONCALL MOVEABLE DISCARDABLE
FILEVERSION 1, 0, 0, 0
PRODUCTVERSION 1, 0, 0, 0
FILEOS VOS__WINDOWS16
FILETYPE VFT_DLL
BEGIN
   BLOCK "StringFileInfo"
   BEGIN
     BLOCK "040904E4"
     BEGIN
       VALUE "CompanyName", "Coriolis Group\000"
       VALUE "FileDescription", "TextFileEdit Control for Visual Basic
and Windows\000"
       VALUE "FileVersion", "1.0.0.0\000"
       VALUE "InternalName", "TEXTEDIT\000"
       VALUE "LegalCopyright", "Copyright © Paul S. Cilwa 1993\000"
       VALUE "OriginalFilename", "textedit.vbx\000"
       VALUE "ProductName", "Windows Programming Power\000"
       VALUE "ProductVersion", "1.0.0.0\000"
       VALUE "Comments", "\000"
     END
   END
END
```

Figures 10.2, 10.3, 10.4, 10.5, and 10.6 provide examples of the Styles dialog template, the Resource Workshop bitmaps, the Visual toolbox bitmaps, the About box, and the control icon, respectively.

**Figure 10.2  The Styles dialog template.**

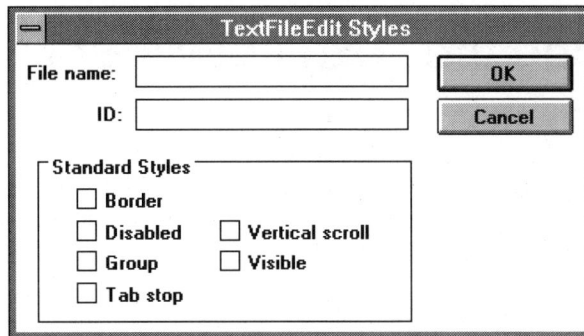

**Figure 10.3  The Resource Workshop toolbox bitmap and cursor.**

**Figure 10.4  The visual environment toolbox bitmaps.**

**Figure 10.5  The TextFileEdit visual environment About box.**

**Figure 10.6  The TextFileEdit official icon.**

# Enhancing the TextFileEdit Control

When we first decided to create the TextFileEdit control, we wanted to make it as full-featured as the standard edit control. This goal turned out to be unreachable for two reasons. First, it would have been a heck of a lotta work. Second, *explaining* the amount of code such a project required would take up half a book the size of this one.

Still, with TextFileEdit as a starting point, you could—in your spare time—make improvements to enhance TextFileEdit. Here are some suggestions:

• Provide a "double-clicking" feature so that the word the cursor is on could easily be selected.

• Add formatting information to the *Line* object to permit italics, boldface, and even font changes within a line.

• Enhance text insertion operations by setting up the control so that only the affected portions of the window were invalidated instead of the whole control.

Although there are many other enhancements you could make, these suggestions should help you get started.

# 11

# The IniData Control

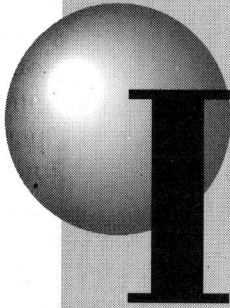

**I**n this final chapter we'll create a useful control for accessing Windows initialization (.INI) files. This control, named IniData, allows your Visual Basic programs to easily display and process the data stored in their private .INI files. We'll be writing this control so that it encapsulates all of the critical management work for processing .INI files, such as initializing buffers, reading files, parsing keys, displaying sections of a .INI file, and so on. As a bonus, we'll also implement an encryption feature so that selected key values can be encrypted to protect users from reading or modifying a program's .INI file.

e'll begin by discussing some important background on Windows initialization files, and then we'll take you inside the design process of the IniData control. Because the control is designed to work with just Visual Basic, you'll find that the work of coding the control is much simpler than many of the other controls we have created in previous chapters.

# Designing the IniData Control

From the beginning, the designers of Windows envisioned that program initialization information should be kept in a consistent and convenient format. In fact, they started out by using a single file, WIN.INI. With this scheme, all Windows apps would be written so that they would share this file to obtain their initialization data. (The SYSTEM.INI file was provided to store data that was too sensitive to withstand even accidental user tampering.) Windows programs could easily access the entries in WIN.INI by using these three functions: *GetProfileString()*, *GetProfileInt()*, and *WriteProfileString()*.

As years passed and the number of Windows apps skyrocketed, the "all purpose" WIN.INI initialization file got too crowded—and too big. With the release of Windows 3.0, Microsoft introduced the concept of "private profiles" along with a matching set of functions: *GetPrivateProfileString()*, *WritePrivateProfileString()*, and so on. Under this scheme, each application, or group of applications from a single vendor, could place its initialization information in a private initialization file. Of course, each private initialization (.INI) file needed to follow a consistent format. This approach allowed a file to be accessed by functions that hide the complexities of file I/O and keyword parsing.

Next came Visual Basic. VB apps were designed to use the same private profile functions as those written in other languages. (They could call the Windows API functions via the proper **Declare** statements.) But the API calls required a peculiar syntax and were therefore awkward to use for VB programmers. Thus, accessing .INI files in a VB program turned out to be quite a chore. For example, before calling *GetPrivateProfileString()*, a VB app had to first pad a String variable with blanks in order to allocate the space that the function would need. VB programmers also had to tell the function how many bytes had been allocated: not a hard thing to do, but somehow out-of-place in a VB application.

Our solution for processing .INI files is to create an IniData control for VB programmers. This control encapsulates the private profile functions and provides us the chance to create a Visual Basic-only control (which uses the "graphical" style to save on system overhead), and to demonstrate a control that is visible only at design time.

## Processing .INI Files

Being a Windows programmer, you're probably familiar with the format of .INI files. As Figure 11.1 shows, they are essentially ASCII files divided into sections. Each section contains one or more keys and their related values. In addition, some key values are actually multiple values. If you read a multiple key value into your program, you'd have to parse it to access its component parts.

We'll provide our control with several sets of properties to simplify the work of processing .INI files. Obviously, we must include a *Filename* property for accessing .INI files. To process and enumerate the sections in a .INI file, we'll use a *Sections* array property. In addition, we've included a *SectionCount* property to tell us how many entries there are in a section.

Once we have processed a section of a .INI file, we need to process the file at the "key" level. The properties for this task include *Keys*, *KeyCount*, *Value*, *ListDelimiter*, *List*, and *ListCount*. Let's look at how these properties are used. After the *Section* property has been set, the *Keys* array will contain

**Figure 11.1   A sample portion of a .INI file with its components labeled.**

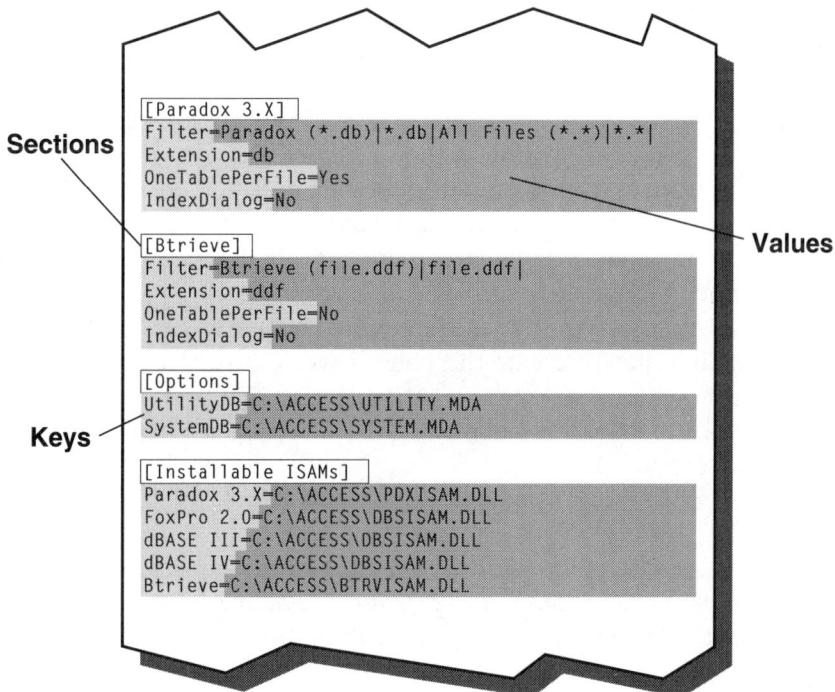

the list of keys for that section, a list with *KeyCount* number of keys. And if a particular *Key* has a value, the value of that key can be read in the *Value* property. (If the key or, for that matter, the section or entire file is missing, the *DefaultValue* property is echoed to the *Value* property.) Finally, if a key has a multi-item value and the user supplies a *ListDelimiter* character, the IniData control will automatically parse the item and fill the *List* array with *ListCount* elements from the value.

Finally, we've tossed in an encryption feature as a bonus. If you set an *EncryptionKey* property to some value, any key value set from your program will be written to the .INI file in a format indecipherable to the average user. On the other hand, if the *EncryptionKey* property is set when your program is reading an encrypted value, the value will be converted and placed in *Value* property as plain text.

## Inside the IniData Control

As we mentioned, the IniData control itself can only be seen at design time. (In this way it is similar to the VB timer control.) Therefore, it provides no useful visible manifestation and we can implement it as an "invisible at run time" control. Furthermore, since we don't need to implement it as an actual window, we can give it the *MODEL_fGraphical* flag. This saves Visual Basic from having to create a true window, and thus preserves precious system resources.

Almost all of the processing features of IniData are implemented using the private profile functions. Although there are only three of them, they can be used to write or obtain values from specified sections and keys, delete sections and keys, and enumerate the keys within a section. These operations are achieved by manipulating the parameters passed to the three profile functions.

Curiously, the Windows API provides no easy way to enumerate sections within a file. To create the control we've just described, we'll have to supply a function that opens a .INI file *as* a file and reads in each line, looking for the lines that begin with the "[" character that signifies the start of a new section.

○ ○ ○

*Since there are no standard C library routines for performing buffered, text-oriented file input—at least, none that we like—we'll implement such functions in a separate, reusable module.*

○ ○ ○

We'll also place the encryption functions in a module of their own. These functions are not heavy-duty, "challenge-the-CIA" encryption algorithms. Actually, since we'll place them in a file by themselves, you're welcome to exchange them with any encryption scheme you like. Ours is a simple substitution algorithm that should be adequate to hide, say, registration codes from all but the most determined snoops.

# Creating the IniData Control

The IniData control is implemented in C with the following modules:

```
ENCRYPT.H/ENCRYPT.C
TEXTFILE.H/TEXTFILE.C
INTERNAL.H
MAIN.C
VISUAL.C
HELP.C
FILEPROP.C
INIDATA.RC
INIDATA.DEF
```

Since the IniData control is implemented as a visual custom control, you'll also need to include VBAPI.LIB in the list of libraries to be linked into the end-product DLL.

## ENCRYPT.H

The encryption files provide for the IniData control's encryption feature. We've packaged this code so that it can be used in other projects as well. Here is the entire header file, ENCRYPT.H:

```
#ifndef __ENCRYPT_H__
#define __ENCRYPT_H__

#include <windows.h>
#include <string.h>
#include <ctype.h>

void far pascal Encrypt_Text
    (
    LPSTR Key,
    LPSTR PlainText,
    LPSTR EncryptedText
    );
```

```
BOOL far pascal Decrypt_Text
    (
    LPSTR Key,
    LPSTR PlainText,
    LPSTR EncryptedText
    );

#endif
```

The **#ifndef/#endif** structure used here prevents ENCRYPT.H from being included more than once. This is the same trick many commercially provided header files use.

The guts of the header file consist of the prototypes for the two functions that this component makes public: *EncryptText()* and *DecryptText()*.

# ENCRYPT.C

Turning to the source code in ENCRYPT.C, though, we find that a non-public function is defined first:

```
#include "encrypt.h"

static void near pascal InitTable
    (
    LPSTR Key,
    LPSTR Subst
    )
    {

    register i;
    register l = lstrlen (Key);
    register j = 0;

    _fstrupr (Key);
    Subst[0] = 0;

    for (i = 0; i < l; i++)
        if (isalpha (Key[i]))
            if (! strchr (Subst, Key[i]))
                {
                Subst[j++] = Key[i];
                Subst[j] = 0;
                }

    for (i = 26-1; i >= 0; i-)
        if (! strchr (Subst, 'A'+i))
            {
```

```
    Subst[j++] = (char) ('A' + i);
    Subst[j] = 0;
    }

}
```

This function, *InitTable()*, initializes a substitution table. It takes each unique alphabetic character from the *Key* that is passed in as a parameter and places the character into a 26-character string (*Subst*). The remaining string is then filled with unused characters.

○ ○ ○

*A key that is longer and contains a variety of letters will work better with our encryption algorithm. For example, the key "NORTHERN EXPO-SURE" would encrypt more effectively than the key "EEEEE".*

○ ○ ○

You'll notice that the substitution table stores only upper-case characters. Numbers and punctuation marks in the input string (*Key*) will *not* be converted in the substitution table. If you want to encrypt *fancy* blocks of text, you'll have to look for an algorithm elsewhere.

Here's the function, *Encrypt_Text()*, that is called to actually perform the encryption:

```
void far pascal Encrypt_Text
    (
    LPSTR Key,
    LPSTR PlainText,
    LPSTR EncryptedText
    )
{

char Subst[37];
register i;
register l = lstrlen (PlainText);

InitTable (Key, Subst);
_fstrupr (PlainText);
EncryptedText[0] = '0';
EncryptedText[1] = '1';
EncryptedText[2] = 0;

for (i = 0; i < l; i++)
    {
    if (isalpha (PlainText[i]))
        EncryptedText[i+2] = Subst[PlainText[i]-'A'];
    else
```

```
    EncryptedText[i+2] = PlainText[i];
  EncryptedText[i+2+1] = 0;
  }

}
```

After calling *InitTable()* to initialize the substitution table and translate the input string to upper case, *Encrypt_Text()* places the characters '01' at the start of the output buffer (*EncryptedText*). These two characters serve as a signature, a sign to the decryption routine that the string being examined has really been encrypted by *Encrypt_Text()*. The signature can also be used as a version indicator, allowing you to enhance this routine later and yet still be able to recognize—and translate—the older, simpler encryptions.

After the signature, each qualifying character—that is, the letters—are used as indexes into the substitution array to derive a new output character. Non-alpha characters are passed on as is.

The decryption function, *Decrypt_Text()*, is just as simple:

```
BOOL far pascal Decrypt_Text
    (
    LPSTR Key,
    LPSTR PlainText,
    LPSTR EncryptedText
    )
{

char Subst[27];
register i;
register l = lstrlen (EncryptedText);

if (EncryptedText[0] != '0' ||
    EncryptedText[1] != '1')
    {
    PlainText[0] = 0;
    return FALSE;
    }

InitTable (Key, Subst);
_fstrupr (EncryptedText);
PlainText[0] = 0;

for (i = 0; i < l; i++)
    {
    if (isalpha (EncryptedText[i+2]))
        PlainText[i] =
            (char) ('A' + (strchr (Subst, EncryptedText[i+2]) - Subst));
    else
```

```
      PlainText[i] = EncryptedText[i+2];
   PlainText[i+1] = 0;
   }

return TRUE;

}
```

Once the signature of the encrypted text has been verified and the substitution table initialized, the encrypted text is analyzed and each letter is used to reconstruct the original letters. (As before, non-alpha characters are passed through unchanged.)

## TEXTFILE.H

Since the standard C library doesn't provide satisfactory routines for buffered, text-oriented file input, we've supplied a few in this utility module. As with ENCRYPT.C, TEXTFILE.C comes with a separate header file so that it can easily be used with other projects.

Here is the TEXTFILE.H header file:

```
#ifndef __TEXTFILE_H__
#define __TEXTFILE_H__

#include <windows.h>

typedef struct
   {
   WORD FileSize;
   WORD Offset;
   LPSTR Block;
   } TFCB;

typedef TFCB far * LPTFCB;

BOOL far pascal TextFile_Open (LPTFCB Tfcb, LPSTR Pathname);
BOOL far pascal TextFile_Read (LPTFCB Tfcb, LPSTR Buffer);
void far pascal TextFile_Close (LPTFCB Tfcb);

#endif
```

The *TFCB* structure is a "text file control block." In Windows, you are not supposed to keep a file open longer than the time required to process a single message. (This is because of the limited number of file handles, and the fact that many Windows applications may be running at once.) By using buffered input and our *TFCB*, we can read the entire file into memory at once, then break out the individual lines of text. The *Offset* field in *TFCB* will keep track of where the next line starts in the buffer.

## TEXTFILE.C

The first function in the TEXTFILE.C source file, *TextFile_Open()*, opens the desired text file:

```
#include "textfile.h"
#include <dos.h>
#include <fcntl.h>
#include <io.h>

BOOL far pascal TextFile_Open (LPTFCB Tfcb, LPSTR Pathname)
  {
  HFILE FileNo;
  Tfcb->Offset = 0;
  FileNo = _lopen (Pathname, READ);
  if (FileNo != HFILE_ERROR)
    {
    HANDLE h;
    Tfcb->FileSize = filelength (FileNo);
    h = GlobalAlloc (GMEM_MOVEABLE, Tfcb->FileSize);
    Tfcb->Block = GlobalLock (Tfcb->hBlock);
    _lread (FileNo, Tfcb->hBlock, Tfcb->FileSize);
    _lclose (FileNo);
    return TRUE;
    }
  return FALSE;
  }
```

The once-undocumented Windows function *_lopen()* is used here to physically open the disk file. This function will return a file handle if it succeeds. If it fails, it returns the defined value *HFILE_ERROR*.

Assuming the operation succeeds, *TextFile_Open()* then fills in the proper values in the *TFCB* structure. It also allocates a global block of memory to serve as the input buffer. This routine will operate properly on a file up to 64K in size—more than adequate for any .INI file.

○   ○   ○

*Note that in the "old" days, we would have saved the handle to the global block and unlocked it between uses. Now, with Windows running only in protected mode, we don't have to.*

○   ○   ○

After the "open" operation—which in reality opens, reads into memory, and closes the physical file—the caller will invoke *TextFile_Read()* as many times as it takes to extract all the lines from the memory buffer:

```
BOOL far pascal TextFile_Read (LPTFCB Tfcb, LPSTR Buffer)
  {
  register WORD i = Tfcb->Offset, j = 0;
  if ((Tfcb->Offset == Tfcb->FileSize) ||
      (Tfcb->Block[i] == 0x1A))
    return FALSE;
  while ((i < Tfcb->FileSize) &&
      (Tfcb->Block[i] != 0x0D) &&
      (Tfcb->Block[i] != 0x1A))
    Buffer[j++] = Tfcb->Block[i++];
  if ((i < Tfcb->FileSize) && (Tfcb->Block[i] == 0x0D))
    i++;
  if ((i < Tfcb->FileSize) && (Tfcb->Block[i] == 0x0A))
    i++;
  Tfcb->Offset = i;
  Buffer[j] = 0;
  return TRUE;
  }
```

In addition to accepting lines terminated with a carriage return, *TextFile_Read()* also understands that ASCII files are sometimes terminated with a Ctrl-Z. It also handles optional line feeds after the carriage return.

Eventually, *TextFile_Read()* will finish reading all of the lines in the file and it will return *FALSE*. At that point the caller will invoke the next function, *TextFile_Close()*:

```
void far pascal TextFile_Close (LPTFCB Tfcb)
  {
  HANDLE h = LOWORD (GlobalHandle (HIWORD (Tfcb->Block)));
  GlobalFree (h);
  Tfcb->Block = NULL;
  }
```

Of course, this function doesn't *really* close anything. The physical file gets closed at the end of *TextFile_Open()*. But it does maintain the illusion for the caller, and it gives us a chance to free the global buffer we previously allocated.

# INTERNAL.H

We're now ready to examine the header file that is used by all the "regular" (non-utility, non-object) code modules in the project. Here is the entire file:

```
#include <windows.h>
#include <vbapi.h>
#include <custcntl.h>
#include <string.h>
#include <stdlib.h>
#include <dir.h>
#include "encrypt.h"
#include "textfile.h"

#ifdef MAIN
HINSTANCE LibInstance = 0;
char far * ClassName = "IniData";
#else
extern HINSTANCE LibInstance;
extern char far * ClassName;
#endif

HSZ far pascal GetAboutPropertyString (HCTL Control);
HWND far pascal PopupAbout (void);
void far pascal RegisterVbPopups (void);
void far pascal UnregisterVbPopups (void);
LPSTR far pascal HelpFileName (void);
BOOL far pascal vbm_Help
    (
    HWND Window,
    BYTE HelpType,
    BYTE i,
    PPROPINFO Properties[],
    PEVENTINFO Events[]
    );


void far pascal RegisterFileDlgPopup (void);
void far pascal UnregisterFileDlgPopup (void);
HWND far pascal PopupFileDlg
    (
    HCTL Control_,
    HWND Window,
    LPSTR Title,
    int PropertyIndex_,
    LPSTR Filters,
    int FilterIndex,
    LPSTR DefaultExt,
    DWORD Flags
    );
```

Because the IniData control cannot be used as a standard control, there is no window procedure in MAIN.C and therefore no *MyData* structure, either. Even though we've added the function prototypes for the Popup File Dialog, our INTERNAL.H file is pretty bare. So let's move on to the next module.

## MAIN.C

MAIN.C is also very simple because the IniData control requires no underlying child window. In fact, the only function in the file is the *LibMain()* routine that will be invoked each time the DLL is loaded:

```
#define MAIN
#include "Internal.H"

#pragma argsused
int far pascal LibMain
    (
    HINSTANCE hInstance,
    WORD DataSeg,
    WORD HeapSize,
    LPSTR CommandLine
    )
    {
    if (HeapSize > 0)
      UnlockData (0);
    LibInstance = hInstance;
    return TRUE;
    }
```

## VISUAL.C

MAIN.C is so sparse because all of the action takes place at the visual layer. Therefore it shouldn't surprise you to find that *plenty* is going on in VISUAL.C. Unlike some of our other controls, VISUAL.C has a rich set of local values, stored in the *VBDATA* structure:

```
#include "internal.h"

#define _segment(p) ((unsigned int) (((unsigned long) (void far *) (p)) >>
16L))
#define _offsetin(struc, fld) ((USHORT)&(((struc *)0)->fld))
#define VBERR_BADINDEX 381

static long Boolean[2] = { 0, -1 };

typedef struct
  {
  char FileName[MAXPATH];
  BYTE SectionCount;
  struct
    {
    char Name[32];
```

```
   } Sections[64];
char  Section[32];
BYTE  KeyCount;
char  Key[32];
struct
    {
    char  Name[32];
    } Keys[32];
char  DefaultText[128];
char  EncryptionKey[32];
char  ListDelimiter;
char  ListParsed: 1;
char  ListCount: 7;
struct
    {
    char  Item[32];
    } List[10];
} VBDATA, far * LPVBDATA;
```

In good design, form usually follows function, and so it is with *VBDATA*. The fields are in the order we'll need them. The name of the .INI file comes first, followed by the names of sections in that file. The *specified* section name is followed by the list of keys in that section. Then we add in the *specified* key name and we have enough information to distinguish the specific value the user wants.

However, what if the value—or the file itself—is missing? The private profile functions were written to *mask* this problem from the user. The *DefaultText* property will supply a value if there isn't one in the .INI file.

The remaining fields support our added features: value encryption and the parsing of multiple-item value lists.

## Defining the Properties and Events

Next up comes the list of properties required for the IniData control:

```
PROPINFO Property_About =
  {
  "(About)",
  DT_HSZ | PF_fGetMsg | PF_fNoRuntimeW | PF_fGetHszMsg,
  0, 0, 0, NULL, 0
  };

PROPINFO Property_FileName =
  {
  "FileName",
  DT_HSZ | PF_fSetMsg | PF_fGetMsg | PF_fSaveMsg | PF_fEditable,
  0, 0, 0, NULL, 0
  };
```

```
PROPINFO Property_SectionList =
  {
  "SectionList",
  DT_HSZ | PF_fGetMsg | PF_fNoShow | PF_fPropArray | PF_fNoRuntimeW,
  0, 0, 0, NULL, 0
  };

PROPINFO Property_SectionCount =
  {
  "SectionCount",
  DT_SHORT | PF_fGetMsg | PF_fNoShow | PF_fNoRuntimeW,
  0, 0, 0, NULL, 0
  };

PROPINFO Property_Section =
  {
  "Section",
  DT_HSZ | PF_fSetMsg | PF_fGetMsg | PF_fSaveMsg,
  0, 0, 0, NULL, 0
  };

PROPINFO Property_KeyList =
  {
  "KeyList",
  DT_HSZ | PF_fGetMsg | PF_fNoShow | PF_fPropArray | PF_fNoRuntimeW,
  0, 0, 0, NULL, 0
  };

PROPINFO Property_KeyCount =
  {
  "KeyCount",
  DT_SHORT | PF_fGetMsg | PF_fNoShow | PF_fNoRuntimeW,
  0, 0, 0, NULL, 0
  };

PROPINFO Property_Key =
  {
  "KeyName",
  DT_HSZ | PF_fSetMsg | PF_fGetMsg | PF_fSaveMsg,
  0, 0, 0, NULL, 0
  };

PROPINFO Property_DefaultText =
  {
  "DefaultText",
  DT_HSZ | PF_fSetMsg | PF_fGetMsg | PF_fSaveMsg,
  0, 0, 0, NULL, 0
  };
```

```
PROPINFO Property_Text =
  {
  "Text",
  DT_HSZ | PF_fSetMsg | PF_fGetMsg | PF_fNoShow,
  0, 0, 0, NULL, 0
  };

PROPINFO Property_EncryptionKey =
  {
  "EncryptionKey",
  DT_HSZ | PF_fSetMsg | PF_fGetMsg | PF_fSaveMsg,
  0, 0, 0, NULL, 0
  };

PROPINFO Property_List =
  {
  "List",
  DT_HSZ | PF_fGetMsg | PF_fNoShow | PF_fPropArray | PF_fNoRuntimeW,
  0, 0, 0, NULL, 0
  };

PROPINFO Property_ListCount =
  {
  "ListCount",
  DT_SHORT | PF_fGetMsg | PF_fNoShow | PF_fNoRuntimeW,
  0, 0, 0, NULL, 0
  };

PROPINFO Property_ListDelimiter =
  {
  "ListDelimiter",
  DT_HSZ | PF_fSetMsg | PF_fGetMsg,
  0, 0, 0, NULL, 0
  };

PPROPINFO Properties[] =
  {
  PPROPINFO_STD_NAME,
  PPROPINFO_STD_INDEX,
  PPROPINFO_STD_LEFTNORUN,
  PPROPINFO_STD_TOPNORUN,
  PPROPINFO_STD_TAG,
  PPROPINFO_STD_LAST,
  &Property_About,
  &Property_FileName,
  &Property_SectionList,
  &Property_SectionCount,
  &Property_Section,
  &Property_KeyList,
  &Property_KeyCount,
```

```
&Property_Key,
&Property_DefaultText,
&Property_Text,
&Property_EncryptionKey,
&Property_List,
&Property_ListCount,
&Property_ListDelimiter,
NULL
};

typedef enum
    {
    IPROPINFO_STD_NAME,
    IPROPINFO_STD_INDEX,
    IPROPINFO_STD_LEFT,
    IPROPINFO_STD_TOP,
    IPROPINFO_STD_TAG,
    IPROPINFO_STD_LAST,
    IPROPINFO_About,
    IPROPINFO_Filename,
    IPROPINFO_SectionList,
    IPROPINFO_SectionCount,
    IPROPINFO_Section,
    IPROPINFO_KeyList,
    IPROPINFO_KeyCount,
    IPROPINFO_Key,
    IPROPINFO_DefaultText,
    IPROPINFO_Text,
    IPROPINFO_EncryptionKey,
    IPROPINFO_List,
    IPROPINFO_ListCount,
    IPROPINFO_ListDelimiter,
    IPROPINFO_End
    } PROPSIX;
```

Although there are quite a few properties, only one event is needed:

```
EVENTINFO Event_Change = { "Change", 0, 0, NULL, NULL };

PEVENTINFO Events[] =
    {
    &Event_Change,
    NULL
    };

typedef enum
    {
    IPEVENTINFO_Change,
    IPEVENTINFO_End
    } EVENTSIX;
```

The *Change* event will be triggered by the receipt of a *WM_WININICHANGE* message. This message notifies a VB application that, perhaps, a key's value has changed. Applications responding to the *Change* event should probably reload their initialization values.

## Building the Sections List

The private profile functions allow you to list keys in a section, obtain values, and even delete keys and entire sections from an .INI file. Since there is no provision for enumerating section names of a .INI file, our IniData control must actually open and read the .INI file in question. We've already presented the low-level mechanism for reading files in the TEXTFILE.C module. Now let's look at how that module is used to enumerate the section names:

```
static void near pascal BuildSectionList (LPVBDATA VbData)
  {
  if (! VbData->SectionCount)
    {
    char PathName[MAXPATH];
    TFCB IniFile;
    if (VbData->FileName[1] == ':' && VbData->FileName[2] == '\\')
      lstrcpy (PathName, VbData->FileName);
    else
      {
      GetWindowsDirectory (PathName, sizeof PathName);
      lstrcat (PathName, "\\");
      lstrcat (PathName, VbData->FileName);
      }
    if (TextFile_Open (&IniFile, PathName))
      {
      char Buffer[256];
      while (TextFile_Read (&IniFile, Buffer))
        {
        if (Buffer[0] == '[')
          {
          LPSTR t;
          if ((t = strchr (Buffer, ']')) != NULL)
            {
            *t = 0;
            lstrcpy (VbData->Sections[VbData->SectionCount++].Name,
              &Buffer[1]);
            }
          }
        Buffer[0] = 0;
        }
```

```
        TextFile_Close (&IniFile);
        }
    }
}
```

Notice first that this code is *only* exercised if *VbData->SectionCount* is equal to zero. *BuildSectionList()* is actually called from several places; the real-life order will depend on the sequence in which a VB app sets the IniData properties. Actually reading the file every time would take too long, however. So we check for a special condition: If the count of sections is equal to zero, we know that the list has not been filled in yet. On subsequent calls to *BuildSectionList()*, the list will be referenced but not actually rebuilt. (You can force a rebuild by setting *VbData->SectionCount* to zero, which happens automatically if the filename is changed, and on command if the VB app invokes IniData's *Refresh* method, as we'll see shortly.)

The first block of actual code, after the variable definitions, qualifies the filename. Windows does not locate .INI files the way it finds other files. If the filename is not fully qualified, Windows looks in the Windows directory—the one you get when you invoke *GetWindowsDir()*. If the name *is* fully qualified, Windows will look in the specified location. Either way, Windows looks no further.

The next code block opens the file and reads each line. Information is saved from only those lines that begin and end with brackets. The file is then "closed." (Remember that the TEXTFILE.C functions don't open and close the file when you would expect.)

## Building the Key List

When a VB app places a name in the *Section* property of its initialization file, the IniData control loads the set of keys available for that section. Fortunately, this task is much easier to perform than it is to list sections. One call to *GetPrivateProfileString()*, with the *Key* parameter missing, supplies the whole list at once. The items in the list are *NULL*-terminated; the list itself ends with a double *NULL*. Thus, the following function retrieves and parses the list:

```
static void near pascal BuildKeyList (LPVBDATA VbData)
    {
    if (! VbData->KeyCount)
        {
        LPSTR Temp = malloc (2048);
        GetPrivateProfileString (VbData->Section,
            NULL, NULL, Temp, 2048, VbData->FileName);
        while (Temp[0])
```

```
      {
      lstrcpy (VbData->Keys[VbData->KeyCount++].Name,  Temp);
      Temp = &Temp[lstrlen (Temp)+1];
      }
    free (Temp);
    }
  }
```

## Implementing the Text Property

The *Text* property is interesting to code because it may, or may not, have to deal with data encryption:

```
static void near pascal GetText (LPVBDATA VbData, LPSTR Buffer)
  {
  char PlainBuffer[128];
  char EncryptedBuffer[128];
  LPSTR Ptr;
  Ptr = (! VbData->EncryptionKey[0]) ? PlainBuffer : EncryptedBuffer;
  if (! VbData->Key[0])
    Ptr[0] = 0;
  else
    GetPrivateProfileString (VbData->Section,
      VbData->Key, VbData->DefaultText, Ptr, 128, VbData->FileName);
  if (VbData->EncryptionKey[0])
    {
    Decrypt_Text (VbData->EncryptionKey, PlainBuffer, EncryptedBuffer);
    Ptr = PlainBuffer;
    }
  lstrcpy (Buffer, Ptr);
  }
```

*GetPrivateProfileString()* again forms the centerpiece of this function. It is supplied with the filename, section, and key names, and it does almost all the work (except for the decryption). Note the use of the *DefaultText* field of *VbData*. That facility is built into *GetPrivateProfileString()*; we just have to supply a default value for it to work. (And, of course, the actual default value is loaded as a property by the VB application.)

## Parsing a Multi-Item Value

Many values in a typical .INI file are actually *multiple* values. For example, the colors in WIN.INI are expressed as three numbers; one each for the red, green, and blue components of the color.

Sometimes multiple values are delimited by a space or a comma. Some applications even use semicolons! That's why we've provided a *ListDelimiter* property for a VB app to set. The following function obtains the value for the current section/key combination, decrypted if necessary, and breaks it into its component parts at each occurrence of the delimiter:

```
static void near pascal ParseList (LPVBDATA VbData)
  {
  char Buffer[128];
  register WORD i = 0;
  register WORD j = 0;
  BOOL NewItem = FALSE;

  VbData->ListCount = 0;
  GetText (VbData, Buffer);

  while (Buffer[i] && VbData->ListCount <= 10)
    {
    while (Buffer[i] == VbData->ListDelimiter)
      {
      NewItem = TRUE;
      i++;
      }
    if (NewItem)
      {
      VbData->List[VbData->ListCount].Item[j] = 0;
      VbData->ListCount++;
      j = 0;
      NewItem = FALSE;
      }
    if (j || (Buffer[i] != ' '))
      VbData->List[VbData->ListCount].Item[j++] = Buffer[i];
    i++;
    }
  if (j)
    {
    VbData->List[VbData->ListCount].Item[j] = 0;
    VbData->ListCount++;
    }

  VbData->ListParsed = TRUE;
  }
```

## Creating the Control Data

IniData processes the *WM_NCREATE* message to place initial values in the more sensitive fields of the *VBDATA* structure:

```
#pragma argsused
static void near pascal wm_NcCreate
```

```
    (
    HCTL  Control,
    LPCREATESTRUCT  Create
    )
  {
  LPVBDATA VbData = (LPVBDATA) VBDerefControl (Control);
  lstrcpy (VbData->FileName, "win.ini");
  VbData->ListDelimiter = ' ';
  VbData->SectionCount = 0;
  VbData->Section[0] = 0;
  VbData->KeyCount = 0;
  VbData->Key[0] = 0;
  VbData->ListCount = 0;
  }
```

Since no memory is allocated as part of the initialization, we don't need to process the *WM_NCDESTROY* message.

## Waiting for the WIN.INI File to Change

If a change is made to the WIN.INI file, the maker of that change is supposed to broadcast the fact that the change was made to all applications. This broadcast is achieved using a *WM_WININICHANGE* message, which may or may not include the name of the specific section that was changed. In true VB control fashion, we use this message as an excuse to trigger the *Change* event, and so pass its handling on to the VB app:

```
static void near pascal wm_WinIniChange (HCTL Control, LPSTR Section)
  {
  LPVBDATA VbData = (LPVBDATA) VBDerefControl (Control);
  if ((! Section) || (lstrcmpi (VbData->Section, Section)==0))
    {
    VBFireEvent (Control, IPEVENTINFO_Change, NULL);
    VbData->SectionCount = 0;
    VbData->KeyCount = 0;
    }
  }
```

We don't completely ignore it, though. We set our section and key counts to zero, forcing those lists to be rebuilt if the VB app queries them.

According to the documentation, the *WM_WININICHANGE* message is sent only for changes in the WIN.INI file. No equivalent message is provided for changes to other .INI files. In the world of C applications, it would be easy to register a new message for use by a family of applications sharing the same .INI file, whenever one of them made a change. This is trickier to accomplish in Visual Basic, however. We suggest that if you expect many copies of your application to be running at once, or if you are writing a suite of applications that will share a .INI file, you should use the *WM_WININICHANGE* message anyway, and respond to the *Change* event. As you'll see in the next function and again later, that behavior is built into the IniData control.

## Removing a Key From a Section

The only custom method IniData supports is *RemoveItem*. This method, you may recall, was originally invented for use with listboxes. It is invoked with the index of the item to be removed.

By documenting that an index of -1 deletes the current section, and a number higher than that deletes the key in the *KeyList* of that index, we can provide a VB application with as much control as possible:

```
typedef struct
    {
    long Count;
    long Index;
    } REMOVEITEM;
typedef REMOVEITEM far * LPREMOVEITEM;

static long near pascal vbm_Method
    (
    HCTL Control,
    HWND Window,
    USHORT Method,
    void far * Args
    )
    {
    LPVBDATA VbData = (LPVBDATA) VBDerefControl (Control);
    LPSTR Text;
    LPREMOVEITEM RemoveItem = Args;
    switch (Method)
        {
        case METH_REMOVEITEM:
            {
            register int i;
            i = (RemoveItem->Count == 2) ? (int) RemoveItem->Index : -1;
            if (i < 0)
                WritePrivateProfileString (VbData->Section,
                    NULL, NULL, VbData->FileName);
            else if (i < VbData->KeyCount)
                WritePrivateProfileString (VbData->Section,
                    VbData->Keys[i].Name, NULL, VbData->FileName);
            }
```

```
      VbData->SectionCount = 0;
      SendMessage (-1, WM_WININICHANGE,
        0, (long) (LPSTR) VbData->Section);
      return 0;
   default:
      return VBDefControlProc (Control, Window, VBM_METHOD,
        Method, (long) Args);
   }
}
```

Note that this change to the .INI file does not go unnoticed by other
applications; a *WM_WININICHANGE* message is broadcast to all applications.
That's what the first parameter (-1) of the *SendMessage()* function is used for.

## Setting and Getting Property Values

Except for the *(About)* property, all our properties can be set at run time as
well as design time—guaranteeing a full *vbm_SetProperty()* function:

```
#pragma argsused
static BOOL near pascal vbm_SetProperty
    (
    HCTL Control,
    HWND Window,
    USHORT Property,
    LPSTR Value,
    long far * Error
    )
{
LPVBDATA VbData = (LPVBDATA) VBDerefControl (Control);
switch (Property)
    {
    case IPROPINFO_Filename:
       lstrcpy (VbData->FileName, Value);
       VbData->KeyCount = 0;
       VbData->SectionCount = 0;
       VbData->ListParsed = FALSE;
       return TRUE;
    case IPROPINFO_Section:
       lstrcpy (VbData->Section, Value);
       VbData->KeyCount = 0;
       VbData->ListParsed = FALSE;
       return TRUE;
    case IPROPINFO_Key:
       lstrcpy (VbData->Key, Value);
       VbData->ListParsed = FALSE;
       return TRUE;
```

```
    case IPROPINFO_DefaultText:
      lstrcpy (VbData->DefaultText, Value);
      VbData->ListParsed = FALSE;
      return TRUE;
    case IPROPINFO_Text:
      if (VbData->Key[0])
        {
        char EncryptedBuffer[128];
        LPSTR Buffer;
        if (! VbData->EncryptionKey[0])
          Buffer = Value;
        else
          {
          Encrypt_Text (VbData->EncryptionKey,
            (LPSTR) Value,
            EncryptedBuffer);
          Buffer = EncryptedBuffer;
          }
        WritePrivateProfileString (VbData->Section,
          VbData->Key, Buffer, VbData->FileName);
        VbData->ListParsed = FALSE;
        }
      return TRUE;
    case IPROPINFO_EncryptionKey:
      lstrcpy (VbData->EncryptionKey, Value);
      VbData->ListParsed = FALSE;
      return TRUE;
    case IPROPINFO_ListDelimiter:
      if (Value[0])
        VbData->ListDelimiter = Value[0];
      else
        VbData->ListDelimiter = ' ';
      VbData->ListParsed = FALSE;
      return TRUE;
    default:
      return FALSE;
    }
  }
```

Since these properties are all string-type ones and the parameter passed as part of the *VBM_SETPROPERTY* message passes a pointer to a C string on such property types, it's easy for us to set these values. *Reading* them is a little harder because we'll have to allocate memory to copy the text into the Visual Basic HSZ (handle to null-terminated string) functions:

```
#pragma argsused
static BOOL near pascal vbm_GetProperty
    (
```

```
  HCTL Control,
  HWND Window,
  USHORT Property,
  LPVOID Value,
  long far * Error
  )
{
LPVBDATA VbData = (LPVBDATA) VBDerefControl (Control);
switch (Property)
  {
  case IPROPINFO_Filename:
    *(HSZ far *)Value = VBCreateHsz (_segment (Control), VbData->FileName);
    return TRUE;
  case IPROPINFO_SectionList:
    {
    LPDATASTRUCT Data = Value;
    long i = Data->index[0].data;
    BuildSectionList (VbData);
    if ((i < 0) || (i >= VbData->SectionCount))
      {
      *Error = VBERR_BADINDEX;
      return TRUE;
      }
    Data->data = (long) VBCreateHsz (_segment(Control),
      VbData->Sections[i].Name);
    }
    return TRUE;
  case IPROPINFO_SectionCount:
    BuildSectionList (VbData);
    *(long far *)Value = VbData->SectionCount;
    return TRUE;
  case IPROPINFO_Section:
    *(HSZ far *)Value = VBCreateHsz (_segment (Control), VbData->Section);
    return TRUE;
  case IPROPINFO_Key:
    *(HSZ far *)Value = VBCreateHsz (_segment (Control), VbData->Key);
    return TRUE;
  case IPROPINFO_KeyList:
    {
    LPDATASTRUCT Data = Value;
    long i = Data->index[0].data;
    BuildKeyList (VbData);
    if ((i < 0) || (i >= VbData->KeyCount))
      {
      *Error = VBERR_BADINDEX;
      return TRUE;
      }
    Data->data = (long) VBCreateHsz (_segment(Control),
      VbData->Keys[i].Name);
```

```
      }
    return TRUE;
  case IPROPINFO_KeyCount:
    BuildKeyList (VbData);
    *(long far *)Value = VbData->KeyCount;
    return TRUE;
  case IPROPINFO_DefaultText:
    *(HSZ far *)Value = VBCreateHsz (_segment (Control),
      VbData->DefaultText);
    return TRUE;
  case IPROPINFO_Text:
    {
    char Buffer[128];
    GetText (VbData, Buffer);
    *(HSZ far *)Value = VBCreateHsz (_segment (Control), Buffer);
    }
    return TRUE;
  case IPROPINFO_EncryptionKey:
    *(HSZ far *)Value = VBCreateHsz (_segment (Control),
      VbData->EncryptionKey);
    return TRUE;
  case IPROPINFO_List:
    {
    LPDATASTRUCT Data = Value;
    long i = Data->index[0].data;
    if (! VbData->ListParsed)
      ParseList (VbData);
    if ((i < 0) || (i >= VbData->ListCount))
      {
      *Error = VBERR_BADINDEX;
      return TRUE;
      }
    Data->data = (long) VBCreateHsz (_segment(Control),
      VbData->List[(WORD)i].Item);
    }
    return TRUE;
  case IPROPINFO_ListCount:
    if (! VbData->ListParsed)
      ParseList (VbData);
    *(long far *)Value = VbData->ListCount;
    return TRUE;
  case IPROPINFO_ListDelimiter:
    if (VbData->ListDelimiter == ' ')
      *(HSZ far *)Value = VBCreateHsz (_segment (Control), "");
    else
      {
      char Buffer[2];
      Buffer[0] = VbData->ListDelimiter;
      Buffer[1] = 0;
```

```
          *(HSZ far *)Value = VBCreateHsz (_segment (Control), Buffer);
        }
      return TRUE;
    default:
      return FALSE;
    }
}
```

## Loading and Storing Property Values

Since many of our properties are string properties, it makes sense to place the code to read strings efficiently from the form in a function of its own:

```
static void near pascal ReadFormData
    (
    HFORMFILE FormFile,
    LPSTR Buffer
    )
{
WORD ByteCount;
VBReadFormFile (FormFile, (LPVOID) &ByteCount, sizeof ByteCount);
VBReadFormFile (FormFile, (LPVOID) Buffer, ByteCount);
Buffer[ByteCount] = 0;
}
```

The routine simply reads the length of the string first, then the string itself. This makes it a lot easier to load the various properties on demand:

```
#pragma argsused
static BOOL near pascal vbm_LoadProperty
    (
    HCTL Control,
    HWND Window,
    USHORT Property,
    HFORMFILE FormFile,
    long far * Error
    )
{
LPVBDATA VbData = (LPVBDATA) VBDerefControl (Control);
switch (Property)
    {
    case IPROPINFO_Filename:
      ReadFormData (FormFile, VbData->FileName);
      return TRUE;
    case IPROPINFO_Section:
      ReadFormData (FormFile, VbData->Section);
      return TRUE;
```

```
      case IPROPINFO_Key:
        ReadFormData (FormFile, VbData->Key);
        return TRUE;
      case IPROPINFO_DefaultText:
        ReadFormData (FormFile, VbData->DefaultText);
        return TRUE;
      case IPROPINFO_EncryptionKey:
        ReadFormData (FormFile, VbData->EncryptionKey);
        return TRUE;
      default:
        return FALSE;
      }
    }
```

Likewise, we'll need a companion function to write the strings out in the format that *ReadFormData()* expects:

```
static void near pascal WriteFormData
    (
    HFORMFILE FormFile,
    LPSTR Buffer
    )
  {
  WORD ByteCount = lstrlen (Buffer);
  VBWriteFormFile (FormFile, (LPVOID) &ByteCount, sizeof ByteCount);
  VBWriteFormFile (FormFile, (LPVOID) Buffer, ByteCount);
  }
```

This allows us to store the properties as easily as we can load them:

```
#pragma argsused
static BOOL near pascal vbm_SaveProperty
    (
    HCTL Control,
    HWND Window,
    USHORT Property,
    HFORMFILE FormFile,
    long far * Error
    )
  {
  LPVBDATA VbData = (LPVBDATA) VBDerefControl (Control);
  switch (Property)
    {
    case IPROPINFO_Filename:
      WriteFormData (FormFile, VbData->FileName);
      return TRUE;
    case IPROPINFO_Section:
```

```
      WriteFormData (FormFile, VbData->Section);
      return TRUE;
   case IPROPINFO_Key:
      WriteFormData (FormFile, VbData->Key);
      return TRUE;
   case IPROPINFO_DefaultText:
      WriteFormData (FormFile, VbData->DefaultText);
      return TRUE;
   case IPROPINFO_EncryptionKey:
      WriteFormData (FormFile, VbData->EncryptionKey);
      return TRUE;
   default:
      return FALSE;
   }
}
```

## Wrapping up the Visual Module

We're now ready for the control procedure, *CtlProc()*. This function serves as the heart of any control, especially one like IniData that is not based on an existing window:

```
long far pascal _export CtlProc
    (
    HCTL Control,
    HWND Window,
    USHORT Msg,
    USHORT wParam,
    long lParam
    )
{
long Error = 0;
switch (Msg)
    {
    case WM_NCCREATE:
      wm_NcCreate (Control, (LPCREATESTRUCT) lParam);
      break;
    case WM_WININICHANGE:
      wm_WinIniChange (Control, (LPSTR) lParam);
      break;
    case VBM_METHOD:
      return vbm_Method (Control, Window, wParam, (void far *) lParam);
    case VBN_COMMAND:
      switch (HIWORD (lParam))
         {
         default:
           break;
         }
```

```
        break;
case  VBM_SETPROPERTY:
    if (vbm_SetProperty (Control, Window,
        wParam, (LPSTR) lParam, &Error))
      return Error;
    break;
case  VBM_GETPROPERTY:
    if (vbm_GetProperty (Control, Window,
        wParam, (LPVOID) lParam, &Error))
      return Error;
    break;
case  VBM_LOADPROPERTY:
    if (vbm_LoadProperty (Control, Window,
        wParam, (HFORMFILE) lParam, &Error))
      return Error;
    break;
case  VBM_SAVEPROPERTY:
    if (vbm_SaveProperty (Control, Window,
        wParam, (HFORMFILE) lParam, &Error))
      return Error;
    break;
case  VBM_GETPROPERTYHSZ:
    switch (wParam)
      {
      case  IPROPINFO_About:
        *((HSZ far *) lParam) = GetAboutPropertyString (Control);
        break;
      }
    return 0;
case  VBM_INITPROPPOPUP:
    switch (wParam)
      {
      case  IPROPINFO_About:
        return PopupAbout ();
      case  IPROPINFO_Filename:
        return PopupFileDlg (Control,
          Window,
          "Select Initialization File",
          IPROPINFO_Filename,
          ".INI  files\0*.ini\0All  files\0*.*\0",
            1, "ini", 0);
      }
    break;
case  VBM_HELP:
    if (vbm_Help (Window,
        LOBYTE (wParam),
        HIBYTE (wParam),
        Properties, Events))
      return 0;
```

```
        break;
    case WM_DESTROY:
        WinHelp (Window, HelpFileName (), HELP_QUIT, 0);
        break;
    }
    return VBDefControlProc (Control, Window, Msg, wParam, lParam);
}
```

Note that the *FileName* property, as in the TextFileView and TextFileEdit controls, uses the *PopupFileDlg()* function to assist the VB programmer in supplying a filename at design time.

Next, we set up the *MODEL* structure. We haven't talked much about this structure since the Skeleton chapter because we've been using it without any major changes. Note the new flags that have been added now:

```
MODEL Model =
    {
    VB_VERSION,
    MODEL_fFocusOk | MODEL_fArrows | MODEL_fGraphical | MODEL_fInvisAtRun,
    (PCTLPROC) CtlProc,
    CS_VREDRAW | CS_HREDRAW,
    WS_BORDER,
    sizeof (VBDATA),
    8000,
    NULL,
    NULL,
    NULL,
    Properties,
    Events,
    IPROPINFO_STD_NAME,
    IPEVENTINFO_Change,
    -1
    };
```

The new flags are *MODEL_fGraphical* and *MODEL_fInvisAtRun*. The first flag tells the visual environment that this control is not only *not based* on an existing window class; it *has* no underlying window, ever, not even one supplied by the environment. The flag was intended for use with simple display controls like the Image control that comes with Visual Basic 3.0. Such a control cannot respond to mouse clicks or even mouse movements; they are intended for their visual effects alone.

The second flag states that this control will be invisible at run time. At first glance, it might seem that these two flags conflict. But if you think about it, any "control" which simply encapsulates related function calls, does not need an underlying window and does not need to be displayed at run time. These two flags, then, are perfect for IniData.

The only thing left to do in this module is to supply the initialization and termination hooks that the visual environments require:

```
#pragma argsused
BOOL far pascal _export VBINITCC
    (
    USHORT  Version,
    BOOL  Runtime
    )
  {
  if (! Runtime)
    {
    RegisterVbPopups ();
    RegisterFileDlgPopup ();
    }
  Model.npszDefCtlName =
  Model.npszClassName = (PSTR) ClassName;
  Model.npszParentClassName = NULL;
  return VBRegisterModel (LibInstance, &Model);
  }

VOID FAR PASCAL _export VBTERMCC (void)
  {
  UnregisterVbPopups ();
  UnregisterFileDlgPopup ();
  }
```

## FILEPROP.C

This module is unchanged from the TextFileView and TextFileEdit controls; simply copy it to the IniData control project.

## HELP.C

This module is unchanged from the Skeleton control; simply copy it to the IniData control project.

## INIDATA.DEF

The module definition file for the IniData control is somewhat abbreviated since it doesn't have to export the functions required by a control that is going to be part of a "standard" Windows application:

```
LIBRARY INIDATA
EXETYPE WINDOWS
```

```
CODE PRELOAD MOVEABLE DISCARDABLE
DATA PRELOAD MOVEABLE SINGLE
HEAPSIZE  0
EXPORTS
        WEP        RESIDENTNAME
```

Remember that *WEP* should be marked *PRIVATE* instead of *RESIDENTNAME* if you are using the newer Microsoft linker.

## INIDATA.RC

The IniData resources are derived from the Skeleton resources as well. We don't have to support the Dialog Editor, so the first entries in the .RC file are provided for the Visual Basic environment:

```
#include "internal.h"

// For Visual Basic
8000 BITMAP MOVEABLE PURE "8000.BMP"
8001 BITMAP MOVEABLE PURE "8001.BMP"
8003 BITMAP MOVEABLE PURE "8003.BMP"
8006 BITMAP MOVEABLE PURE "8006.BMP"

ABOUT DIALOG 41, 45, 192, 125
STYLE DS_MODALFRAME | WS_POPUP | WS_CAPTION
CAPTION "About IniData Custom Control"
FONT 8, "MS Sans Serif"
BEGIN
  CONTROL "IniData Custom Control", 0, "STATIC", SS_CENTER | WS_CHILD |
WS_VISIBLE, 0, 8, 190, 8
  CONTROL "by Paul S. Cilwa", 0, "STATIC", SS_CENTER | WS_CHILD |
WS_VISIBLE, 0, 16, 190, 8
  ICON "MAIN", 0, 87, 29, 18, 20
  CONTROL "Version 1.0", 0, "STATIC", SS_CENTER | WS_CHILD | WS_VISIBLE,
0, 59, 190, 8
  CONTROL "\2511993 by Paul S. Cilwa", 0, "STATIC", SS_CENTER | WS_CHILD
| WS_VISIBLE, 0, 79, 190, 8
  CONTROL "All Rights Reserved", 0, "STATIC", SS_CENTER | WS_CHILD |
WS_VISIBLE, 0, 88, 190, 8
  PUSHBUTTON "OK", IDOK, 74, 102, 45, 15
END

MAIN ICON "INIDATA.ICO"
```

The four visual toolbox bitmaps are shown in Figure 11.2. The About box is shown in Figure 11.3, and the IniData icon is shown in Figure 11.4.

**Figure 11.2 IniData bitmaps are from left to right: 8000, 8001, 8003, and 8006 for Visual Basic.**

**Figure 11.3 The IniData About box for Visual Basic.**

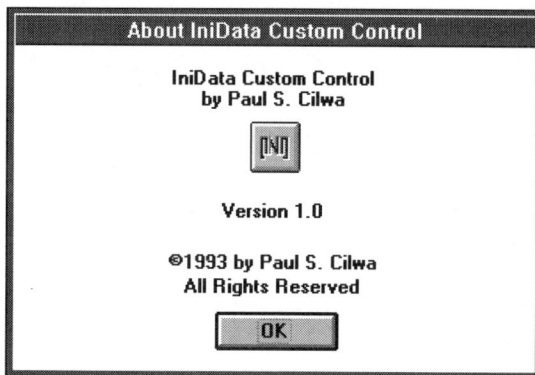

**Figure 11.4 The IniData icon.**

As always, don't forget the following version control information:

```
1 VERSIONINFO LOADONCALL MOVEABLE DISCARDABLE
FILEVERSION 1, 0, 0, 0
PRODUCTVERSION 1, 0, 0, 0
FILEOS VOS__WINDOWS16
FILETYPE VFT_DLL
BEGIN
  BLOCK "StringFileInfo"
  BEGIN
    BLOCK "040904E4"
    BEGIN
      VALUE "CompanyName", "Coriolis Group\000"
      VALUE "FileDescription", "IniData Custom Control for Visual Basic
and Windows\000"
```

```
        VALUE "FileVersion", "1.0.0.0\000"
        VALUE "InternalName", "INIDATA\000"
        VALUE "LegalCopyright", "Copyright © Paul S. Cilwa 1993\000"
        VALUE "OriginalFilename", "inidata.vbx\000"
        VALUE "ProductName", "Windows Programming Power\000"
        VALUE "ProductVersion", "1.0.0.0\000"
        VALUE "Comments", "\000"
      END
    END
END
```

# Enhancing the IniData Control

Frankly, we can't think of any way this control can be improved. This doesn't happen often, but when it does it we realize that these are the golden moments we strive for as programmers.

If *you* can think of an improvement, go for it. You've got the source code, and now you should have the skills to work with the control and make any changes you like. Better still—you can create your *own* custom controls from scratch, or at least from the Skeleton we've provided in Chapter 3.

Because, in the final analysis, improving IniData—or any of the other controls presented in this book—is just part of that ongoing effort, the one that started 500,000 years ago when one of our ancestors first chipped a piece of flint and thought there might be some use for it. Ever since, we've been improving our tools. Blaise Pascal did it when he designed his Mathematical Engine. Grace Hopper did it when she guided the team that created the first useful, business-oriented programming language. Cooper Software did it when they created Visual Basic. And those of us who write custom controls for the new environments continue the task still.

Go, thou, and do likewise.

# Appendix A

# Using the Custom Controls

This appendix provides instructions to help you use each of the custom controls presented in this book. Whenever appropriate, we'll show you how to use a control from both standard and visual environments.

# How to Use This Guide

This guide is organized into the following sections to help you use the controls:

- *Supported Custom Controls* presents a quick description of each custom control presented in this appendix.
- *Using Controls in Standard Windows Apps* provides all of the instructions required for using the controls with standard Windows apps.
- *Using Controls in Visual Environments* provides all of the instructions required for using the controls in both Visual Basic applications and applications constructed in other visual environments.
- *Using the ... Control* presents information on each custom control, including details for each style, message, and notification (standard apps), and each property, method, and event (visual apps).

**Note:** Make sure you first read the sections on using the controls with standard apps and visual environments before you try to use the controls.

# Supported Custom Controls

Here is the complete list of custom controls that are presented:

| Control | Description |
| --- | --- |
| Panel | Provides a 3-D panel similar to the one provided with Visual Basic. This control is designed to work with non-visual environments. |
| Virtual Listbox | Provides a listbox capable of displaying up to 32K items. |
| Pagelist | Provides a selector for accessing pages in a document. |
| Browser | Provides a Browser tool for viewing database records. This control is designed to work with Visual Basic. |
| TextFileView | Provides a useful text viewer for displaying up to 32K lines of text directly from a disk file. |
| TextFileEdit | Provides a useful text editor for editing up to 32K lines of text directly from a disk file. |
| IniData | Provides a tool for accessing an application's initialization file (or WIN.INI). This control is designed to work with the visual programming environments. |

# Using Controls in Standard Windows Apps

The following controls can be incorporated into "standard" Windows applications:

- Panel
- Virtual Listbox
- Pagelist
- TextFileView
- TextFileEdit

To incorporate one of these controls in a standard Windows app, you'll need to follow these four steps:

1.  Compile and link the control as a DLL. This operation is explained in detail in Chapter 3. You can skip this step by using the .DLL or .VBX provided on the companion disk. If the control will also be used in a visual development environment, you must rename the .DLL to a .VBX extension.

2.  Include the *LoadLibrary()* function call in the application that will be using the control. The following statement is required to load and save the instance handle of the control's DLL:

    ```
    LibHandle = LoadLibrary ("libname");
    ```

    Here *libname* must be the actual name of the custom control .DLL or .VBX you are using. *LibHandle* is the variable used to save the control's instance handle. (It will be used later to free the library.) As an example, if you were loading the Panel control, the statement would look like:

    ```
    PanelDLL = LoadLibrary("PANEL.DLL");
    ```

3.  Include the control in a dialog template in a resource file, or create the control dynamically in your program by calling the *CreateWindow()* function. (We'll include specific examples of how this is done when we present each control.)

4.  Unload the custom control library before your application terminates by using the instance handle you saved in step 2:

    ```
    FreeLibrary (LibHandle);
    ```

    That's all there is to it. (Well, almost.)

## Using Styles

When you use a custom control in a standard Windows app, you can assign it certain *styles*. The styles are assigned when you define the control in a resource file or create the control dynamically by calling the *CreateWindow()* function. For example, to display a control with a standard border, you use the *WS_BORDER* style. To include a horizontal scroll bar with a control, you use the *WS_HSCROLL* style. Most of the styles we use are standard ones that can be applied to any control. However, we do use some unique custom styles which will be discussed as each control is presented.

## Using Messages

A standard Windows app communicates with a custom control by sending it *messages*. Most messages are standard messages that can be sent to any window. Other messages are unique to the control. The special messages that are used with our controls will be discussed as each control is presented.

## Using Notifications

A custom control notifies its parent window of certain events, such as keystrokes or mouse clicks, by sending its parent *notifications* when the events occur. All notifications are defined specifically for the control that issues them. The notifications generated by each control will also be discussed when we present each control.

## Using a Resource Editor

Standard custom controls can be added to most resource editors, such as Microsoft's Dialog Editor (included with the Windows SDK) and Borland's Resource Workshop. To add a control, you use the *Options..Install Code Library* (or equivalent) command to identify and add the custom control .DLL or .VBX file to the resource editor's list of custom controls.

○ ○ ○

*Note: Microsoft has abandoned the standard it created, and it no longer supports standard controls in its development environments such as Visual C++.*

○ ○ ○

# Using Controls in Visual Environments

You can add a custom control to Visual Basic by using the *File..Add File to Project* command. Once the control has been added to a project, the control icon is added to the toolbox and can then be selected and added to a form (dialog) like any other control. When selected, the control's properties can be accessed from the properties window normally, and its events will be listed in the code window.

Visual C++ works a little differently. The Visual C++ "App Studio" facility also has a *File..Add File to Project* command for adding Visual Basic-style custom controls. However, Visual C++ Version 1.0 does not support Visual Basic version 3.0 controls such as the ones presented in this book. App Studio also does not support the older-style custom controls that follow the standard that Microsoft previously set. To use our .VBX controls, you'll need a version of Visual C++ that supports Visual Basic version 3.0 controls. You'll also be limited to applications based on the Microsoft Foundation Classes because one of these classes is needed to translate between the Visual Basic layer and the underlying standard layer that C++ applications understand.

## Using Properties

A custom control used in a Visual Basic application has certain *properties.* Some of these properties get set when the control is created, and others are set programmatically at run time. For example, the *Border* property is used to specify that a control will be displayed with a standard border. Most of the properties used are standard ones that are common to any control, although some are unique. The documentation for each of our controls in this appendix lists the properties used, and notes any properties that are non-standard, or standard properties that have non-standard behavior.

## Using Methods

A Visual Basic application communicates with a custom control by invoking its *methods.* We aren't using any custom methods with our controls, although the action each method performs is based on the function of the control. The documentation for each control lists its methods, and notes any non-standard behavior.

## Using Events

A custom control notifies its Visual Basic application of certain *events* (such as keystrokes or mouse clicks). Most of the events used are standard ones that are common to any control, although some are unique. The documentation for each control lists the events that it may report.

# Using the Panel Control

The Panel control creates the effect of a 3-D panel having one or two bevels, each of which can be either "raised above" or "sunken into" the plane of an application's window. It displays single or multi-line text aligned vertically at the top, middle, or bottom; and horizontally to the left, center, or right. It also supports flood fills to create a progress bar.

Figure A.1 presents a sample Panel control, and Table A.1 shows the Panel's vital statistics.

**Figure A.1   A sample Panel control with its key components labeled.**

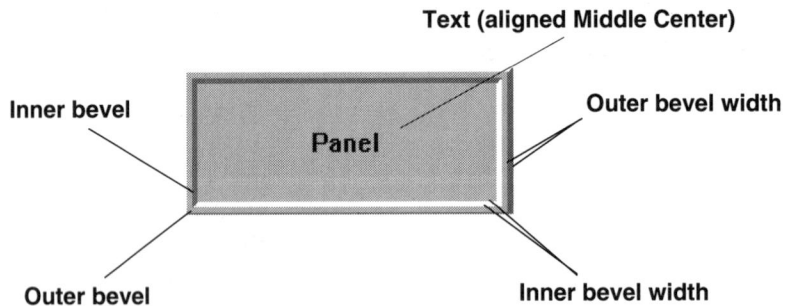

**Table A.1   The Panel Control at a Glance.**

| | |
|---|---|
| Implementation file | PANEL.DLL |
| Class name | "Panel" |
| Toolbox representation |  |
| On-line documentation | PANEL.HLP |
| Can be used in a standard Windows app | Yes |
| Can be used in a Visual Basic app | No |

# Using Panel in a Standard Windows App

The Panel control can be used in a standard Windows app in one of two ways: by including it as a control in a dialog template or by creating one by calling the *CreateWindow()* function. Let's look at both approaches.

Here's an example dialog template for including a Panel control:

```
MAIN DIALOG PRELOAD MOVEABLE DISCARDABLE -32768, -43, 312, 130
STYLE WS_OVERLAPPED | WS_CAPTION | WS_SYSMENU | WS_MINIMIZEBOX
CLASS "MAIN"
CAPTION "Import Old Collection Accounts"
FONT 8, "MS Sans Serif"
  BEGIN
      ▼
      ▼
   CONTROL "", 9999, "Panel", PNLS_CENTER | PNLS_MIDDLE | WS_CHILD |
WS_VISIBLE, 6, 115, 299, 12
   END
```

And here's an example of how to create a Panel control dynamically by calling *CreateWindow()*:

```
PanelWnd = CreateWindow ("Panel",
   "My Text",
   PNLS_CENTER | PNLS_MIDDLE | WS_CHILD | WS_VISIBLE,
   6, 115, 299, 12,
   Window, 9999,
   hInstance, NULL);
```

In both cases, notice that the class name of the control is "Panel." Also notice that different styles are used to modify the control's appearance.

## Styles

This section includes a complete description of each custom style flag used in the Panel control. (You use these flags when you define a Panel control in a resource file or create one dynamically by calling *CreateWindow()*. These flags can be combined with the logical ( | ) operator. The flags which are mutually exclusive, such as *PNLS_TOP* and *PNLS_BOTTOM*, should not be combined.

### PNLS_TOP

This style indicates that text should be placed vertically at the top of the text rectangle. Do not combine with *PNLS_MIDDLE* or *PNLS_BOTTOM*.

**PNLS_MIDDLE**

This style indicates that text should be placed vertically at the center of the text rectangle. Do not combine with *PNLS_TOP* or *PNLS_BOTTOM*.

**PNLS_BOTTOM**

This style indicates that text should be placed vertically at the bottom of the text rectangle. Do not combine with *PNLS_MIDDLE* or *PNLS_BOTTOM*.

**PNLS_LEFT**

This style indicates that text should be left-justified within the text rectangle. Do not combine with *PNLS_CENTER* or *PNLS_RIGHT*.

**PNLS_CENTER**

This style indicates that text should be centered within the text rectangle. Do not combine with *PNLS_TOP* or *PNLS_RIGHT*.

**PNLS_RIGHT**

This style indicates that text should be right-justified within the text rectangle. Do not combine with *PNLS_TOP* or *PNLS_CENTER*.

**PNLS_INNERBEVELRAISED**

This style indicates that the inner bevel will appear "raised from" the surface of the application.

**PNLS_INNERBEVELSUNK**

This style indicates that the inner bevel will appear "sunken into" the surface of the application.

**PNLS_INNERBEVELWIDTH(n)**

This style specifies the width of the inner bevel. Valid values for $n$ are from 0-7, with zero indicating that there will be no inner bevel.

**PNLS_OUTERBEVELRAISED**

This style indicates that the outer bevel will appear "raised from" the surface of the application.

**PNLS_OUTERBEVELSUNK**

This style indicates that the outer bevel will appear "sunken into" the surface of the application.

**PNLS_OUTERBEVELWIDTH(n)**

This style specifies the width of the outer bevel. Valid values for $n$ are from 0-7, with zero indicating that an outer bevel will not be displayed.

### PNLS_INTERBEVELWIDTH(n)

This style specifies the distance between the inner and outer bevels. Valid values for *n* are from 0-3.

### PNLS_BEVELTEXTBORDER(n)

This style specifies the distance between the inner bevel and the text. The value *n* is used to create a rectangular region where text can appear. The position of the text in the rectangle will be determined by the alignment flags. For example, if the *PNLS_CENTER* and *PNLS_MIDDLE* flags are used (ORed together), the text border will probably not have any effect.

## Messages

The custom messages supported by the Panel control are presented in this section.

### PNLM_SETUPPERRANGE

This message sets the upper value of the flood fill function. When the current position equals the upper range, the flood will fill 100 percent of the text rectangle. This value defaults to zero. When it is greater than zero, the flood fill operation is in effect. Also, a percentage value will be displayed in the center of the panel regardless of the text alignment flags.

| Parameter | Value |
|-----------|-------|
| *wParam* | The new upper range value |
| *lParam* | Ignored; should be zero |

### PNLM_SETLOWERRANGE

This message sets the lower value of the flood fill function. Although this value is zero by default, you can change it if you want to display a flood fill percentage where zero percent does not equal a value of zero.

| Parameter | Value |
|-----------|-------|
| *wParam* | The new lower range value |
| *lParam* | Ignored; should be zero |

### PNLM_SETPOS

This message sets the current value from which the flood fill percentage will be calculated *if* the upper value is greater than zero. If so, and if the new percentage is not the same as the previous percentage, the text rectangle will be re-flooded and the percentage figure updated.

| Parameter | Value |
| --- | --- |
| *wParam* | The new value |
| *lParam* | Ignored; should be zero |

### PNLM_SETFILLCOLOR

This message sets a color for the flood fill. (By default, this color is the same as *COLOR_BTNTEXT.*)

| Parameter | Value |
| --- | --- |
| *wParam* | Ignored; should be zero |
| *lParam* | An RGB value indicating the desired color |

## Notifications

Since the Panel is primarily a decorative control, it generates no notification messages.

# Using the Virtual Listbox Control

The Virtual Listbox control can be used by both standard and visual Windows apps. As Figure A.2 shows, it appears to the user as a standard, single-selection listbox. The items that it lists are not stored internally. Instead, your application must "tell" the Virtual Listbox how many items it contains. The listbox then notifies the application each time it must display one of those items, allowing the application to supply the text. The vital statistics for this control are provided in Table A.2.

**Figure A.2  A Virtual Listbox control looks just like a standard listbox.**

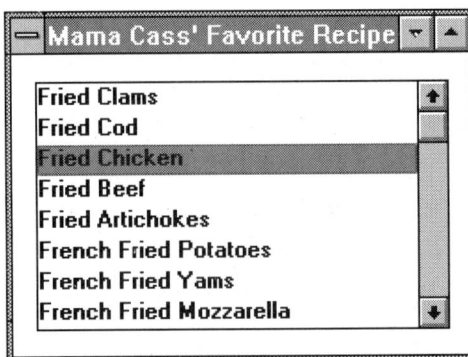

**Table A.2   The Virtual Listbox Control at a Glance**

| | |
|---|---|
| Implementation file | VLISTBOX.VBX |
| Class name | "VListbox" |
| Toolbox representation | |
| On-line documentation | VLISTBOX.HLP |
| Can be used in a standard Windows app | Yes |
| Can be used in a Visual Basic app | Yes |

## Using Virtual Listbox in a Standard App

The Virtual Listbox control can be used in a standard Windows app, either by including it as a control in a dialog template or by explicitly creating one by calling the *CreateWindow()* function.

Here's an example dialog template to include a Virtual Listbox control:

```
MAIN DIALOG PRELOAD MOVEABLE DISCARDABLE -32768, -43, 312, 130
STYLE WS_OVERLAPPED | WS_CAPTION | WS_SYSMENU | WS_MINIMIZEBOX
CLASS "MAIN"
CAPTION "Import Old Collection Accounts"
FONT 8, "MS Sans Serif"
  BEGIN
     ▼
     ▼
  CONTROL "", 1001, "VListbox", WS_CHILD | WS_VISIBLE, 6, 115, 299, 12
  END
```

And here's an example of how to create an equivalent Virtual Listbox control dynamically:

```
VListboxWnd = CreateWindow ("VListbox",
  NULL,
  PNLS_CENTER | PNLS_MIDDLE | WS_CHILD | WS_VISIBLE,
  6, 115, 299, 12,
  Window, 9999,
  hInstance, NULL);
```

## Styles

In addition to the standard Windows styles, Virtual Listbox controls can be created with the following unique style:

### VLS_INTEGRALHEIGHT

If this style is specified, the Virtual Listbox will adjust its size so that only complete items can appear within its borders. Unlike standard listboxes, this is *not* the default case. This style is therefore the opposite of the standard listbox's *LBS_NOINTEGRALHEIGHT* style.

## Messages

As with all controls, an application manipulates Virtual Listbox controls by sending them messages. In addition to the standard Windows (*WM_*) messages, Virtual Listboxes respond to the following messages:

### VL_SETCOUNT

This message sets the count of items the listbox is to display. Since a Virtual Listbox does not store any items, there is no message analogous to the standard listbox's *LB_ADDSTRING*. *VL_SETCOUNT* is therefore the only way to "load" a Virtual Listbox.

| Parameter | Description |
|---|---|
| *wParam* | The number of items the Virtual Listbox is to display |
| *lParam* | Not used |

#### Comment

The *VL_SETCOUNT* message is used to control the range values of the vertical scroll bar. It can be sent as often as needed.

### VL_GETCOUNT

This message returns the count of items the Virtual Listbox is to display. It is simply the last number supplied by a *VL_SETCOUNT* message, and is analogous to the *LB_GETCOUNT* message of standard listboxes.

| Parameter | Description |
|---|---|
| *wParam* | Not used |
| *lParam* | Not used |

| Returns | Description |
|---|---|
| *Count* | The value last passed to the Virtual Listbox in a *VL_SETCOUNT* message |

### VL_SETCURSEL

This message selects the specified Virtual Listbox item by index, or de-selects all items. Valid indeces range from zero through the value returned by *VL_GETCOUNT* - 1.

| Parameter | Description |
|---|---|
| wParam | The index of the item to be selected, or -1 if all items are to be de-selected |
| lParam | Not used |

## VL_GETCURSEL

This message returns the index of the currently selected item in a Virtual Listbox control, or -1 if no item is currently selected. Valid indexes range from zero through the value returned by *VL_GETCOUNT*- 1.

| Parameter | Description |
|---|---|
| wParam | Not used |
| lParam | Not used |

| Returns | Description |
|---|---|
| Index | The index of the currently selected item, or -1 if no item is currently selected |

## VL_SETTABSTOPS

This message sets the location of tab stops in a multi-column Virtual Listbox.

| Parameter | Description |
|---|---|
| wParam | Count of tab stops pointed to by *lParam* |
| lParam | Far pointer to an array of 16-bit values, each of which specifies the next tab stop in the set |

### Comment

Tabs must be ordered from lowest to highest $x$ value. The Virtual Listbox calculates the number of columns it needs to display as one greater than the number of tab stops specified. This message can be sent as often as needed.

## VL_GETTABSTOPS

This message returns the array of tabs passed to the Virtual Listbox in the most recent *VL_SETTABSTOPS* message.

| Parameter | Description |
|---|---|
| wParam | Maximum number of tab stops to be copied into the array pointed to by *lParam* |
| lParam | Far pointer to an array of 16-bit values, each of which specifies the next tab stop in the set |

| Returns | Description |
|---|---|
| Count | The actual number of tab stops copied into the array pointed to by lParam |

### VL_QUERYITEM

This message is sent to a Virtual Listbox by an application during its processing of the *VLN_READYITEM* notification.

| Parameter | Description |
|-----------|-------------|
| *wParam*  | Not used |
| *lParam*  | Not used |

| Returns | Description |
|---------|-------------|
| *QueryItem* | Far Pointer to a *QueryItem* structure |

**Comment**

When an application receives a *VLN_READYITEM* notification, it should send the notifying Virtual Listbox a *VL_QUERYITEM* message to obtain a pointer to the *QueryItem* structure. This structure has the following definition:

```
typedef struct
  {
  int Index;
  char Buffer[128];
  BYTE Column;
  BYTE Align;
  } QUERYITEM, far * LPQUERYITEM;
```

After receiving the structure, the application should use the *Index* and *Column* members to determine and place the appropriate text in the *Buffer* member. Optionally, the application can change the *Align* member to one of the following values, defined in WINDOWS.H: *DT_LEFT, DT_RIGHT,* or *DT_CENTER.* The *Align* member contains *DT_LEFT* by default.

A Virtual Listbox initially sends a *VLN_READYITEM* for column "0"; that is, the entire item. The application is permitted to place the entire item in *Buffer*, with multiple columns separated by tab characters. (In a single-column Virtual Listbox, the application can place the item in *Buffer* at this time.)

If no text is placed into *Buffer* when *Column* equals zero, the Virtual Listbox will send *VLN_READYTEXT* notifications for each column, starting with column one. The number of columns is calculated as being one more than the number of tab stops sent in the most recent *VL_SETTABSTOPS* message.

## Notifications

Like most controls, the Virtual Listbox allows the application to monitor its status by sending the application notification messages. Notification messages are *WM_COMMAND* messages in which the *wParam* and low and high-order words of the *lParam* parameters have certain, pre-defined meanings.

The Virtual Listbox control provides the following notification messages:

### VLN_SELCHANGE

This notification is sent whenever a selection is changed, whether programmatically or by user action. The parent window of the Virtual Listbox receives this notification message through a *WM_COMMAND* message. Upon receipt of this notification, the application can use the *VL_GETCURSEL* message to determine the new selection.

| Parameter | Description |
|-----------|-------------|
| *wParam* | Specifies the control ID of the Virtual Listbox |
| *lParam* | Specifies the handle of the Virtual Listbox in the low-order word, and specifies the *VLN_SELCHANGE* notification message in the high-order word |

### VLN_DBLCLK

This notification message is sent when the user double-clicks a string in a Virtual Listbox. The parent window of the Virtual Listbox receives this notification message through a *WM_COMMAND* message.

| Parameter | Description |
|-----------|-------------|
| *wParam* | Specifies the control ID of the Virtual Listbox |
| *lParam* | Specifies the handle of the Virtual Listbox in the low-order word, and specifies the *VLN_DBLCLK* notification message in the high-order word |

### VLN_KILLFOCUS

This notification message is sent when a Virtual Listbox loses the input focus. The parent window of the Virtual Listbox receives this notification message through a *WM_COMMAND* message.

| Parameter | Description |
|-----------|-------------|
| *wParam* | Specifies the control ID of the Virtual Listbox |
| *lParam* | Specifies the handle of the Virtual Listbox in the low-order word, and specifies the *VLN_KILLFOCUS* notification message in the high-order word |

### VLN_SETFOCUS

This notification message is sent when a Virtual Listbox gains the input focus. The parent window of the Virtual Listbox receives this notification message through a *WM_COMMAND* message.

| Parameter | Description |
|-----------|-------------|
| *wParam* | Specifies the control ID of the Virtual Listbox |
| *lParam* | Specifies the handle of the Virtual Listbox in the low-order word, and specifies the *VLN_SETFOCUS* notification message in the high-order word |

### VLN_READYITEM

This notification is sent as each item "in" the Virtual Listbox must be displayed. Moreover, if the parent window does not respond to the first notification of each item (which is for the item as a whole), *VLN_READYITEM* notifications will be sent for each *column* of that item. The parent window of the Virtual Listbox receives this notification message through a *WM_COMMAND* message. The application should respond to this notification by sending a *VL_QUERYITEM* message to obtain a pointer to a *QueryItem* structure, then it places the text to be displayed in that structure.

| Parameter | Description |
|-----------|-------------|
| *wParam* | Specifies the control ID of the Virtual Listbox |
| *lParam* | Specifies the handle of the Virtual Listbox in the low-order word, and specifies the *VLN_READYITEM* notification message in the high-order word |

## Using Virtual Listbox in a Visual App

To use this control in a visual app, include the Virtual Listbox control in your visual IDE by using the *File..Add File to Project* command or equivalent. Select a Virtual Listbox from the toolbox and apply it to a form just as you would any other control. Virtual Listboxes are managed with the properties, events, and methods described next.

## Properties

A Virtual Listbox control supports the following properties:

```
*(About)
BackColor
BorderStyle
Enabled
.FontBold
FontItalic
FontName
```

```
FontSize
ForeColor
Height
HelpContextID
Index
Left
*ListCount
ListIndex
Name
Parent
TabIndex
*TabCount
TabStop
*TabStops
Tag
Top
Visible
Width
```

The properties marked with an asterisk are either unique to this control or they require special consideration when used with the control. These properties will be presented here. The other properties are documented in Visual Basic's on-line help and in the Visual Basic *Custom Control Reference* (see the section "Standard Properties, Events, and Methods" in Appendix A).

### (About)

This pseudo-property provides version and copyright information for the Virtual Listbox DLL. This information is available only at design time by clicking on the "..." button in the Properties window.

### ListCount

This property allows the number of items "in" the Virtual Listbox to be set or read.

#### *Usage*
`[Form.]VListbox.ListCount [ = count]`

#### *Remarks*
Since a Virtual Listbox does not store any items, no method analogous to the standard listbox's *AddItem* is available. Using the *ListCount* property is therefore the only way to "load" a Virtual Listbox.

### TabStops

This property provides a list of tab stops for a multi-column Virtual Listbox. This property is an array property, available at run time only.

### Usage

```
[form.]VListbox.TabStops(index) = n
```

| Setting | Value |
|---------|-------|
| *n* | A 16-bit value which specifies the next tab stop in the set. Tab stops must be provided in order of increasing distance from the left edge of the Virtual Listbox. |

### See Also
TabCount

## TabCount

This property provides a count of defined tab stops. The number of columns is one greater than this value. Tab stops can be cleared by assigning a zero to this property. This property is available only at run time.

### Usage

```
[form.]Browser.TabCount
```

### See Also
TabStops

## Events

A Virtual Listbox supports the following events:

```
Click
DblClick
DragDrop
DragOver
*GetText
GotFocus
LostFocus
MouseDown
MouseMove
MouseUp
```

The *GetText* event is the only one that is unique to this control. The remaining events are documented in Visual Basic's on-line help and in the Visual Basic *Custom Control Reference* (see the section "Standard Properties, Events, and Methods" in Appendix A).

### GetText

This event is triggered as each item "in" the Virtual Listbox is to be displayed.

#### Usage

Sub *ctlname*_GetText (*ListIndex* as Integer, *Column* as Integer, *Text* as String, *Alignment* as Integer)

| Parameter | Value |
|-----------|-------|
| *ListIndex* | A value indicating the index of the item that is to be rendered. The first item has a *ListIndex* of zero. |
| *Column* | A value from 1 to *n*, where *n* is the number of fields retrieved by the Data control, or 1 if the Browser's *DataField* contains a value. |
| *Text* | When the event is triggered, this is the text that is about to be displayed. You may format or change it in any way you like. |
| *Alignment* | When the event is triggered, this variable contains 0 (left justified). You may change it to 1 (centered) or 2 (right justified) if you prefer. |

#### Remarks

A Virtual Listbox initially triggers this event for *Column* = 0; that is, the entire item. The application is permitted to place the entire item in *Text*, with multiple columns separated by tab characters. (In a single-column Virtual Listbox, the application can place the item in *Text* at this time.)

If no string is assigned to *Text* when *Column* equals 0, the Virtual Listbox will trigger a *GetText* event for each column, starting with *Column* = 1. The number of columns is calculated as being one more than the value of *TabCount*.

#### See also

TabStops
TabCount

## Methods

A Virtual Listbox supports the following methods:

```
Drag
LinkExecute
LinkPoke
LinkRequest
```

```
LinkSend
Move
Refresh
SetFocus
ZOrder
```

None of these methods require special consideration when used with the Virtual Listbox.

# Using the Pagelist Control

The Pagelist control behaves as a standard, single, or multiple-selection listbox, but it does not display the stored items. Instead, each item is represented by an icon of a document page, printed with a number indicating the item's position within the list. The first item is numbered "1". Figure A.3 shows two examples of a Pagelist control. The vital statistics for the Pagelist control are provided in Table A.3.

**Figure A.3  Two examples of a Pagelist control.**

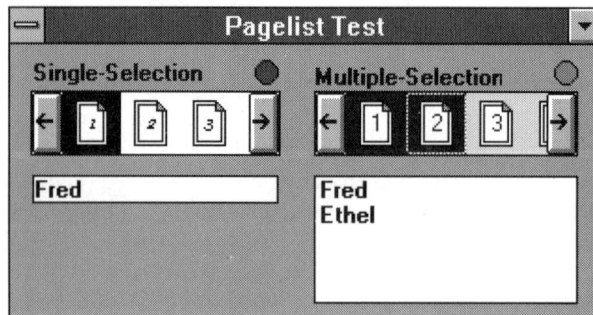

**Table A.3  The Pagelist Control at a Glance**

| | |
|---|---|
| Implementation file | PAGELIST.VBX |
| Class name | "Pagelist" |
| Toolbox representation |  |
| On-line documentation | PAGELIST.HLP |
| Can be used in a standard Windows app | Yes |
| Can be used in a Visual Basic app | Yes |

# Using Pagelist in a Standard App

The Pagelist control can be used in a standard Windows app by including it as a control in a dialog template or by explicitly creating one using the *CreateWindow()* function.

Here's an example dialog template to include a Pagelist control:

```
MAIN DIALOG PRELOAD MOVEABLE DISCARDABLE -32768, -43, 312, 130
STYLE WS_OVERLAPPED | WS_CAPTION | WS_SYSMENU | WS_MINIMIZEBOX
CLASS "MAIN"
CAPTION "Import Old Collection Accounts"
FONT 8, "MS Sans Serif"
  BEGIN
    ▼
    ▼
  CONTROL "", 1001, "PAGELIST", WS_CHILD | WS_VISIBLE, 6, 115, 299, 32
  END
```

And here's an example of how you can create an equivalent Pagelist control dynamically:

```
PagelistWnd = CreateWindow ("PAGELIST",
  NULL,
  PNLS_CENTER | PNLS_MIDDLE | WS_CHILD | WS_VISIBLE,
  6, 115, 299, 32,
  Window, 9999,
  hInstance, NULL);
```

## Messages

As with all controls, an application manipulates Pagelist controls by sending them messages. In addition to the standard Windows (*WM_*) messages, Pagelist controls respond to the messages presented in this section.

### PL_ADDITEM

This message adds an item to the Pagelist control. Although Pagelist does not display the text that is added to it, the text is stored and can be retrieved later with the *PL_GETTEXT* message. Items are appended to the list.

| Parameter | Description |
| --- | --- |
| *wParam* | Not used |
| *lParam* | A far pointer to the text of the item to be added to the Pagelist |

| Returns | Description |
| --- | --- |
| *Index* | The new, zero-based index of the appended item, or *PL_ERR* if an error occurs |

**See also**
PL_INSERTTEXT

## PL_DELETEITEM

This message causes the Pagelist control to delete a specified item from its internal list. Items are referenced by their position, with the first item indexed as zero (even though Pagelist displays that item as "page 1"). After the deletion, items following the deleted item are automatically renumbered to one less than their previous numbers.

| Parameter | Description |
| --- | --- |
| *wParam* | The zero-based index of the item to be removed |
| *lParam* | Not used |

| Returns | Description |
| --- | --- |
| Count | The count of items remaining in the list, or *PL_ERR* if *wParam* is out of range |

**See also**
PL_ADDITEM
PL_INSERTTEXT

## PL_GETCARETINDEX

This message returns the index of the item that currently has the focus caret. This item may or may not be selected, especially if the Pagelist has the *PLS_MUTLIPLESEL* or *PLS_EXTENDEDSEL* styles. The message is particularly useful in a multiple-selection Pagelist in response to a *PLN_SELCHANGE* notification because it returns the item the user just "touched." A *PL_SETSEL* message can then determine whether the item was selected or de-selected, without the program's having to iterate through every item to determine the new selection list.

| Parameter | Description |
| --- | --- |
| *wParam* | Not used |
| *lParam* | Not used |

| Returns | Description |
| --- | --- |
| *Index* | The zero-based index of the item with the focus caret |

*See also*
PL_GETCURSEL
PL_SETCARETINDEX

## PL_GETCOUNT

This message returns the number of items that the Pagelist control contains.

| Parameter | Description |
| --- | --- |
| *wParam* | Not used |
| *lParam* | Not used |

| Returns | Description |
| --- | --- |
| *Count* | A value representing the number of items placed in Pagelist by *PL_ADDSTRING* messages |

## PL_GETCURSEL

This message returns the index of the currently selected item in a Pagelist control, or -1 if no item is currently selected. Valid indeces range from zero through the value returned by *PL_GETCOUNT* - 1.

| Parameter | Description |
| --- | --- |
| *wParam* | Not used |
| *lParam* | Not used |

| Returns | Description |
| --- | --- |
| *Index* | The index of the currently selected item, or -1 if no item is currently selected |

*See also*
PL_GETSEL
PL_SETCURSEL

## PL_GETSEL

This message is used to query the selection state of a particular item. This message may only be sent to a Pagelist with the *PLS_MULTIPLESEL* or *PLS_EXTENDEDSEL* style.

| Parameter | Description |
| --- | --- |
| *wParam* | Index of item being queried |
| *lParam* | Not used |

| Returns | Description |
| --- | --- |
| Selected | TRUE if the item referenced by *wParam* is selected; otherwise *FALSE* |

**See also**
PL_GETCURSEL
PL_SETSEL

## PL_GETSELCOUNT

This message returns the number of items selected in a multiple-selection Pagelist.

| Parameter | Description |
| --- | --- |
| *wParam* | Not used |
| *lParam* | Not used |

| Returns | Description |
| --- | --- |
| *Count* | The number of items selected, or *PL_ERR* if the Pagelist is not multiple-selection |

**See also**
PL_GETSELITEMS

## PL_GETSELITEMS

This message fills an array with the indeces of items currently selected in a multiple-selection Pagelist.

| Parameter | Description |
| --- | --- |
| *wParam* | Maximum number of items to be placed in the array pointed to by *lParam* |
| *lParam* | A far pointer to a *WORD* array to be filled with indexes to selected items |

| Returns | Description |
| --- | --- |
| *Count* | The number of items placed in the array pointed to by *lParam*, or *PL_ERR* if the Pagelist is not multiple-selection |

**Comments**

If *wParam* was less than the number of items selected, *Count* may be less than the actual number of items selected. Typically, a program uses the *PL_GETSELCOUNT* message to first determine how many items are selected, and then allocates exactly enough space for the selection list. Another approach is to supply an array buffer large enough for all items.

**See also**
PL_SETSELITEMS

### PL_GETTEXT

This message returns the text of a specified item. The text is the same as that placed in the Pagelist control by a previous *PL_ADDITEM* or *PL_INSERTTITEM* message.

| Parameter | Description |
| --- | --- |
| *wParam* | The zero-based index of an item whose text is to be retrieved |
| *lParam* | Far pointer to a buffer into which the text is to be placed |

| Returns | Description |
| --- | --- |
| *Count* | The number of bytes, excluding the terminating *NULL*, copied into the buffer pointed to by *lParam*, or *PL_ERR* if *wParam* is out of range |

**See also**
PL_GETTEXTLEN

### PL_GETTEXTLEN

This message retrieves the size of the text of a specified item. The text is the same as that placed in the Pagelist by a previous *PL_ADDITEM* or *PL_INSERTTITEM* message.

| Parameter | Description |
| --- | --- |
| *wParam* | The zero-based index of the item whose size is being queried |
| *lParam* | Not used |

| Returns | Description |
| --- | --- |
| *Count* | The number of bytes, excluding the terminating *NULL*, of the item being queried or *PL_ERR* if *wParam* is out of range |

**See also**
PL_GETTEXT

### PL_GETTOPINDEX

This message returns the index of the first visible item in the Pagelist display, if any. No item will be visible if the Pagelist is empty.

| Parameter | Description |
| --- | --- |
| *wParam* | Not used |
| *lParam* | Not used |

| Returns | Description |
|---------|-------------|
| *Index* | The zero-based index of the first item currently visible in the Pagelist |

### See also
PL_GETCURSEL
PL_GETCARETINDEX
PL_SETTOPINDEX

## PL_INSERTITEM

This message inserts an item into a specified position in the Pagelist. Items which follow the new item are automatically renumbered.

| Parameter | Description |
|-----------|-------------|
| *wParam* | The zero-based index which indicates where the item will be inserted |
| *lParam* | A far pointer to the string that is to be inserted into the Pagelist |

### See also
PL_ADDITEM
PL_DELETEITEM
PL_GETTEXT

## PL_RESETCONTENT

This message causes the Pagelist to be emptied of its contents.

| Parameter | Description |
|-----------|-------------|
| *wParam* | Not used |
| *lParam* | Not used |

### See also
PL_DELETEITEM

## PL_SELITEMRANGE

This message programmatically selects one or more items at once in a multiple-selection Pagelist.

| Parameter | Description |
|-----------|-------------|
| *wParam* | If *TRUE*, the items in the range are selected; if *FALSE* they are de-selected |
| *lParam* | The *LOWORD* contains the zero-based index of the first item to set. The *HIWORD* contains the zero-based index of the last item to set. |

*See also*
PL_SELECTSTRING
PL_SETSEL

## PL_SETCARETINDEX

This message sets the focus caret to a specified item in the Pagelist. If that item is not currently visible, it is scrolled into view.

| Parameter | Description |
| --- | --- |
| *wParam* | The zero-based index of the item to receive the focus caret |
| *lParam* | If *TRUE*, the specified item will be scrolled into full view; if *FALSE*, the item will be scrolled into at least partial view |

### Comments

The *lParam* flag is meaningful only if the width of the Pagelist is such that a non-integral number of items may be visible at one time.

### See also

PL_GETCARETINDEX
PL_SETCURSEL

## PL_SETCURSEL

This message selects the specified Pagelist item by index, or de-selects all items. Valid index ranges are from zero through the value returned by *PL_GETCOUNT* - 1. This message should be sent only to single-selection Pagelist controls.

| Parameter | Description |
| --- | --- |
| *wParam* | The index of the item to be selected, or -1 if all items are to be de-selected |
| *lParam* | Not used |

### See also

PL_GETCURSEL
PL_SETCARETINDEX
PL_SETSEL

## PL_SETSEL

This message selects or de-selects a specified item in the Pagelist. It should be sent only to multiple-selection Pagelist controls.

| Parameter | Description |
|-----------|-------------|
| wParam | If *TRUE*, the item will be selected; if *FALSE*, it will be de-selected |
| lParam | The zero-based index of the item to be set |

*See also*
PL_GETSEL
PL_SELITEMRANGE
PL_SETCARETINDEX
PL_SETCURSEL

## PL_SETTOPINDEX

This message makes the specified item the first one visible in the Pagelist, if possible. (If the specified item's index is less than the number of items that are visible in the Pagelist at the same time, the item cannot be made visible.)

| Parameter | Description |
|-----------|-------------|
| wParam | The index of the item to be made visible first |
| lParam | Not used |

## Notifications

Like most controls, the Pagelist control allows an application to monitor its status by sending the application notification messages. Recall that the notification messages are *WM_COMMAND* messages in which the *wParam* and low and high-order words of the *lParam* parameters have certain pre-defined meanings.

The Pagelist control provides the notification messages presented next.

### PLN_SELCHANGE

This notification is sent whenever a selection is changed, whether programmatically or by user action. The parent window of the Pagelist receives this notification message through a *WM_COMMAND* message. Upon receipt of this notification, the application can use the *PL_GETCURSEL* message to determine the new selection.

| Parameter | Description |
|-----------|-------------|
| wParam | Specifies the control ID of the Pagelist |
| lParam | Specifies the handle of the Pagelist in the low-order word, and specifies the *PLN_SELCHANGE* notification message in the high-order word |

### PLN_DBLCLK

This notification message is sent when the user double-clicks a string in a Pagelist. The parent window of the Pagelist receives this notification message through a *WM_COMMAND* message.

| Parameter | Description |
| --- | --- |
| *wParam* | Specifies the control ID of the Pagelist |
| *lParam* | Specifies the handle of the Pagelist in the low-order word, and specifies the *PLN_DBLCLK* notification message in the high-order word |

### PLN_SETFOCUS

This notification message is sent when a Pagelist gains the input focus. The parent window of the Pagelist receives this notification message through a *WM_COMMAND* message.

| Parameter | Description |
| --- | --- |
| *wParam* | Specifies the control ID of the Pagelist |
| *lParam* | Specifies the handle of the Pagelist in the low-order word, and specifies the *PLN_SETFOCUS* notification message in the high-order word |

### PLN_KILLFOCUS

This notification message is sent when a Pagelist loses the input focus. The parent window of the Pagelist receives this notification message through a *WM_COMMAND* message.

| Parameter | Description |
| --- | --- |
| *wParam* | Specifies the control ID of the Pagelist |
| *lParam* | Specifies the handle of the Pagelist in the low-order word, and specifies the *PLN_KILLFOCUS* notification message in the high-order word |

## Using Pagelist in a Visual App

To use Pagelist in a visual app, you include the Pagelist control in your visual IDE via the *File..Add File to Project* command or equivalent. Next, select a Pagelist from the toolbox and apply it to a form just as you would any other control. Pagelists are managed using the properties, events, and methods described next.

## Properties

A Pagelist control supports the following properties:

```
*About
BackColor
BorderStyle
Enabled
FontBold
FontItalic
FontName
FontSize
ForeColor
Height
HelpContextID
Index
Left
*List
ListCount
ListIndex
Name
Parent
TabIndex
TabStop
Tag
Top
*TopIndex
Visible
Width
```

The properties marked with an asterisk are either unique to this control, or they require special consideration when used with the control. These properties are presented next. The remaining properties are documented in Visual Basic's on-line help and in the Visual Basic *Custom Control Reference* (see the "Standard Properties, Events, and Methods" section in Appendix A).

### (About)

This pseudo-property provides version and copyright information for the Pagelist DLL. This information is available only at design time by clicking on the "..." button in the Properties window.

### List

This array property provides read-only access to the items in the Pagelist. This property is not available at design time.

#### *Usage*
```
[Form.]PageList.List  (Index)
```

***Remarks***

Use the *AddItem* method to place items in the Pagelist. Remember, these items are not displayed—just the number of the "page" of each item appears on-screen.

### TopIndex

This property determines which item appears first in a Pagelist. It is not available at design time. *TopIndex* cannot guarantee that an item is *actually* first; the order depends on how many items can be viewed at the same time. *TopIndex* does guarantee that the specified item will be visible.

## Events

A Pagelist supports the following events:

```
Click
DblClick
DragDrop
DragOver
GotFocus
LostFocus
MouseDown
MouseMove
MouseUp
```

The Pagelist control does not require any special events. You can find descriptions of these events in Visual Basic's on-line help and in the Visual Basic *Custom Control Reference* (see the "Standard Properties, Events, and Methods" section in Appendix A).

## Methods

A Pagelist supports the following methods:

```
*AddItem
*Clear
Drag
LinkExecute
LinkPoke
LinkRequest
Move
Refresh
*RemoveItem
SetFocus
ZOrder
```

The methods marked with an asterisk are either unique to this control or they require special consideration when used with the control. These methods are presented next. You can find descriptions of the other methods in Visual Basic's on-line help and in the Visual Basic *Custom Control Reference* (see the "Standard Properties, Events, and Methods" section in Appendix A).

### AddItem

This method is used to add an item to the Pagelist control.

#### *Usage*

```
control.AddItem item [, index ]
```

| Component | Value |
|-----------|-------|
| *control* | Pagelist control |
| *item* | Specifies the string expression to add to the control |
| *index* | Integer representing the position within the control where the new item is placed. For the first item, *index* is set to zero |

### Clear

This method is used to remove all the items from a Pagelist control with a single statement.

#### *Usage*

```
control.Clear
```

| Component | Value |
|-----------|-------|
| *control* | Pagelist control |

### RemoveItem

This method removes a specified item from a Pagelist. Items that follow the removed item are automatically renumbered.

#### *Usage*

```
control.RemoveItem item , index
```

| Component | Value |
|-----------|-------|
| *control* | Pagelist control |
| *index* | Integer representing the item within the control that is to be removed. For the first item, *index* is set to zero. |

# Using the Browser Control

The Browser control is designed to work in concert with Visual Basic's most powerful control—the Data control. While Visual Basic's other "bound" controls allow you to manipulate one record at a time, the Browser control provides listbox-style access to one or more fields from an entire database table at once.

Figure A.4 shows an example of a Browser control and Table A.4 provides the vital statistics for this control.

## Using Browser in a Visual App

To access this control, include it in your visual IDE using the *File..Add File to Project* command or equivalent. Select a Browser from the toolbox and apply it to a form just as you would any other control. Browsers are managed by using the properties, events, and methods described next.

**Figure A.4   A Browser control looks and acts just like a standard listbox, but binds to a Data control and displays one or more fields of an entire table.**

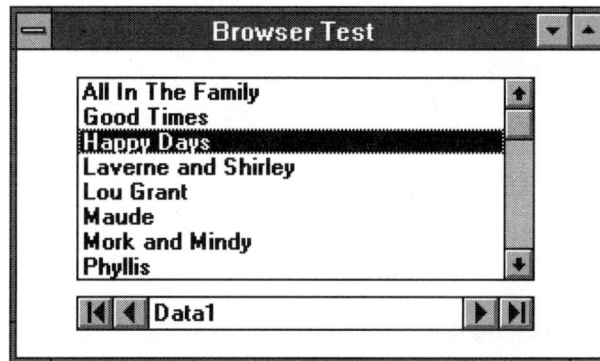

**Table A.4   The Browser Control at a Glance**

| | |
|---|---|
| Implementation file | BROWSER.VBX |
| Class name | "Browser" |
| Toolbox representation | |
| On-line documentation | BROWSER.HLP |
| Can be used in a standard Windows app | No |
| Can be used in a Visual Basic app | Yes |

## Properties

A Browser control supports the following properties:

```
*About
Align
*AutoSelect
BackColor
BorderStyle
*DataField
DataSource
Enabled
FontBold
FontItalic
FontName
FontSize
ForeColor
Height
HelpContextID
Index
Left
*ListCount
ListIndex
Name
Parent
TabIndex
*TabCount
TabStop
*TabStops
Tag
Top
Visible
Width
```

The properties marked with an asterisk are either unique to this control or they require special consideration when used with the control. These properties are presented next. The other properties are documented in Visual Basic's on-line help, and in the Visual Basic *Custom Control Reference* (see the "Standard Properties, Events, and Methods" section in Appendix A).

### (About)

This pseudo-property provides version and copyright information for the Browser Listbox VBX. This information is available only at design time by clicking on the "..." button in the Properties window.

## AutoSelect

When the value of this property is *True*, changing a selection in the Browser changes the current record in the Data control to which it is bound. The default value is *False*.

### Usage
```
[Form.]Browser.AutoSelect [ = new value ]
```

### Remarks
If you set this value to True, the Browser duplicates the visual function of the Data control. The Data control is still required, but you can set its *Visible* property to False to avoid the redundancy.

## DataField

This property binds a Browser to a specific field. Read/write attributes are available at both design time and run time. If not specified, the Browser will display all fields retrieved by the control specified in the *DataSource* property.

### Usage
```
[Form.]Browser.DataField [ = fieldname]
```

### Remarks
A Browser provides read-only access to data in your database. The *DataSource* property specifies a valid Data control name, and the *DataField* property specifies either a valid field name in the Data control's *RecordSet* property, or is blank (in which case all fields will be displayed). A *DataField* property should be specified if the Data control is set to retrieve more than eight fields—the maximum number a Browser can display.

## ListCount

This property provides a count of items in the Browser and, therefore, in the Data control's current RecordSet. This property is not available at design time and is read-only at run time.

### Usage
```
[form.]Browser.ListCount
```

## TabStops

This property provides a list of tab stops for a multi-column Browser. This array property is not available at design time.

### Usage
```
[form.]Browser.TabStops(index) = n
```

| Setting | Value |
|---|---|
| *n* | A 16-bit value which specifies the next tab stop in the set. Tab stops must be provided in order of increasing distance from the left edge of the Browser. |

*See Also*
TabCount

## TabCount

Provides a count of defined tab stops. The number of columns is one greater than this value. Tab stops can be cleared by assigning a zero to this property. This property is available only at run time.

*Usage*
```
[form.]Browser.TabCount
```

*See Also*
TabStops

## Events

A Browser supports the following events:

```
Click
DblClick
DragDrop
DragOver
*FormatField
GotFocus
LostFocus
MouseDown
MouseMove
MouseUp
```

Only one unique event is used with the Browser control: *FormatField*. The remaining events are documented in Visual Basic's on-line help and in the Visual Basic *Custom Control Reference* (see the "Standard Properties, Events, and Methods" section in Appendix A).

### FormatField

This event is triggered each time the Browser is about to paint a single field. It provides a Visual Basic program an opportunity to provide special formatting for the field, or special alignment, prior to its being painted.

***Usage***

```
Sub Browser_FormatField (Column As Integer, Text As String,
Alignment As Integer)
```

| Parameter | Value |
|---|---|
| *Column* | A value from 1 to *n*, where *n* is the number of fields retrieved by the Data control or if the Browser's DataField contains a value |
| *Text* | The text that is about to be displayed when the event is triggered. You may format or change it in any way you like. |
| *Alignment* | When the event is triggered, this variable contains 0 (left justified). You may change it to 1 (centered) or 2 (right justified) if you prefer. |

## Methods

The Browser control supports the following methods:

```
Drag
LinkExecute
LinkPoke
LinkRequest
LinkSend
Move
Refresh
SetFocus
ZOrder
```

None of the methods require special consideration when used with the Browser. They are documented in Visual Basic's on-line help, and in the Visual Basic *Custom Control Reference* (see the "Standard Properties, Events, and Methods" section in Appendix A).

# Using the TextFileView Control

The Text File Viewer control (TextFileView) provides instant access to any text file. Where Windows' standard edit control must be "loaded" and is limited to 32K of data, the TextFileView control is available as soon as it is given a filename, and it supports as many as 32K *lines* of text.

Figure A.5 shows an example of a TextFileView control, and Table A.5 provides the vital statistics for this control.

**Figure A.5   An example of a TextFileView control.**

**Table A.5   The TextFileView Control at a Glance**

| | |
|---|---|
| Implementation file | TEXTVIEW.VBX |
| Class name | "TextFileView" |
| Toolbox representation | 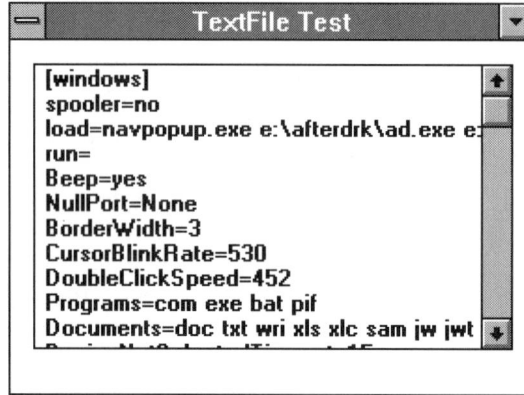 |
| On-line documentation | TEXTVIEW.HLP |
| Can be used in a standard Windows app | Yes |
| Can be used in a Visual Basic app | Yes |

## Using TextFileView in a Standard App

The TextFileView control can be used in a standard Windows app by including it as a control in a dialog template or by explicitly creating one using the *CreateWindow()* function.

Here's an example dialog template to include a TextFileView control:

```
MAIN DIALOG PRELOAD MOVEABLE DISCARDABLE -32768, -43, 312, 130
STYLE WS_OVERLAPPED | WS_CAPTION | WS_SYSMENU | WS_MINIMIZEBOX
CLASS "MAIN"
CAPTION "Import Old Collection Accounts"
FONT 8, "MS Sans Serif"
  BEGIN
     ▼
     ▼
  CONTROL "", 9999, "TextFileView", WS_BORDER | WS_CHILD | WS_VISIBLE, 6,
115, 299, 12
  END
```

And here's an example of how to create an equivalent TextFileView control dynamically:

```
TFVWnd = CreateWindow ("TextFileView",
   "",
   WS_BORDER | WS_CHILD | WS_VISIBLE,
   6, 115, 299, 12,
   Window, 9999,
   hInstance, NULL);
```

## Styles

The TextFileView control does not require any custom styles.

## Messages

As with all controls, an application manipulates TextFileView controls by sending them messages. In addition to the standard Windows (*WM_*) messages, TextFileView controls respond to the messages presented in this section.

### WM_SETTEXT

This message clears the control of its current contents and loads the text of the specified file.

| Parameter | Description |
|-----------|-------------|
| *wParam* | Not used |
| *lParam* | A far pointer to the name of the text file that is to be displayed in the control |

### WM_GETTEXT

This message obtains the name of the file currently being displayed.

| Parameter | Description |
|-----------|-------------|
| *wParam* | Not used |
| *lParam* | A far pointer to a buffer in which the name of the text file that is displayed in the control is to be placed |

## Notifications

Since the TextFileView control behaves much like a giant static control, it does not generate any notification messages.

## Using TextFileView in a Visual App

To use the TextFileView control in a visual app, include the control in your visual IDE by using the *File..Add File to Project* command or equivalent. Then, select the control from the toolbox and apply it to a form just as you would any other control. TextFileView controls are managed using the properties, events, and methods described next.

### Properties

A TextFileView control supports the following properties:

```
*About
BackColor
BorderStyle
Enabled
*FileName
FontBold
FontItalic
FontName
FontSize
ForeColor
Height
HelpContextID
Index
Left
Name
Parent
TabIndex
TabStop
Tag
Top
Visible
Width
```

The properties marked with an asterisk are either unique to this control or they require special consideration when used with the control. The other properties are documented in Visual Basic's on-line help and in the Visual Basic *Custom Control Reference* (see the "Standard Properties, Events, and Methods" section in Appendix A).

### (About)

This pseudo-property provides version and copyright information for the TextFileView DLL. This information is available only at design time by clicking on the "..." button in the Properties window.

**FileName**

This property sets or gets the name of the file whose contents the control is to display.

***Usage***

```
[form].TextFileView.FileName [ = newvalue ]
```

## Events

A TextFileView supports no non-standard events.

## Methods

A Text File Viewer supports the following methods:

```
Drag
LinkExecute
LinkPoke
LinkRequest
LinkSend
Move
Refresh
SetFocus
ZOrder
```

None of the methods require special consideration when used with the TextFileView control. They are documented in Visual Basic's on-line help and in the Visual Basic *Custom Control Reference* (see the "Standard Properties, Events, and Methods" section in Appendix A).

# Using the TextFileEdit Control

The TextFileEdit control provides a basic text editor that supports up to 32K lines (not characters) of text. With this control you'll be able to read in text files and perform basic editing operations.

Figure A.6 shows a sample TextFileEdit control and Table A.6 presents the vital statistics for this control.

## Using TextFileEdit in a Standard App

The TextFileEdit control can be used in a standard Windows app by including it as a control in a dialog template or by explicitly creating one using the *CreateWindow()* function.

**Figure A.6  An example of a TextFileEdit control.**

**Table A.6  The TextFileEdit Control at a Glance**

| | |
|---|---|
| Implementation file | TEXTEDIT.VBX |
| Class name | "TextFileEdit" |
| Toolbox representation | 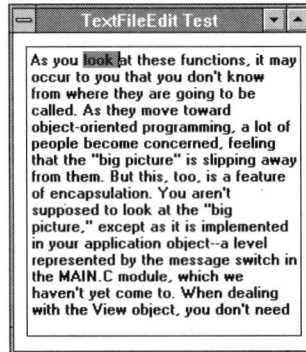 |
| On-line documentation | TEXTEDIT.HLP |
| Can be used in a standard Windows app | Yes |
| Can be used in a Visual Basic app | Yes |

Here's an example dialog template to include in a TextFileEdit control:

```
MAIN DIALOG PRELOAD MOVEABLE DISCARDABLE -32768, -43, 312, 130
STYLE WS_OVERLAPPED | WS_CAPTION | WS_SYSMENU | WS_MINIMIZEBOX
CLASS "MAIN"
CAPTION "Import Old Collection Accounts"
FONT 8, "MS Sans Serif"
   BEGIN
      ▼
      ▼
   CONTROL "", 9999, "TextFileEdit", WS_BORDER | WS_CHILD | WS_VISIBLE, 6,
115, 299, 12
   END
```

And here's an example of how to create an equivalent TextFileEdit control dynamically:

```
TFEWnd = CreateWindow ("TextFileEdit",
   "",
```

```
WS_BORDER | WS_CHILD | WS_VISIBLE,
6, 115, 299, 12,
Window, 9999,
hInstance, NULL);
```

## Styles

The TextFileEdit control requires no custom styles.

## Messages

As with all standard controls, an application manipulates TextFileEdit controls by sending them messages. In addition to the standard Windows (*WM_*) messages, TextFileEdit controls respond to the message presented in this section.

### TEM_GETMODIFIED

This message retrieves the state of the control's Modified flag.

| Parameter | Description |
|-----------|-------------|
| *wParam* | Not used |
| *lParam* | Not used |

*Returns*

TRUE if the text in the control has been changed since it was loaded; and FALSE if it has not.

### TEM_GETSEL

This message retrieves the current selected character positions.

| Parameter | Description |
|-----------|-------------|
| *wParam* | Not used |
| *lParam* | A far pointer to a *RECT* structure in which the *top* and *bottom* fields point to the first and last lines selected, and the *right* and *left* fields point to the first selected character in the top line, and the last selected character in the bottom line. |

### TEM_REPLACESEL

This message replaces the current selection with the text you specify.

| Parameter | Description |
|-----------|-------------|
| *wParam* | Not used |
| *lParam* | A far pointer to a buffer in which the replacement text is supplied |

### TEM_SETMODIFIED

This message retrieves the state of the control's Modified flag.

| Parameter | Description |
|---|---|
| *wParam* | The new value of the Modified flag |
| *lParam* | Not used |

### TEM_SETSEL

This message programmatically sets the selected characters to the ones you specify.

| Parameter | Description |
|---|---|
| *wParam* | Not used |
| *lParam* | A far pointer to a *RECT* structure in which the *top* and *bottom* fields point to the first and last lines selected, and the *right* and *left* fields point to the first selected character in the top line, and the last selected character in the bottom line |

### TEM_STOREDATA

This message causes the contents of the TextFileEdit control to be written back to the disk file that originally loaded it. It also resets the Modified flag to FALSE.

| Parameter | Description |
|---|---|
| *wParam* | Not used |
| *lParam* | Not used; must be zero |

### WM_SETTEXT

This message clears the control of its current contents and loads the text of the specified file.

| Parameter | Description |
|---|---|
| *wParam* | Not used |
| *lParam* | A far pointer to the name of the text file that is to be displayed in the control |

### WM_GETTEXT

This message obtains the name of the file currently being displayed.

| Parameter | Description |
|---|---|
| *wParam* | Not used |
| *lParam* | A far pointer to a buffer in which the name of the text file that is displayed in the control is to be placed |

## Notifications

Like most controls, the TextFileEdit allows the application to monitor its status by sending the application notification messages. Notification messages are *WM_COMMAND* messages in which the *wParam* and low and high-order words of the *lParam* parameters have certain, pre-defined meanings.

The TextFileEdit control provides the following notification messages:

**TEN_CHANGE**

>This notification is generated whenever the user alters the text; for example, by typing a character or deleting the current selection.

**TEN_KILLFOCUS**

>This notification is generated as the TextFileEdit control is losing the input focus.

**TEN_SETFOCUS**

>This notification is generated as the TextFileEdit control is gaining the input focus.

## Using TextFileEdit in a Visual App

To use the TextFileEdit control in a visual app, include the control in your visual IDE by using the *File..Add File to Project* command or equivalent. Select the control from the toolbox and apply it to a form just as you would any other control. TextFileEdit controls are managed using the properties, events, and methods described next.

## Properties

A TextFileEdit control supports the following properties:

```
*About
*Action
BackColor
BorderStyle
Enabled
FontBold
FontItalic
FontName
FontSize
ForeColor
Height
HelpContextID
Index
```

```
Left
*Modified
Name
Parent
*SelStartPos
*SelStartLine
*SelStopPos
*SelStopLine
*SelText
TabIndex
TabStop
Tag
*Text
Top
Visible
Width
```

The properties marked with an asterisk are either unique to this control or they require special consideration when used with the control. They will be described in this section. The other properties are documented in Visual Basic's on-line help and in the Visual Basic *Custom Control Reference* (see the "Standard Properties, Events, and Methods" section in Appendix A).

### (About)

This pseudo-property provides version and copyright information for the TextFileEdit DLL. This information is available only at design time by clicking on the "..." button in the Properties window.

### Action

This psuedo-property is used to provide the missing methods needed by the TextFileEdit control to make the control fully functional.

#### Usage
```
[control.]TextFileEdit.Action [ = ActionCode ]
```

| ActionCode | Value | Description |
| --- | --- | --- |
| TFE_STOREDATA | 1 | Causes the control to save its contents back to disk |

### Modified

This property sets or returns the Modified flag within the control. Unless changed manually, this flag is set to True coincident with the first triggering of a *Change* event.

*Usage*
```
[control.]TextFileEdit.Modified [ = True or False ]
```

## SelStartPos

This property sets or returns the position in its line of the first currently selected character.

*Usage*
```
[control.]TextFileEdit.SelStartPos [ = new selection position ]
```

## SelStartLine

This property sets or returns the number of the line containing the first currently selected character.

*Usage*
```
[control.]TextFileEdit.SelStartLine [ = new selection line ]
```

## SelStopPos

This property sets or returns the position in its line of the last currently selected character.

*Usage*
```
[control.]TextFileEdit.SelStopPos [ = new selection position ]
```

## SelStopLine

This property sets or returns the number of the line containing the last currently selected character.

*Usage*
```
[control.]TextFileEdit.SelStopLine [ = new selection line ]
```

## SelText

This property sets or retrieves the text that is currently selected in the control.

*Usage*
```
[control.]TextFileEdit.SelText [ = new text ]
```

## Text

This property sets or retrieves the entire text of the control. Note that this can conceivably require a great deal of memory if the file being edited by the TextFileEdit control is very large.

*Usage*
```
[control.]TextFileEdit.Text [ = new text ]
```

## Events

A TextFileEdit control supports the following events:

```
Change
Click
DblClick
DragDrop
DragOver
GotFocus
LostFocus
MouseDown
MouseMove
MouseUp
```

None of these events applies *only* to this control. They are documented in Visual Basic's on-line help and in the Visual Basic *Custom Control Reference* (see the "Standard Properties, Events, and Methods" section in Appendix A).

## Methods

A TextFileEditor supports the following methods:

```
Drag
LinkExecute
LinkPoke
LinkRequest
LinkSend
Move
Refresh
SetFocus
ZOrder
```

None of the methods require special consideration when used with the TextFileEditor. They are documented in Visual Basic's on-line help and in the Visual Basic *Custom Control Reference* (see the "Standard Properties, Events, and Methods" section in Appendix A).

# Using the IniData Control

The IniData control allows your Visual Basic programs to easily display and process the data stored in their private .INI files. The control encapsulates all of the critical management work for processing .INI files, such as initial-

**Figure A.7   An example of an IniData control (visible only at design time).**

**Table A.7   The IniData Control at a Glance**

| | |
|---|---|
| Implementation file | INIDATA.VBX |
| Class name | "IniData" |
| Toolbox representation |  |
| On-line documentation | INIDATA.HLP |
| Can be used in a standard Windows app | No |
| Can be used in a Visual Basic app | Yes |

izing buffers, reading files, parsing keys, displaying sections of a .INI file, and so on. The control also provides an encryption feature so that selected key values can be encrypted to protect users from reading or modifying a program's .INI file.

Figure A.7 shows an example of the IniData control, and Table A.7 provides the vital statistics for this control.

## Using IniData in a Visual App

To use the IniData control with a visual app, include the IniData control in your visual IDE using the *File..Add File to Project* command or equivalent. Select an IniData from the toolbox and apply it to a form just as you would any other control. IniData controls are managed using the properties, events, and methods described next.

### Properties

An IniData control supports the following properties:

```
*(About)
*DefaultText
*EncryptionKey
*FileName
Index
*Key
```

```
*KeyCount
*KeyList
Left
*List
*ListCount
*ListDelimiter
Name
Parent
*Section
*SectionCount
*SectionList
TabIndex
TabStop
Tag
*Text
Top
Width
```

The properties marked with an asterisk are either unique to this control or they require special consideration when used with the control. They will be described in this section. The other properties are documented in Visual Basic's on-line help and in the Visual Basic *Custom Control Reference* (see the "Standard Properties, Events, and Methods" section in Appendix A).

## (About)

This pseudo-property provides version and copyright information for the IniData DLL. This information is available only at design time, by clicking on the "..." button in the Properties window.

## DefaultText

This property stores a default value for the current section/key combination. If the .INI file specified by the *FileName* property does not exist, or if the *Section* or *Key* is not present in that file, this property will be echoed as the *Text* property. If the *ListDelimiter* property is supplied, the *DefaultText* will also be parsed into component items available through the *List* property.

### Usage

```
[control.]TextFileEdit.DefaultText [ = new default text ]
```

## EncryptionKey

This property, if supplied, causes values read from the .INI to be decrypted, and values written to it to be encrypted.

### Usage

```
[control.]TextFileEdit.EncryptionKey [ = new key ]
```

**FileName**

This property is the name of the .INI file being managed. The default value of this property is "WIN.INI".

*Usage*
```
[control.]TextFileEdit.FileName [ = new .INI file name ]
```

**Key**

This property specifies the current key, within the section specified by the *Section* property, used to determine the *Text* property.

*Usage*
```
[control.]TextFileEdit.Key [ = new section key ]
```

**KeyCount**

This property supplies the number of keys in the *KeyList* property. These are the keys in the section indicated by the *Section* property, of the .INI file indicated by the *FileName* property.

*Usage*
```
[control.]TextFileEdit.KeyCount
```

*Remarks*
This property is read-only.

**KeyList**

This array property contains a list of keys in the section indicated by the *Section* property of the .INI file indicated by the *FileName* property.

*Usage*
```
[control.]TextFileEdit.KeyList  (Index)
```

*Remarks*
This property is read-only. To add another key to the section, set the *Key* property to the desired key name and assign a value to the *Text* property.

**List**

This array property contains one element for each component of the *Text* property, as delimited by the *ListDelimiter* property.

*Usage*
```
[control.]TextFileEdit.List  (Index)
```

*Remarks*
This property is read-only.

## ListCount

This property contains the number of elements in the *List* array property.

### *Usage*

```
[control.]TextFileEdit.ListCount
```

## ListDelimiter

This property specifies the character used to delimit items in the *Text* property, when the *Text* represents a multiple-item value. The components of *Text* are then enumerated in the *List* property.

### *Usage*

```
[control.]TextFileEdit.ListDelimiter [ = new delimiting character ]
```

### *Remarks*

The default value is a space. The *DelimiterChar* can never be more than a single character.

## Section

This property specifies the section in the .INI file indicated by the *FileName* property being queried. Together with the *Key* value, it fully qualifies a specific *Text*.

### *Usage*

```
[control.]TextFileEdit.Section [ = new section name ]
```

## SectionCount

This property indicates the number of elements in the *Sections* array property.

### *Usage*

```
[control.]TextFileEdit.SectionCount
```

## SectionList

This array property contains an element for each section contained in the .INI file indicated by the *FileName* property.

### *Usage*

```
[control.]TextFileEdit.SectionList  (Index)
```

## Text

This property contains the current value of the item in the .INI file indicated by the *FileName* property, in the section identified by the *Section* property, identified by the *Key* property.

*Usage*
```
[control.]TextFileEdit.Text [ = new text ]
```

## Events

An IniData control supports only the following event:

```
*Change
```

### Change

The *Change* event is triggered whenever the application receives a *WM_WININICHANGE* message from another application in the system.

## Methods

An IniData control supports the following methods:

```
Drag
LinkExecute
LinkPoke
LinkRequest
LinkSend
Move
Refresh
*RemoveItem
SetFocus
ZOrder
```

Only the RemoveItem method requires special consideration when used with the IniData control. The others are documented in Visual Basic's on-line help and in the Visual Basic *Custom Control Reference* (see the "Standard Properties, Events, and Methods" section in Appendix A).

### RemoveItem

This method removes a specific key and item by deleting it from the .INI file.

| Setting | Value |
| --- | --- |
| *-1* | Delete the key and value indicated by the KeyName property |
| *<index>* | Delete the key identified by the index from the Keys array property |

# Index

# READ THE MAGAZINE OF TECHNICAL EXPERTISE!

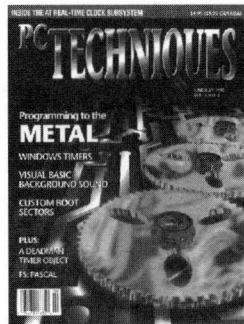

Published by The Coriolis Group

For years, Jeff Duntemann has been known for his crystal-clear, slightly-bemused explanations of programming technology. He's one of the few in computer publishing who has never forgotten that English is the one language we all have in common. Now he's teamed up with author Keith Weiskamp and created a magazine that brings you a selection of readable, practical technical articles six times a year, written by himself and a crew of the very best technical writers working today. Michael Abrash, Tom Swan, Jim Mischel, Keith Weiskamp, David Gerrold, Brett Glass, Michael Covington, Peter Aitken, Marty Franz, Jim Kyle, and many others will perform their magic before your eyes, and then explain how *you* can do it too, in language that you can understand.

If you program under DOS or Windows in C, C++, Pascal, Visual Basic, or assembly language, you'll find code you can use in every issue. You'll also find essential debugging and optimization techniques, programming tricks and tips, detailed product reviews, and practical advice on how to get your programming product finished, polished and ready to roll.

**Don't miss another issue—subscribe today!**

- - - - - - - - - - - - - - - - - - - - - - - - - - - - - - - -

☐  1 Year $21.95                           ☐  2 Years $37.95

☐  $29.95 Canada; $39.95 Foreign          ☐  $53.95 Canada; $73.95 Foreign

Total for subscription _____
Arizona orders please add 6% sales tax _____
Total due, in US funds _____

Name _____
Company _____
Address_____
City/State/ZIP _____
Phone _____

VISA/MC # _____

Signature for charge orders _____

Send to:
*PC TECHNIQUES*
7721 E. Gray Road, #204
Scottsdale AZ 85260

Phone  (602) 483-0192
Fax     (602) 483-0193

Expires _____

**THE CORIOLIS GROUP**

The Coriolis Group warrants the enclosed disk to be free of defects in materials and faulty workmanship under normal use for a period of ninety days after purchase. If a defect is discovered in the disk during this warranty period, a replacement disk can be obtained at no charge by sending the defective disk, postage prepaid, with proof of purchase to:

**Coriolis Group Books**
**7721 E. Gray Road, Suite 204**
**Scottsdale, AZ 85260**
**(602) 483-0192**

After the 90-day period, a replacement will be sent upon receipt of the defective disk and a check or money order for $10.00, payable to Coriolis Group Books.